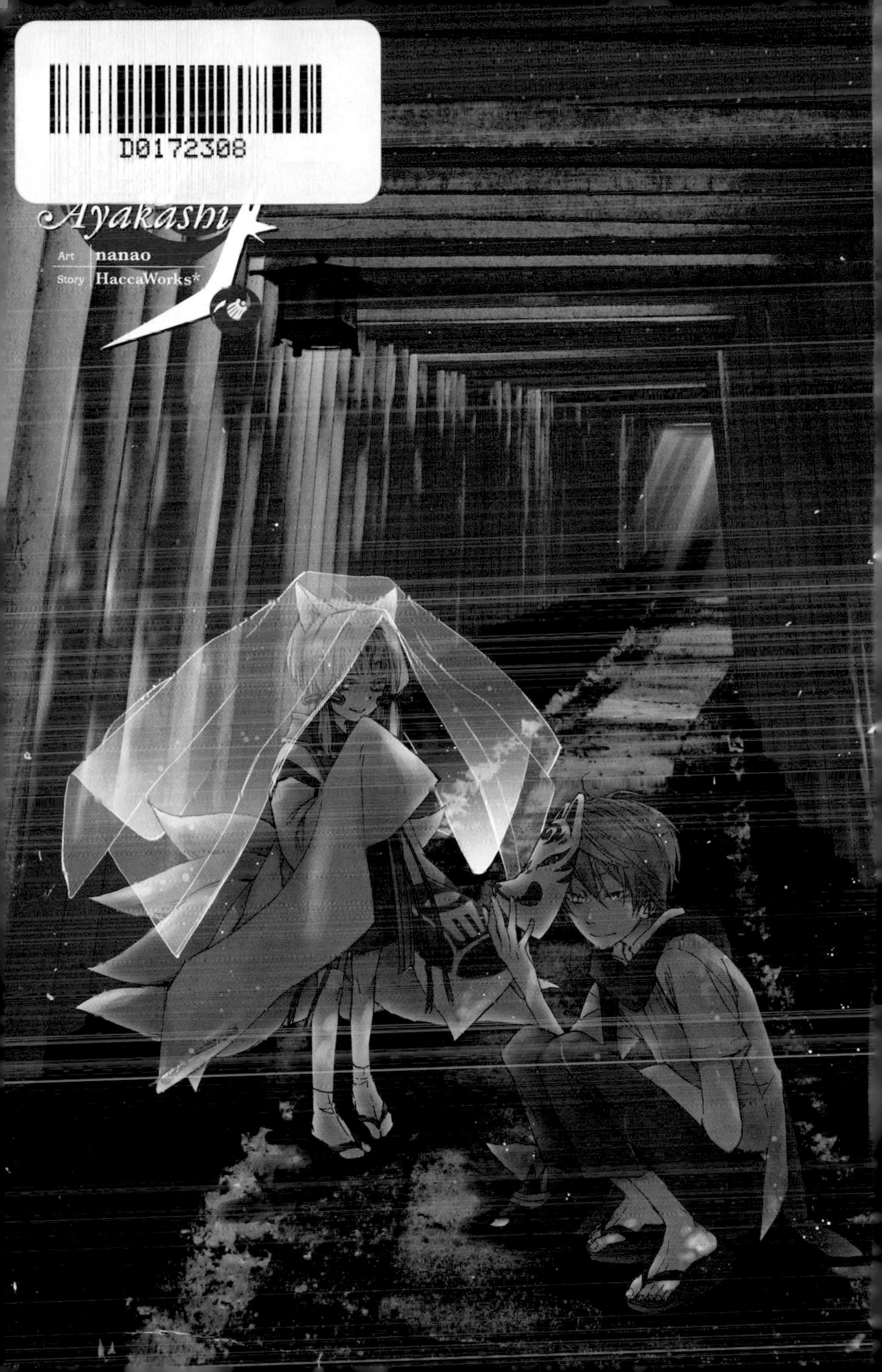
Ayakashi
Art nanao
Story HaccaWorks*

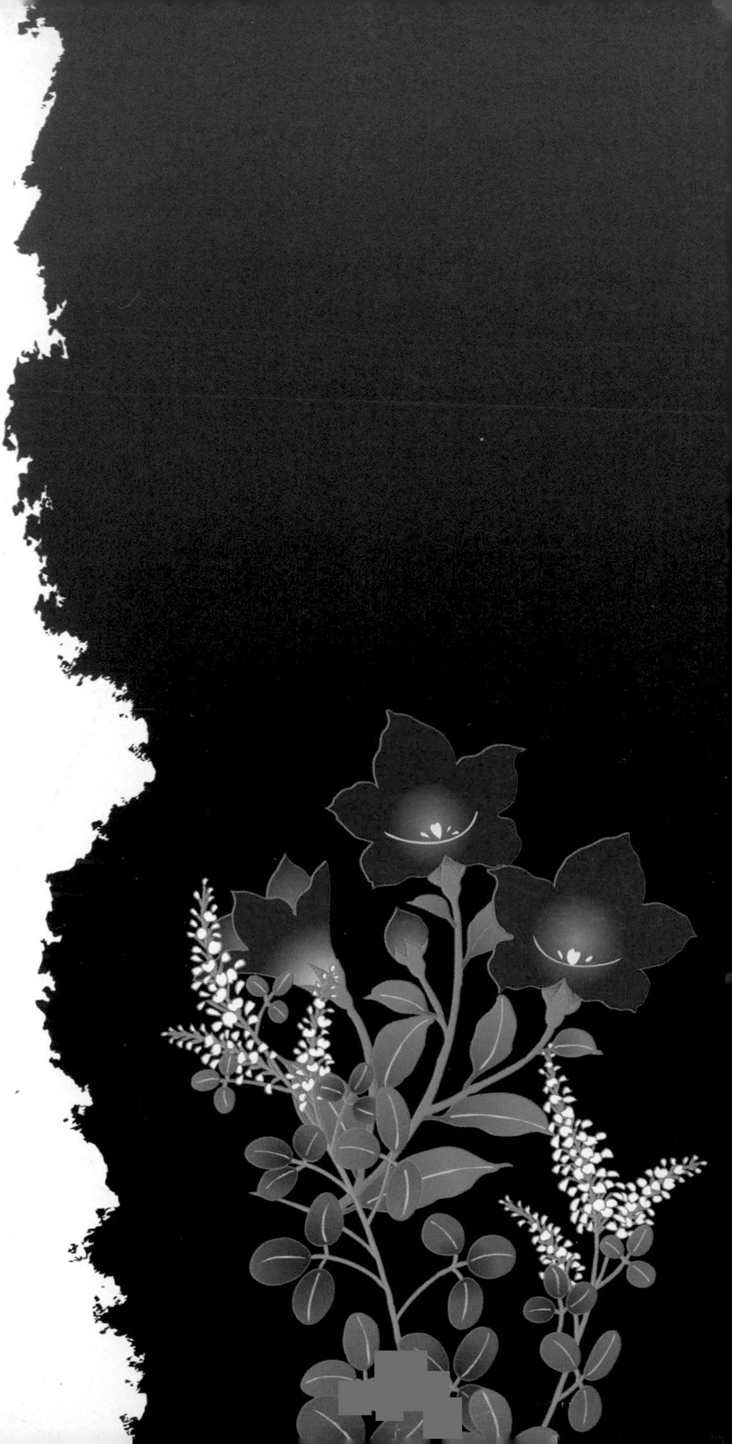

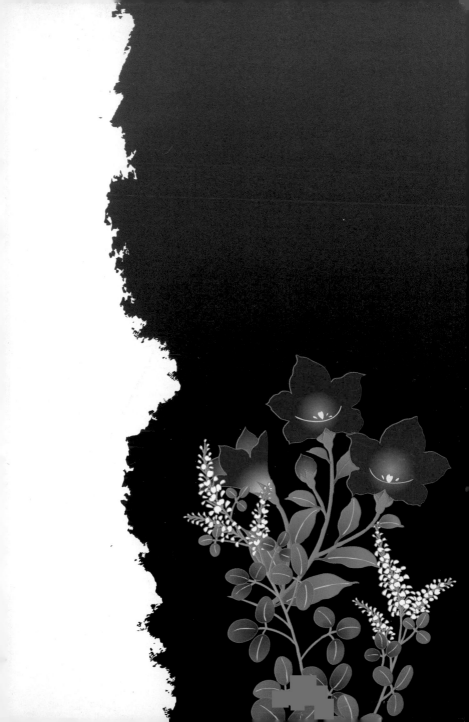

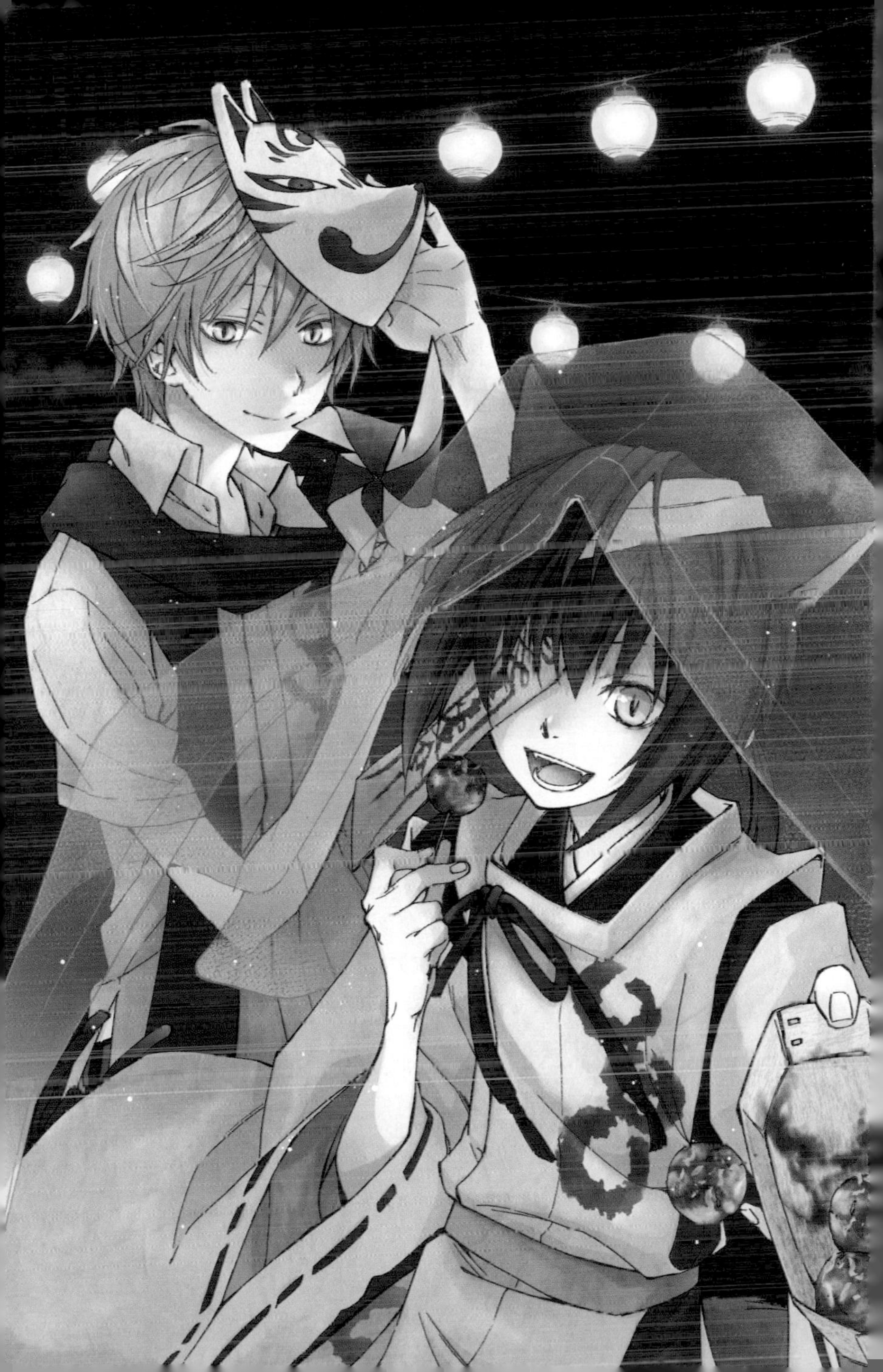

CONTENTS

THE 5.5TH TALE: FEELINGS   005

THE 6TH TALE: INVESTIGATION   023

THE 7TH TALE: SAGANO   053

THE 8TH TALE: FORM   079

THE 9TH TALE: SHIN   101

THE 10TH TALE: UTSUWA   125

UTSUWA SHRINE.
I'VE BEEN HERE EVER SINCE I WAS BORN.
...OR SO I'M TOLD.
THE 5.5TH TALE
FEELINGS
CHUN (CHIRP)
OH!
ONI-GIRI.
A FISH.
NU (LOOM)

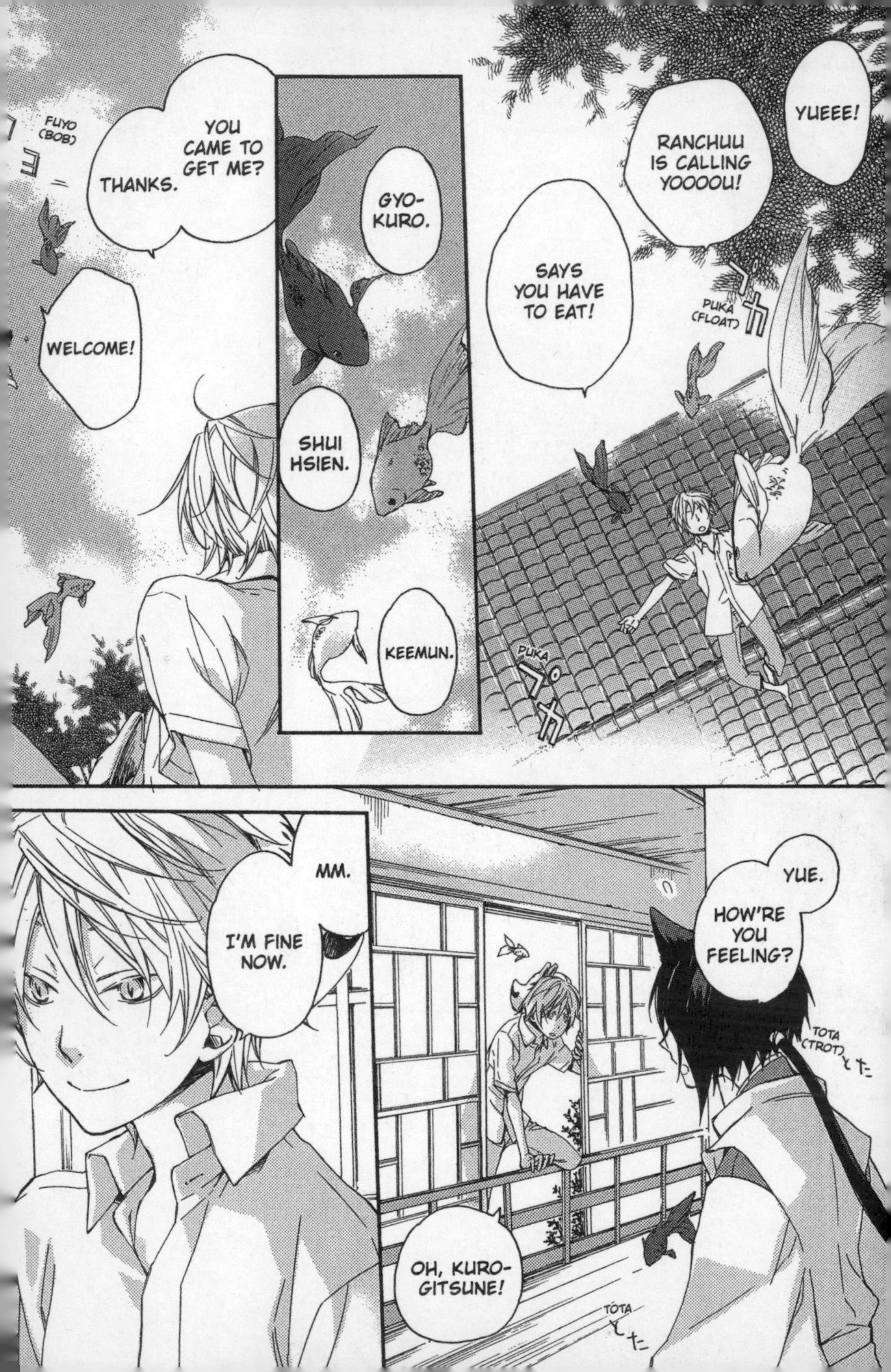
YUEEE!
RANCHUU IS CALLING YOOOOU!
SAYS YOU HAVE TO EAT!
PUKA (FLOAT)
PUKA
GYO-KURO.
SHUI HSIEN.
KEEMUN.
FUYO (BOB)
YOU CAME TO GET ME?
THANKS.
WELCOME!
YUE.
HOW'RE YOU FEELING?
TOTA (TROT)
OH, KURO-GITSUNE!
TOTA
MM.
I'M FINE NOW.

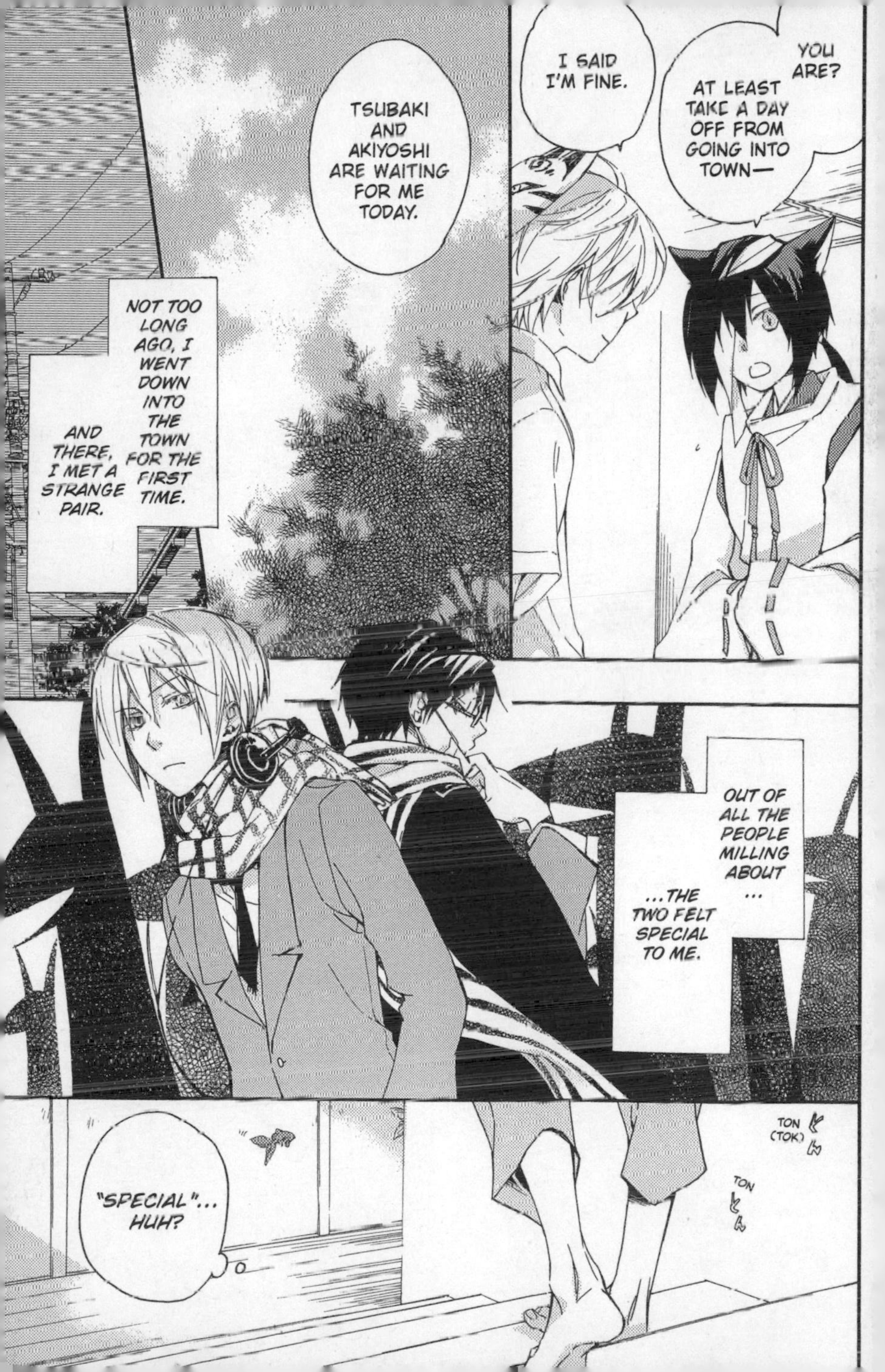
YOU ARE?
AT LEAST TAKE A DAY OFF FROM GOING INTO TOWN—
I SAID I'M FINE.
TSUBAKI AND AKIYOSHI ARE WAITING FOR ME TODAY.
NOT TOO LONG AGO, I WENT DOWN INTO THE TOWN FOR THE FIRST TIME.
AND THERE, I MET A STRANGE PAIR.
OUT OF ALL THE PEOPLE MILLING ABOUT ...
...THE TWO FELT SPECIAL TO ME.
TON (TOK)
TON
"SPECIAL"... HUH?

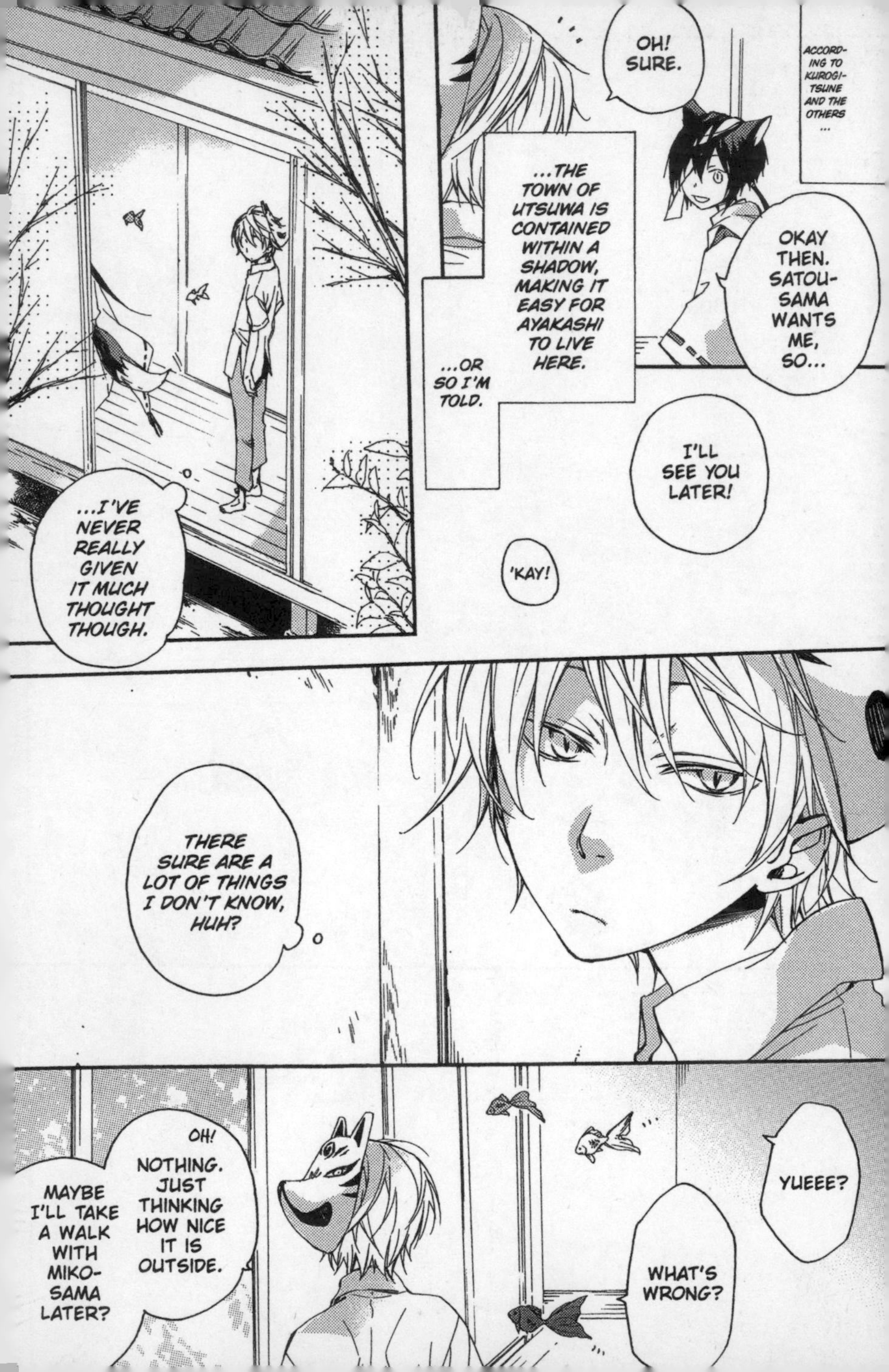
ACCORDING TO KUROGI-TSUNE AND THE OTHERS...
OH! SURE.
OKAY THEN. SATOU-SAMA WANTS ME, SO...
I'LL SEE YOU LATER!
'KAY!
...THE TOWN OF UTSUWA IS CONTAINED WITHIN A SHADOW, MAKING IT EASY FOR AYAKASHI TO LIVE HERE.
...OR SO I'M TOLD.
...I'VE NEVER REALLY GIVEN IT MUCH THOUGHT THOUGH.
THERE SURE ARE A LOT OF THINGS I DON'T KNOW, HUH?
YUEEE?
WHAT'S WRONG?
OH!
NOTHING. JUST THINKING HOW NICE IT IS OUTSIDE.
MAYBE I'LL TAKE A WALK WITH MIKO-SAMA LATER?

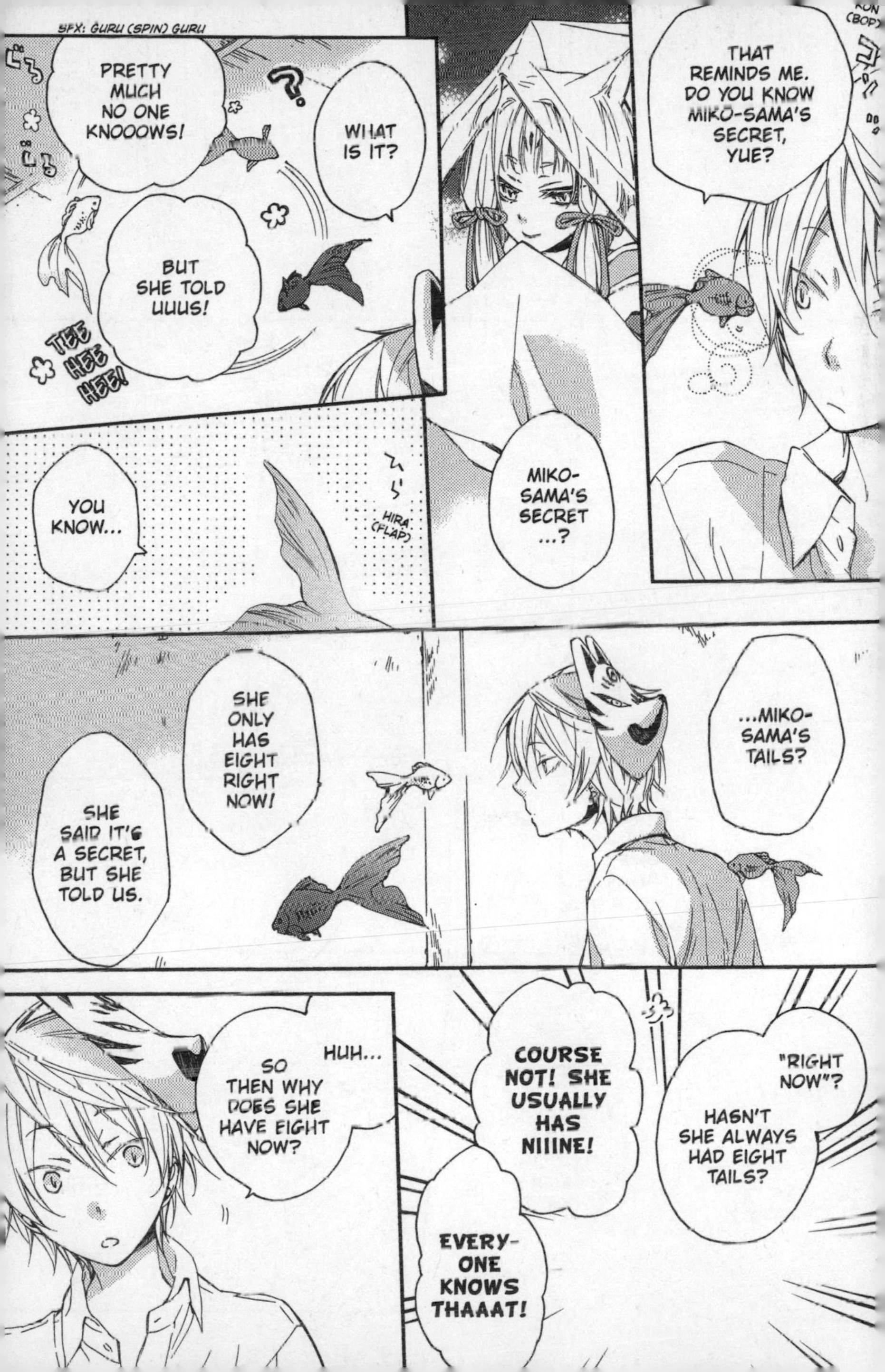
KON (BOP)
THAT REMINDS ME. DO YOU KNOW MIKO-SAMA'S SECRET, YUE?
MIKO-SAMA'S SECRET ...?
WHAT IS IT?
SFX: GURU (SPIN) GURU
PRETTY MUCH NO ONE KNOOOWS!
BUT SHE TOLD UUUS!
TEE HEE HEE!
HIRA (FLAP)
YOU KNOW...
...MIKO-SAMA'S TAILS?
SHE ONLY HAS EIGHT RIGHT NOW!
SHE SAID IT'S A SECRET, BUT SHE TOLD US.
"RIGHT NOW"?
HASN'T SHE ALWAYS HAD EIGHT TAILS?
COURSE NOT! SHE USUALLY HAS NIIINE!
EVERY-ONE KNOWS THAAAT!
HUH...
SO THEN WHY DOES SHE HAVE EIGHT NOW?

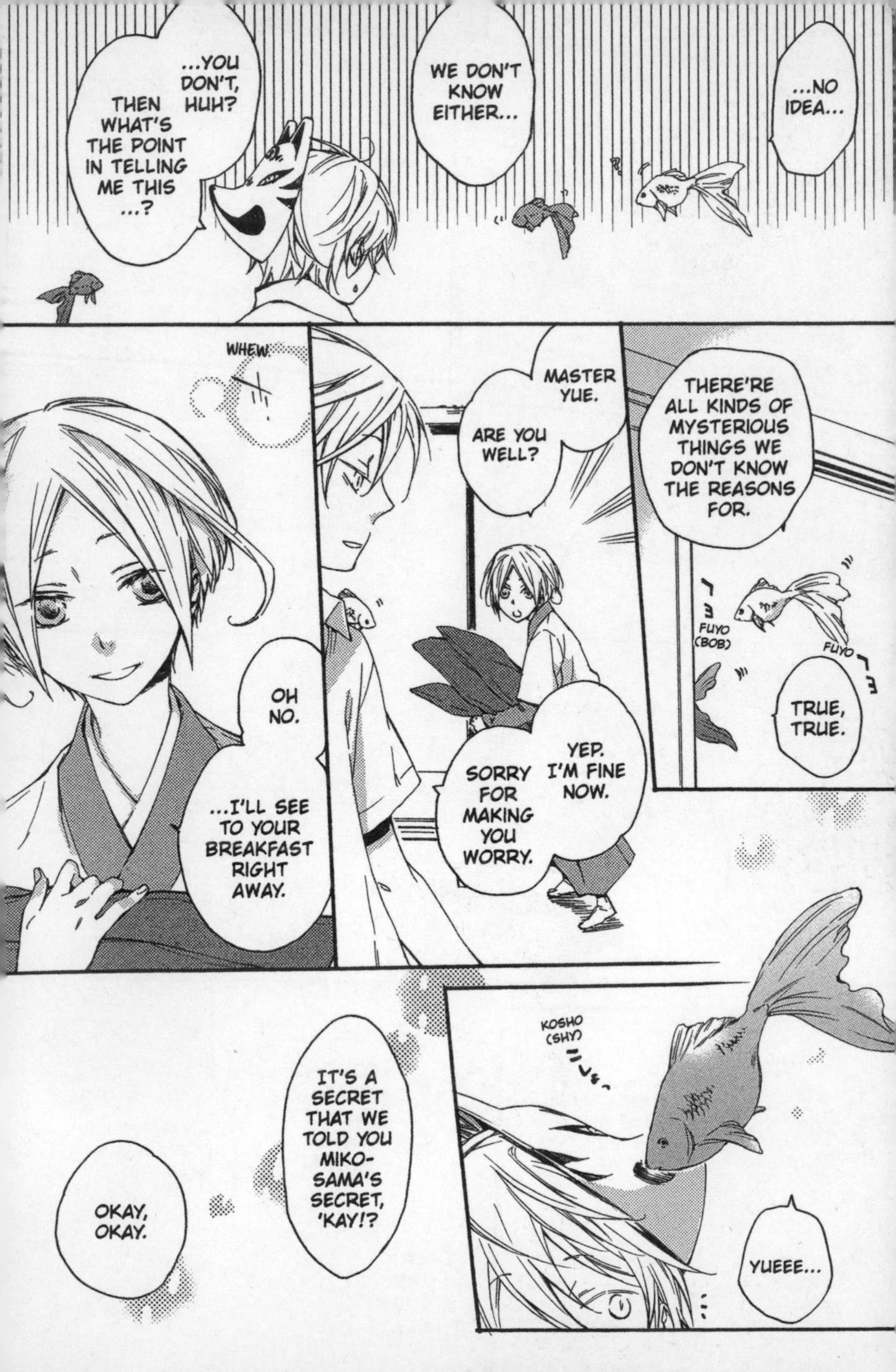
...NO IDEA...
WE DON'T KNOW EITHER...
...YOU DON'T, HUH? THEN WHAT'S THE POINT IN TELLING ME THIS ...?
THERE'RE ALL KINDS OF MYSTERIOUS THINGS WE DON'T KNOW THE REASONS FOR.
FUYO (BOB)
FUYO
TRUE, TRUE.
MASTER YUE.
ARE YOU WELL?
YEP. I'M FINE NOW.
SORRY FOR MAKING YOU WORRY.
WHEW
OH NO.
...I'LL SEE TO YOUR BREAKFAST RIGHT AWAY.
KOSHO (SHY)
YUEEE...
IT'S A SECRET THAT WE TOLD YOU MIKO-SAMA'S SECRET, 'KAY!?
OKAY, OKAY.

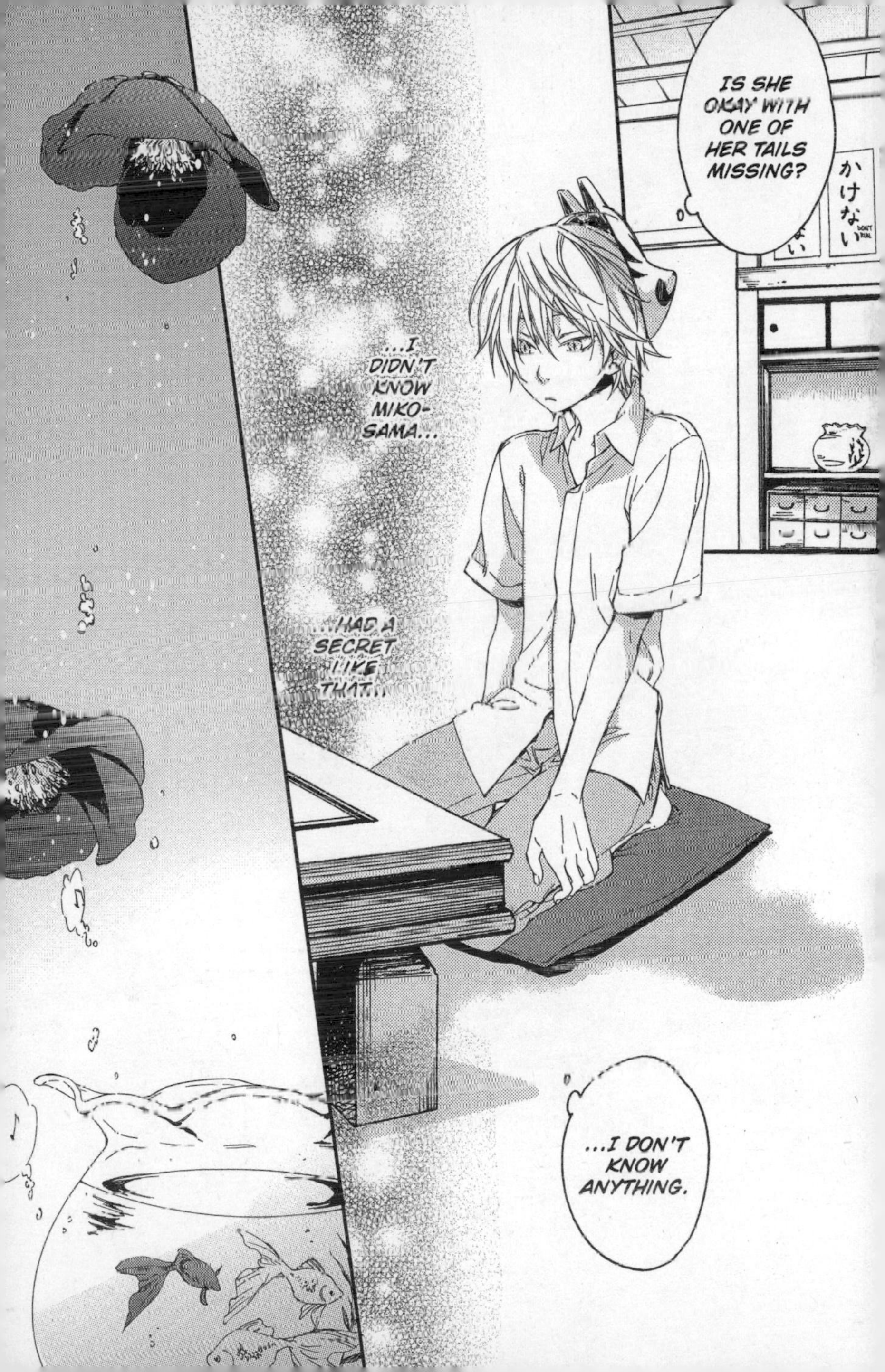
IS SHE OKAY WITH ONE OF HER TAILS MISSING?
かけない
...I DIDN'T KNOW MIKO-SAMA...
...HAD A SECRET LIKE THAT...
...I DON'T KNOW ANYTHING.

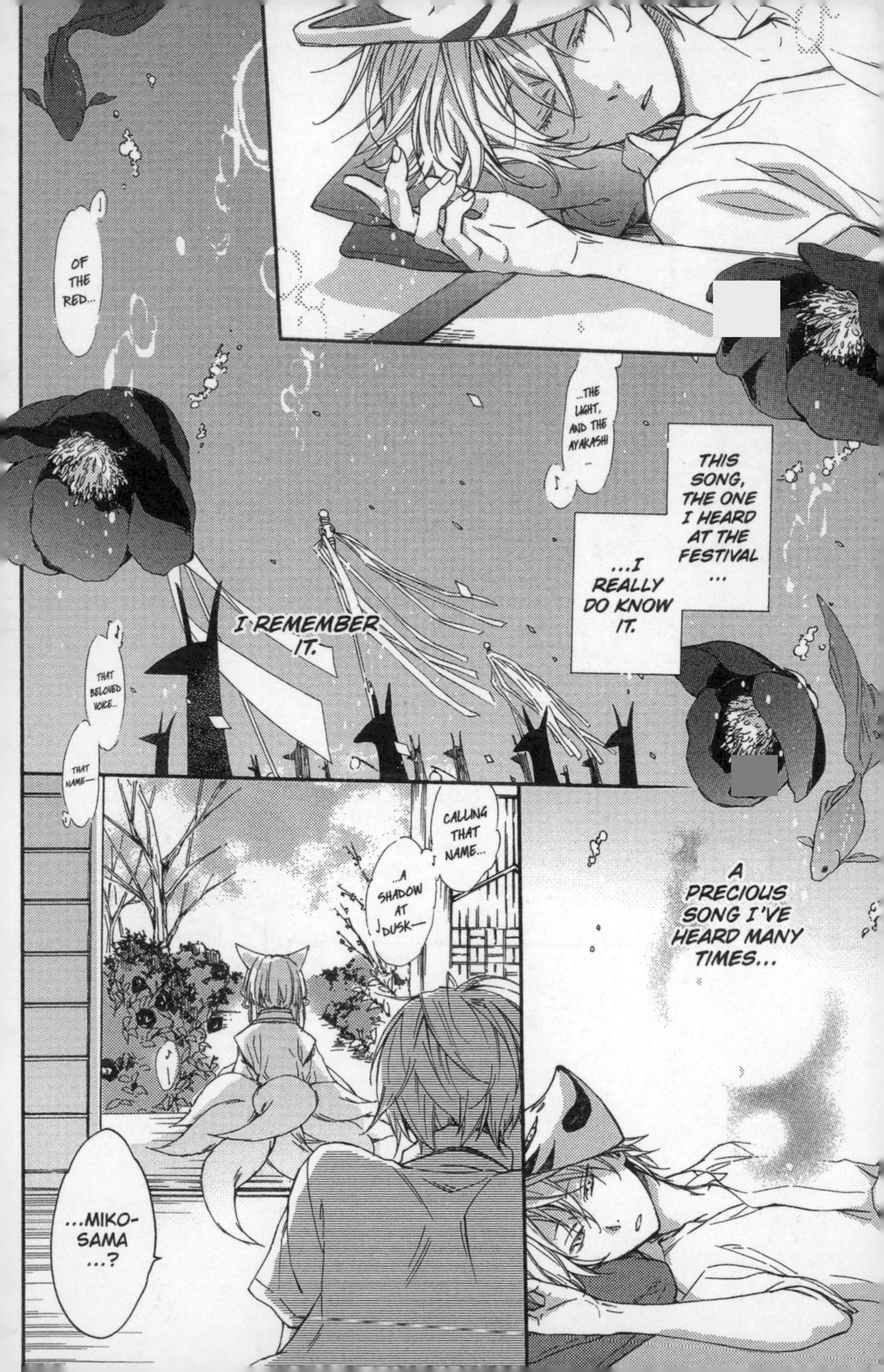
OF THE RED...
...THE LIGHT, AND THE AYAKASHI ...
THIS SONG, THE ONE I HEARD AT THE FESTIVAL ...
...I REALLY DO KNOW IT.
I REMEMBER IT.
THAT BELOVED VOICE...
THAT NAME—
A PRECIOUS SONG I'VE HEARD MANY TIMES...
CALLING THAT NAME...
...A SHADOW AT DUSK—
...MIKO-SAMA ...?

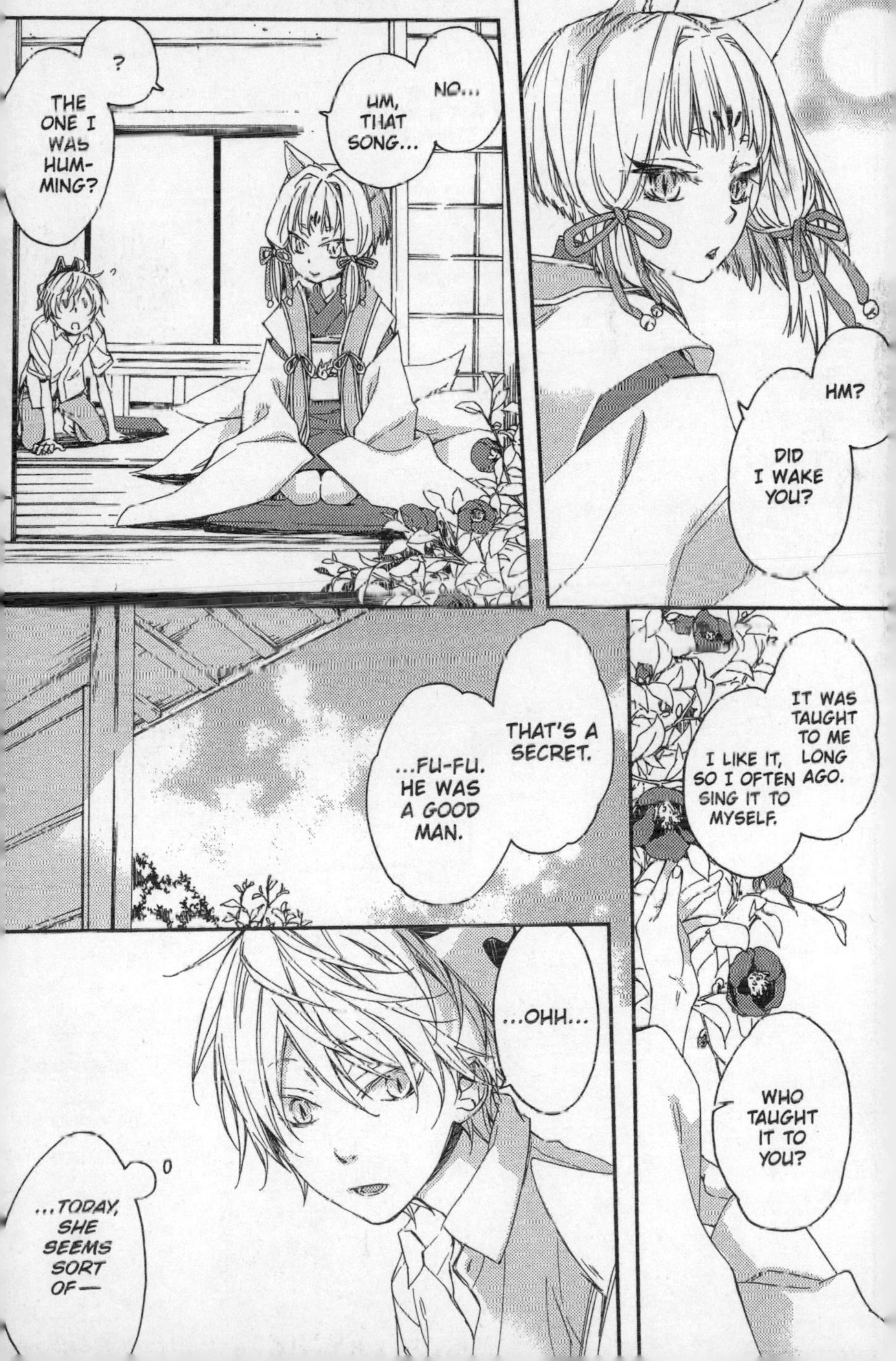
HM?
DID I WAKE YOU?
NO... UM, THAT SONG...
?
THE ONE I WAS HUM-MING?
IT WAS TAUGHT TO ME LONG AGO.
I LIKE IT, SO I OFTEN SING IT TO MYSELF.
WHO TAUGHT IT TO YOU?
THAT'S A SECRET.
...FU-FU. HE WAS A GOOD MAN.
...OHH...
...TODAY, SHE SEEMS SORT OF—

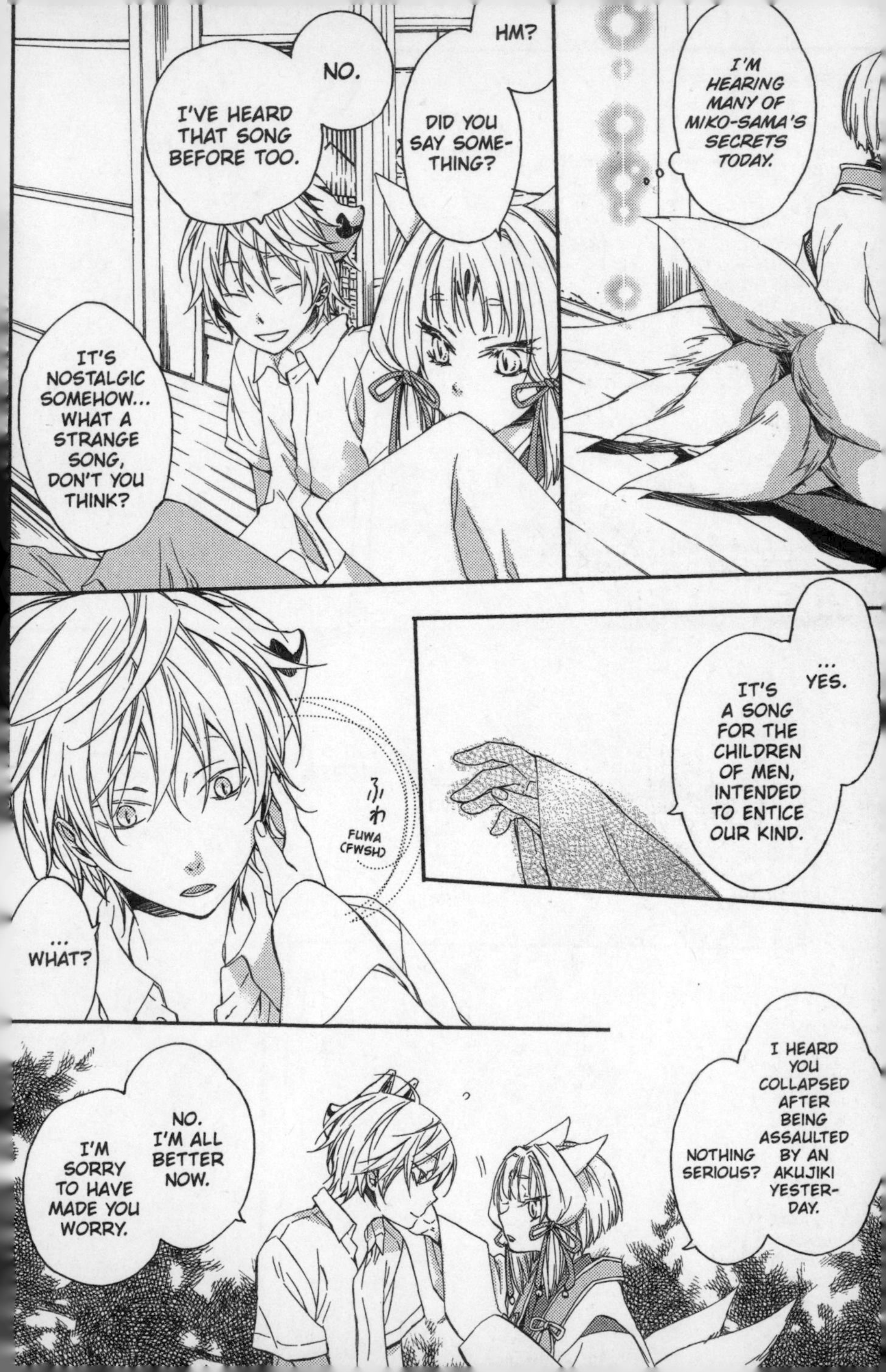
I'M HEARING MANY OF MIKO-SAMA'S SECRETS TODAY.
HM?
DID YOU SAY SOME-THING?
NO.
I'VE HEARD THAT SONG BEFORE TOO.
IT'S NOSTALGIC SOMEHOW... WHAT A STRANGE SONG, DON'T YOU THINK?
... YES.
IT'S A SONG FOR THE CHILDREN OF MEN, INTENDED TO ENTICE OUR KIND.
ふわ
FUWA (FWSH)
... WHAT?
I HEARD YOU COLLAPSED AFTER BEING ASSAULTED BY AN AKUJIKI YESTER-DAY.
NOTHING SERIOUS?
NO. I'M ALL BETTER NOW.
I'M SORRY TO HAVE MADE YOU WORRY.

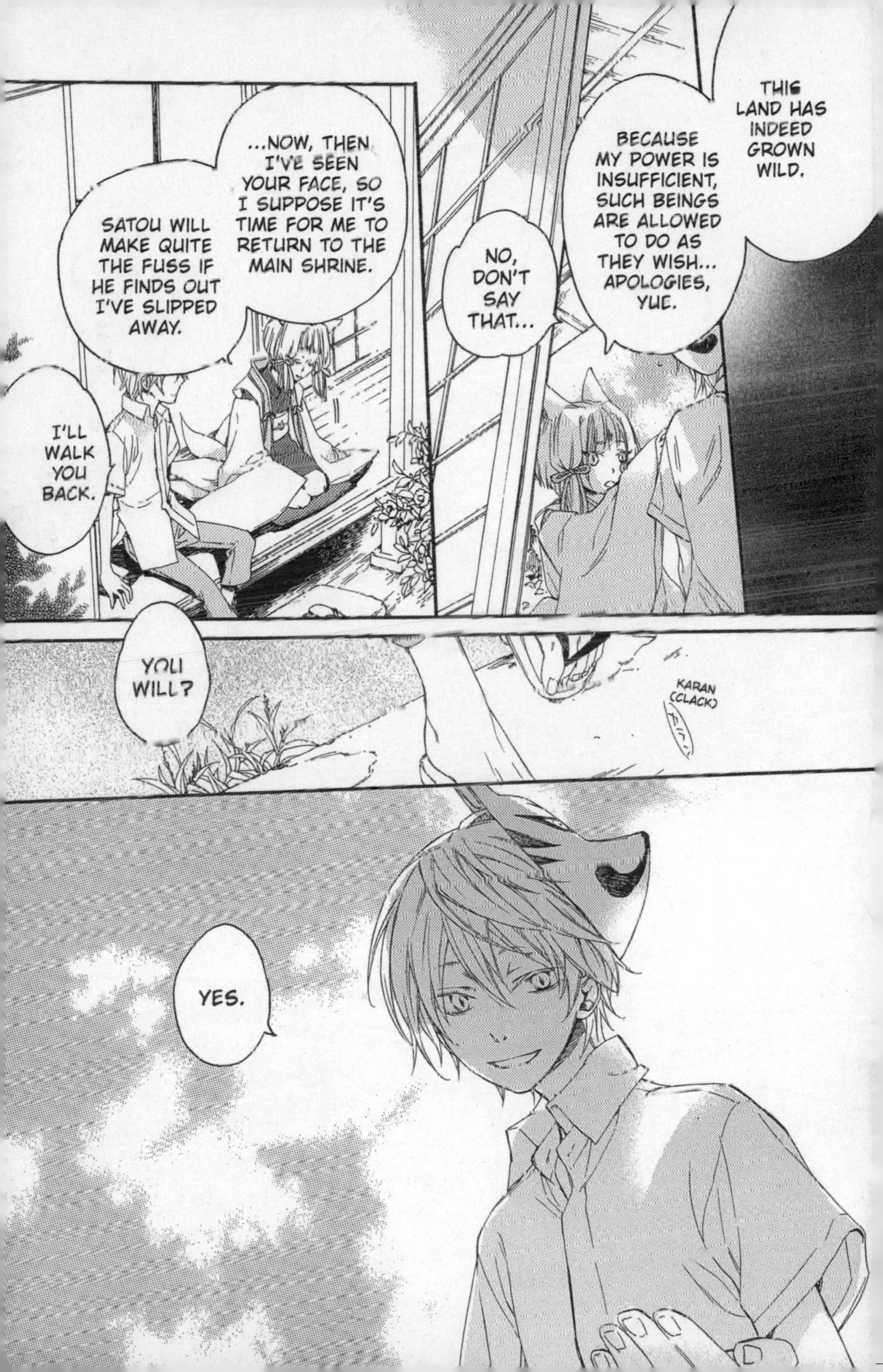
THIS LAND HAS INDEED GROWN WILD.
BECAUSE MY POWER IS INSUFFICIENT, SUCH BEINGS ARE ALLOWED TO DO AS THEY WISH... APOLOGIES, YUE.
NO, DON'T SAY THAT...
...NOW, THEN I'VE SEEN YOUR FACE, SO I SUPPOSE IT'S TIME FOR ME TO RETURN TO THE MAIN SHRINE.
SATOU WILL MAKE QUITE THE FUSS IF HE FINDS OUT I'VE SLIPPED AWAY.
I'LL WALK YOU BACK.
KARAN (CLACK)
YOU WILL?
YES.

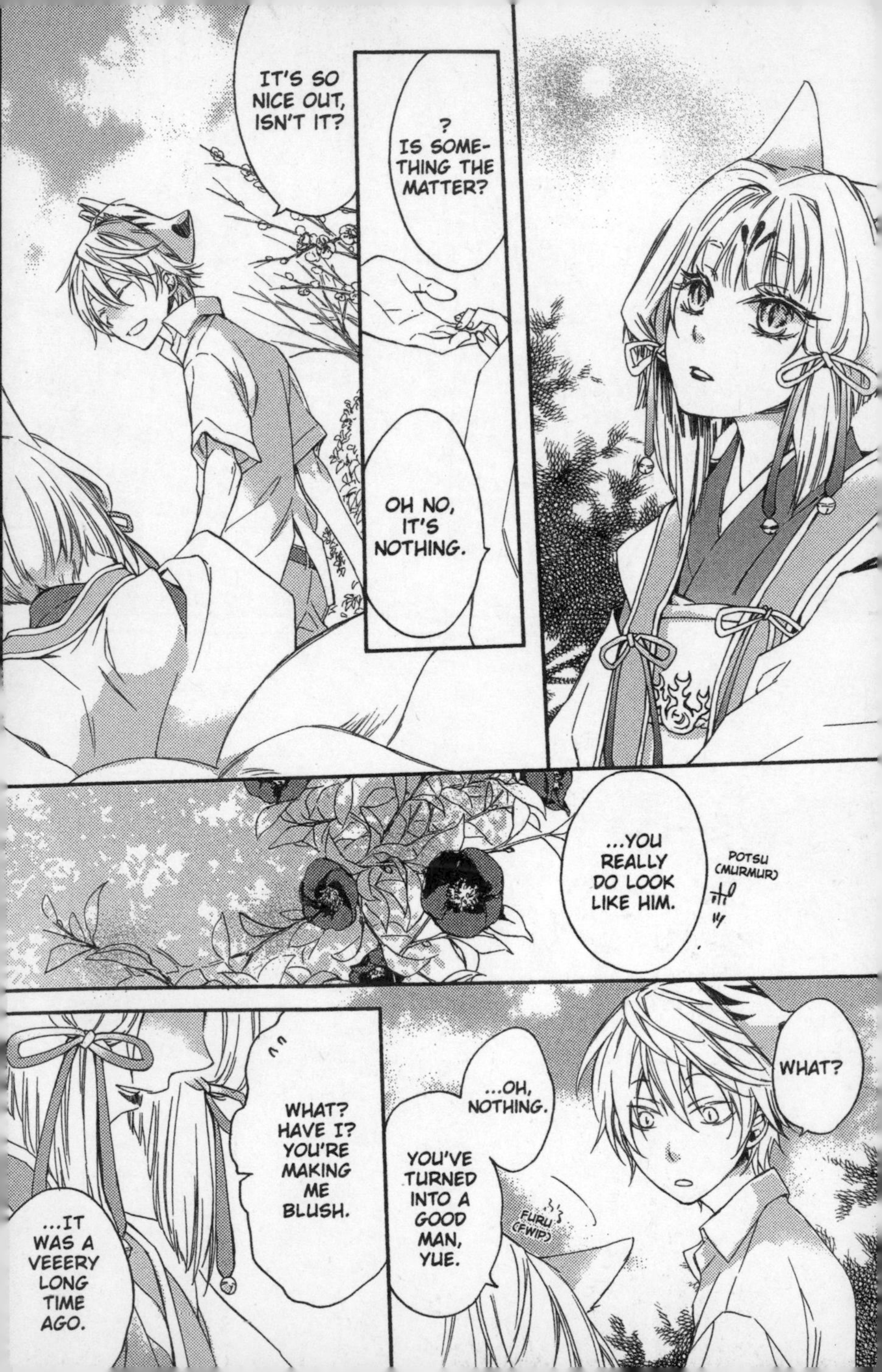
IT'S SO NICE OUT, ISN'T IT?
? IS SOMETHING THE MATTER?
OH NO, IT'S NOTHING.
...YOU REALLY DO LOOK LIKE HIM.
POTSU (MURMUR)
WHAT?
...OH, NOTHING.
YOU'VE TURNED INTO A GOOD MAN, YUE.
FURU (FWIP)
WHAT? HAVE I? YOU'RE MAKING ME BLUSH.
...IT WAS A VEEERY LONG TIME AGO.

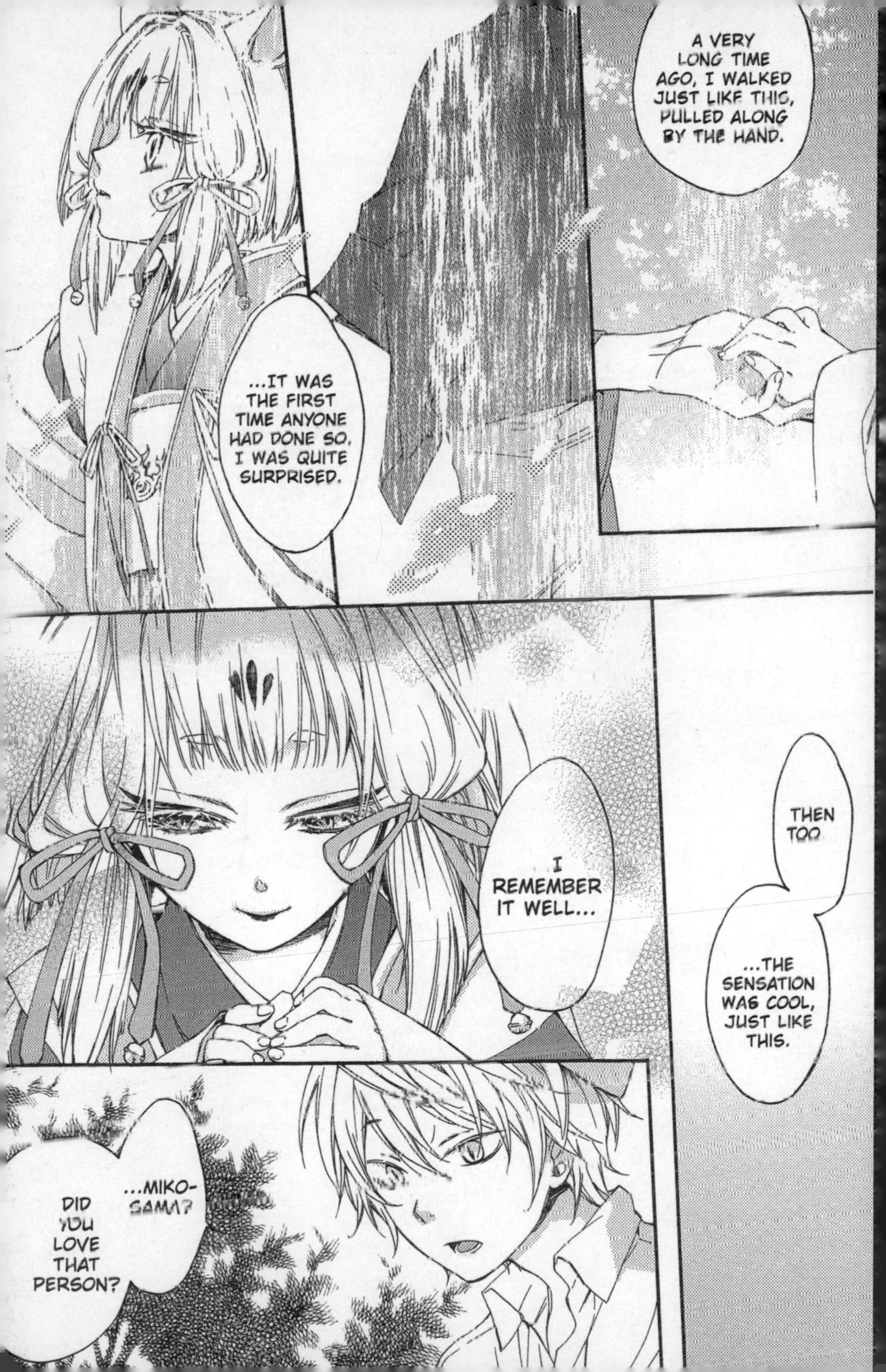
A VERY LONG TIME AGO, I WALKED JUST LIKE THIS, PULLED ALONG BY THE HAND.
...IT WAS THE FIRST TIME ANYONE HAD DONE SO. I WAS QUITE SURPRISED.
THEN TOO
...THE SENSATION WAS COOL, JUST LIKE THIS.
I REMEMBER IT WELL...
...MIKO-SAMA?
DID YOU LOVE THAT PERSON?

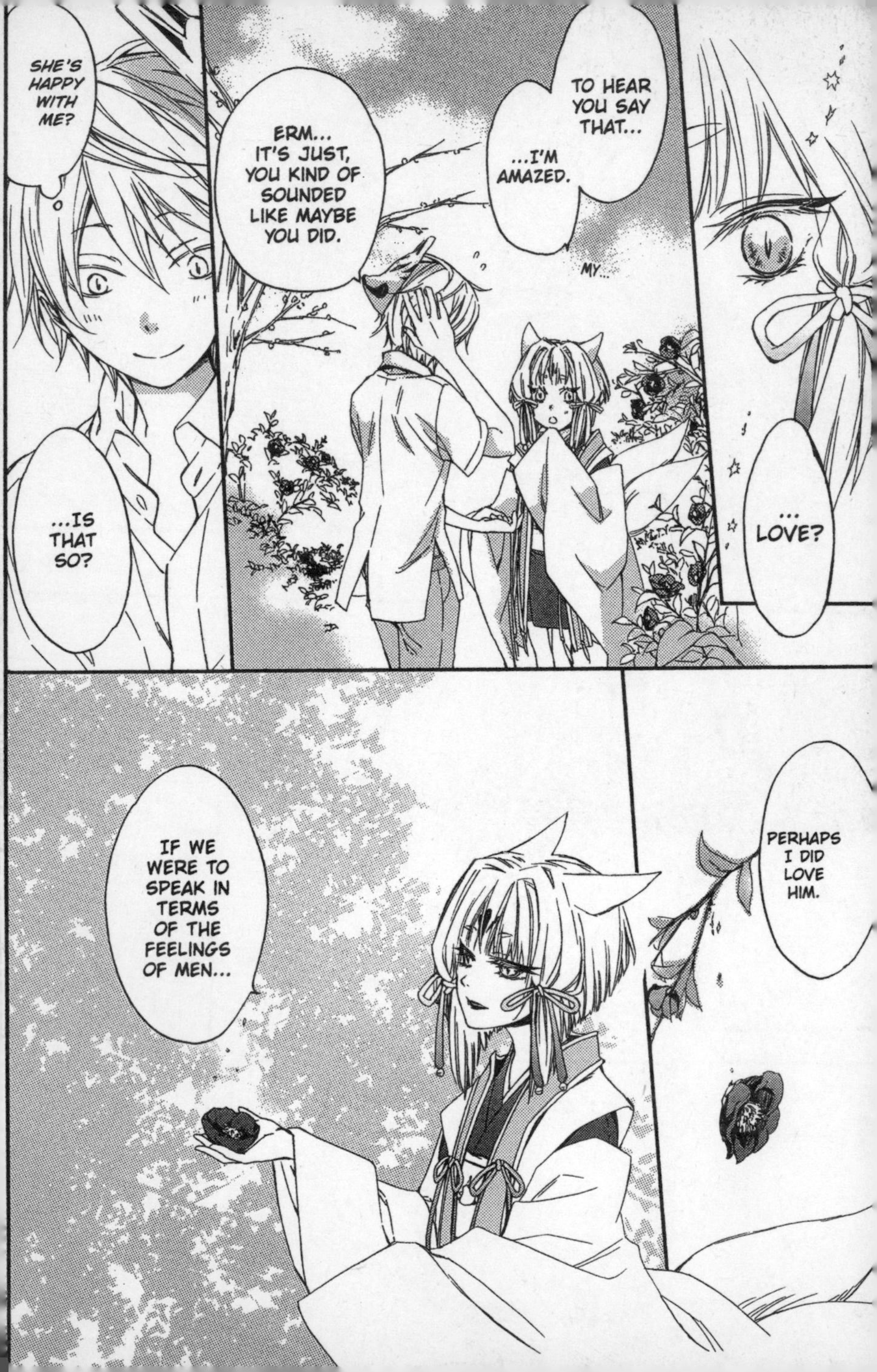

...LOVE?
TO HEAR YOU SAY THAT...
...I'M AMAZED.
MY...
ERM... IT'S JUST, YOU KIND OF SOUNDED LIKE MAYBE YOU DID.
SHE'S HAPPY WITH ME?
...IS THAT SO?
PERHAPS I DID LOVE HIM.
IF WE WERE TO SPEAK IN TERMS OF THE FEELINGS OF MEN...

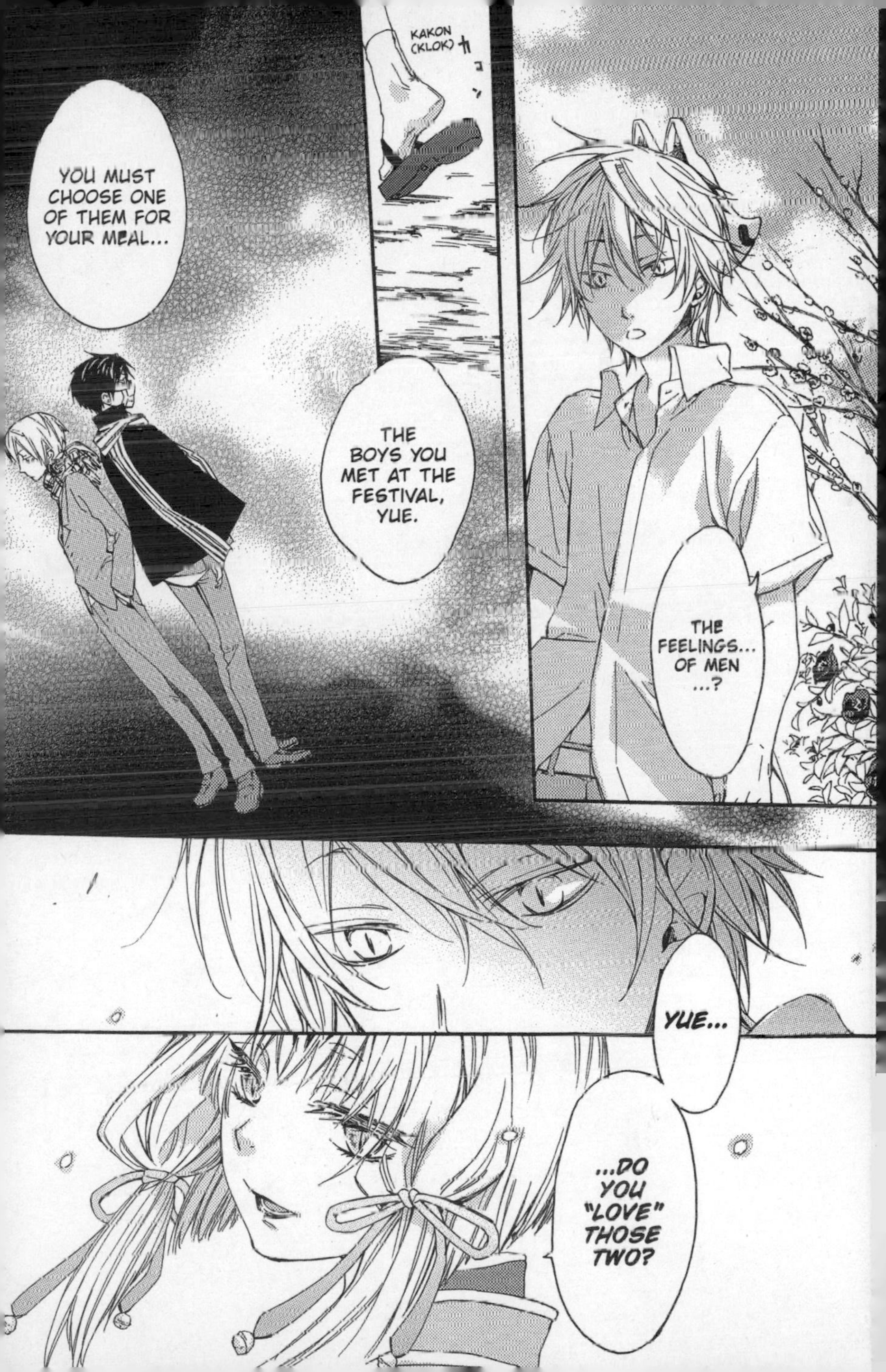
THE FEELINGS... OF MEN ...?
KAKON (KLOK)
YOU MUST CHOOSE ONE OF THEM FOR YOUR MEAL...
THE BOYS YOU MET AT THE FESTIVAL, YUE.
YUE...
...DO YOU "LOVE" THOSE TWO?

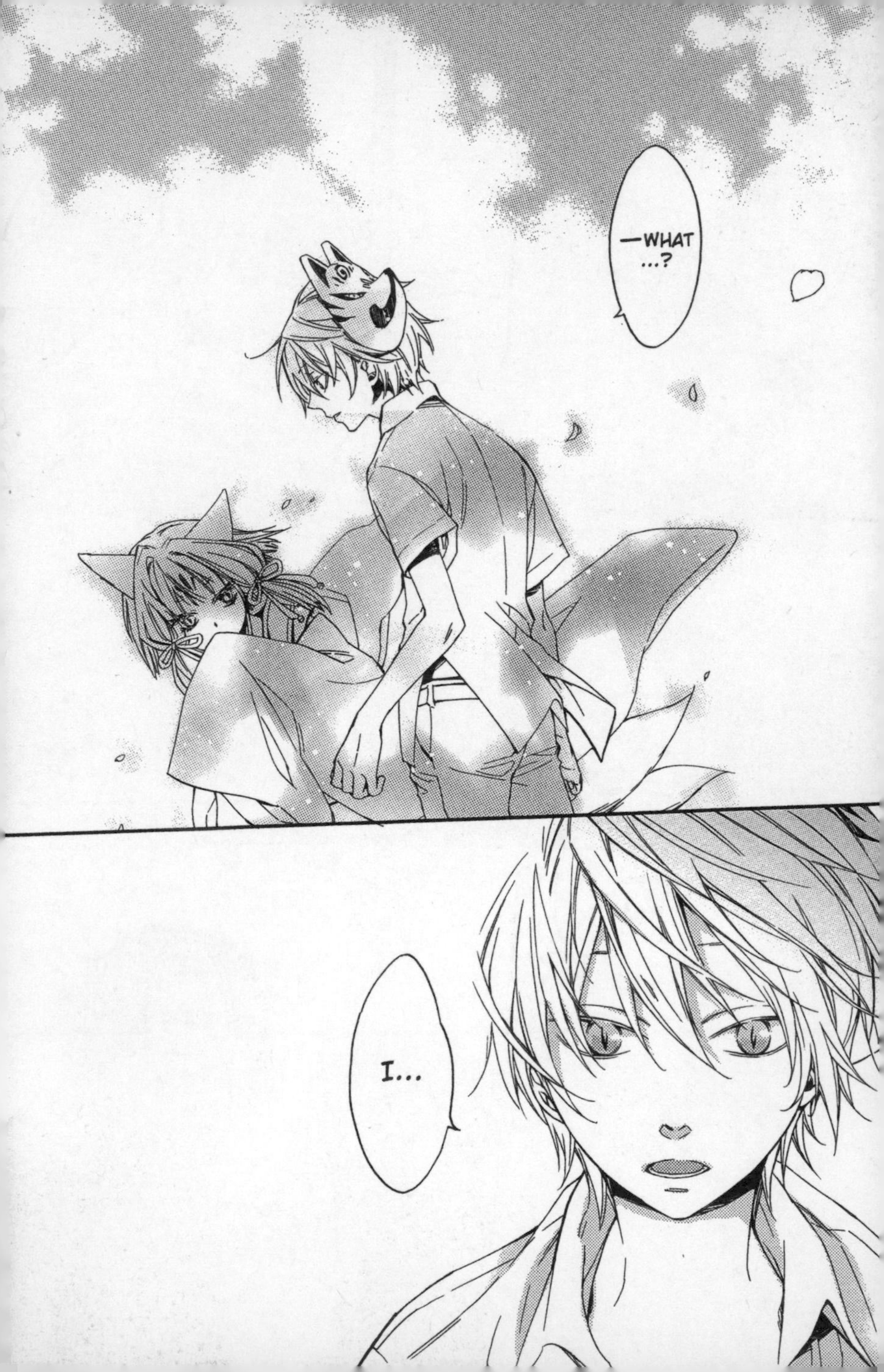
—WHAT ...?
I...

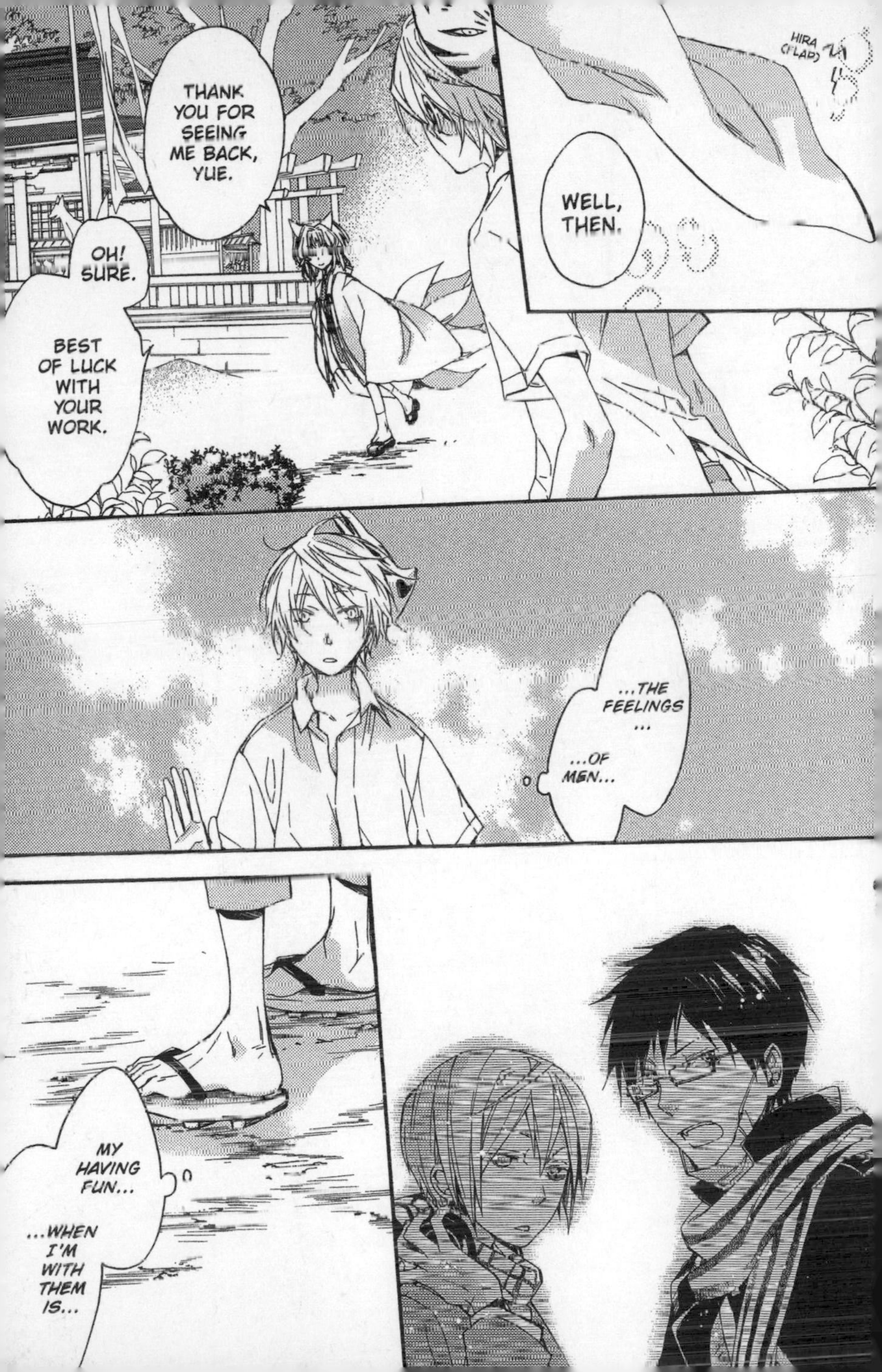
HIRA (FLAP)
WELL, THEN.
THANK YOU FOR SEEING ME BACK, YUE.
OH! SURE.
BEST OF LUCK WITH YOUR WORK.
...THE FEELINGS ...
...OF MEN...
MY HAVING FUN...
...WHEN I'M WITH THEM IS...

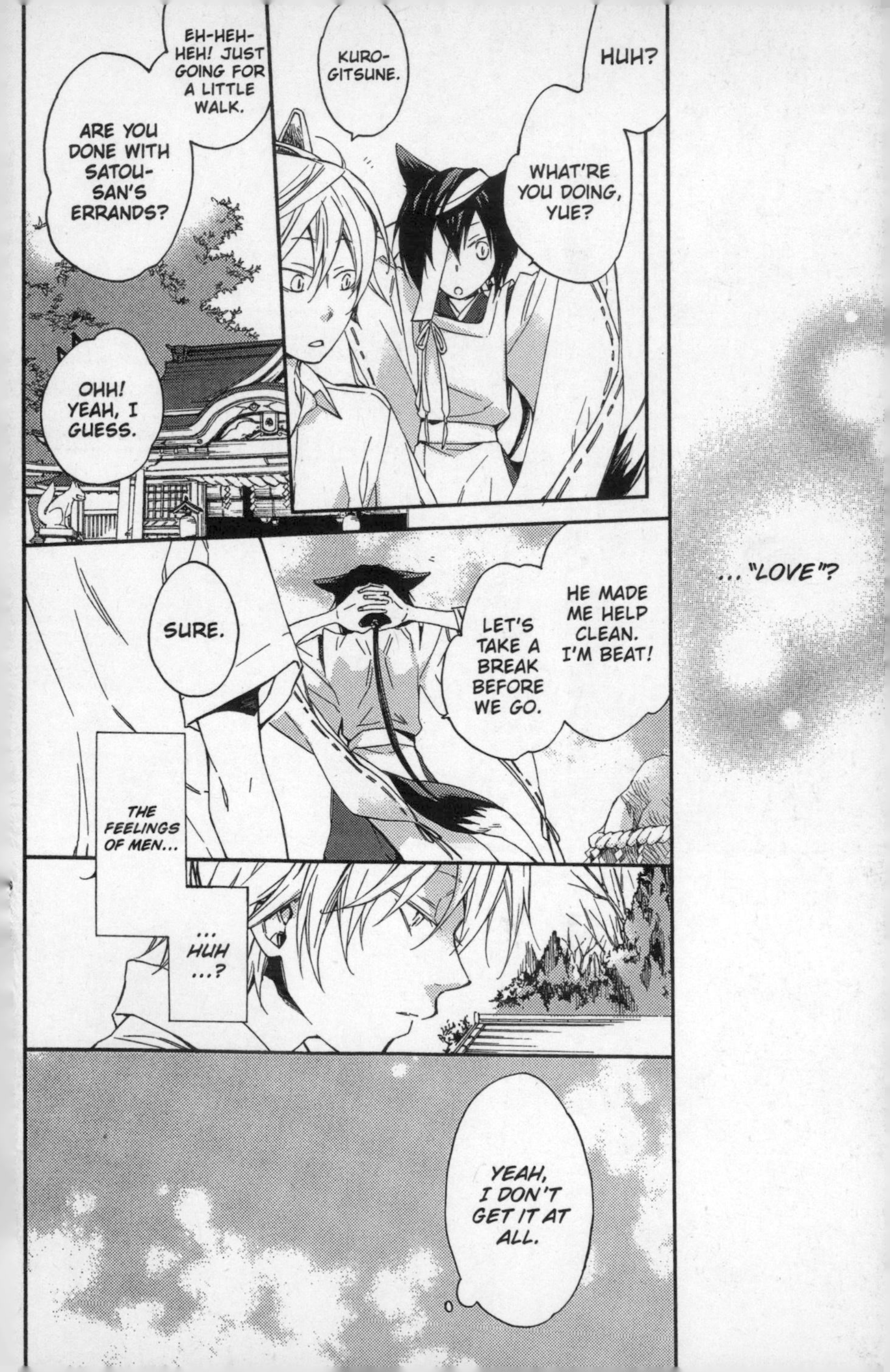
…"LOVE"?
HUH?
KURO-GITSUNE.
WHAT'RE YOU DOING, YUE?
EH-HEH-HEH! JUST GOING FOR A LITTLE WALK.
ARE YOU DONE WITH SATOU-SAN'S ERRANDS?
OHH! YEAH, I GUESS.
HE MADE ME HELP CLEAN. I'M BEAT!
LET'S TAKE A BREAK BEFORE WE GO.
SURE.
THE FEELINGS OF MEN…
…HUH…?
YEAH, I DON'T GET IT AT ALL.

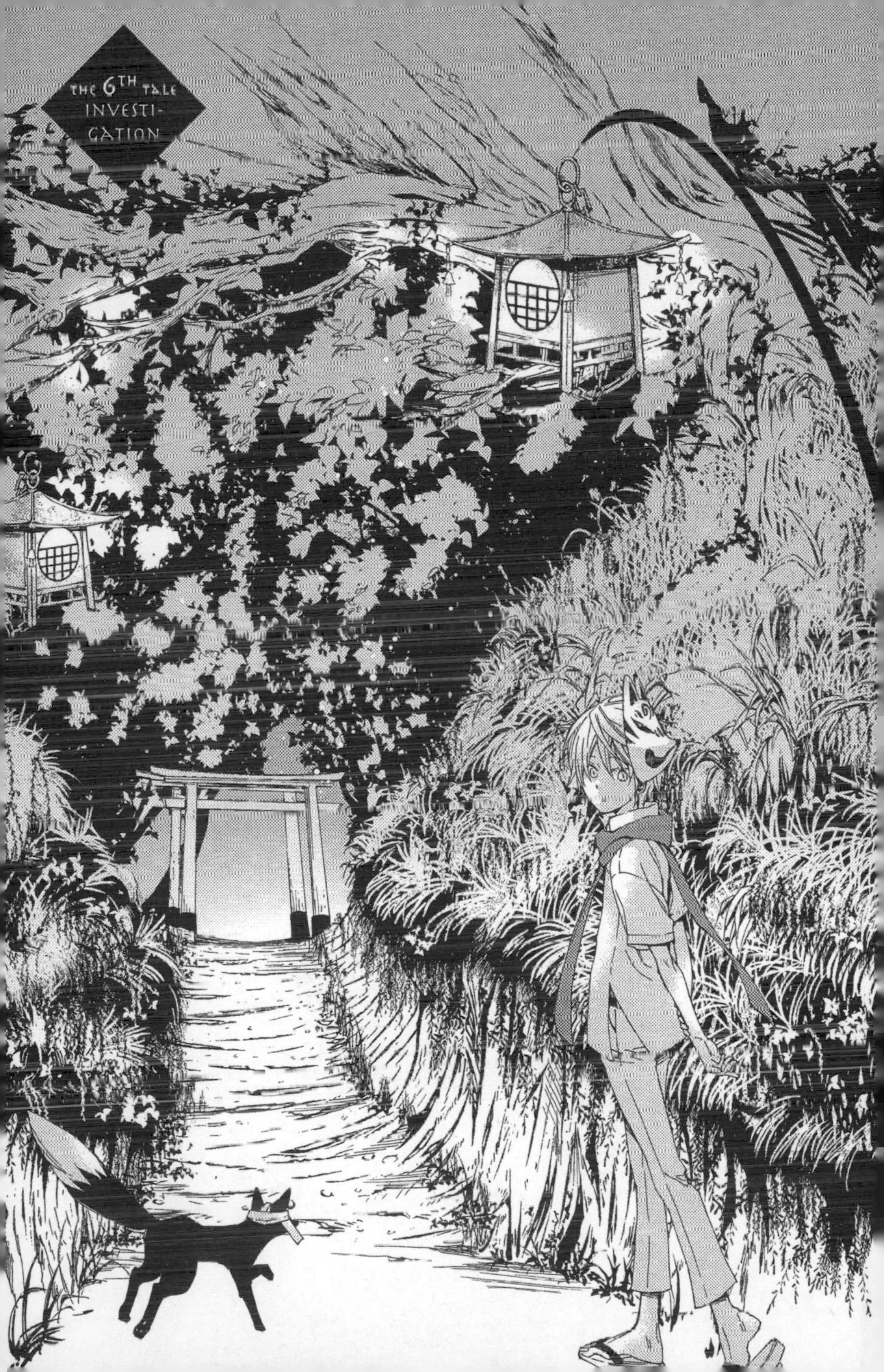
THE 6TH TALE
INVESTIGATION

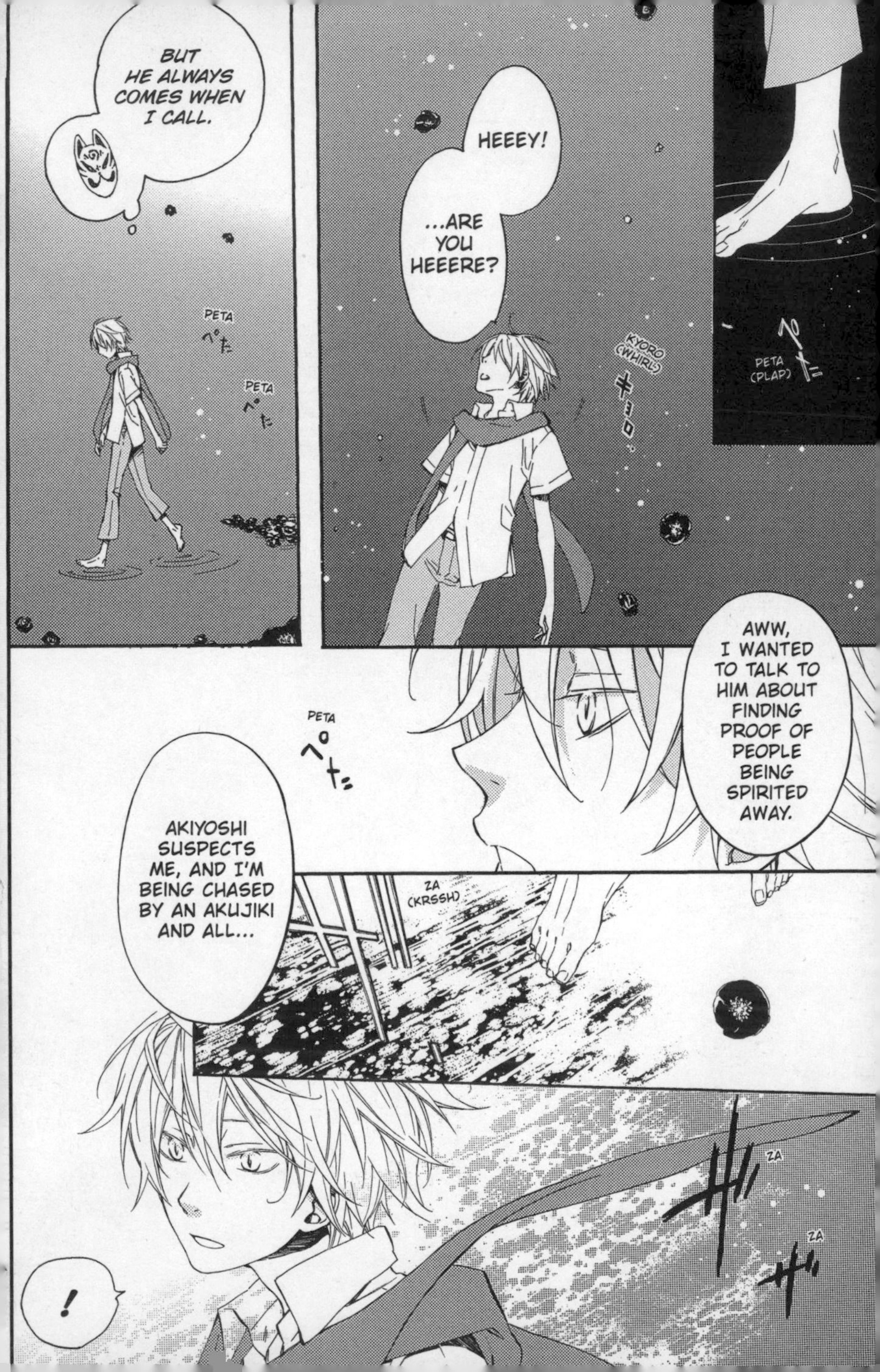

PETA (PLAP)
HEEEY!
...ARE YOU HEEERE?
KYORO (WHIRL)
BUT HE ALWAYS COMES WHEN I CALL.
PETA
PETA
AWW, I WANTED TO TALK TO HIM ABOUT FINDING PROOF OF PEOPLE BEING SPIRITED AWAY.
PETA
AKIYOSHI SUSPECTS ME, AND I'M BEING CHASED BY AN AKUJIKI AND ALL...
ZA (KRSSH)
ZA
ZA
!

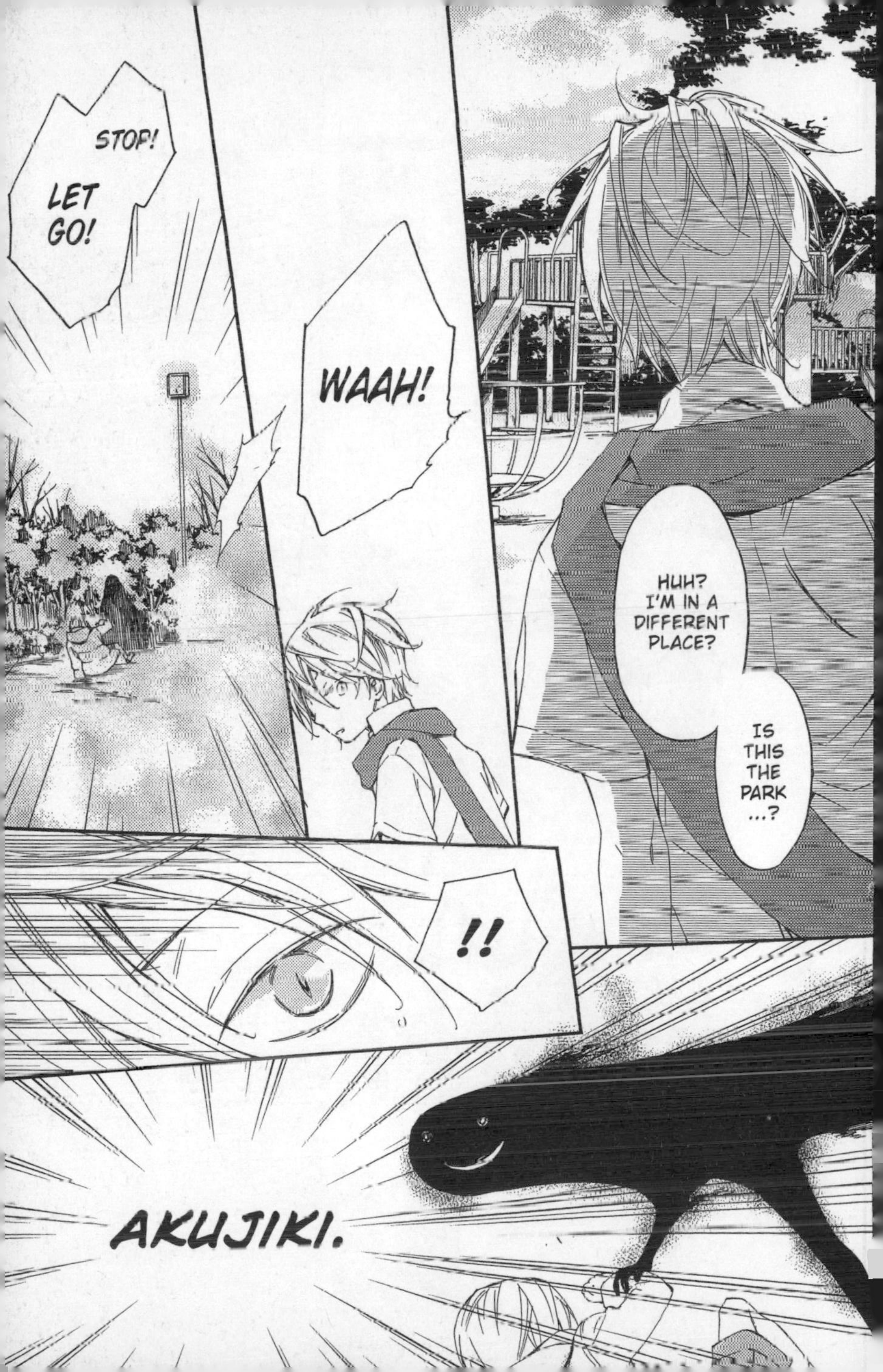
HUH? I'M IN A DIFFERENT PLACE?
IS THIS THE PARK ...?
WAAH!
STOP!
LET GO!
!!
AKUJIKI.

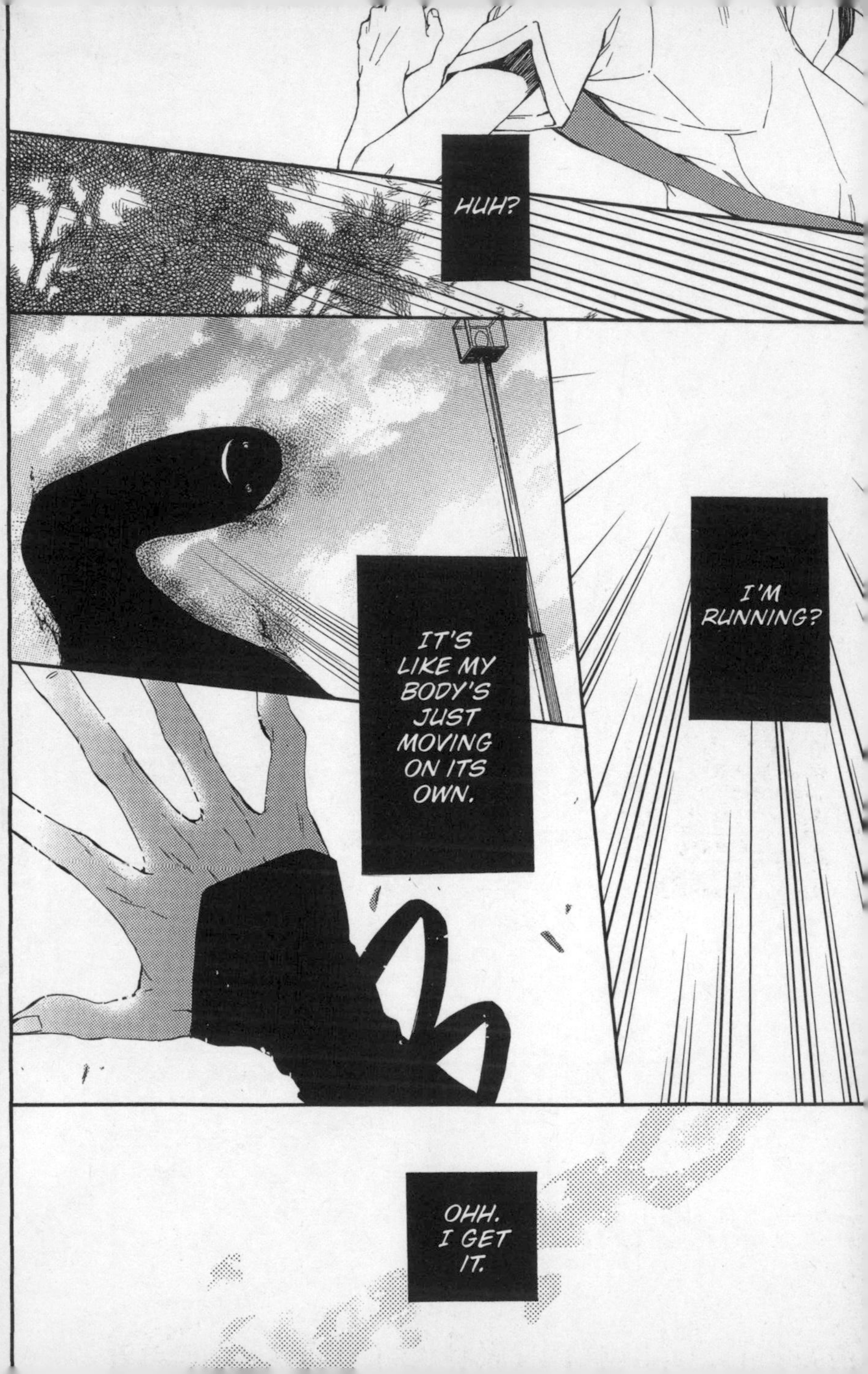
HUH?
I'M RUNNING?
IT'S LIKE MY BODY'S JUST MOVING ON ITS OWN.
OHH. I GET IT.

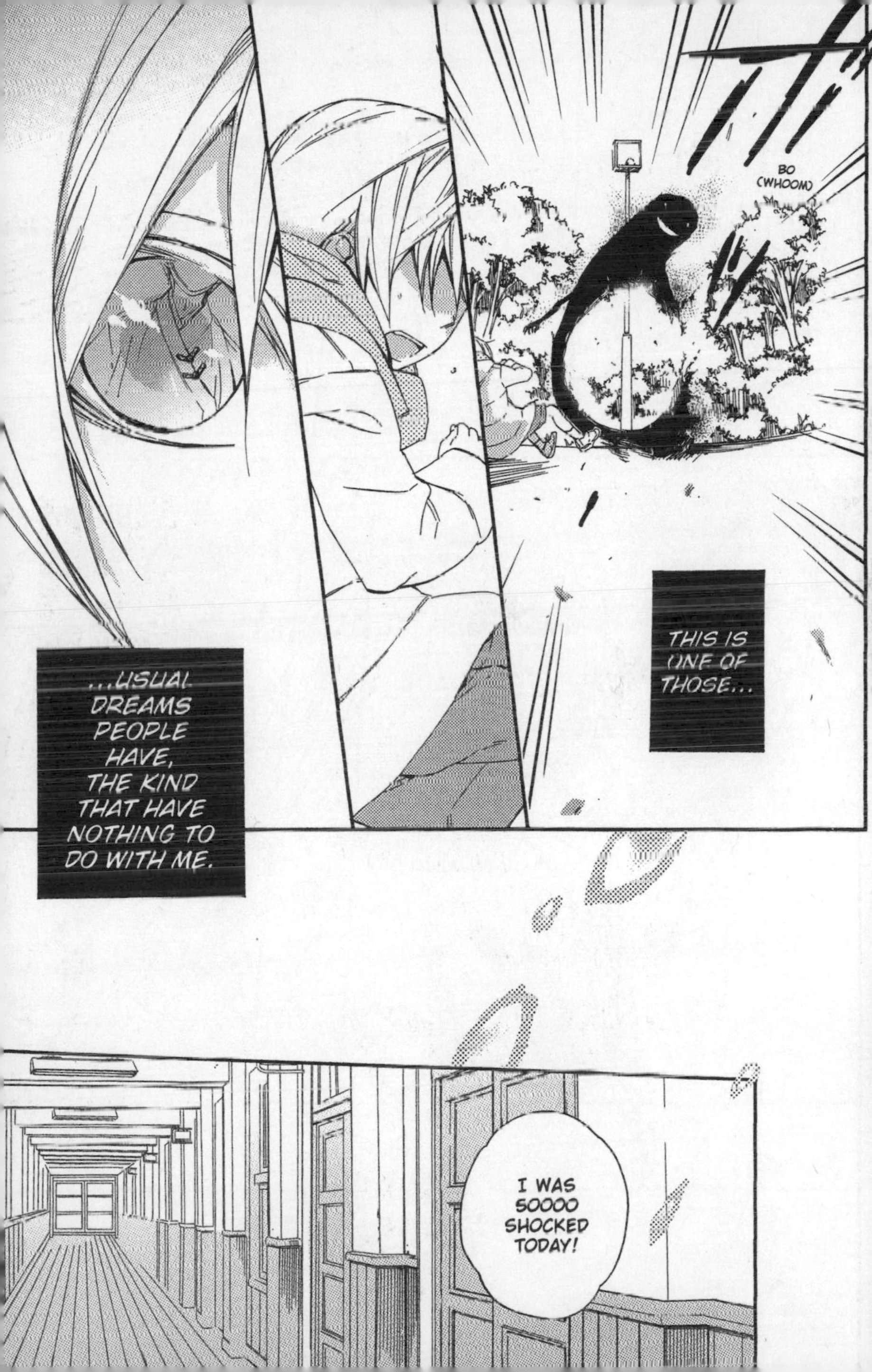
BO (WHOOM)
THIS IS ONE OF THOSE...
...USUAL DREAMS PEOPLE HAVE, THE KIND THAT HAVE NOTHING TO DO WITH ME.
I WAS SOOOO SHOCKED TODAY!

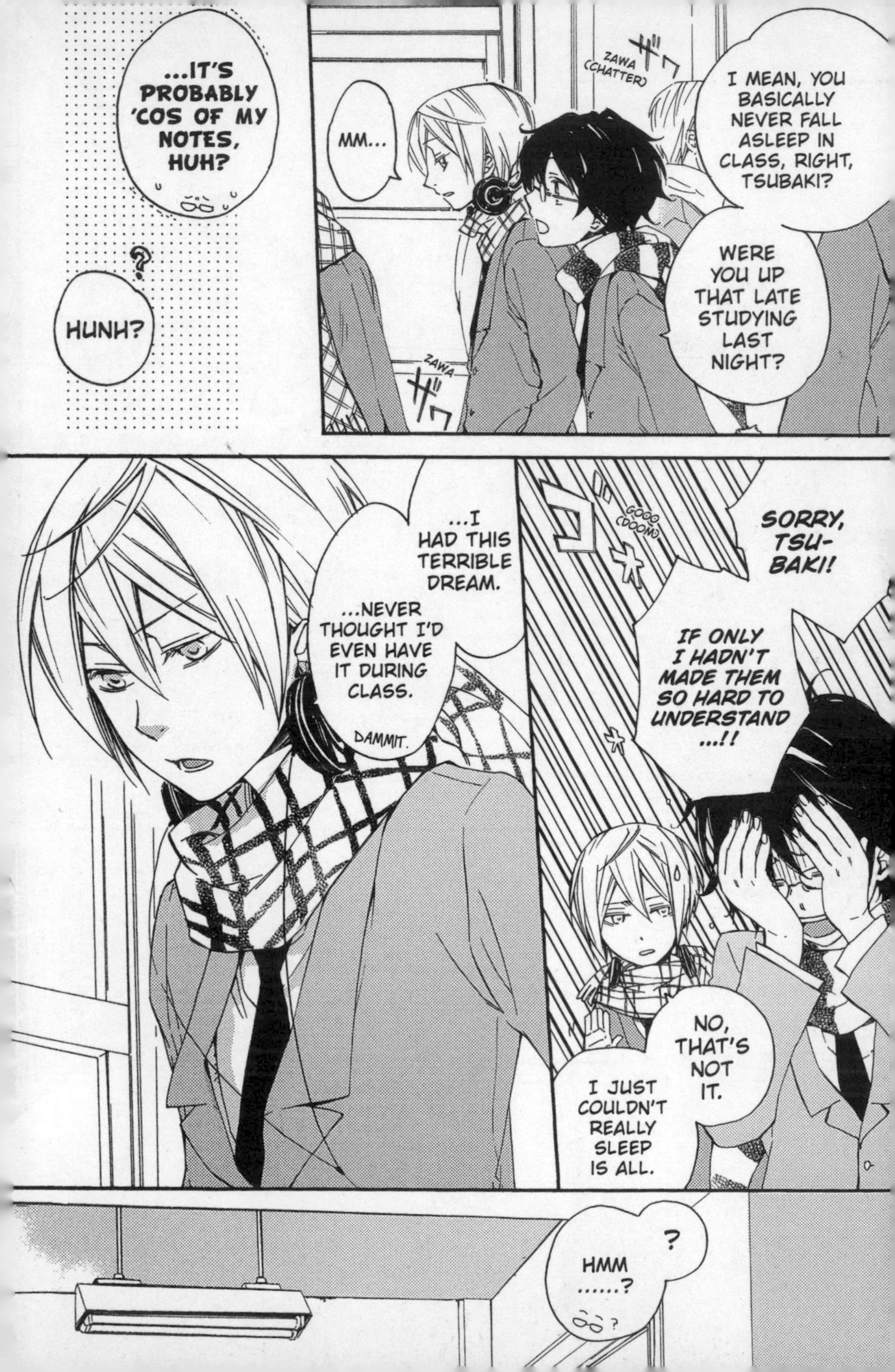
I MEAN, YOU BASICALLY NEVER FALL ASLEEP IN CLASS, RIGHT, TSUBAKI?
ZAWA (CHATTER)
WERE YOU UP THAT LATE STUDYING LAST NIGHT?
MM...
ZAWA
...IT'S PROBABLY 'COS OF MY NOTES, HUH?
HUNH?
SORRY, TSU-BAKI!
GOOO (DOOM)
IF ONLY I HADN'T MADE THEM SO HARD TO UNDERSTAND ...!!
NO, THAT'S NOT IT.
I JUST COULDN'T REALLY SLEEP IS ALL.
...I HAD THIS TERRIBLE DREAM.
...NEVER THOUGHT I'D EVEN HAVE IT DURING CLASS.
DAMMIT.
HMM ......?

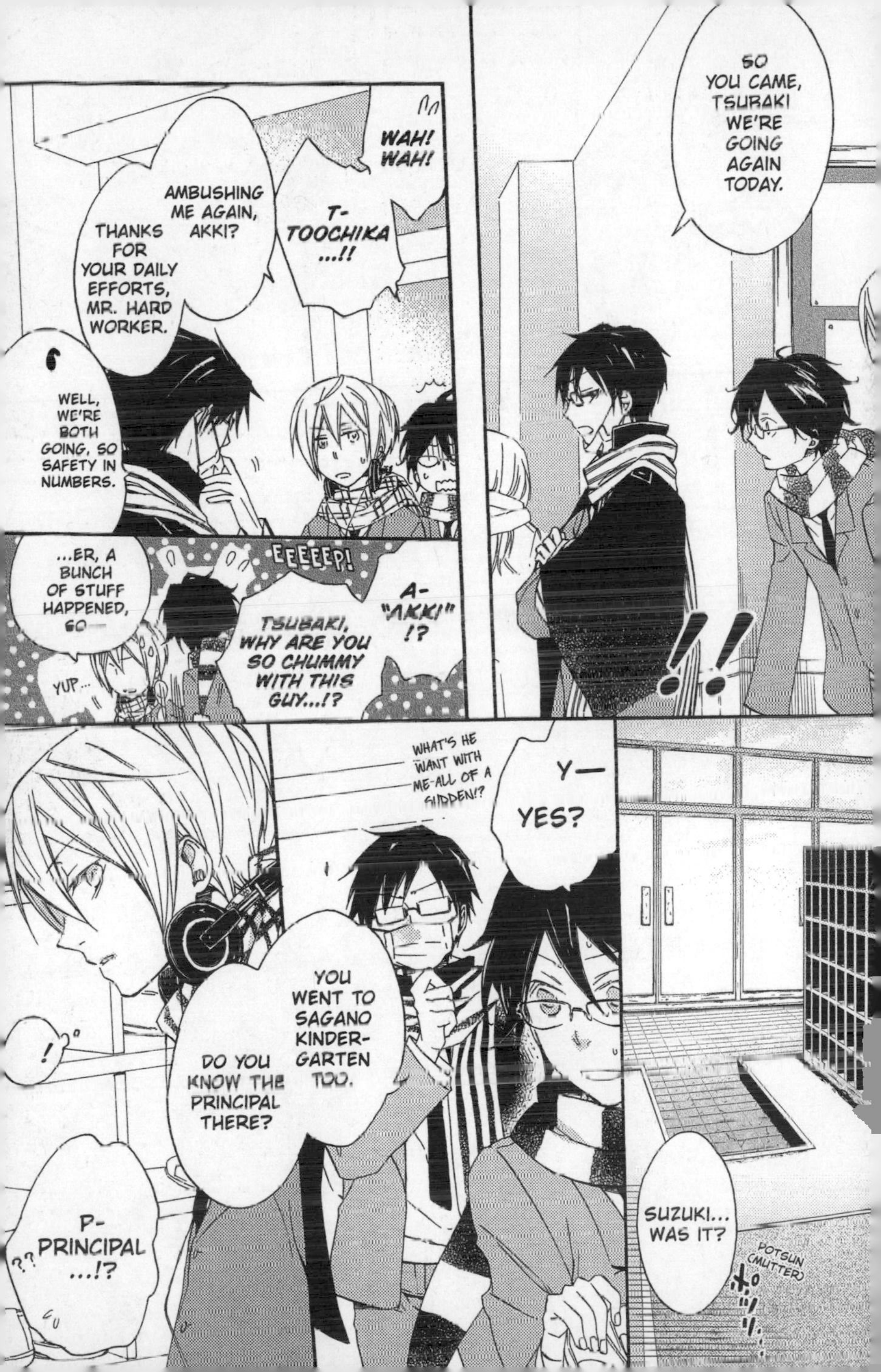
SO YOU CAME, TSUBAKI WE'RE GOING AGAIN TODAY.
WAH! WAH!
T-TOOCHIKA ...!!
AMBUSHING ME AGAIN, AKKI?
THANKS FOR YOUR DAILY EFFORTS, MR. HARD WORKER.
WELL, WE'RE BOTH GOING, SO SAFETY IN NUMBERS.
EEEEEP!
A- "AKKI" !?
TSUBAKI, WHY ARE YOU SO CHUMMY WITH THIS GUY...!?
...ER, A BUNCH OF STUFF HAPPENED, SO—
YUP...
SUZUKI... WAS IT?
POTSUN (MUTTER)
Y—
YES?
WHAT'S HE WANT WITH ME ALL OF A SUDDEN!?
YOU WENT TO SAGANO KINDER-GARTEN TOO.
DO YOU KNOW THE PRINCIPAL THERE?
P-PRINCIPAL ...!?

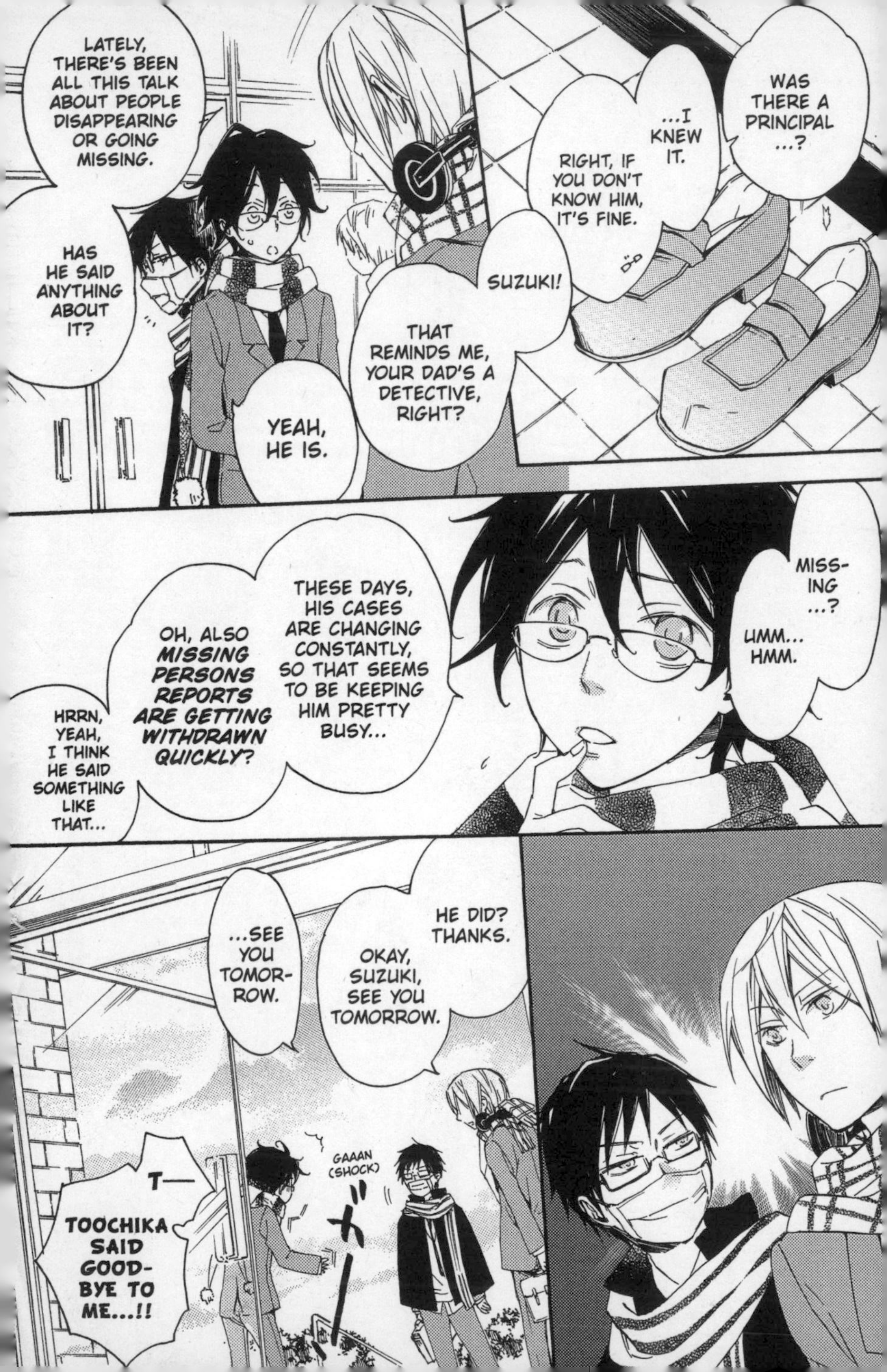
WAS THERE A PRINCIPAL ...?
...I KNEW IT.
RIGHT, IF YOU DON'T KNOW HIM, IT'S FINE.
SUZUKI!
THAT REMINDS ME, YOUR DAD'S A DETECTIVE, RIGHT?
YEAH, HE IS.
LATELY, THERE'S BEEN ALL THIS TALK ABOUT PEOPLE DISAPPEARING OR GOING MISSING.
HAS HE SAID ANYTHING ABOUT IT?
MISS-ING ...?
UMM... HMM.
THESE DAYS, HIS CASES ARE CHANGING CONSTANTLY, SO THAT SEEMS TO BE KEEPING HIM PRETTY BUSY...
OH, ALSO *MISSING PERSONS REPORTS ARE GETTING WITHDRAWN QUICKLY*?
HRRN, YEAH, I THINK HE SAID SOMETHING LIKE THAT...
HE DID? THANKS.
OKAY, SUZUKI, SEE YOU TOMORROW.
...SEE YOU TOMOR-ROW.
GAAAN (SHOCK)
T—
TOOCHIKA SAID GOOD-BYE TO ME...!!

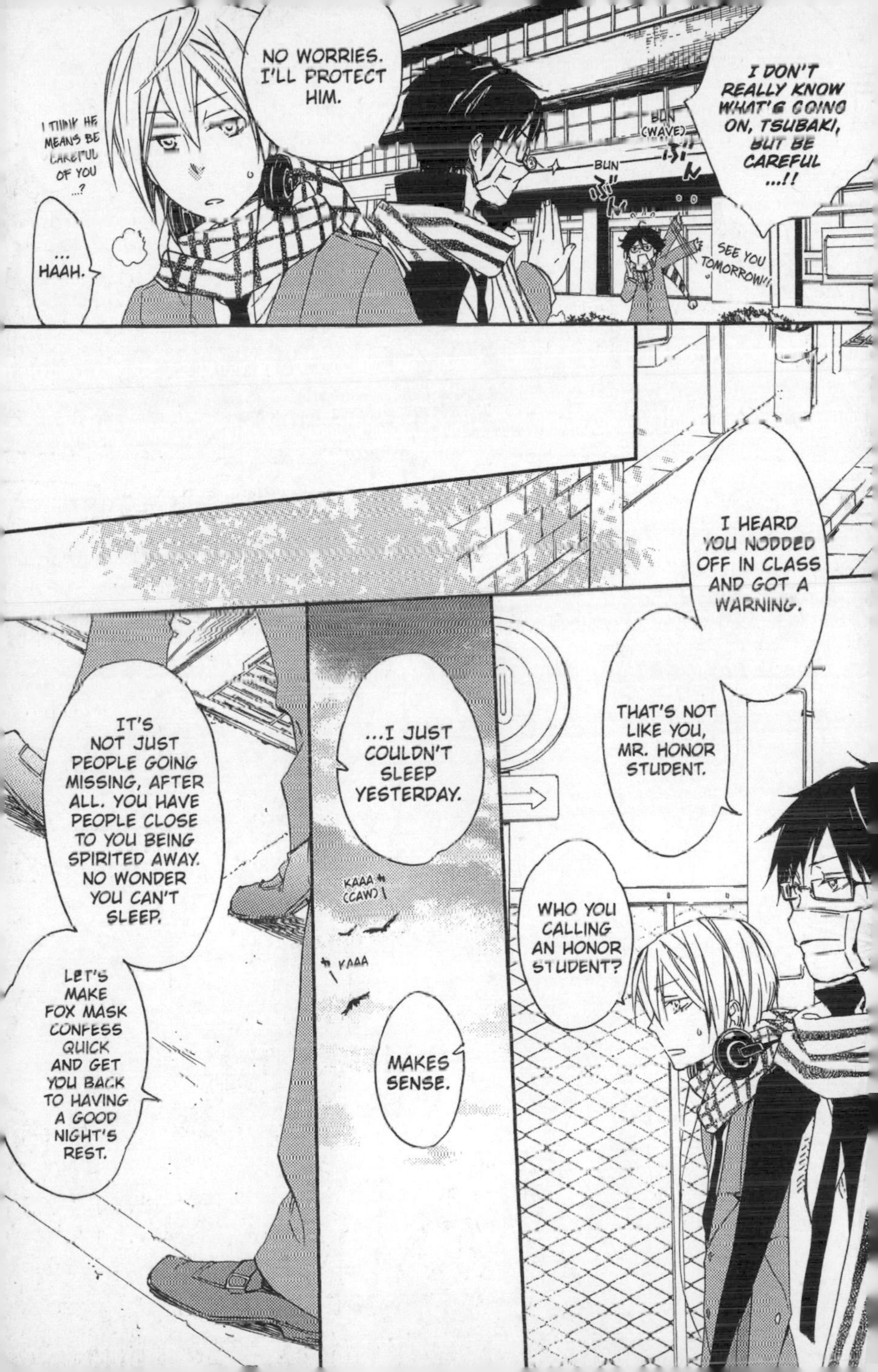
I DON'T REALLY KNOW WHAT'S GOING ON, TSUBAKI, BUT BE CAREFUL ...!!
SEE YOU TOMORROW!!
BUN (WAVE)
BUN
NO WORRIES. I'LL PROTECT HIM.
I THINK HE MEANS BE CAREFUL OF YOU ...?
... HAAH.
I HEARD YOU NODDED OFF IN CLASS AND GOT A WARNING.
THAT'S NOT LIKE YOU, MR. HONOR STUDENT.
WHO YOU CALLING AN HONOR STUDENT?
...I JUST COULDN'T SLEEP YESTERDAY.
KAAA (CAW)
KAAA
MAKES SENSE.
IT'S NOT JUST PEOPLE GOING MISSING, AFTER ALL. YOU HAVE PEOPLE CLOSE TO YOU BEING SPIRITED AWAY. NO WONDER YOU CAN'T SLEEP.
LET'S MAKE FOX MASK CONFESS QUICK AND GET YOU BACK TO HAVING A GOOD NIGHT'S REST.

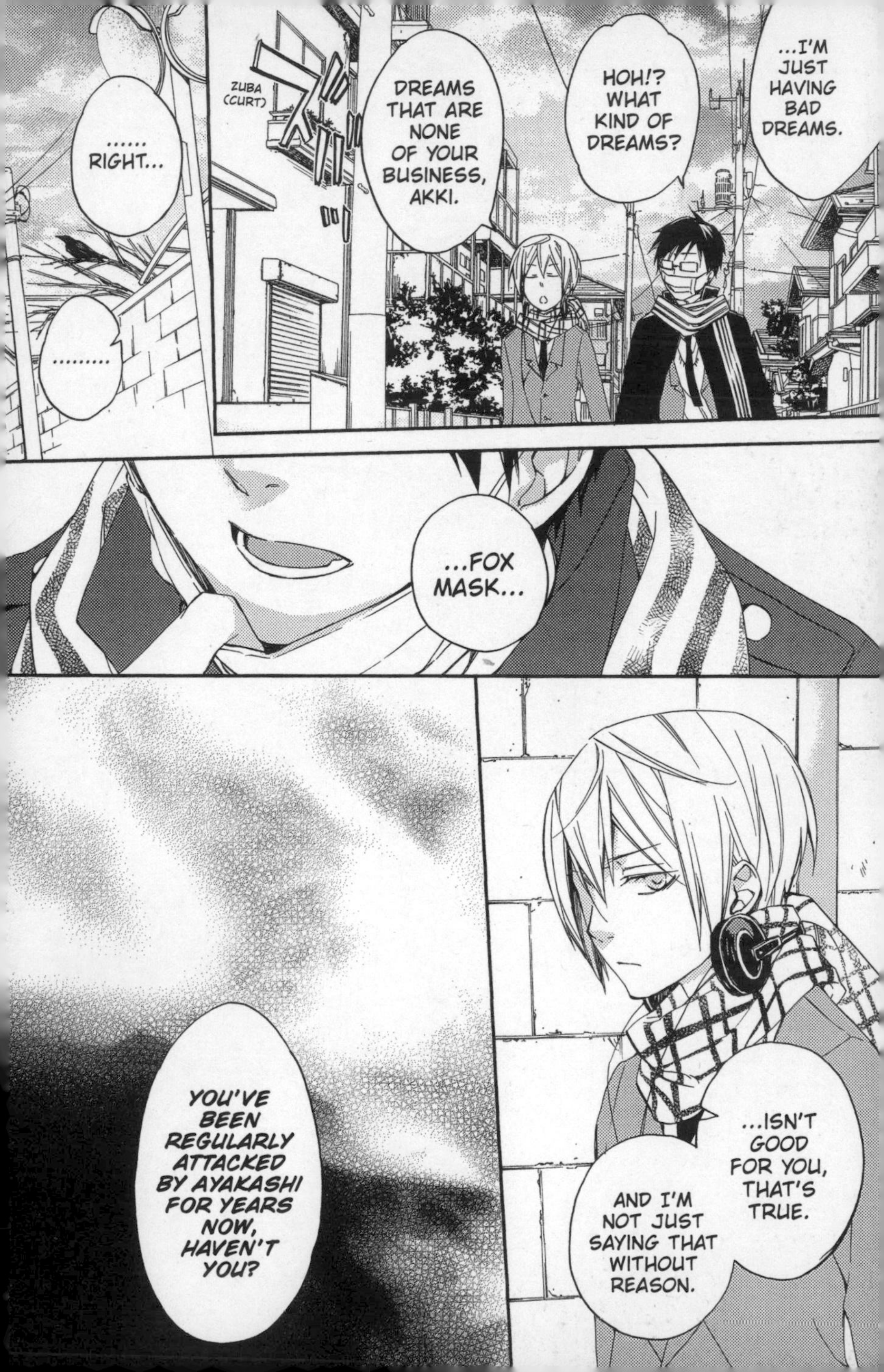
...I'M JUST HAVING BAD DREAMS.
HOH!? WHAT KIND OF DREAMS?
DREAMS THAT ARE NONE OF YOUR BUSINESS, AKKI.
ZUBA (CURT)
...... RIGHT...
....
...FOX MASK...
...ISN'T GOOD FOR YOU, THAT'S TRUE.
AND I'M NOT JUST SAYING THAT WITHOUT REASON.
YOU'VE BEEN REGULARLY ATTACKED BY AYAKASHI FOR YEARS NOW, HAVEN'T YOU?

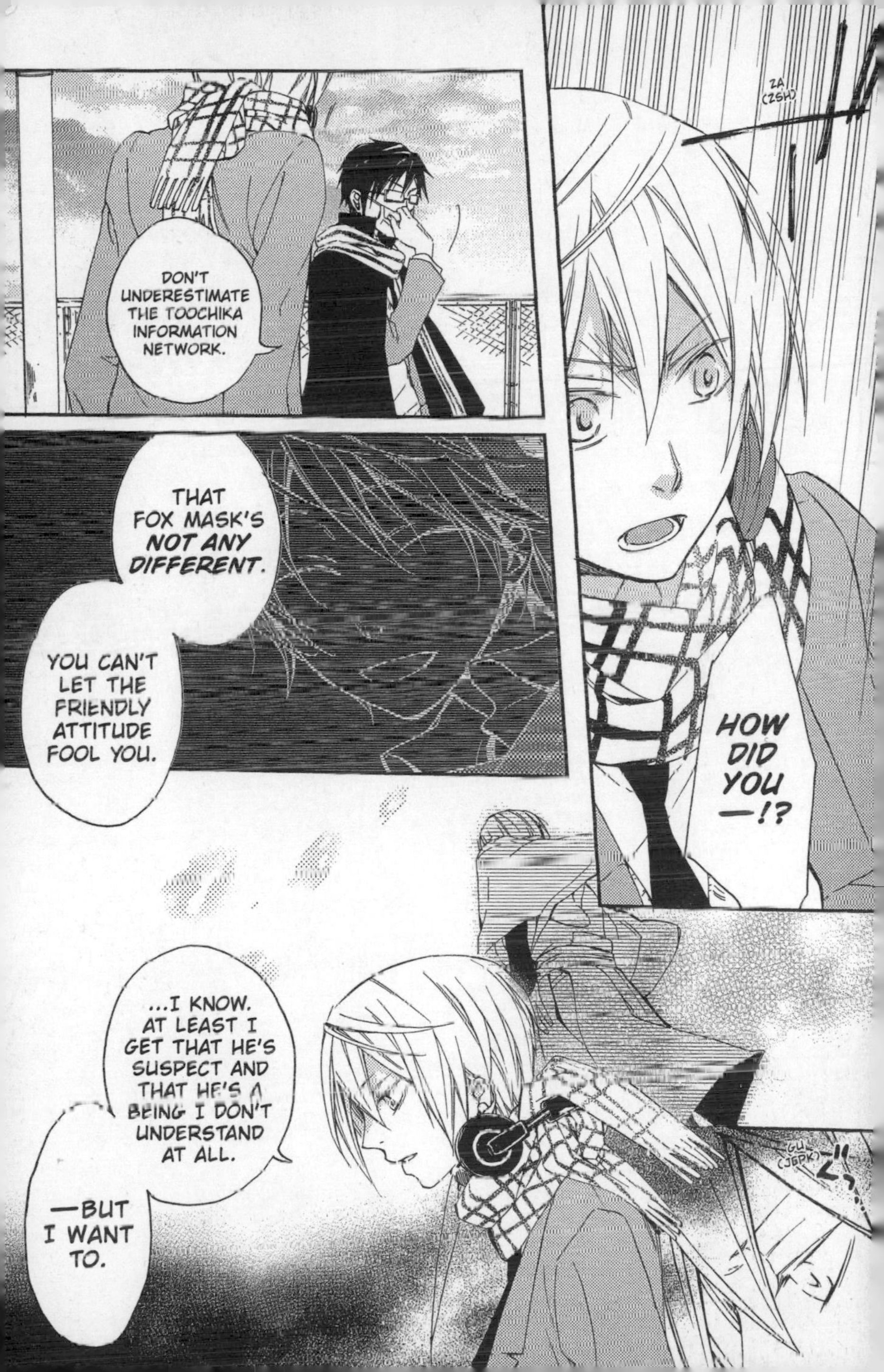
ZA
(ZSH)
HOW DID YOU —!?
DON'T UNDERESTIMATE THE TOOCHIKA INFORMATION NETWORK.
THAT FOX MASK'S ***NOT ANY DIFFERENT***.
YOU CAN'T LET THE FRIENDLY ATTITUDE FOOL YOU.
GU
(JGPK)
...I KNOW. AT LEAST I GET THAT HE'S SUSPECT AND THAT HE'S A BEING I DON'T UNDERSTAND AT ALL.
—BUT I WANT TO.

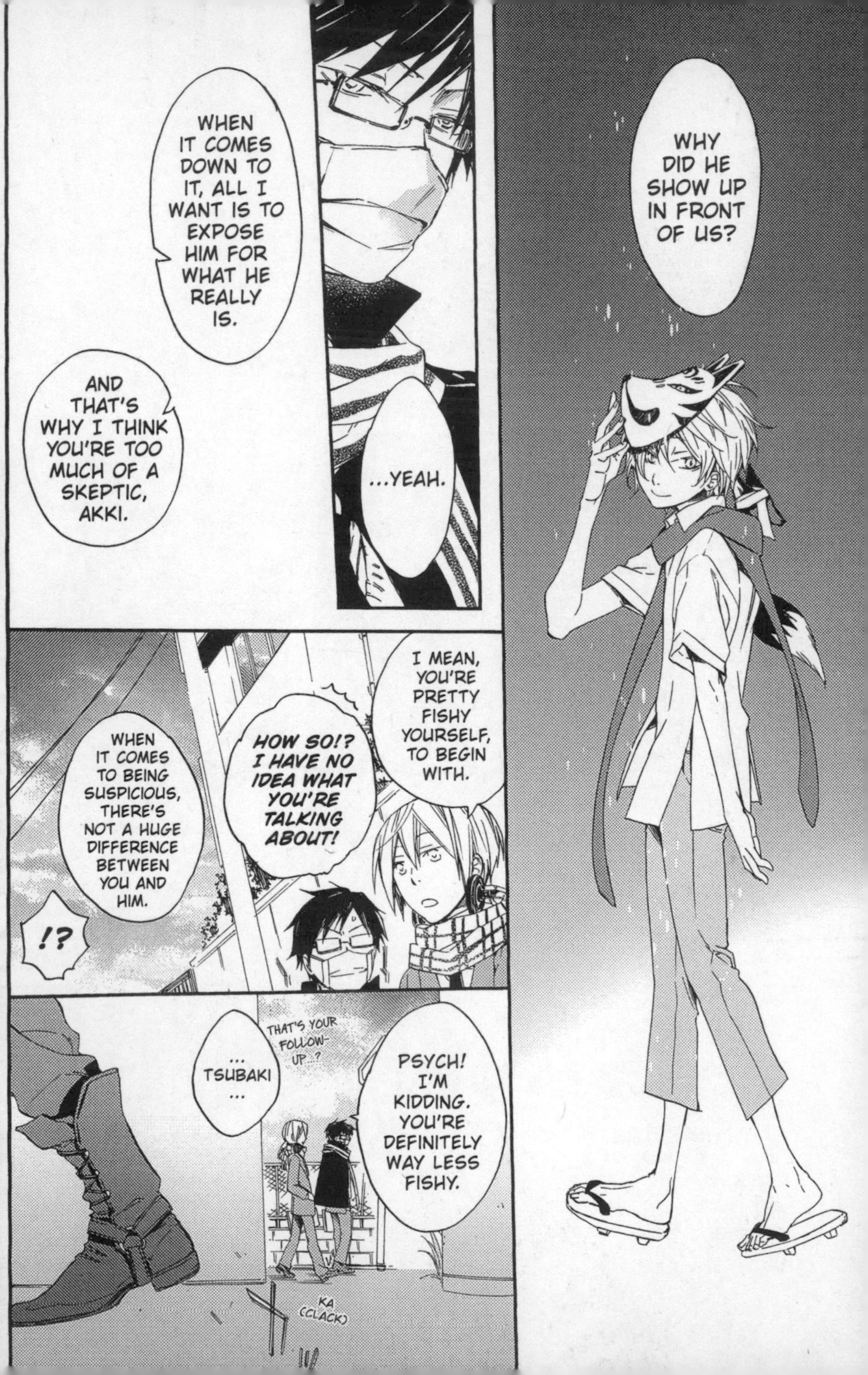
WHY DID HE SHOW UP IN FRONT OF US?
WHEN IT COMES DOWN TO IT, ALL I WANT IS TO EXPOSE HIM FOR WHAT HE REALLY IS.
...YEAH.
AND THAT'S WHY I THINK YOU'RE TOO MUCH OF A SKEPTIC, AKKI.
I MEAN, YOU'RE PRETTY FISHY YOURSELF, TO BEGIN WITH.
HOW SO!? I HAVE NO IDEA WHAT YOU'RE TALKING ABOUT!
WHEN IT COMES TO BEING SUSPICIOUS, THERE'S NOT A HUGE DIFFERENCE BETWEEN YOU AND HIM.
!?
PSYCH! I'M KIDDING. YOU'RE DEFINITELY WAY LESS FISHY.
THAT'S YOUR FOLLOW-UP...?
... TSUBAKI ...
KA (CLACK)

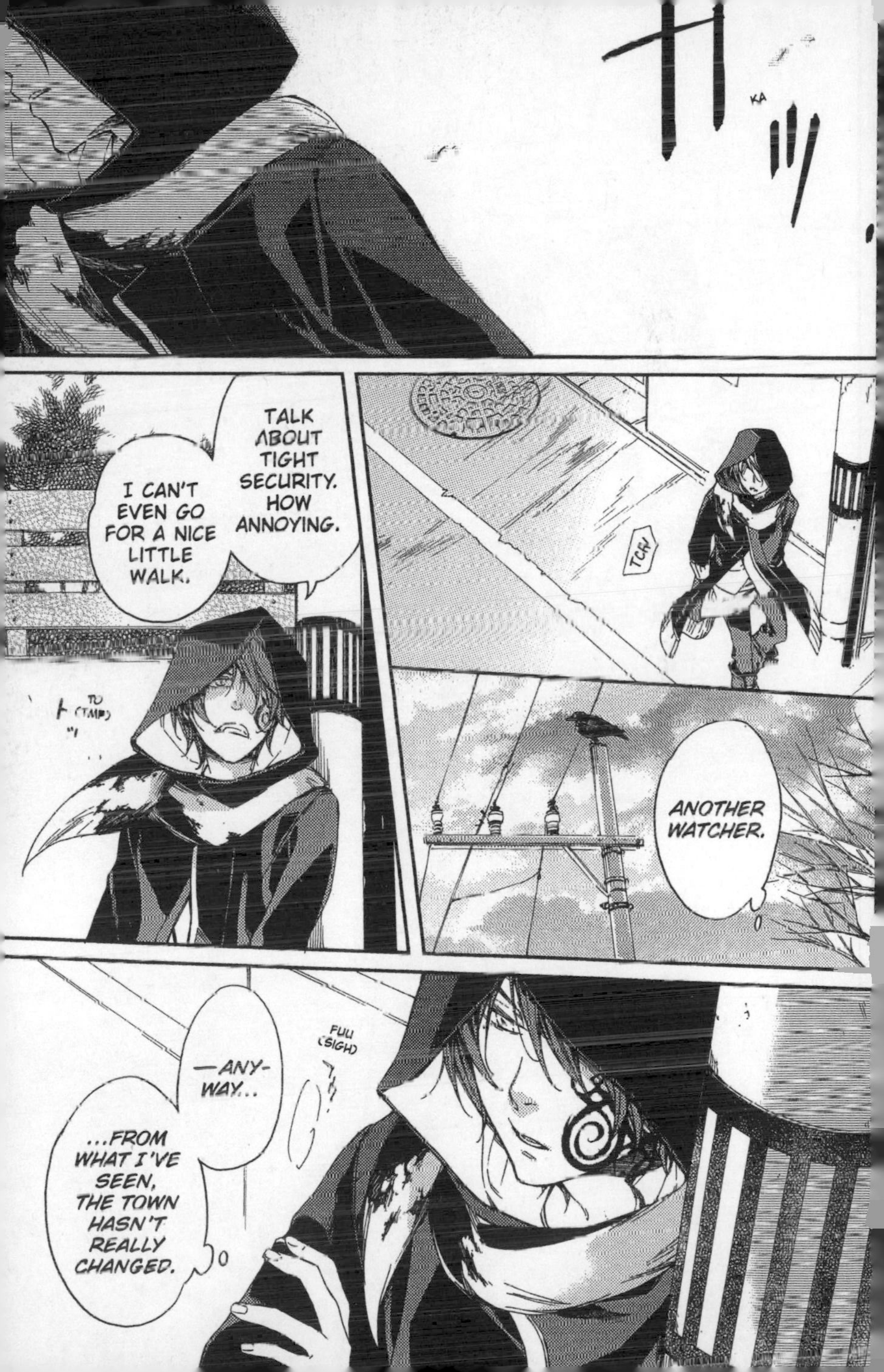
KA
TCH
ANOTHER WATCHER.
TALK ABOUT TIGHT SECURITY. HOW ANNOYING.
I CAN'T EVEN GO FOR A NICE LITTLE WALK.
TO (TMP)
FUU (SIGH)
—ANY-WAY...
...FROM WHAT I'VE SEEN, THE TOWN HASN'T REALLY CHANGED.

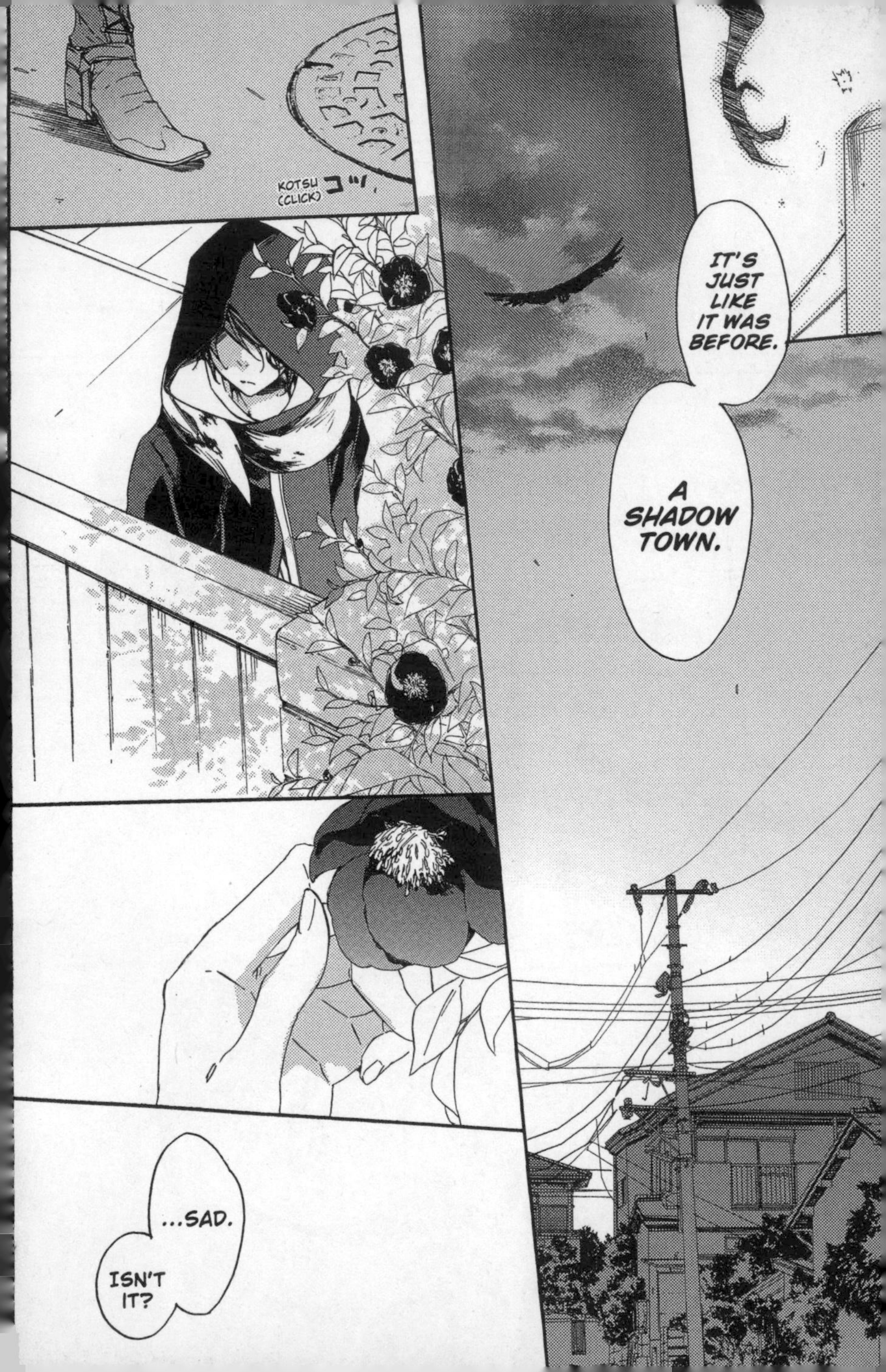
IT'S JUST LIKE IT WAS BEFORE.
A SHADOW TOWN.
KOTSU (CLICK)
...SAD.
ISN'T IT?

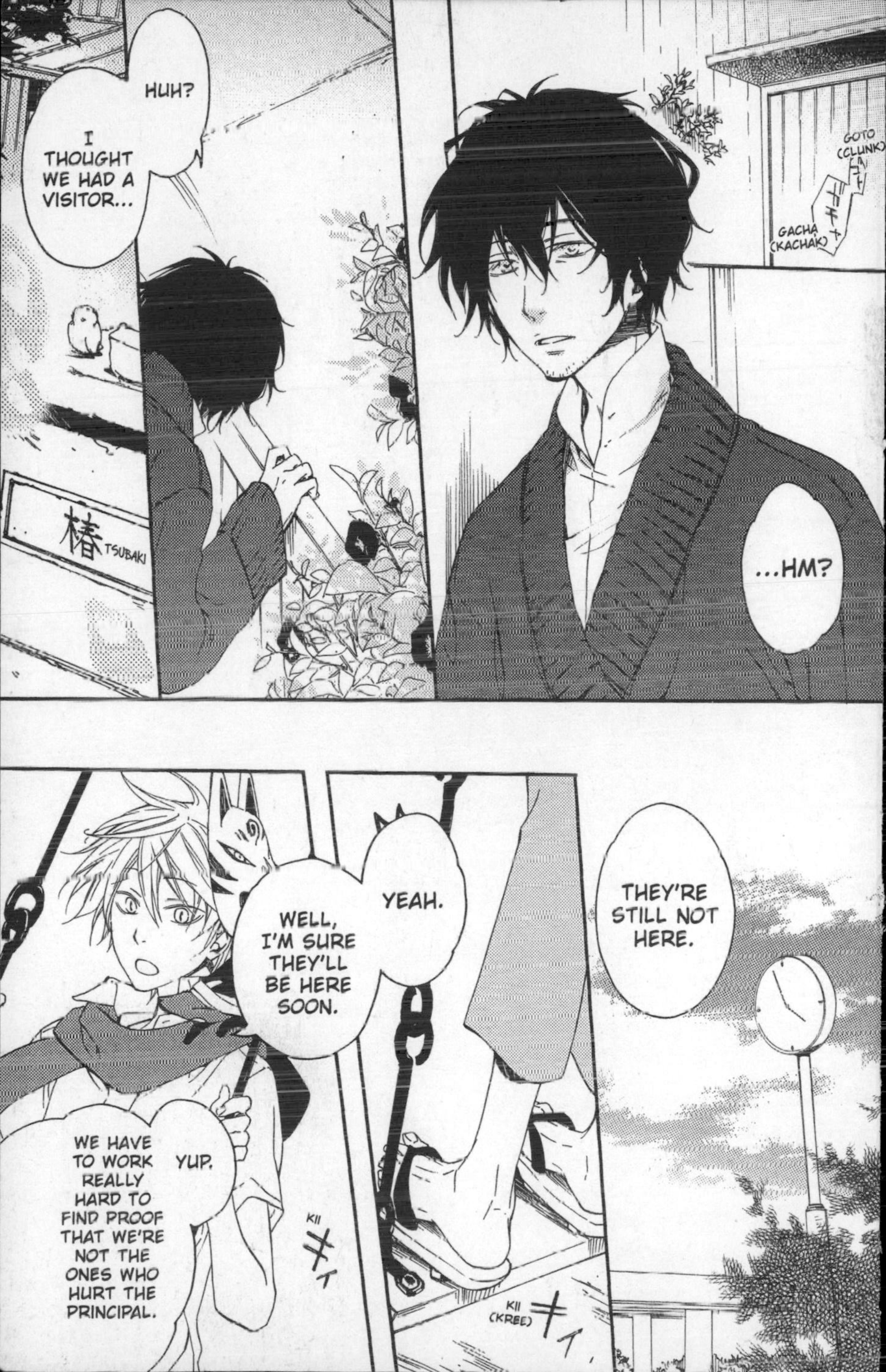
GOTO (CLUNK)
GACHA (KACHAK)
...HM?
HUH?
I THOUGHT WE HAD A VISITOR...
椿 TSUBAKI
THEY'RE STILL NOT HERE.
YEAH.
WELL, I'M SURE THEY'LL BE HERE SOON.
KII (KREE)
YUP.
WE HAVE TO WORK REALLY HARD TO FIND PROOF THAT WE'RE NOT THE ONES WHO HURT THE PRINCIPAL.
KII

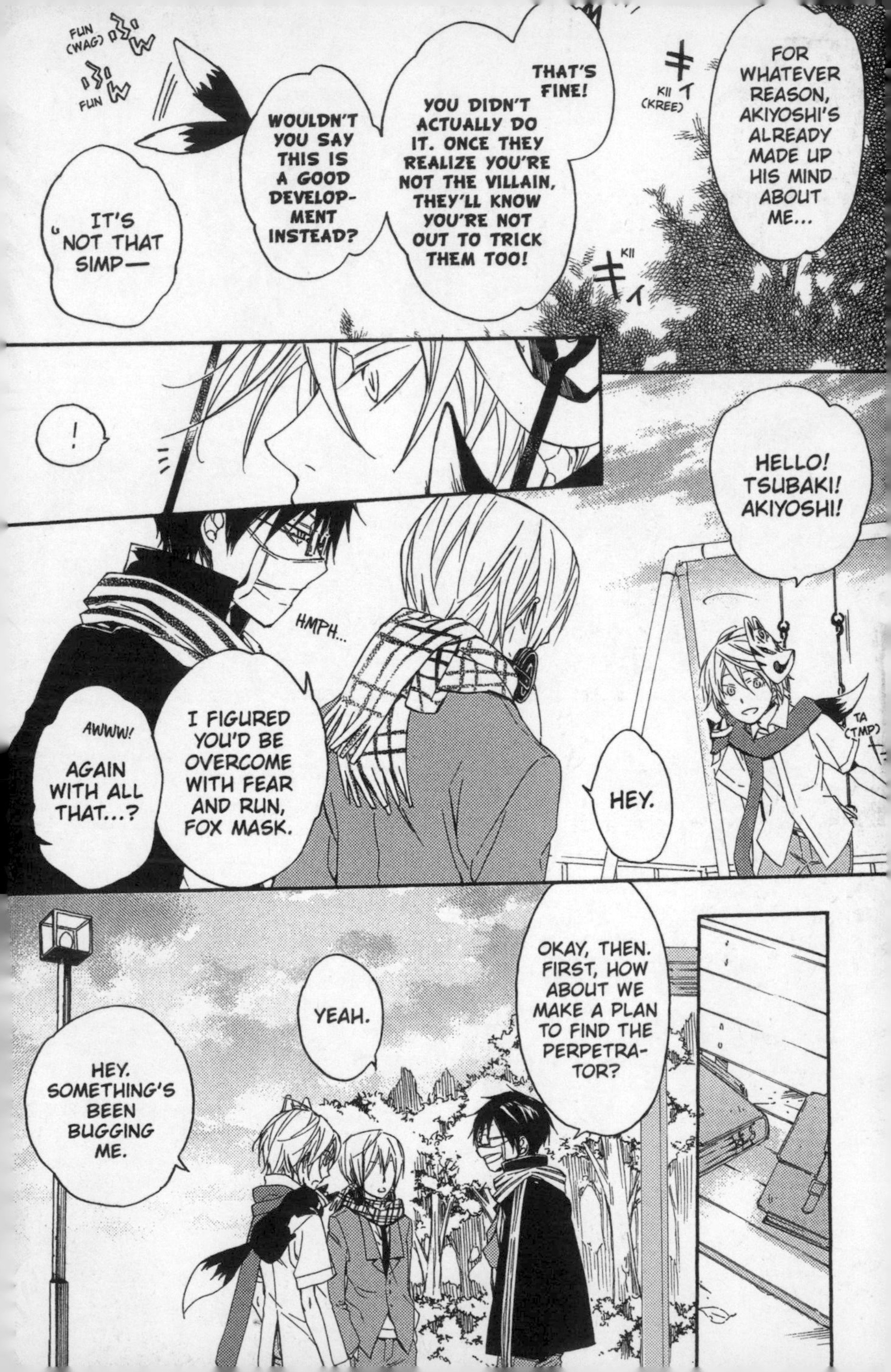
FOR WHATEVER REASON, AKIYOSHI'S ALREADY MADE UP HIS MIND ABOUT ME...
KII (KREE)
KII
THAT'S FINE!
YOU DIDN'T ACTUALLY DO IT. ONCE THEY REALIZE YOU'RE NOT THE VILLAIN, THEY'LL KNOW YOU'RE NOT OUT TO TRICK THEM TOO!
WOULDN'T YOU SAY THIS IS A GOOD DEVELOPMENT INSTEAD?
FUN (WAG)
FUN
IT'S NOT THAT SIMP—
HELLO! TSUBAKI! AKIYOSHI!
TA (TMP)
!
HEY.
HMPH...
I FIGURED YOU'D BE OVERCOME WITH FEAR AND RUN, FOX MASK.
AWWW!
AGAIN WITH ALL THAT...?
OKAY, THEN. FIRST, HOW ABOUT WE MAKE A PLAN TO FIND THE PERPETRATOR?
YEAH.
HEY. SOMETHING'S BEEN BUGGING ME.

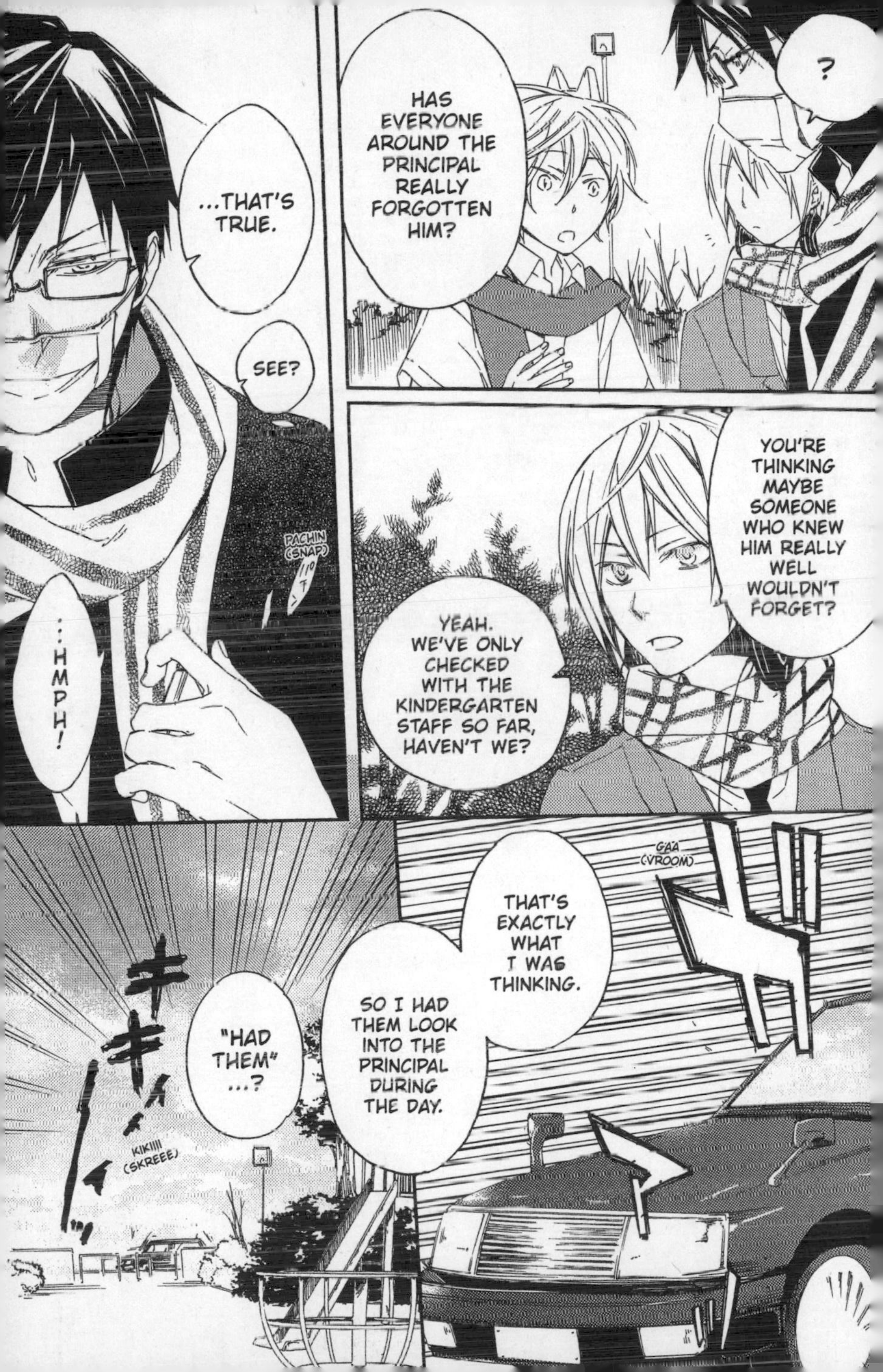
?
HAS EVERYONE AROUND THE PRINCIPAL REALLY FORGOTTEN HIM?
YOU'RE THINKING MAYBE SOMEONE WHO KNEW HIM REALLY WELL WOULDN'T FORGET?
YEAH. WE'VE ONLY CHECKED WITH THE KINDERGARTEN STAFF SO FAR, HAVEN'T WE?
...THAT'S TRUE.
SEE?
PACHIN (SNAP)
...HMPH!
GAA (VROOM)
THAT'S EXACTLY WHAT I WAS THINKING.
SO I HAD THEM LOOK INTO THE PRINCIPAL DURING THE DAY.
"HAD THEM"...?
KIKIIII (SKREEE)

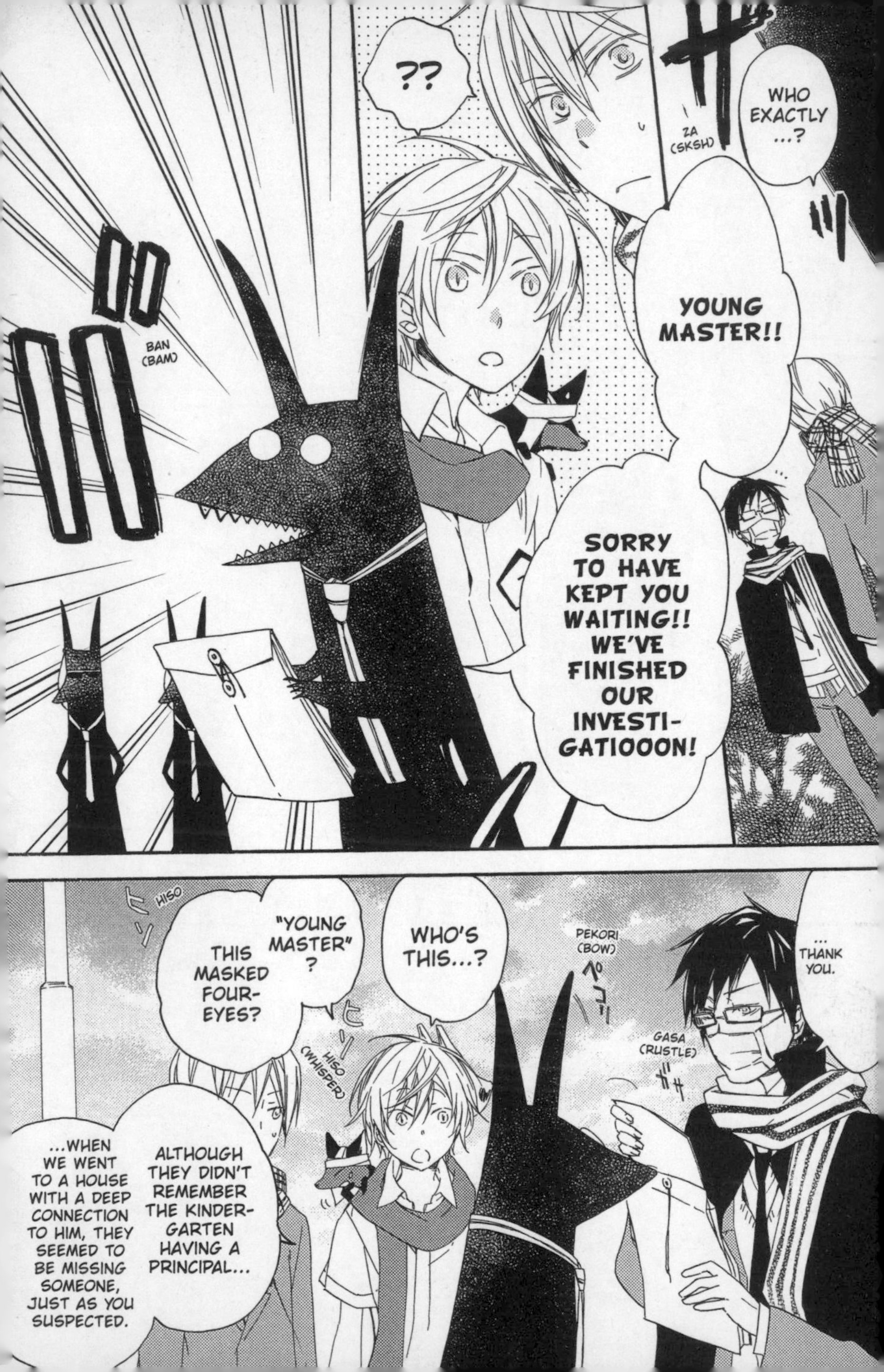
WHO EXACTLY ...?
ZA (SKSH)
??
YOUNG MASTER!!
SORRY TO HAVE KEPT YOU WAITING!! WE'VE FINISHED OUR INVESTI-GATIOOON!
BAN (BAM)
... THANK YOU.
PEKORI (BOW)
WHO'S THIS...?
"YOUNG MASTER"?
THIS MASKED FOUR-EYES?
HISO
HISO (WHISPER)
GASA (RUSTLE)
ALTHOUGH THEY DIDN'T REMEMBER THE KINDER-GARTEN HAVING A PRINCIPAL...
...WHEN WE WENT TO A HOUSE WITH A DEEP CONNECTION TO HIM, THEY SEEMED TO BE MISSING SOMEONE, JUST AS YOU SUSPECTED.

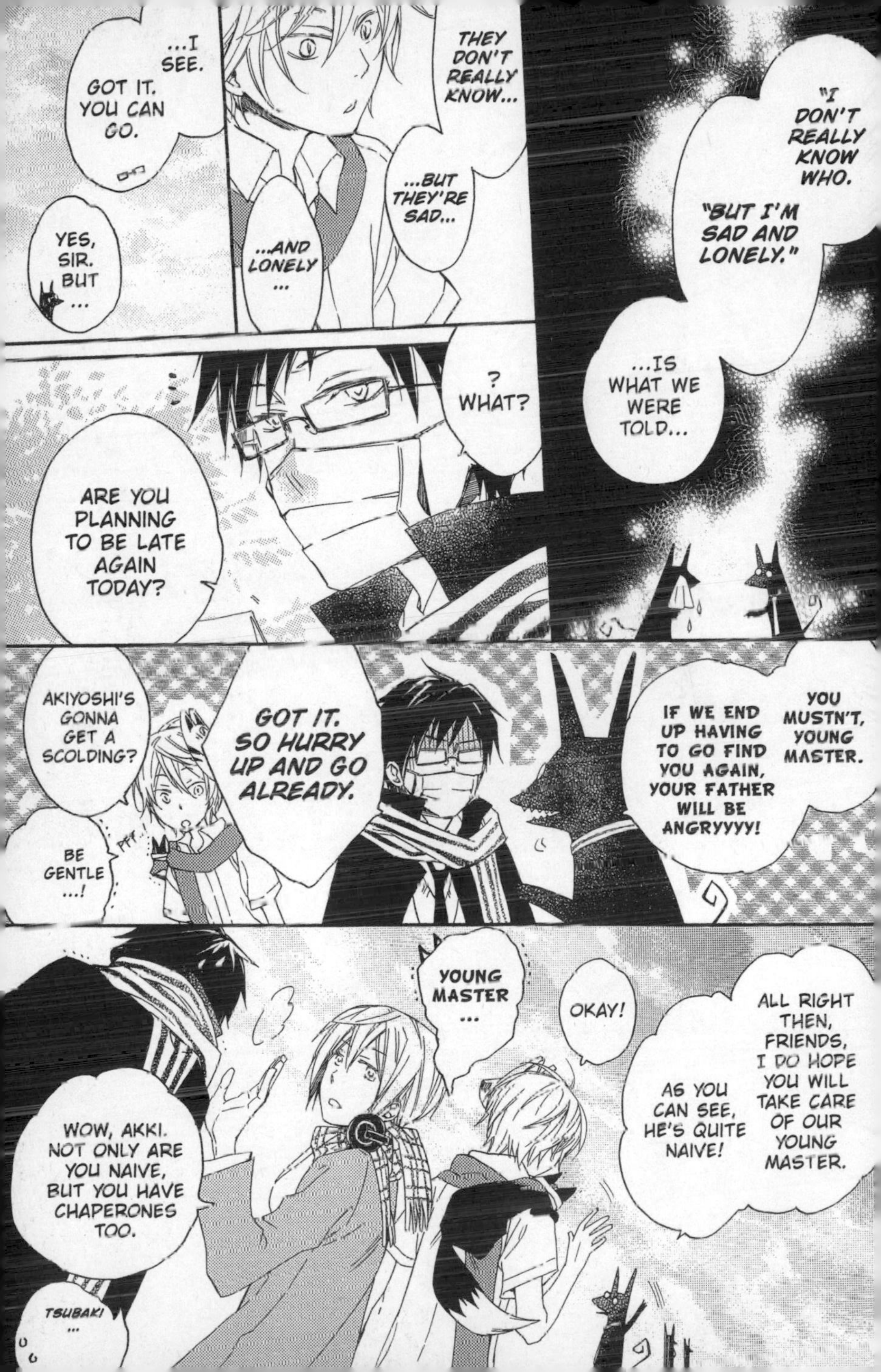
"I DON'T REALLY KNOW WHO.
"BUT I'M SAD AND LONELY."
...IS WHAT WE WERE TOLD...
THEY DON'T REALLY KNOW...
...BUT THEY'RE SAD...
...AND LONELY...
...I SEE.
GOT IT. YOU CAN GO.
YES, SIR. BUT...
? WHAT?
ARE YOU PLANNING TO BE LATE AGAIN TODAY?
YOU MUSTN'T, YOUNG MASTER.
IF WE END UP HAVING TO GO FIND YOU AGAIN, YOUR FATHER WILL BE ANGRYYYY!
GOT IT. SO HURRY UP AND GO ALREADY.
AKIYOSHI'S GONNA GET A SCOLDING?
PFF
BE GENTLE ...!
ALL RIGHT THEN, FRIENDS, I DO HOPE YOU WILL TAKE CARE OF OUR YOUNG MASTER.
AS YOU CAN SEE, HE'S QUITE NAIVE!
OKAY!
YOUNG MASTER...
WOW, AKKI. NOT ONLY ARE YOU NAIVE, BUT YOU HAVE CHAPERONES TOO.
TSUBAKI...

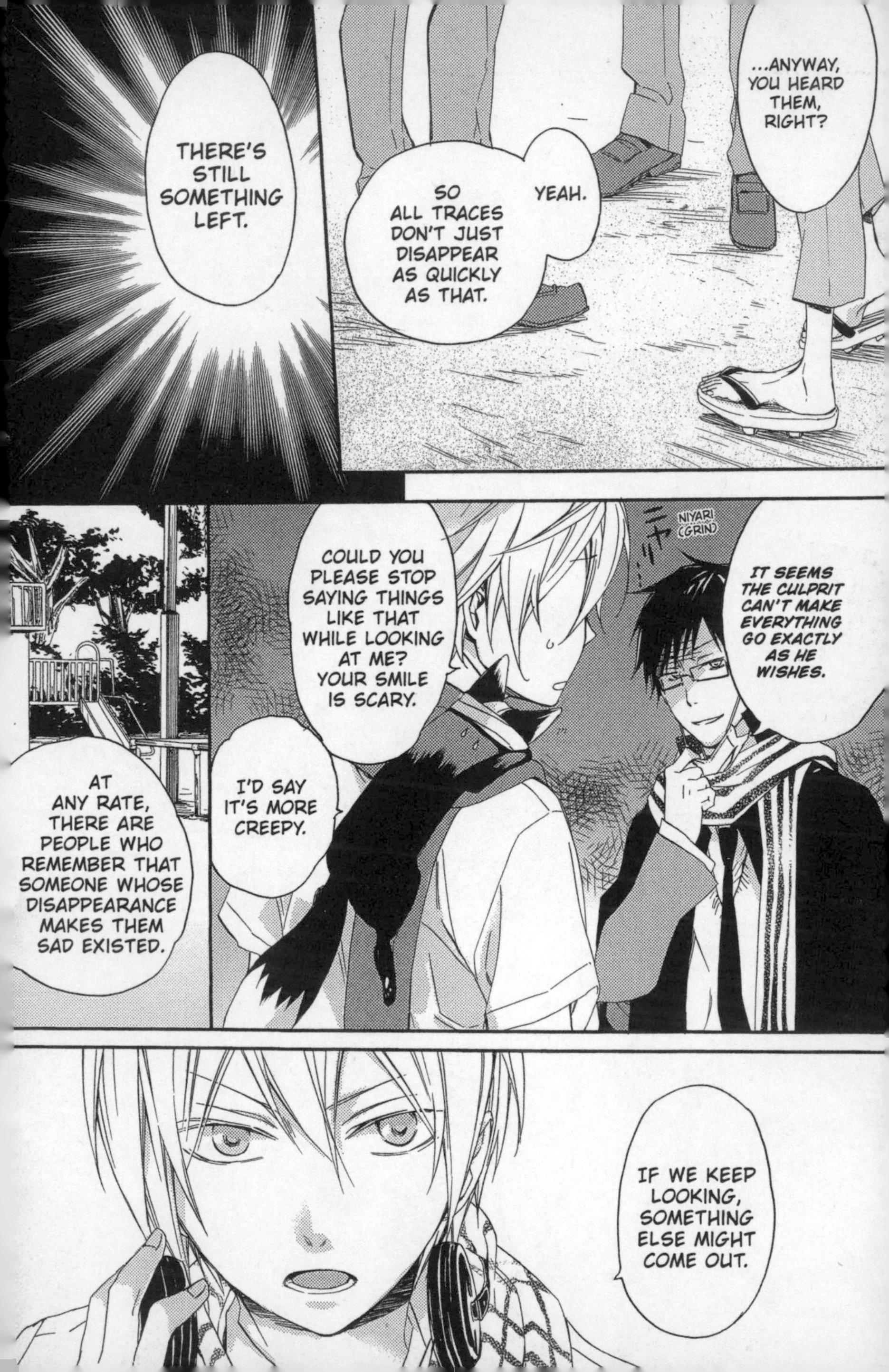
...ANYWAY, YOU HEARD THEM, RIGHT?
YEAH.
SO ALL TRACES DON'T JUST DISAPPEAR AS QUICKLY AS THAT.
THERE'S STILL SOMETHING LEFT.
NIYARI (GRIN)
IT SEEMS THE CULPRIT CAN'T MAKE EVERYTHING GO EXACTLY AS HE WISHES.
COULD YOU PLEASE STOP SAYING THINGS LIKE THAT WHILE LOOKING AT ME? YOUR SMILE IS SCARY.
I'D SAY IT'S MORE CREEPY.
AT ANY RATE, THERE ARE PEOPLE WHO REMEMBER THAT SOMEONE WHOSE DISAPPEARANCE MAKES THEM SAD EXISTED.
IF WE KEEP LOOKING, SOMETHING ELSE MIGHT COME OUT.

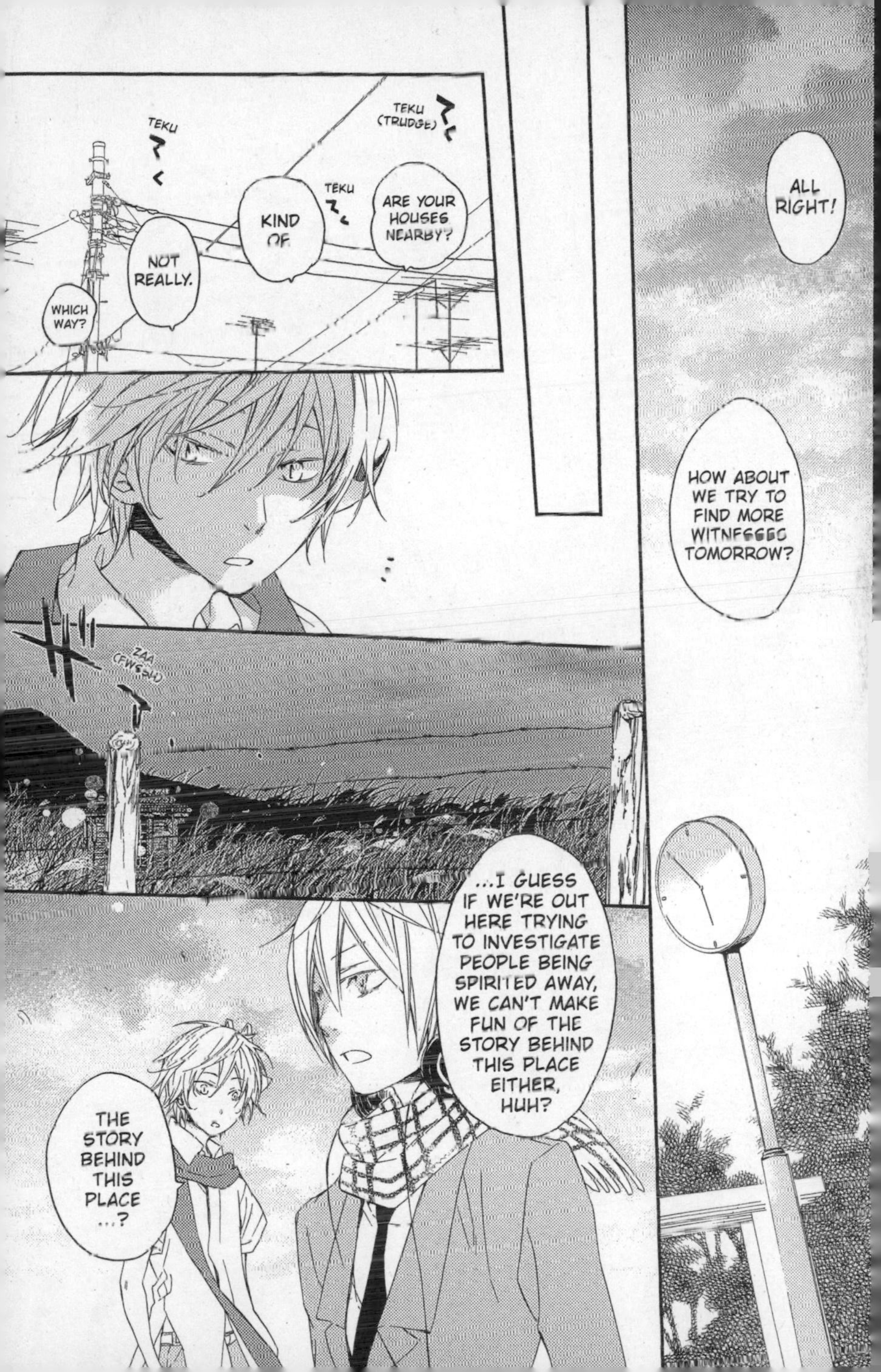
ALL RIGHT!
HOW ABOUT WE TRY TO FIND MORE WITNESSES TOMORROW?
TEKU (TRUDGE)
ARE YOUR HOUSES NEARBY?
TEKU
KIND OF
TEKU
NOT REALLY.
WHICH WAY?
ZAA (FWSSH)
...I GUESS IF WE'RE OUT HERE TRYING TO INVESTIGATE PEOPLE BEING SPIRITED AWAY, WE CAN'T MAKE FUN OF THE STORY BEHIND THIS PLACE EITHER, HUH?
THE STORY BEHIND THIS PLACE ...?

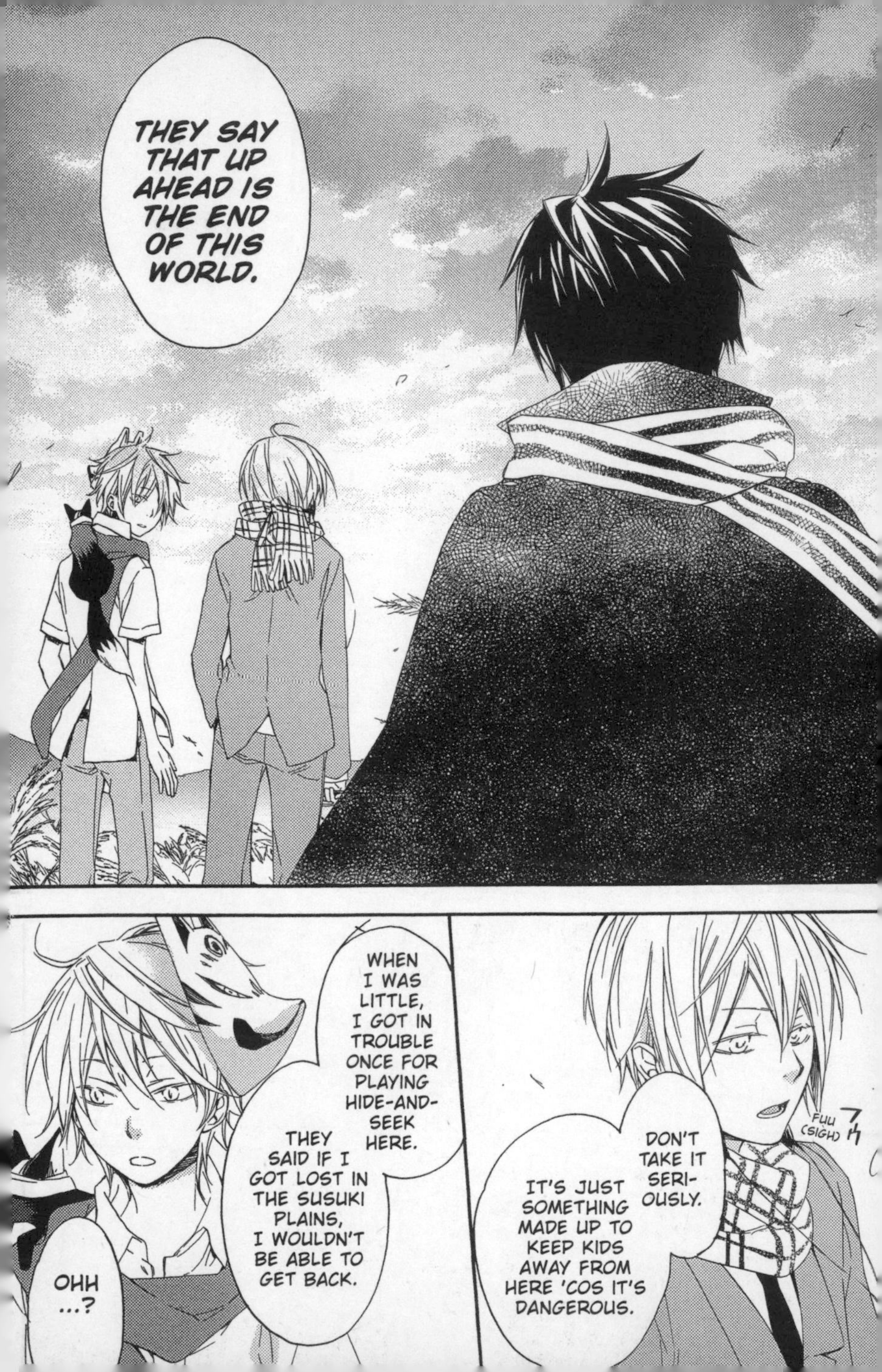
THEY SAY THAT UP AHEAD IS THE END OF THIS WORLD.
FUU (SIGH)
DON'T TAKE IT SERI-OUSLY.
IT'S JUST SOMETHING MADE UP TO KEEP KIDS AWAY FROM HERE 'COS IT'S DANGEROUS.
WHEN I WAS LITTLE, I GOT IN TROUBLE ONCE FOR PLAYING HIDE-AND-SEEK HERE.
THEY SAID IF I GOT LOST IN THE SUSUKI PLAINS, I WOULDN'T BE ABLE TO GET BACK.
OHH ...?

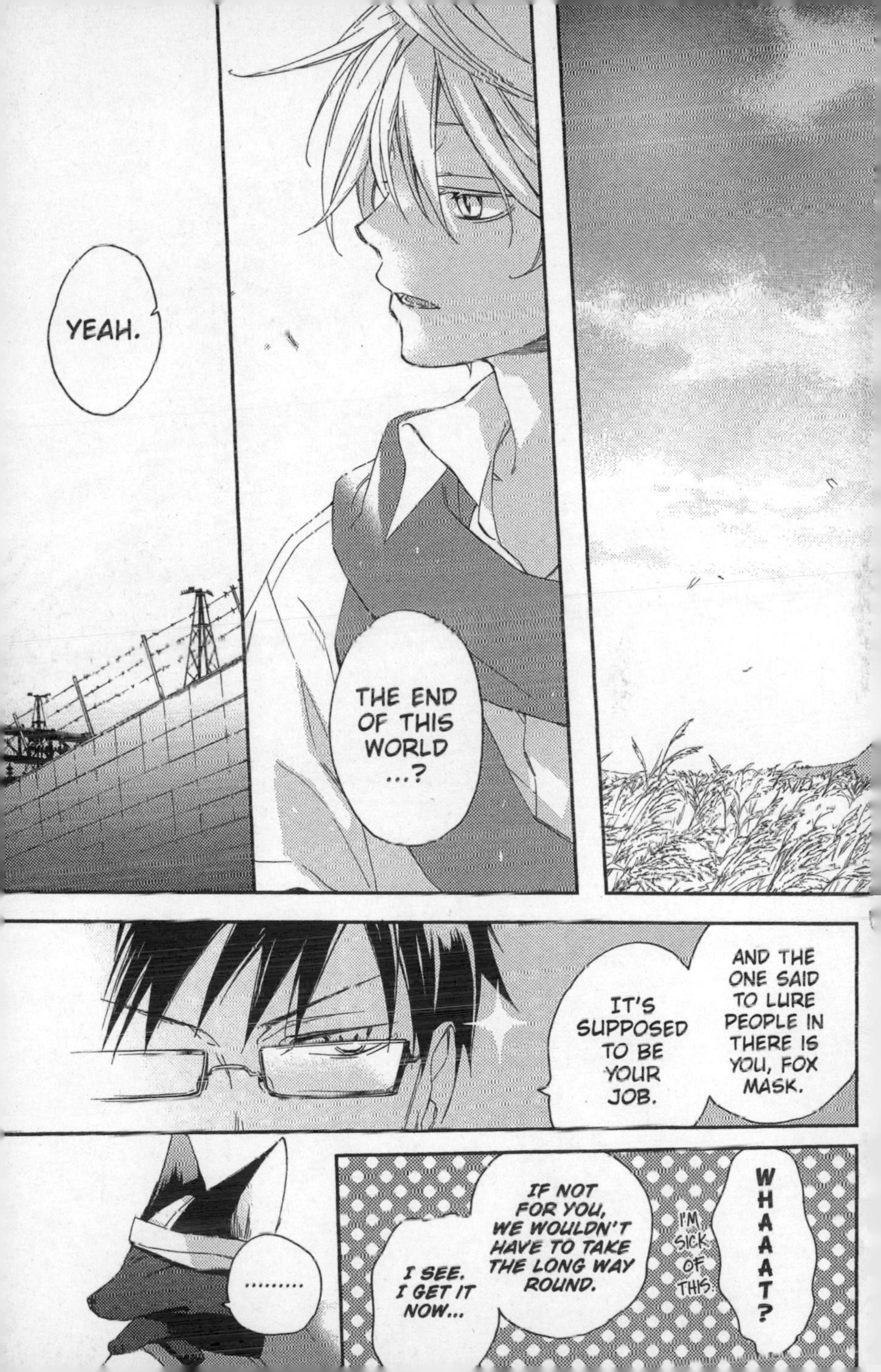
THE END OF THIS WORLD ...?
YEAH.
AND THE ONE SAID TO LURE PEOPLE IN THERE IS YOU, FOX MASK.
IT'S SUPPOSED TO BE YOUR JOB.
WHAAAAT?
I'M SICK OF THIS.
IF NOT FOR YOU, WE WOULDN'T HAVE TO TAKE THE LONG WAY ROUND.
I SEE. I GET IT NOW...
....

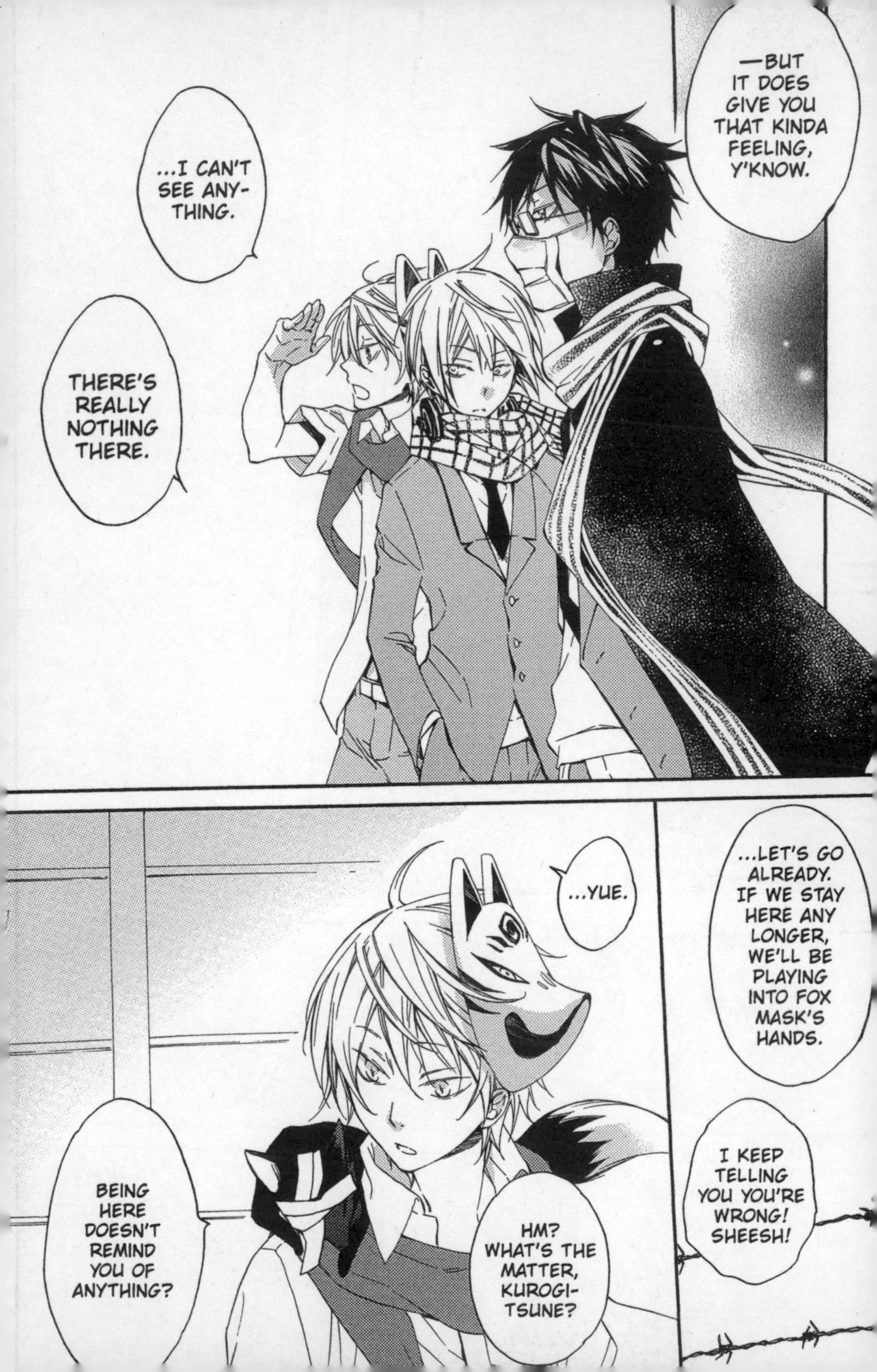
—BUT IT DOES GIVE YOU THAT KINDA FEELING, Y'KNOW.
...I CAN'T SEE ANY-THING.
THERE'S REALLY NOTHING THERE.
...LET'S GO ALREADY. IF WE STAY HERE ANY LONGER, WE'LL BE PLAYING INTO FOX MASK'S HANDS.
I KEEP TELLING YOU YOU'RE WRONG! SHEESH!
...YUE.
HM? WHAT'S THE MATTER, KUROGI-TSUNE?
BEING HERE DOESN'T REMIND YOU OF ANYTHING?

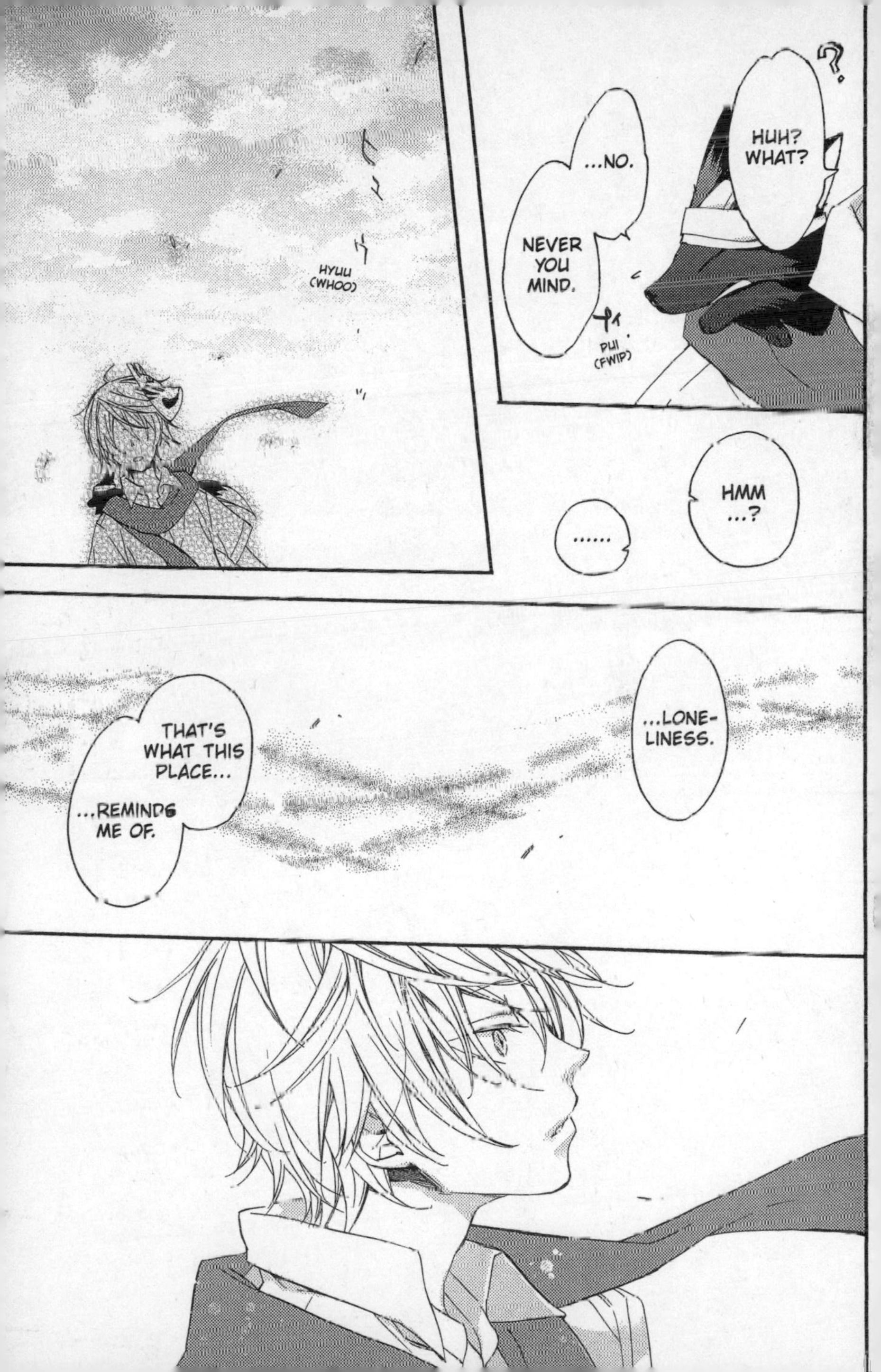
HUH? WHAT?
...NO.
NEVER YOU MIND.
PUI (FWIP)
HMM ...?
......
HYUU (WHOO)
...LONE-LINESS.
THAT'S WHAT THIS PLACE...
...REMINDS ME OF.

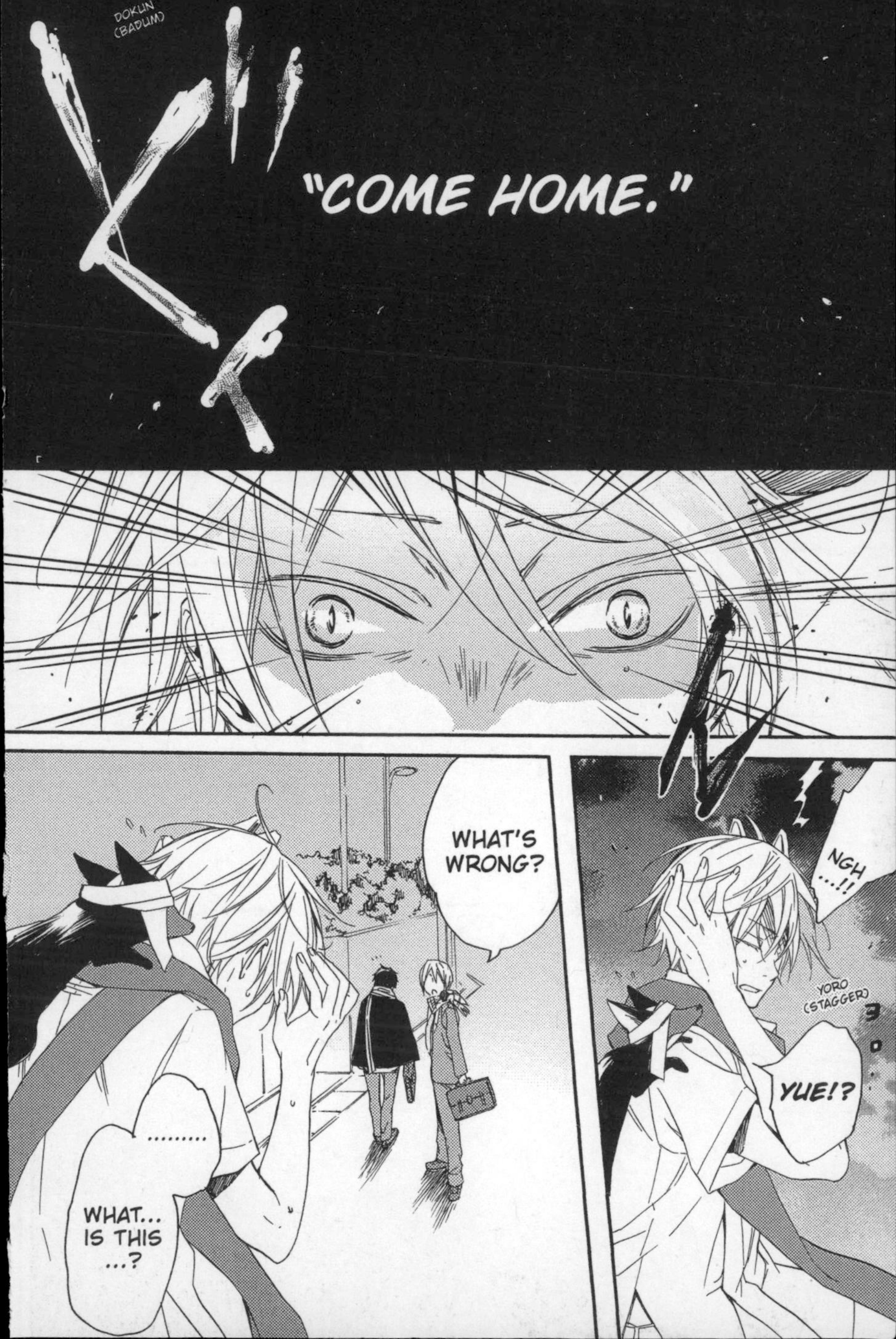
"COME HOME."
DOKUN (BADUM)
NGH ...!!
YORO (STAGGER)
YUE!?
WHAT'S WRONG?
....
WHAT... IS THIS ...?

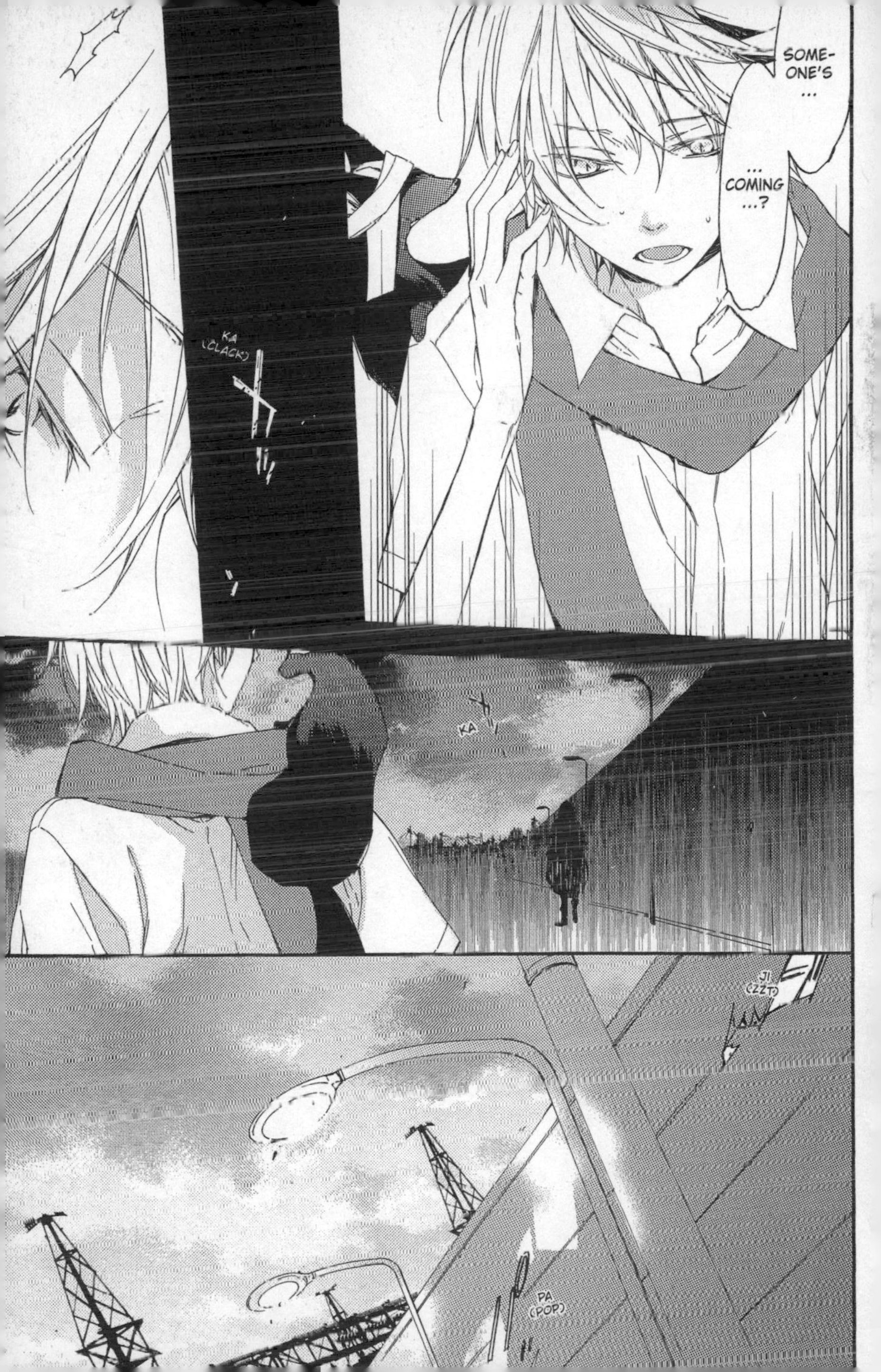
SOME-ONE'S ...
... COMING ...?
KA (CLACK)
KA
JI (ZZZT)
PA (POP)

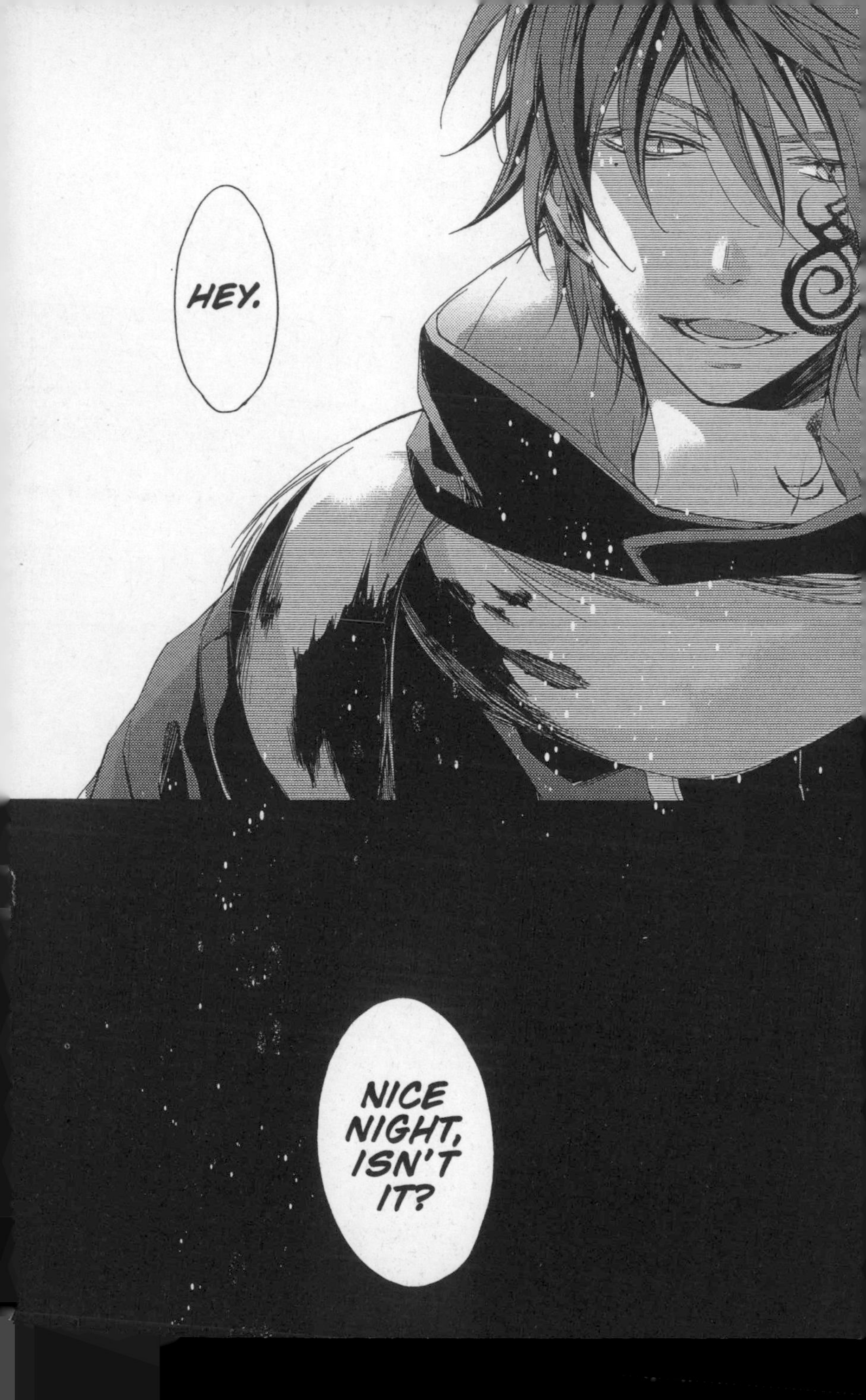
HEY.
NICE NIGHT, ISN'T IT?

Of the Red, the Light, and the Ayakashi

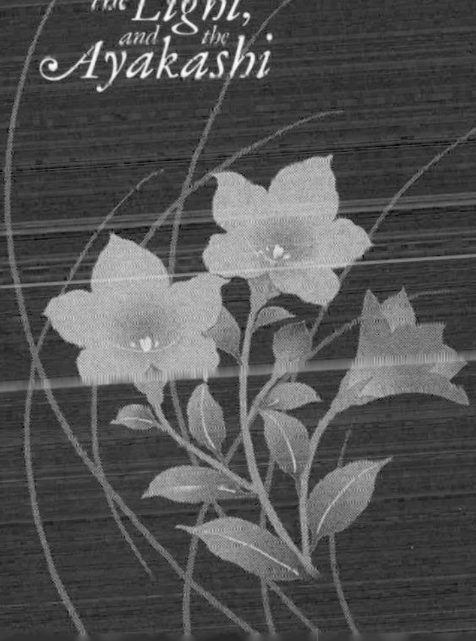

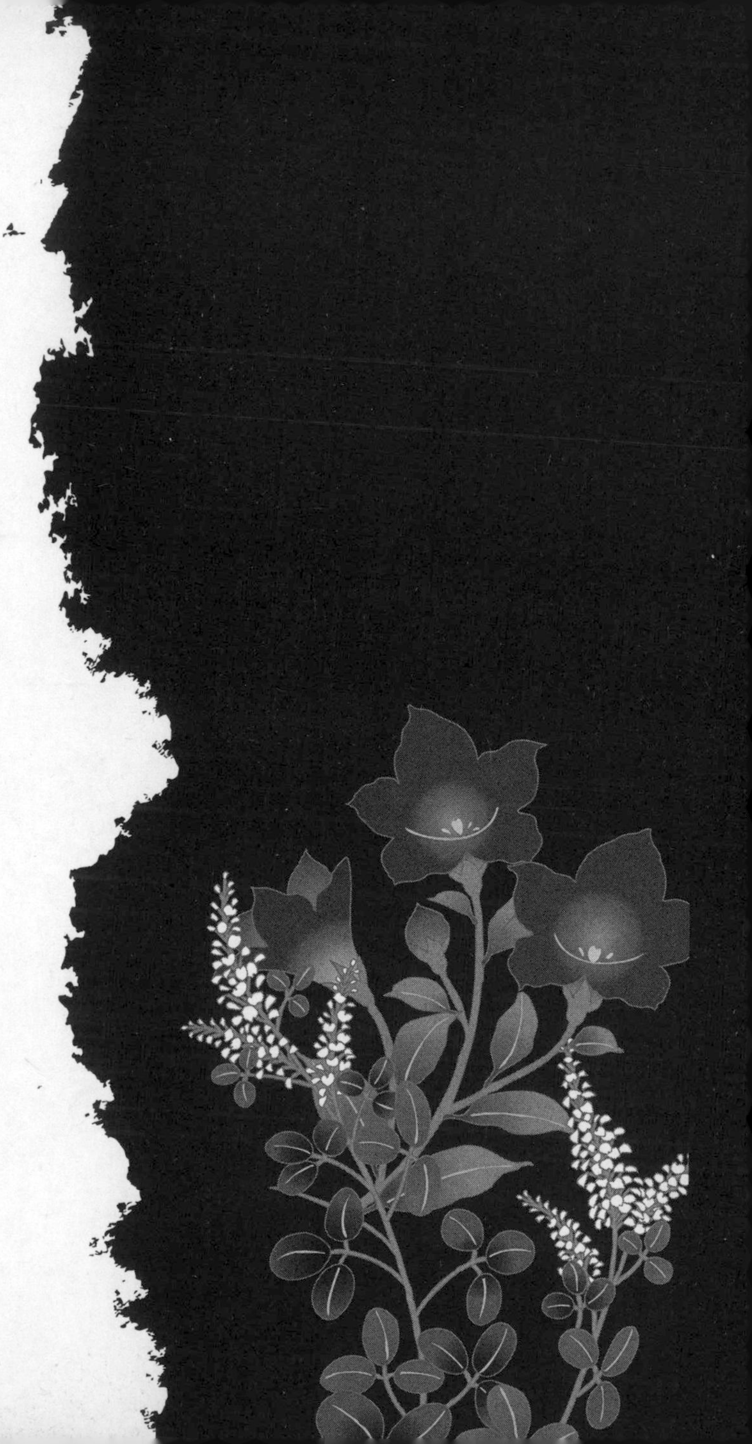

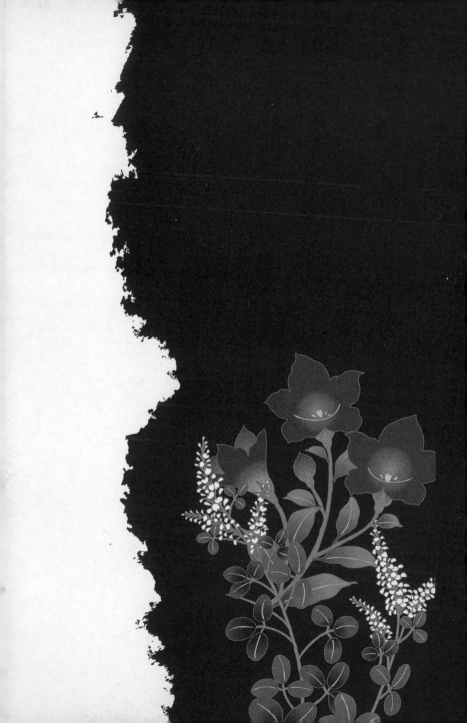

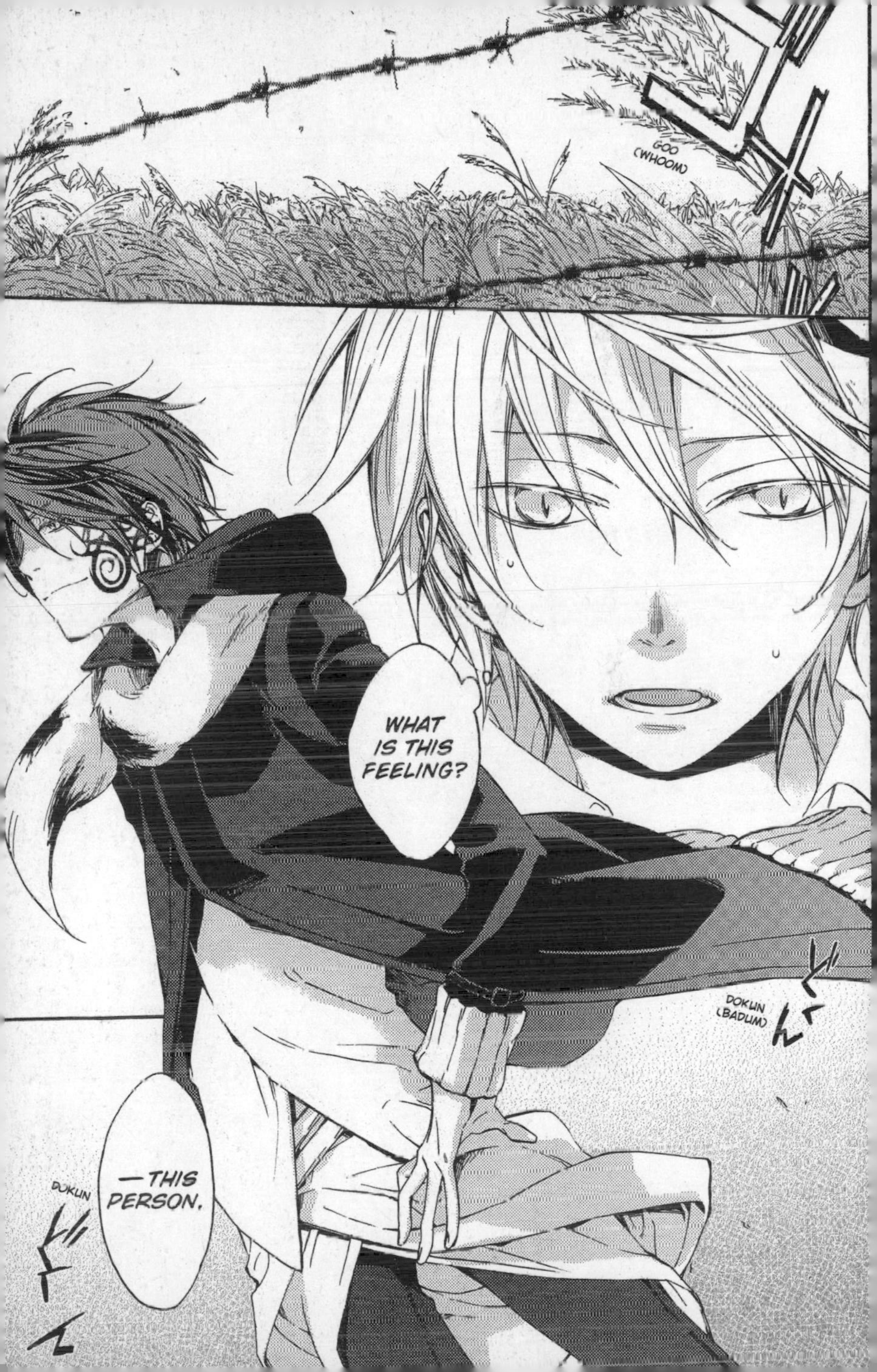
GOO (WHOOM)
WHAT IS THIS FEELING?
DOKUN (BADUM)
—THIS PERSON.
DOKUN

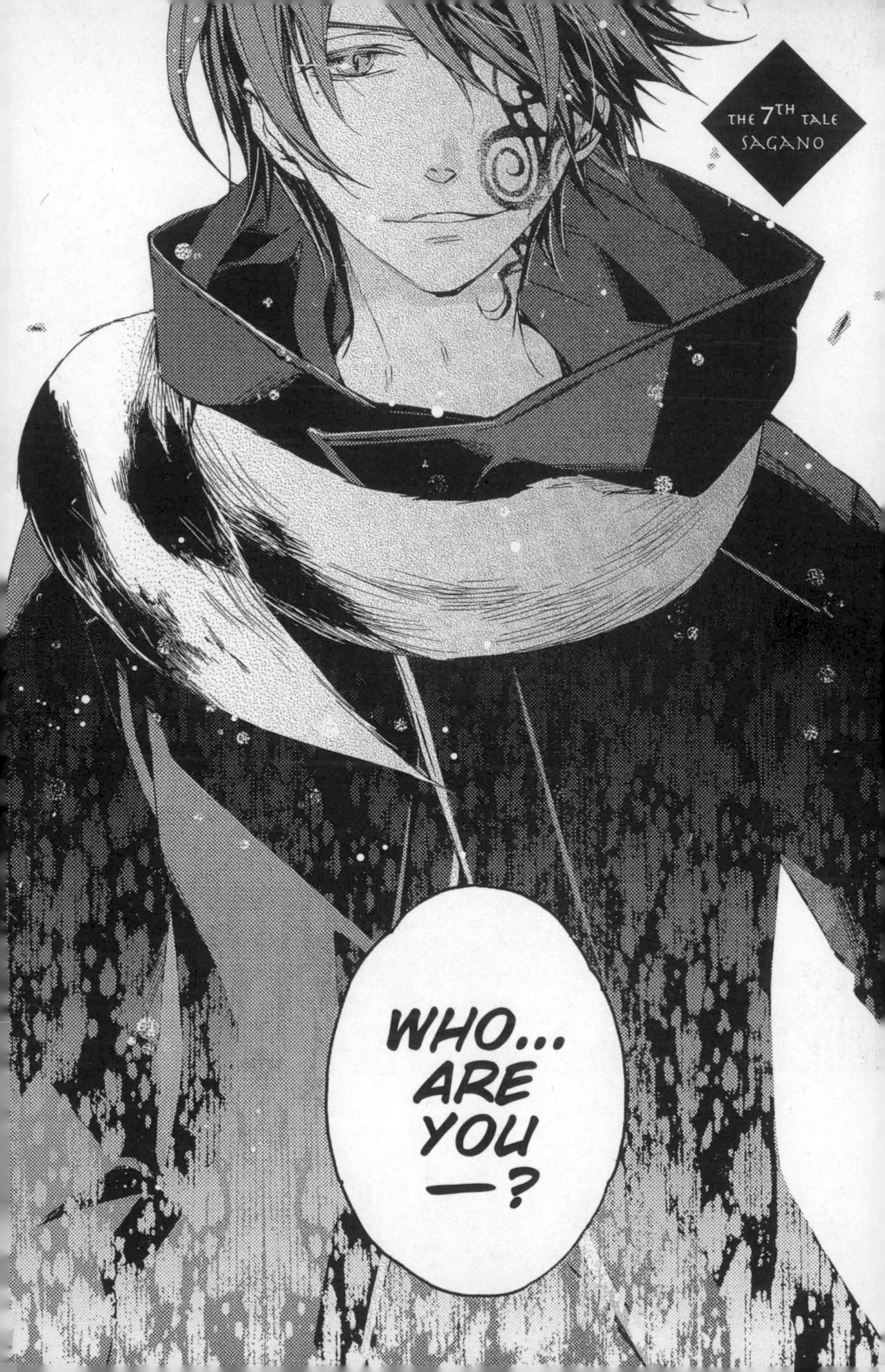
THE 7TH TALE
SAGANO
WHO... ARE YOU —?

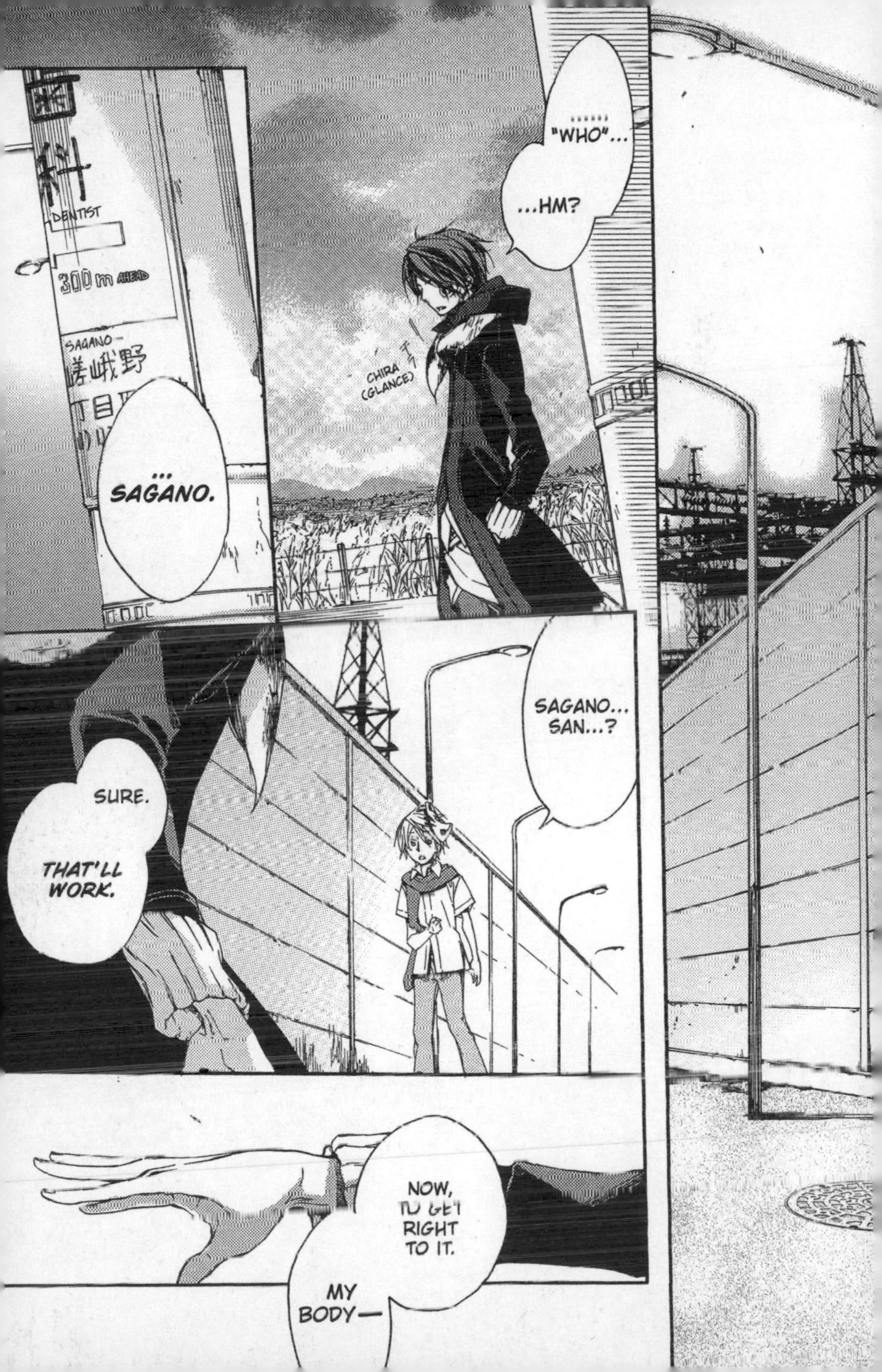
......
"WHO"...
...HM?
CHIRA (GLANCE)
DENTIST
300 m AHEAD
SAGANO-
嵯峨野
...SAGANO.
SAGANO... SAN...?
SURE.
THAT'LL WORK.
NOW, TO GET RIGHT TO IT.
MY BODY—

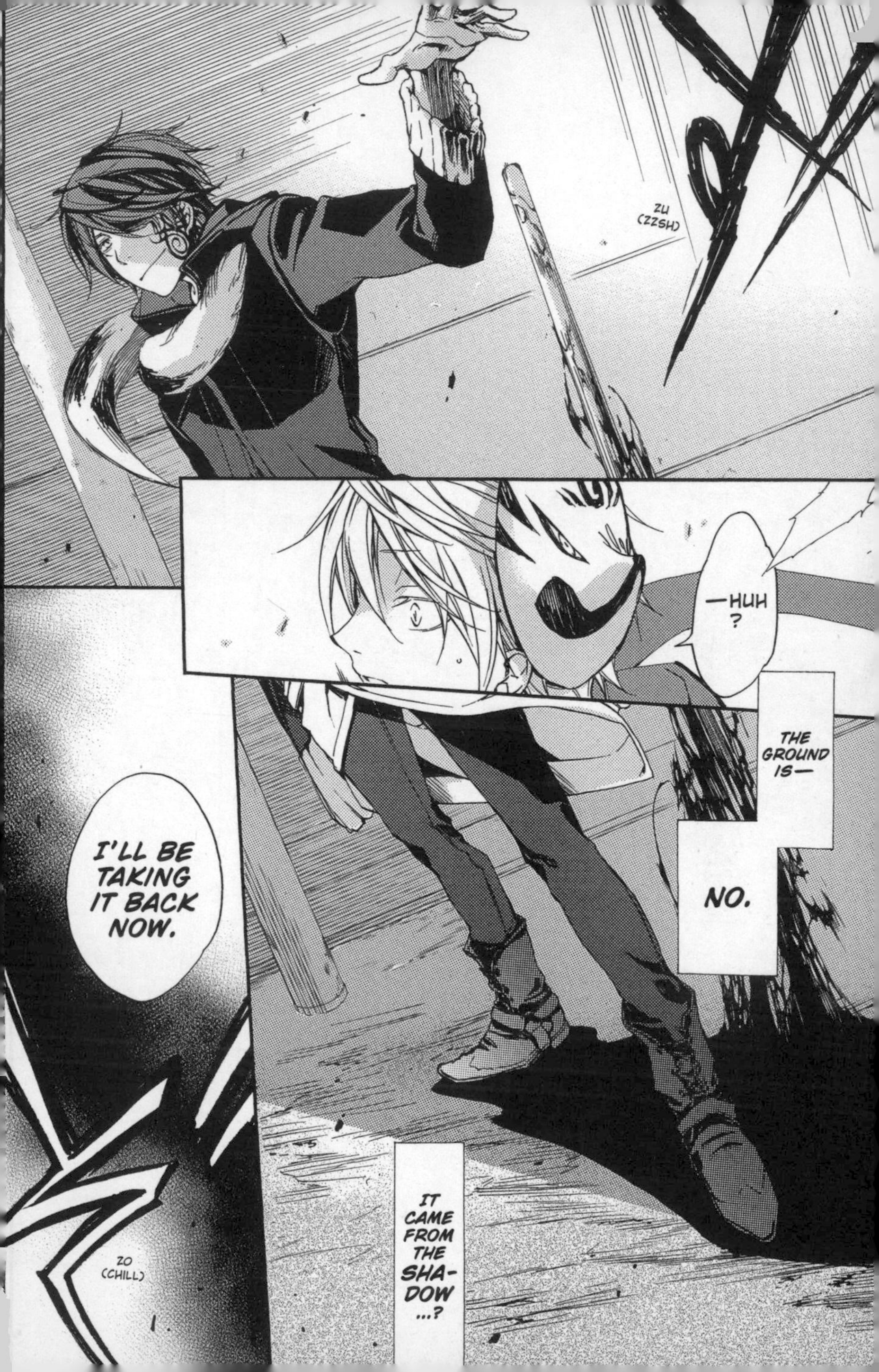
ZU (ZZSH)
—HUH ?
THE GROUND IS—
NO.
IT CAME FROM THE SHA-DOW ...?
I'LL BE TAKING IT BACK NOW.
ZO (CHILL)

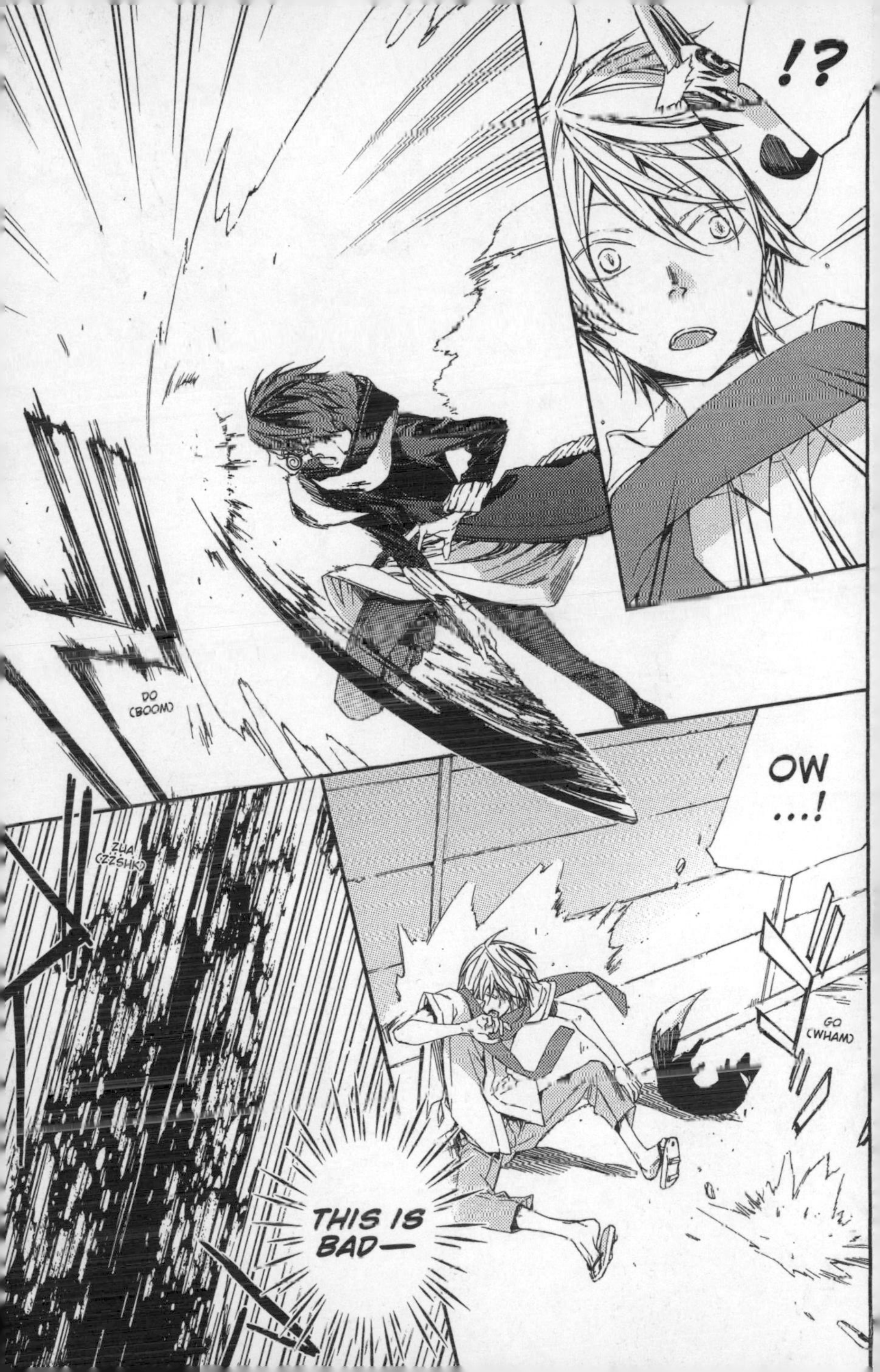
!?
DO (BOOM)
OW ...!
GO (WHAM)
ZUA (ZZSHK)
THIS IS BAD—

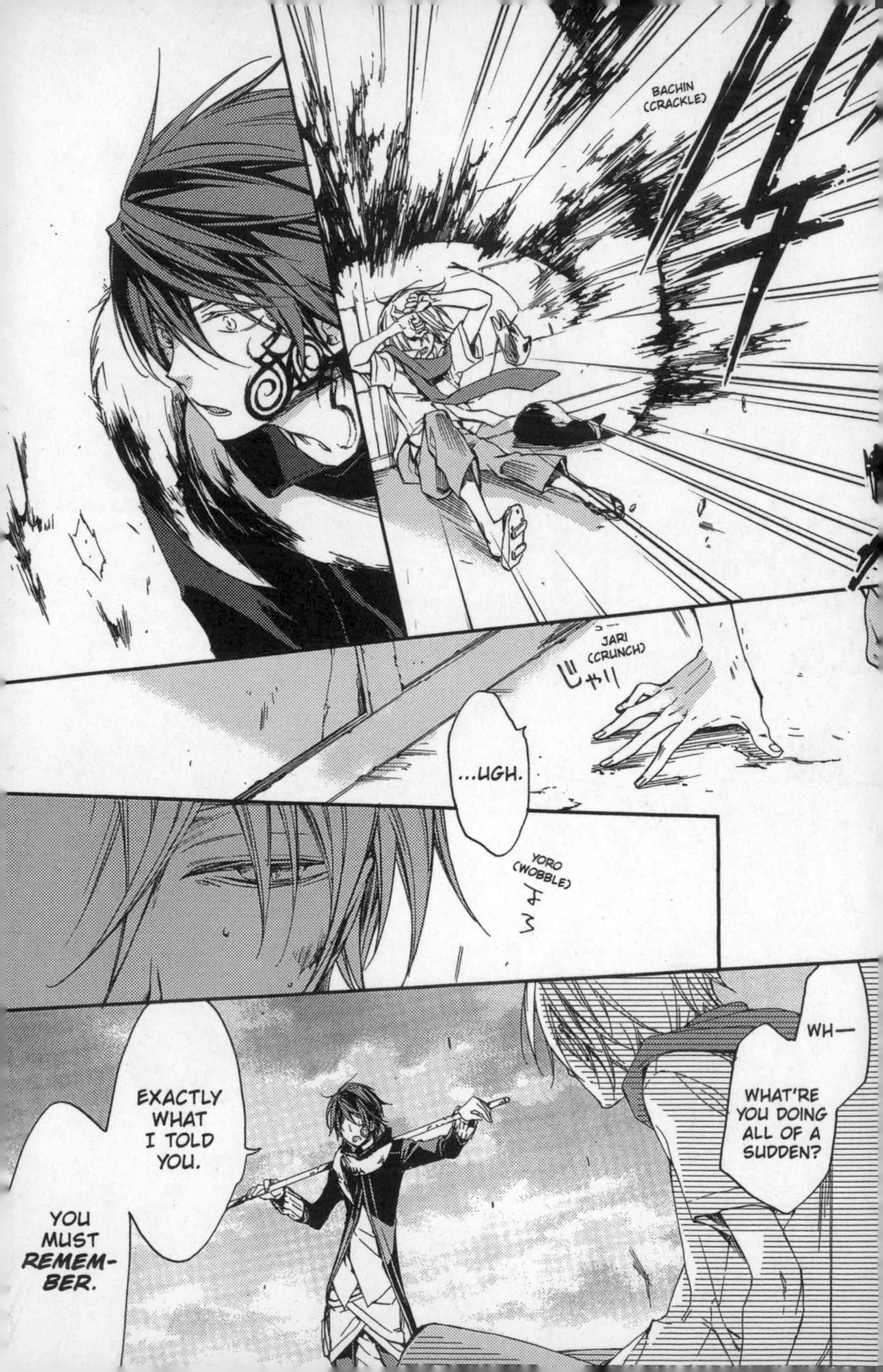
BACHIN (CRACKLE)
JARI (CRUNCH)
じゃり
...UGH.
YORO (WOBBLE)
よろ
WH—
WHAT'RE YOU DOING ALL OF A SUDDEN?
EXACTLY WHAT I TOLD YOU.
YOU MUST *REMEMBER*.

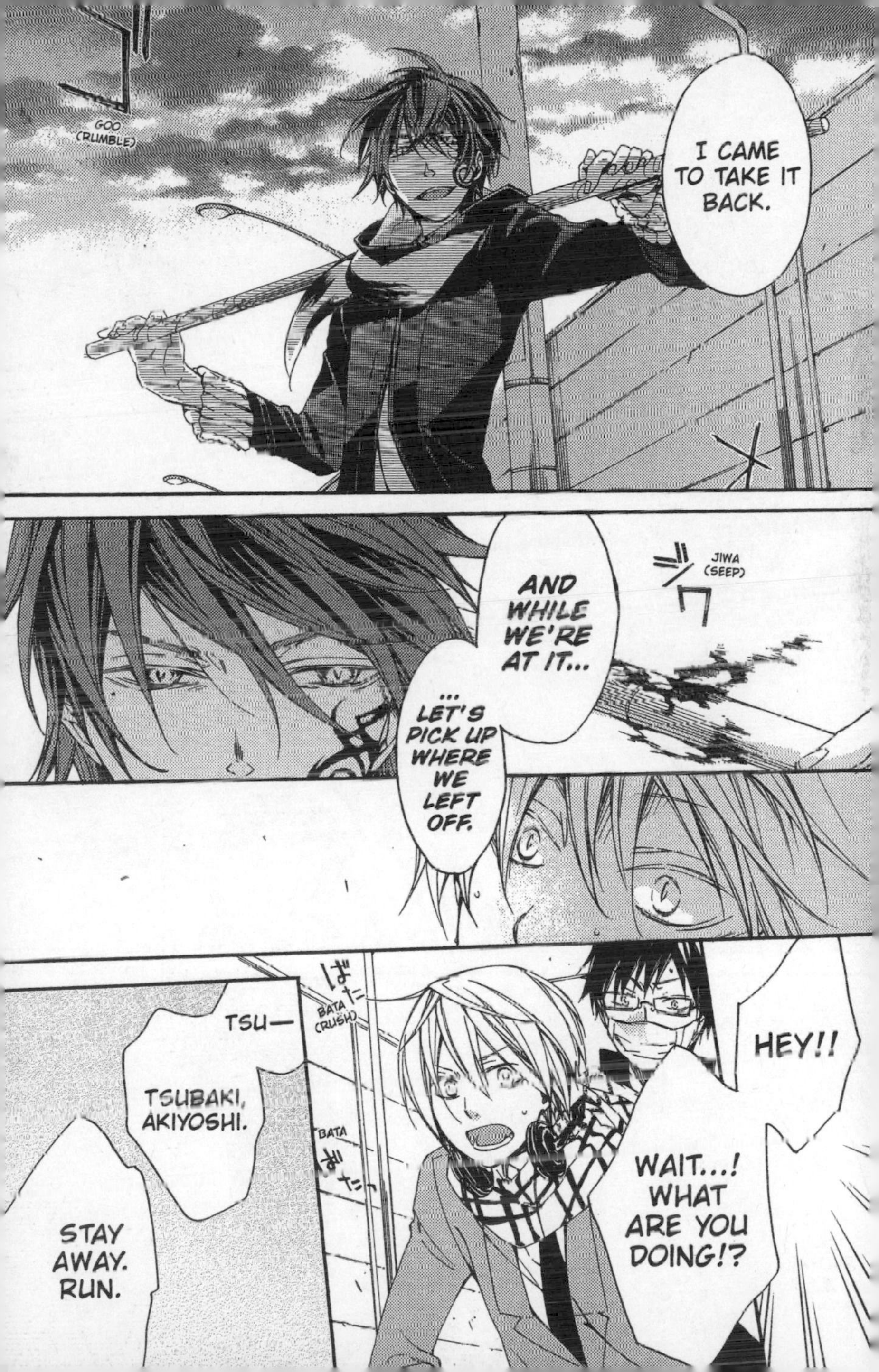
I CAME TO TAKE IT BACK.
GOO (RUMBLE)
JIWA (SEEP)
AND WHILE WE'RE AT IT...
... LET'S PICK UP WHERE WE LEFT OFF.
HEY!!
WAIT...! WHAT ARE YOU DOING!?
BATA (RUSH)
BATA
TSU—
TSUBAKI, AKIYOSHI.
STAY AWAY. RUN.

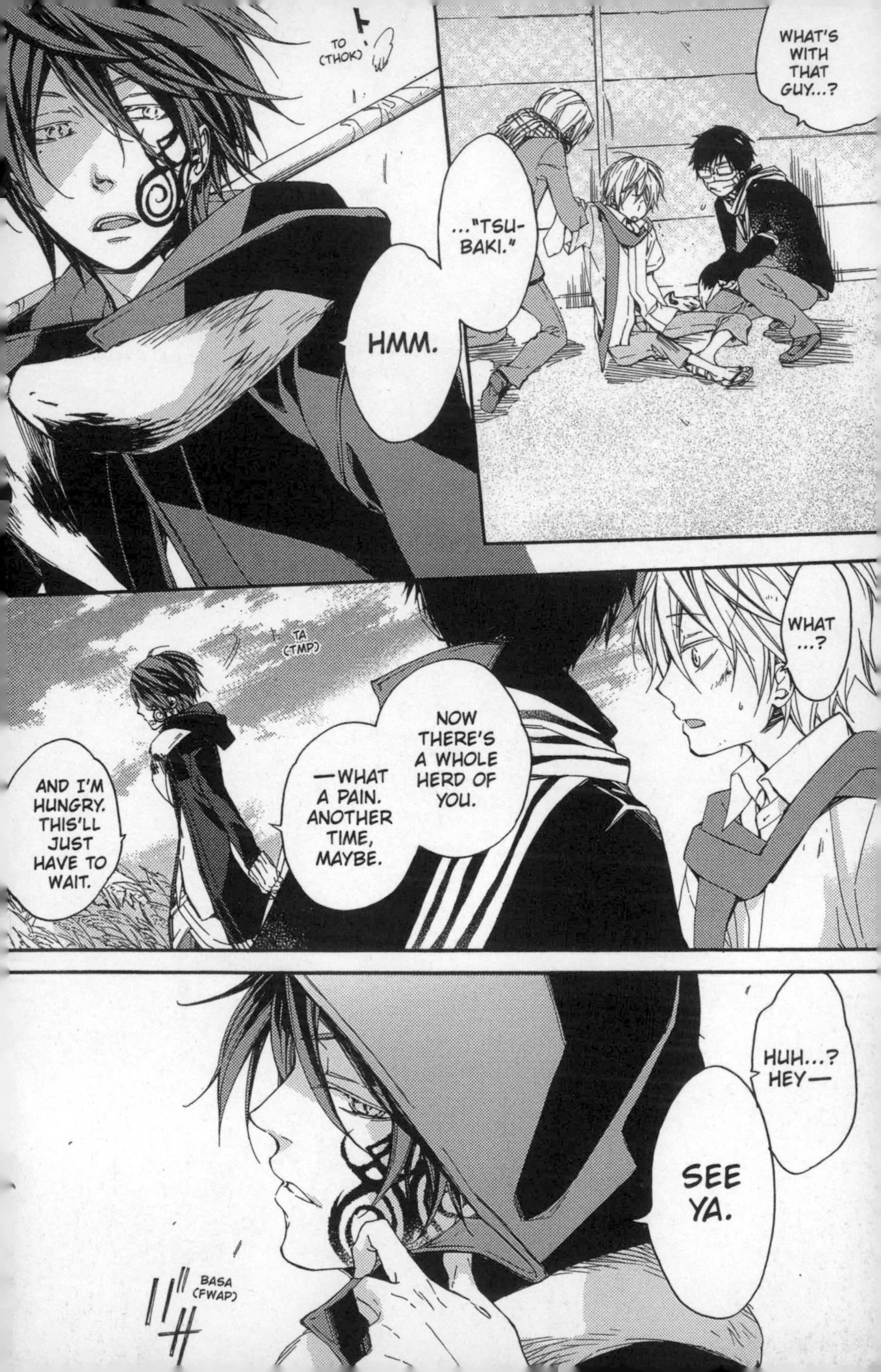
WHAT'S WITH THAT GUY...?
..."TSU-BAKI."
HMM.
TO (THOK)
WHAT ...?
NOW THERE'S A WHOLE HERD OF YOU.
—WHAT A PAIN. ANOTHER TIME, MAYBE.
TA (TMP)
AND I'M HUNGRY. THIS'LL JUST HAVE TO WAIT.
HUH...? HEY—
SEE YA.
BASA (FWAP)

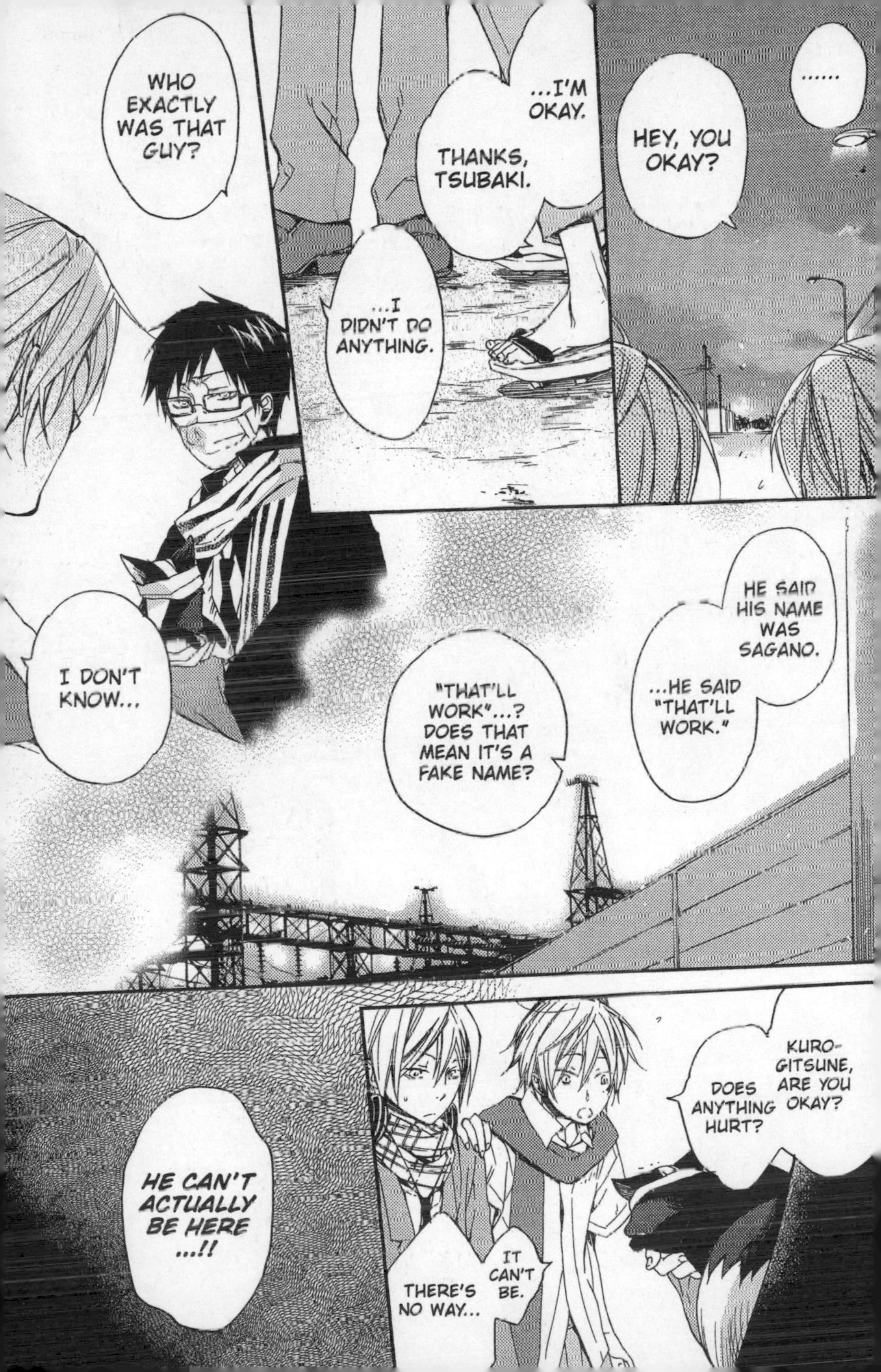
......
HEY, YOU OKAY?
...I'M OKAY.
THANKS, TSUBAKI.
...I DIDN'T DO ANYTHING.
WHO EXACTLY WAS THAT GUY?
HE SAID HIS NAME WAS SAGANO.
...HE SAID "THAT'LL WORK."
"THAT'LL WORK"...? DOES THAT MEAN IT'S A FAKE NAME?
I DON'T KNOW...
KURO-GITSUNE, ARE YOU OKAY?
DOES ANYTHING HURT?
IT CAN'T BE.
THERE'S NO WAY...
HE CAN'T ACTUALLY BE HERE ...!!

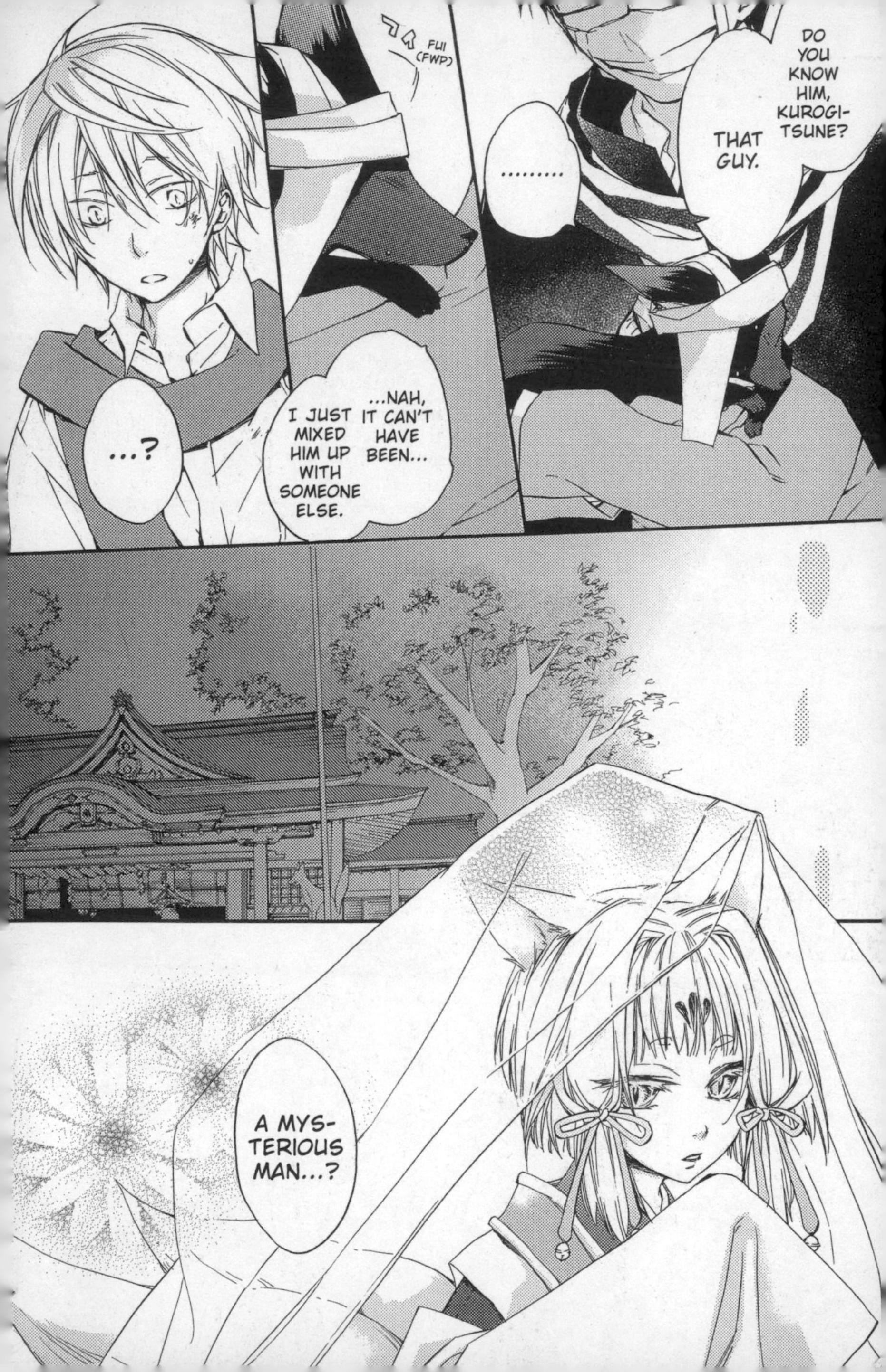
DO YOU KNOW HIM, KUROGI-TSUNE?
THAT GUY.
....
FUII (FWP)
...NAH, IT CAN'T HAVE BEEN...
I JUST MIXED HIM UP WITH SOMEONE ELSE.
...?
A MYS-TERIOUS MAN...?

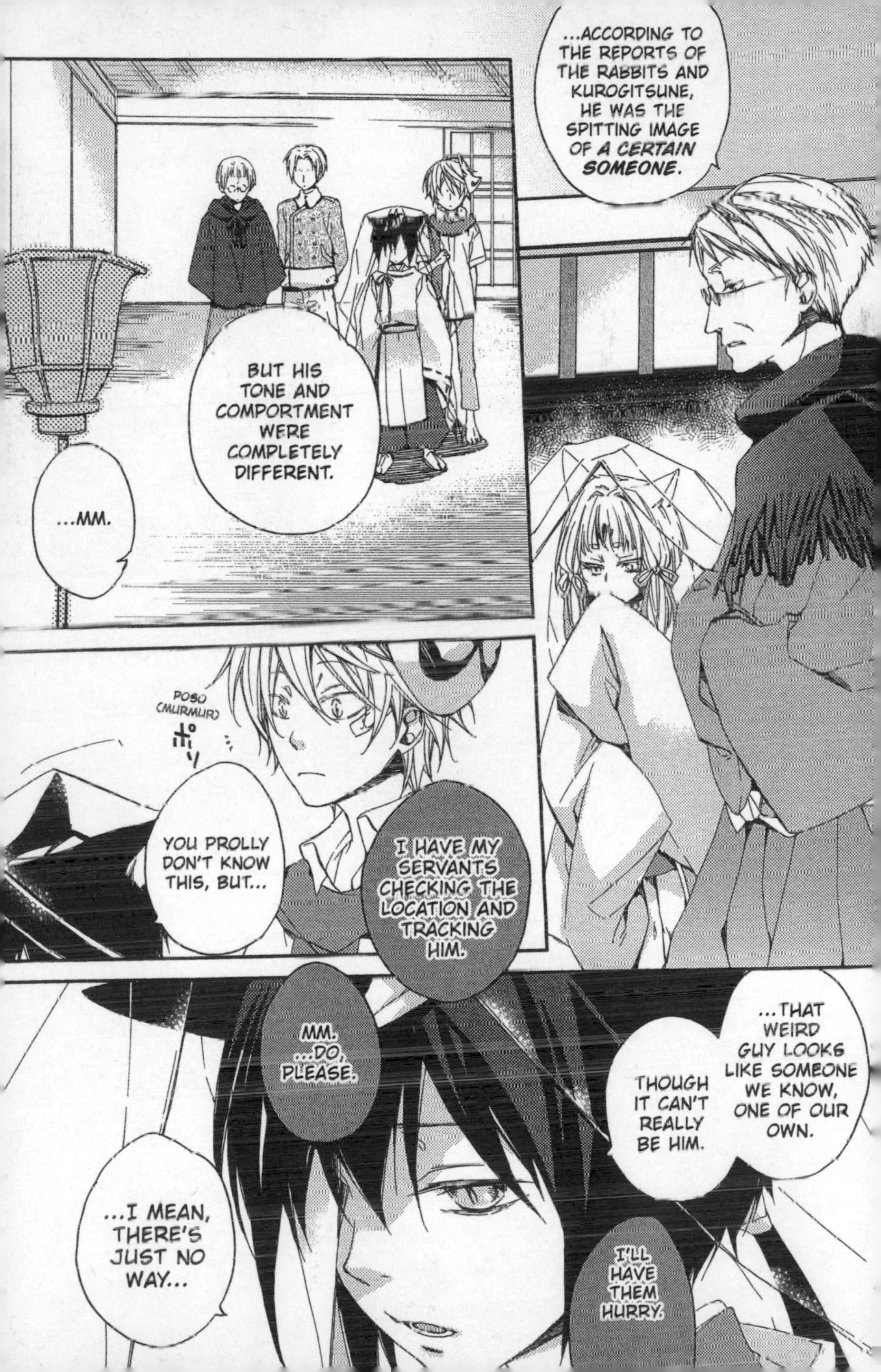
...ACCORDING TO THE REPORTS OF THE RABBITS AND KUROGITSUNE, HE WAS THE SPITTING IMAGE OF *A CERTAIN SOMEONE*.
BUT HIS TONE AND COMPORTMENT WERE COMPLETELY DIFFERENT.
...MM.
I HAVE MY SERVANTS CHECKING THE LOCATION AND TRACKING HIM.
POSO (MURMUR)
YOU PROLLY DON'T KNOW THIS, BUT...
...THAT WEIRD GUY LOOKS LIKE SOMEONE WE KNOW, ONE OF OUR OWN.
THOUGH IT CAN'T REALLY BE HIM.
MM. ...DO, PLEASE.
...I MEAN, THERE'S JUST NO WAY...
I'LL HAVE THEM HURRY.

"I'LL BE TAKING MY BODY BACK."
TAKING HIS BODY BACK...
...AND PICKING UP WHERE WE LEFT OFF... WHAT DID HE MEAN?
"SEE YA."
WHAT A STRANGE PERSON...
UGGGH!
IT'S ANOTHER ALL-NIGHTER TONIGHT, HUUUH?
BOSO (WHISPER)
HISO (WHISPER)
AND YOU MADE UP FOR IT BY SLEEPING LIKE A LOG THIS AFTERNOON.
ALL-NIGHTERS OR NOT, YOU SLEEP TOO MUCH, MASHIRO.
I CAN'T HELP IT. I MEAN, THERE'S NO TELLING WHEN I'LL BE ABLE TO GET ANOTHER GOOD NIGHT'S SLEEP!
YOU GOTTA SLEEP WHEN YOU CAN.
HAAA (SIGH)

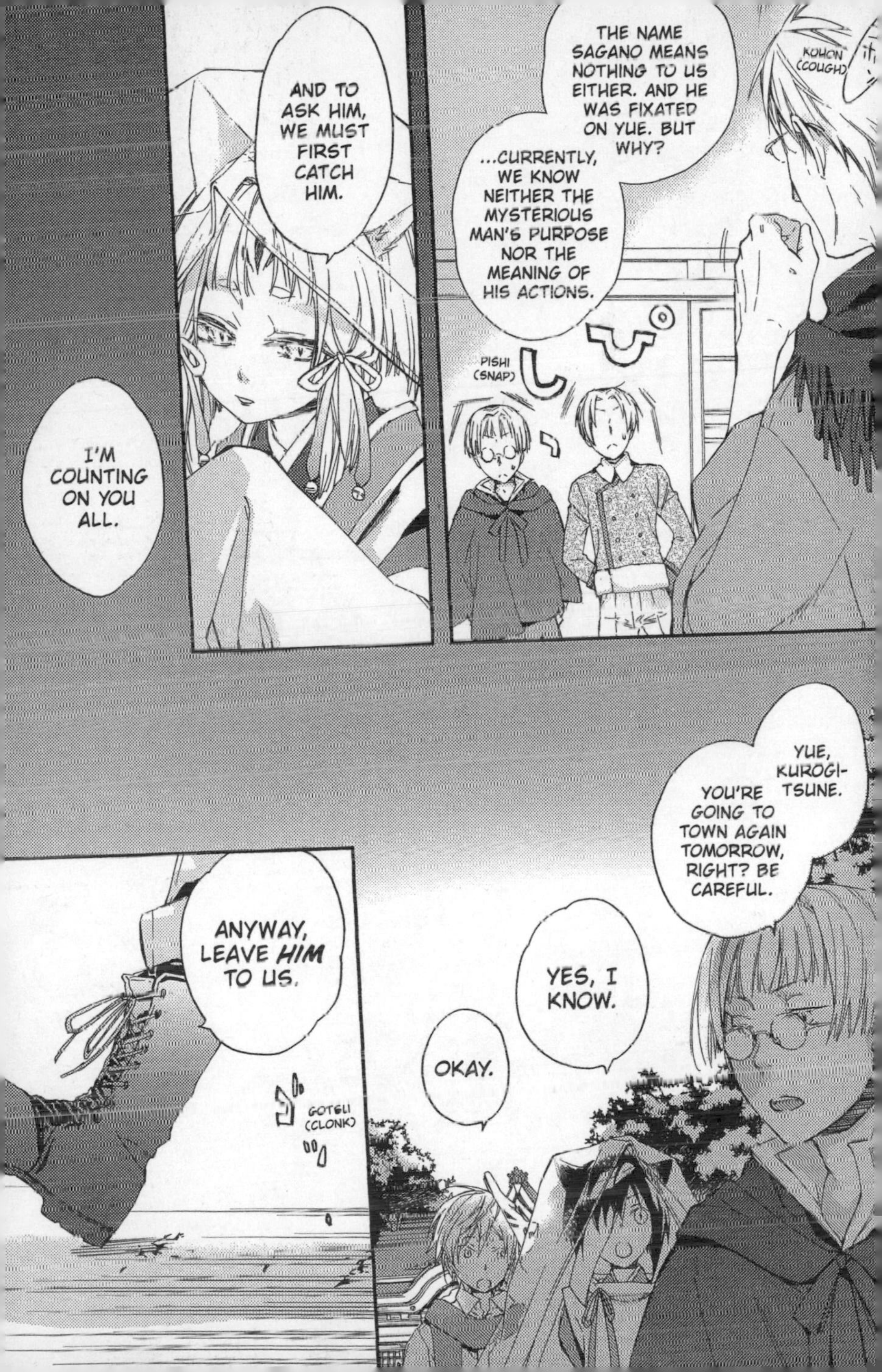
KOHON (COUGH)
THE NAME SAGANO MEANS NOTHING TO US EITHER. AND HE WAS FIXATED ON YUE. BUT WHY?
...CURRENTLY, WE KNOW NEITHER THE MYSTERIOUS MAN'S PURPOSE NOR THE MEANING OF HIS ACTIONS.
PISHI (SNAP)
AND TO ASK HIM, WE MUST FIRST CATCH HIM.
I'M COUNTING ON YOU ALL.
YUE, KUROGI-TSUNE.
YOU'RE GOING TO TOWN AGAIN TOMORROW, RIGHT? BE CAREFUL.
YES, I KNOW.
OKAY.
ANYWAY, LEAVE *HIM* TO US.
GOTSU (CLONK)

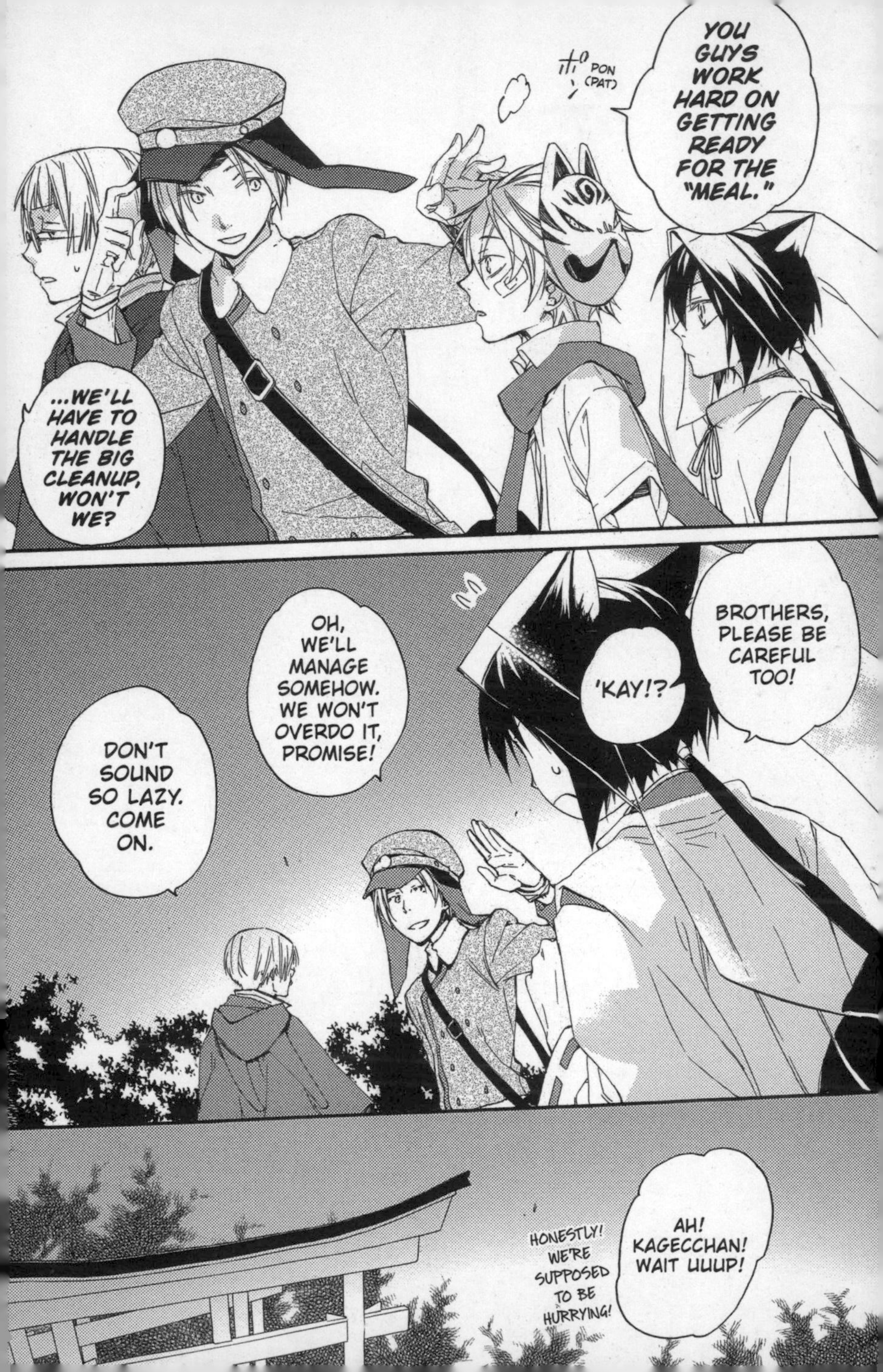
YOU GUYS WORK HARD ON GETTING READY FOR THE "MEAL."
PON (PAT)
...WE'LL HAVE TO HANDLE THE BIG CLEANUP, WON'T WE?
BROTHERS, PLEASE BE CAREFUL TOO!
'KAY!?
OH, WE'LL MANAGE SOMEHOW. WE WON'T OVERDO IT, PROMISE!
DON'T SOUND SO LAZY. COME ON.
AH! KAGECCHAN! WAIT UUUP!
HONESTLY! WE'RE SUPPOSED TO BE HURRYING!

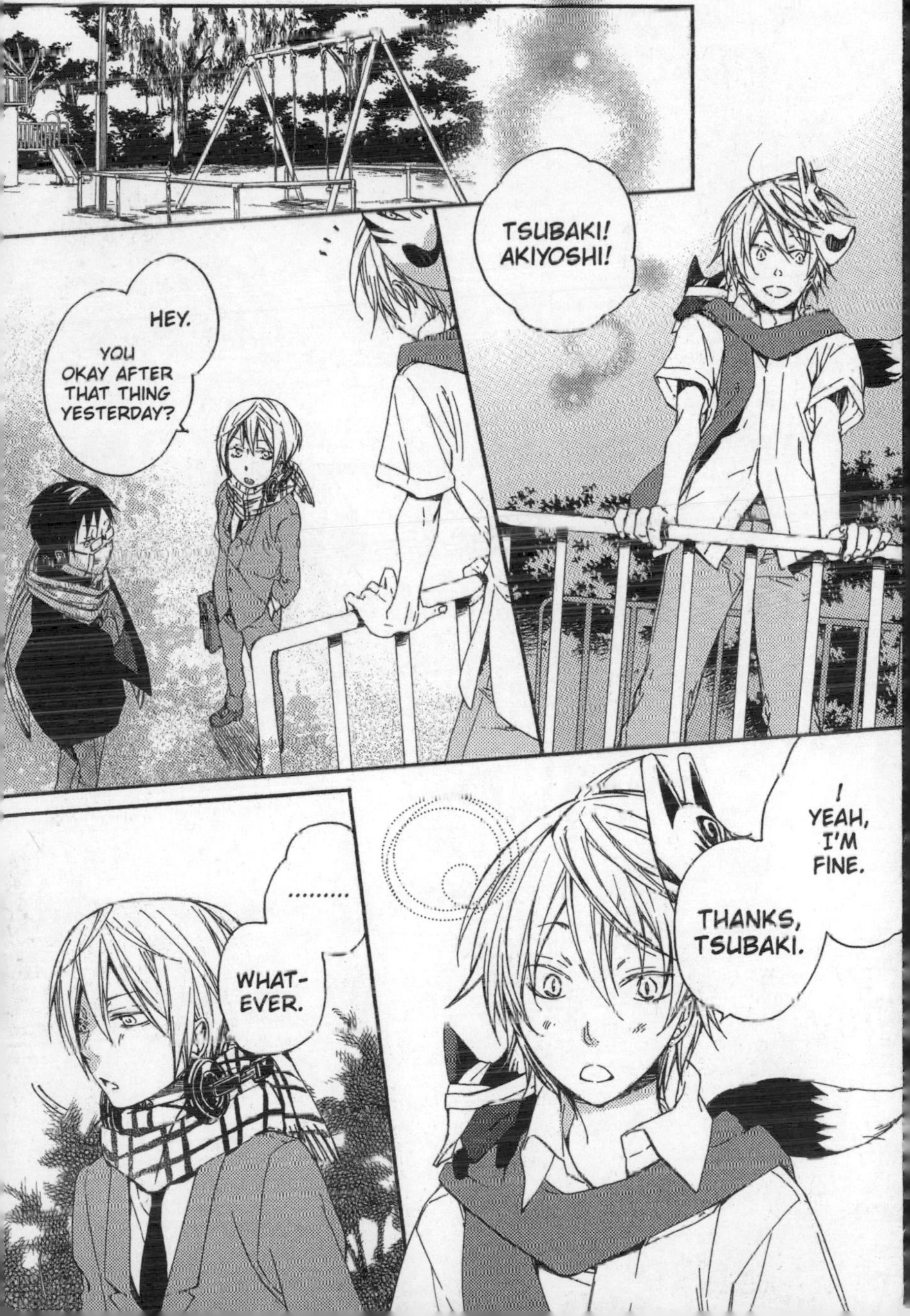
TSUBAKI! AKIYOSHI!
HEY.
YOU OKAY AFTER THAT THING YESTERDAY?
! YEAH, I'M FINE.
THANKS, TSUBAKI.
....
WHAT-EVER.

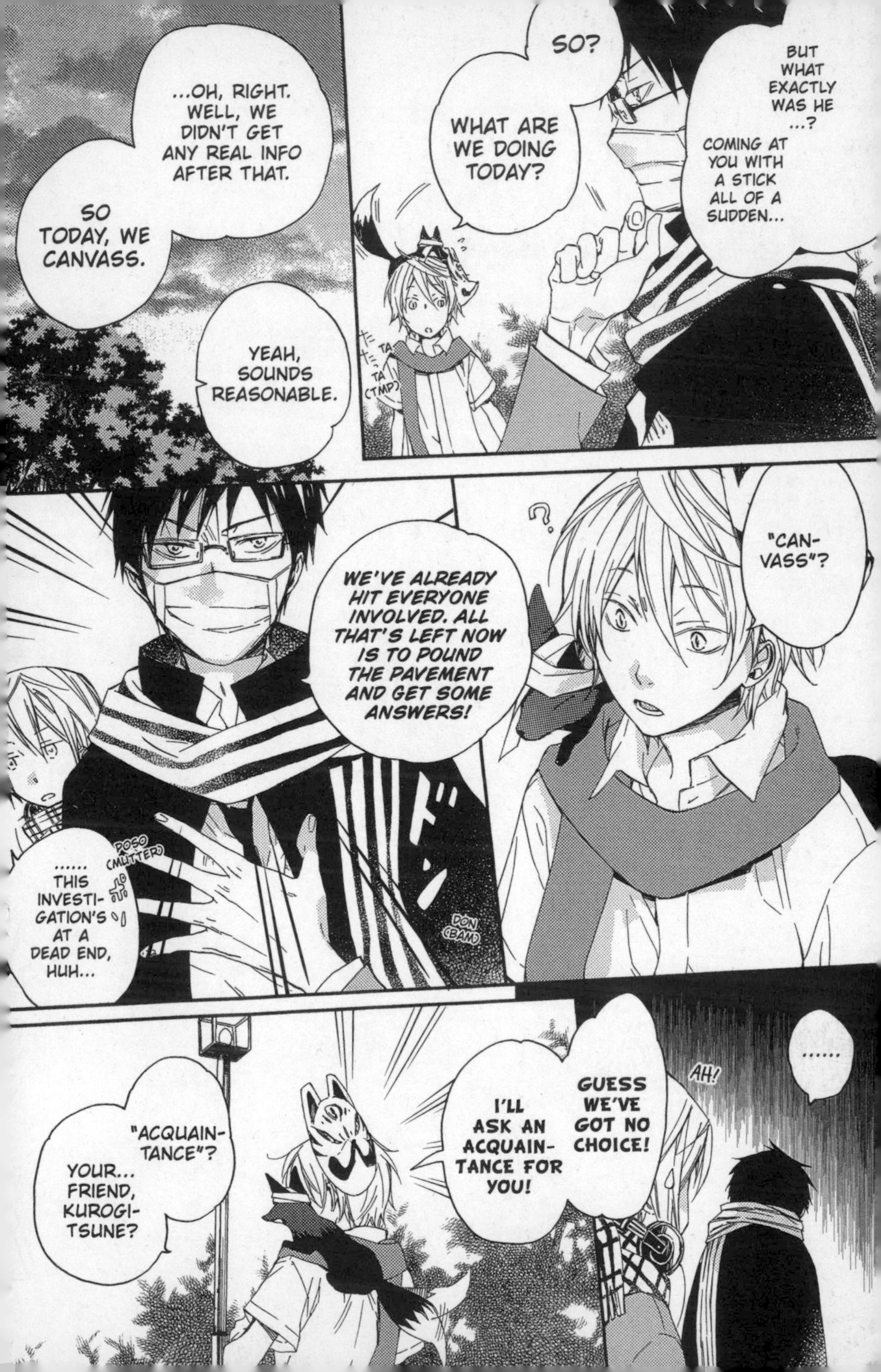
BUT WHAT EXACTLY WAS HE ...?
COMING AT YOU WITH A STICK ALL OF A SUDDEN...
SO?
WHAT ARE WE DOING TODAY?
TA TA (TMP)
...OH, RIGHT. WELL, WE DIDN'T GET ANY REAL INFO AFTER THAT.
SO TODAY, WE CANVASS.
YEAH, SOUNDS REASONABLE.
"CAN-VASS"?
WE'VE ALREADY HIT EVERYONE INVOLVED. ALL THAT'S LEFT NOW IS TO POUND THE PAVEMENT AND GET SOME ANSWERS!
DON (BAM)
POSO (MUTTER)
...... THIS INVESTIGATION'S AT A DEAD END, HUH...
......
AH!
GUESS WE'VE GOT NO CHOICE!
I'LL ASK AN ACQUAINTANCE FOR YOU!
"ACQUAINTANCE"?
YOUR... FRIEND, KUROGITSUNE?

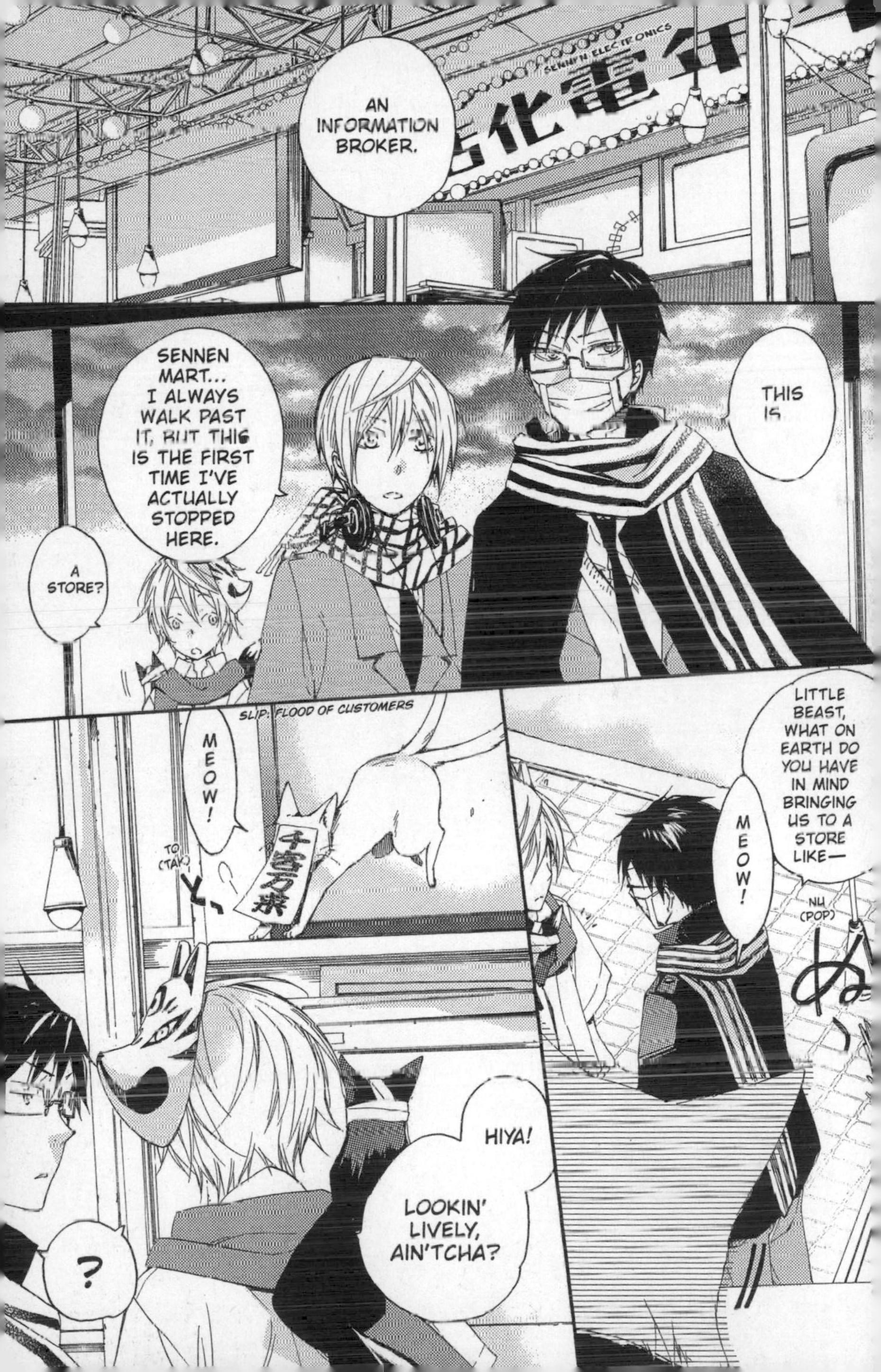
SENNEN ELECTRONICS
AN INFORMATION BROKER.
THIS IS
SENNEN MART... I ALWAYS WALK PAST IT, BUT THIS IS THE FIRST TIME I'VE ACTUALLY STOPPED HERE.
A STORE?
LITTLE BEAST, WHAT ON EARTH DO YOU HAVE IN MIND BRINGING US TO A STORE LIKE—
MEOW!
NU (POP)
SLIP: FLOOD OF CUSTOMERS
MEOW!
TO (TAK)
HIYA!
LOOKIN' LIVELY, AIN'TCHA?
?

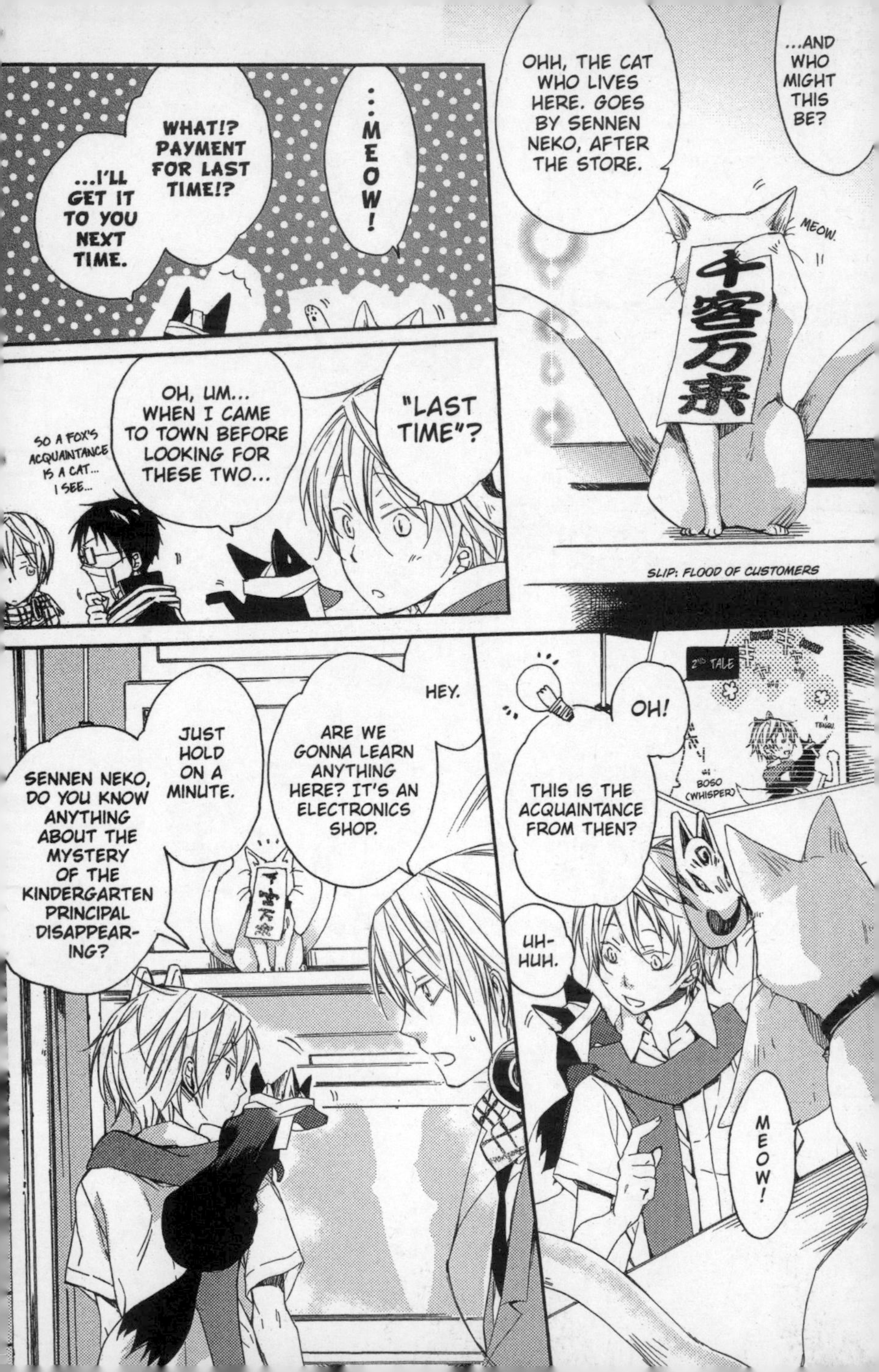
...AND WHO MIGHT THIS BE?
OHH, THE CAT WHO LIVES HERE. GOES BY SENNEN NEKO, AFTER THE STORE.
MEOW.
千客万来
SLIP: FLOOD OF CUSTOMERS
...MEOW!
WHAT!? PAYMENT FOR LAST TIME!?
...I'LL GET IT TO YOU NEXT TIME.
"LAST TIME"?
OH, UM... WHEN I CAME TO TOWN BEFORE LOOKING FOR THESE TWO...
SO A FOX'S ACQUAINTANCE IS A CAT... I SEE...
2ND TALE
A TENGU
BOSO (WHISPER)
OH!
THIS IS THE ACQUAINTANCE FROM THEN?
UH-HUH.
MEOW!
HEY.
ARE WE GONNA LEARN ANYTHING HERE? IT'S AN ELECTRONICS SHOP.
JUST HOLD ON A MINUTE.
SENNEN NEKO, DO YOU KNOW ANYTHING ABOUT THE MYSTERY OF THE KINDERGARTEN PRINCIPAL DISAPPEARING?

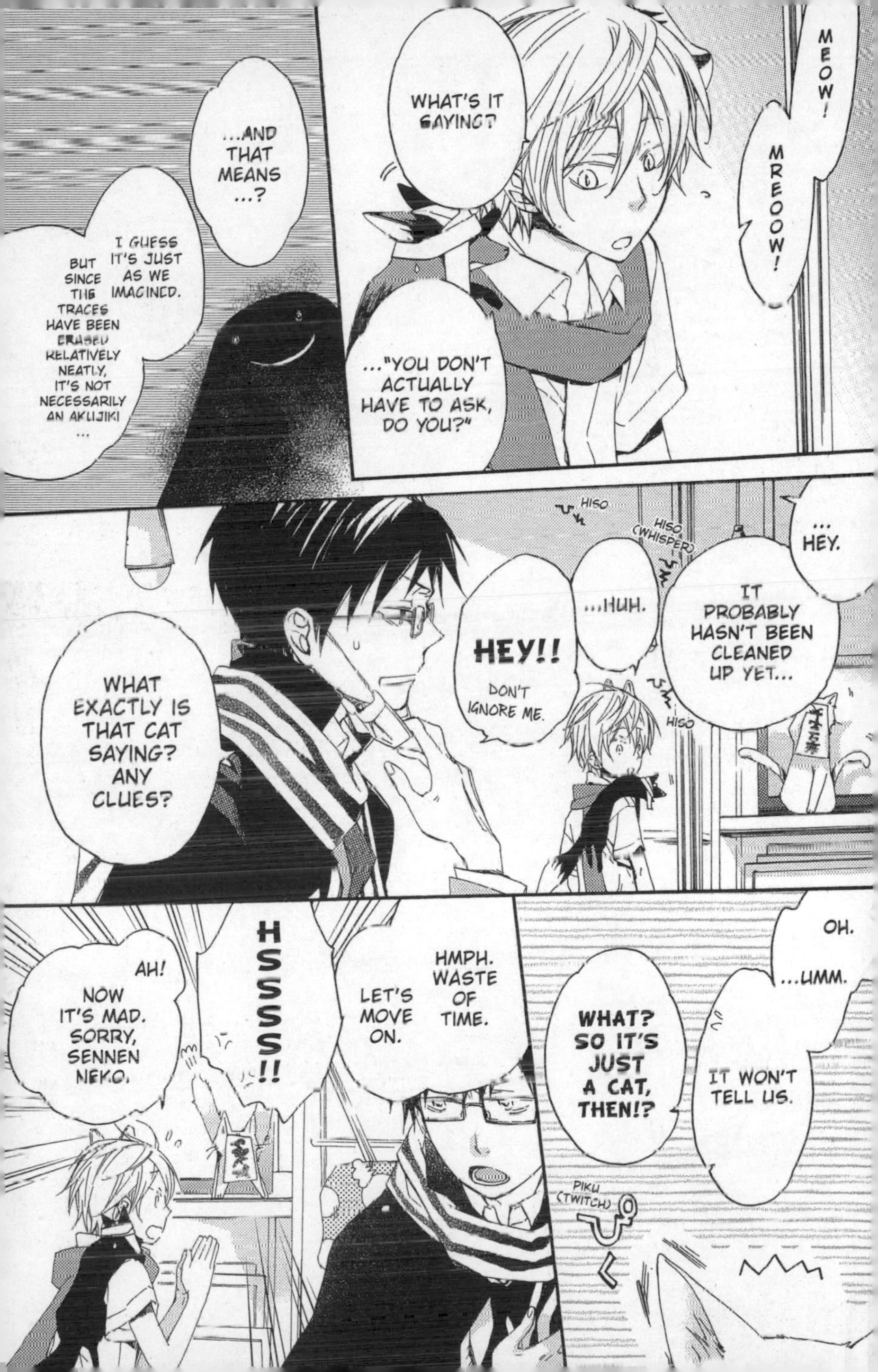
MEOW! MREOOW!
WHAT'S IT SAYING?
..."YOU DON'T ACTUALLY HAVE TO ASK, DO YOU?"
...AND THAT MEANS ...?
I GUESS IT'S JUST AS WE IMAGINED.
BUT SINCE THE TRACES HAVE BEEN ERASED RELATIVELY NEATLY, IT'S NOT NECESSARILY AN AKUJIKI ...
... HEY.
IT PROBABLY HASN'T BEEN CLEANED UP YET...
HISO (WHISPER)
HISO
HISO
...HUH.
HEY!!
DON'T IGNORE ME.
WHAT EXACTLY IS THAT CAT SAYING? ANY CLUES?
OH.
...UMM.
IT WON'T TELL US.
WHAT? SO IT'S JUST A CAT, THEN!?
PIKU (TWITCH)
HMPH. WASTE OF TIME.
LET'S MOVE ON.
HSSSS!!
AH!
NOW IT'S MAD. SORRY, SENNEN NEKO.

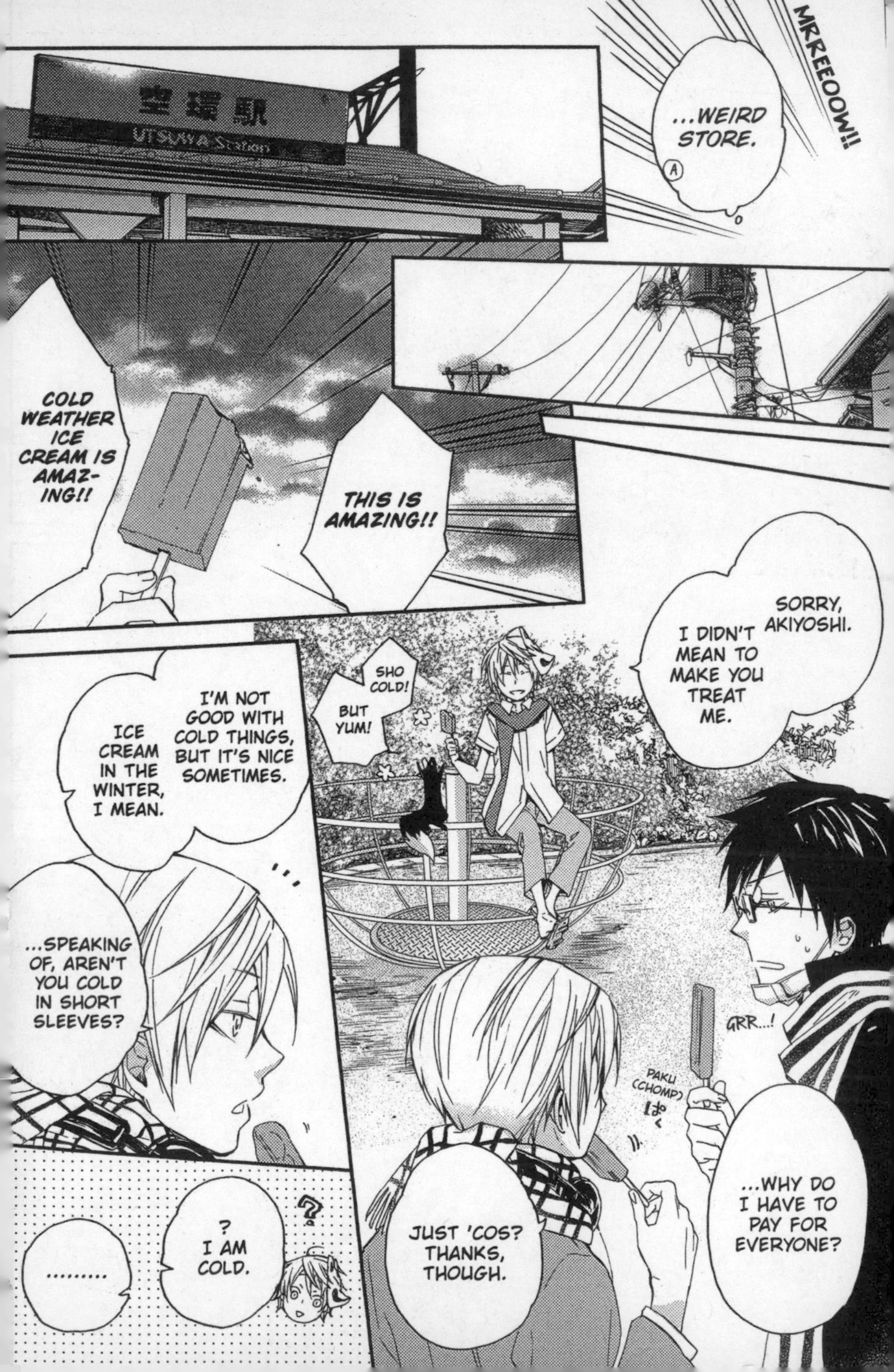

MRREEOOW!!
...WEIRD STORE.
空環駅
UTSUWA Station
THIS IS AMAZING!!
COLD WEATHER ICE CREAM IS AMAZING!!
SORRY, AKIYOSHI. I DIDN'T MEAN TO MAKE YOU TREAT ME.
SHO COLD!
BUT YUM!
I'M NOT GOOD WITH COLD THINGS, BUT IT'S NICE SOMETIMES.
ICE CREAM IN THE WINTER, I MEAN.
GRR...!
PAKU (CHOMP)
ぱく
...WHY DO I HAVE TO PAY FOR EVERYONE?
JUST 'COS? THANKS, THOUGH.
...SPEAKING OF, AREN'T YOU COLD IN SHORT SLEEVES?
? I AM COLD.
....

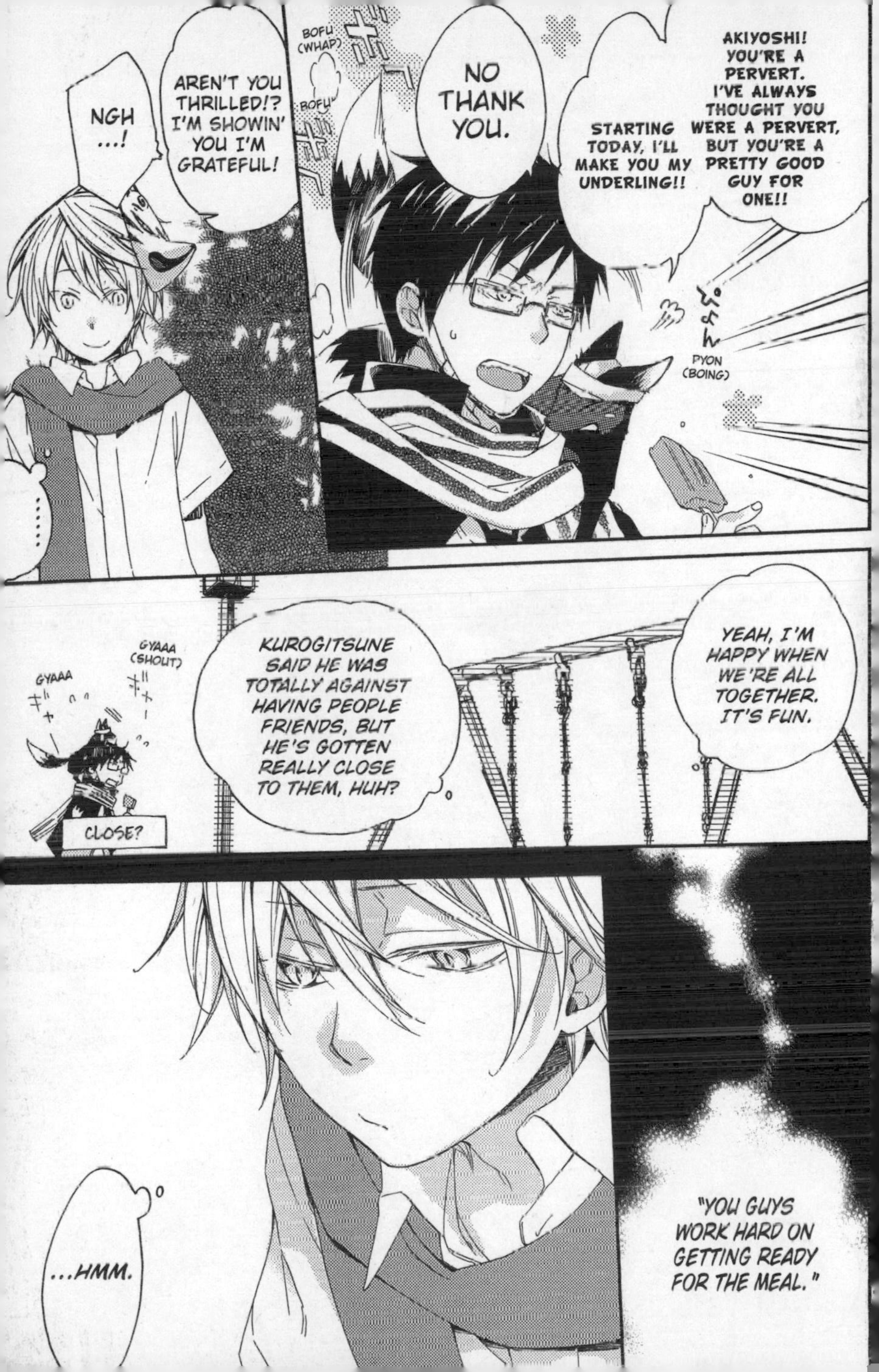
AKIYOSHI! YOU'RE A PERVERT. I'VE ALWAYS THOUGHT YOU WERE A PERVERT, BUT YOU'RE A PRETTY GOOD GUY FOR ONE!!
STARTING TODAY, I'LL MAKE YOU MY UNDERLING!!
NO THANK YOU.
BOFU (WHAP)
BOFU
PYON (BOING)
AREN'T YOU THRILLED!? I'M SHOWIN' YOU I'M GRATEFUL!
NGH ...!
YEAH, I'M HAPPY WHEN WE'RE ALL TOGETHER. IT'S FUN.
KUROGITSUNE SAID HE WAS TOTALLY AGAINST HAVING PEOPLE FRIENDS, BUT HE'S GOTTEN REALLY CLOSE TO THEM, HUH?
GYAAA (SHOUT)
GYAAA
CLOSE?
"YOU GUYS WORK HARD ON GETTING READY FOR THE MEAL."
...HMM.

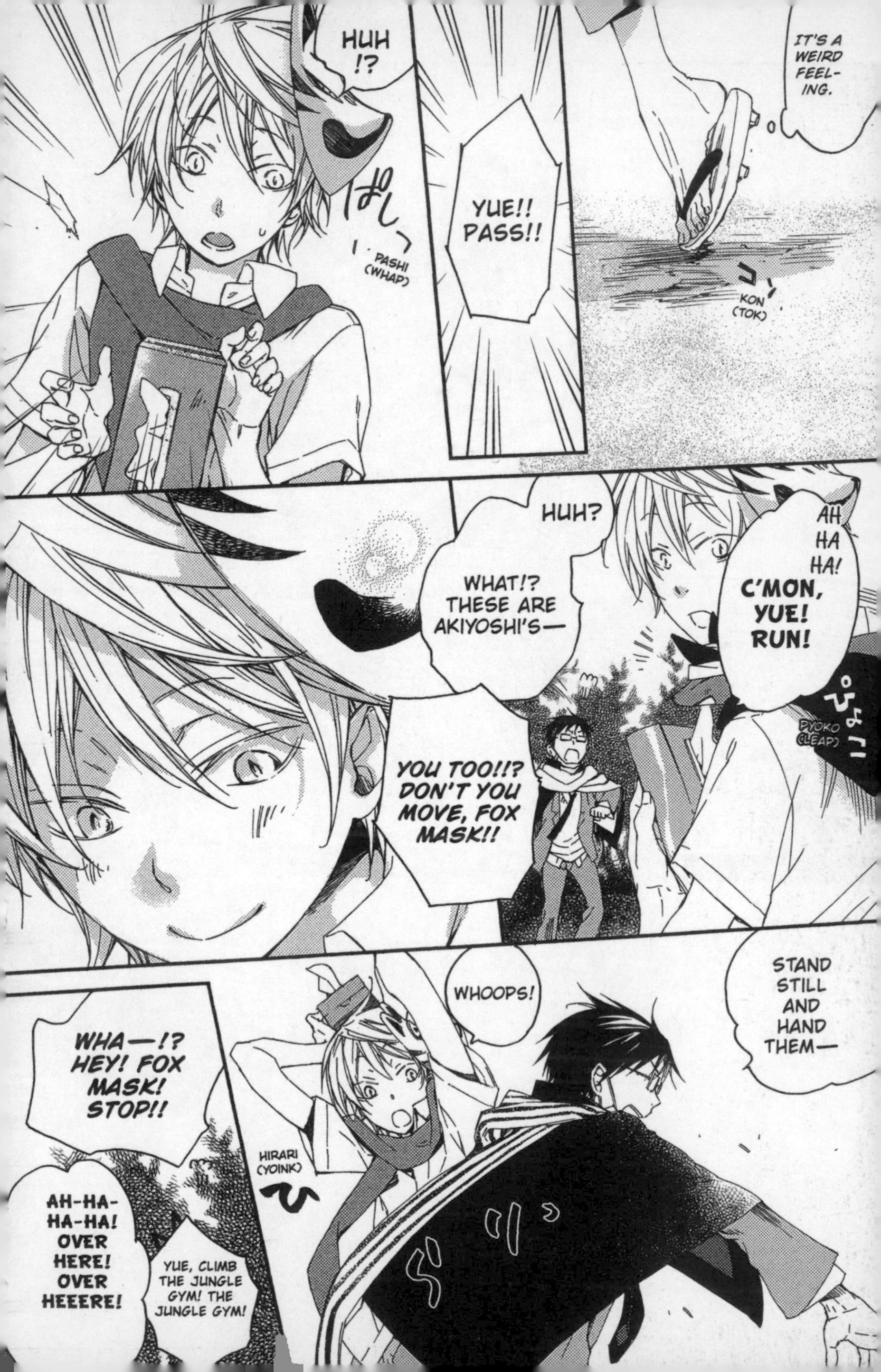
IT'S A WEIRD FEEL-ING.
KON (TOK)
YUE!! PASS!!
HUH !?
PASHI (WHAP)
HUH?
AH HA HA! C'MON, YUE! RUN!
WHAT!? THESE ARE AKIYOSHI'S—
PYOKO (LEAP)
YOU TOO!!? DON'T YOU MOVE, FOX MASK!!
STAND STILL AND HAND THEM—
WHOOPS!
HIRARI (YOINK)
WHA—!? HEY! FOX MASK! STOP!!
AH-HA-HA-HA! OVER HERE! OVER HEEERE!
YUE, CLIMB THE JUNGLE GYM! THE JUNGLE GYM!

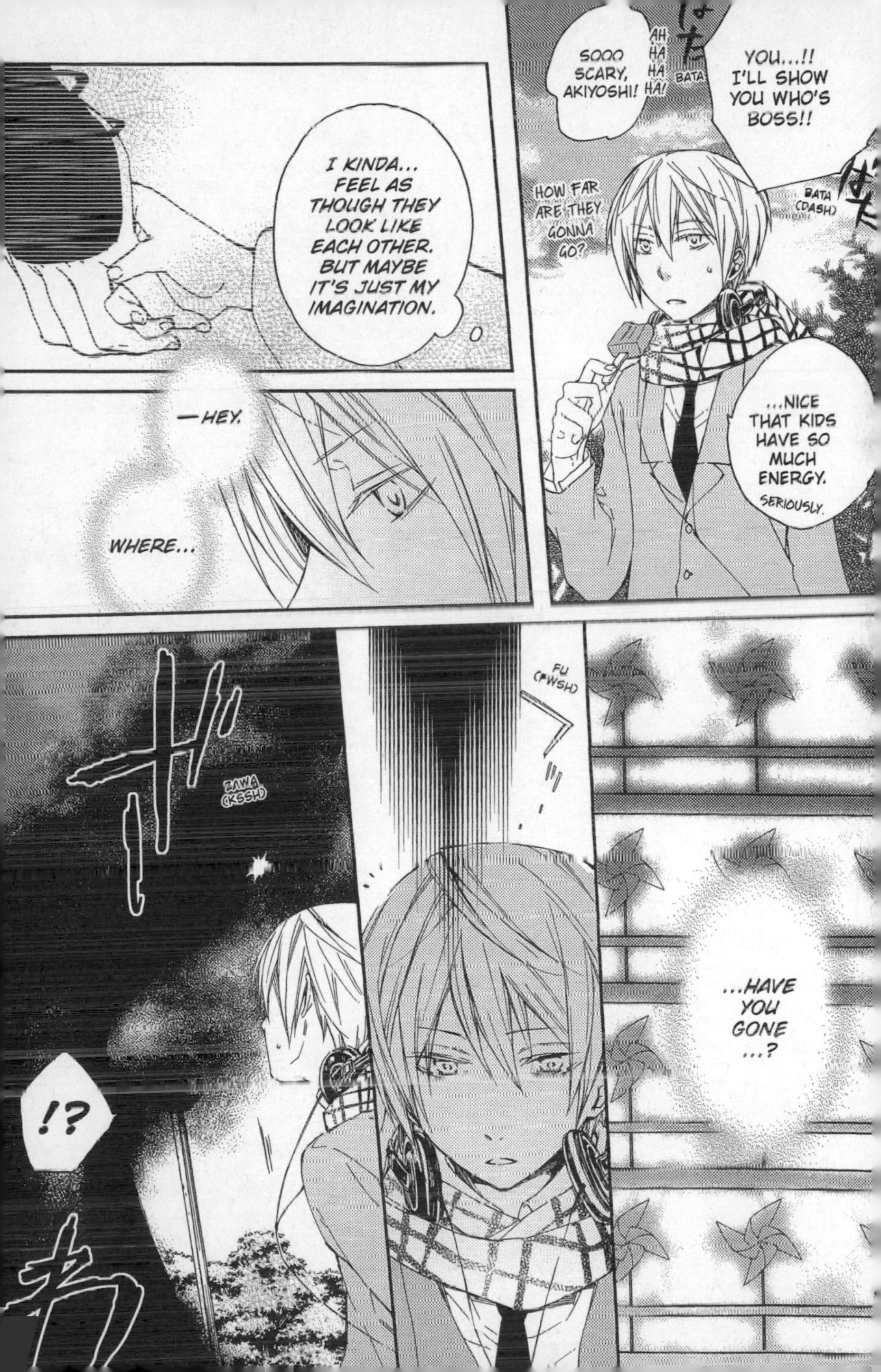
YOU...!! I'LL SHOW YOU WHO'S BOSS!!
BATA
AH HA HA HA!
SOOO SCARY, AKIYOSHI!
BATA (DASH)
HOW FAR ARE THEY GONNA GO?
...NICE THAT KIDS HAVE SO MUCH ENERGY.
SERIOUSLY.
I KINDA... FEEL AS THOUGH THEY LOOK LIKE EACH OTHER. BUT MAYBE IT'S JUST MY IMAGINATION.
—HEY.
WHERE...
...HAVE YOU GONE ...?
FU (PWSH)
ZAWA (KSSH)
!?

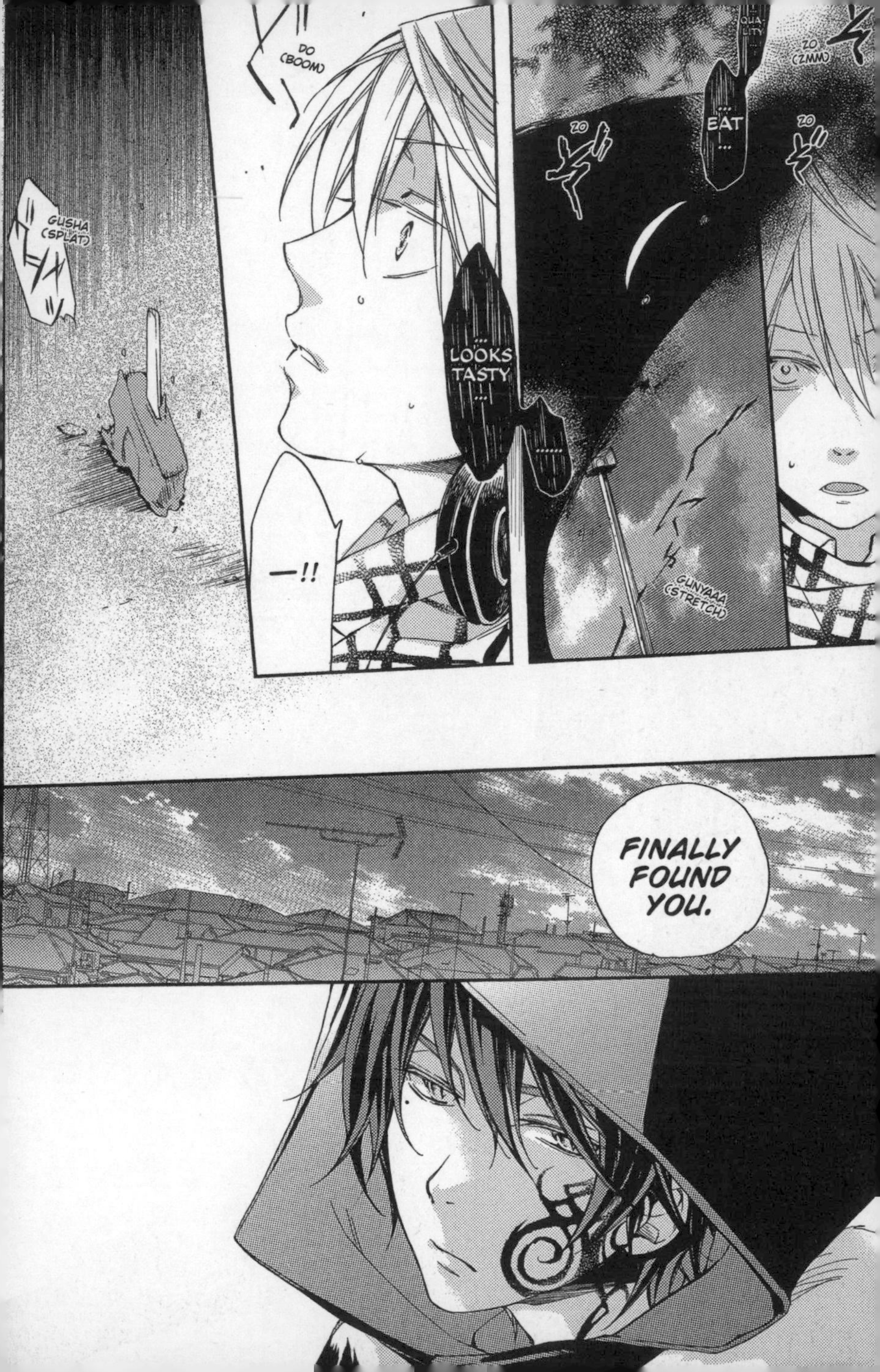
ZO (ZMM)
QUALITY
... EAT ...
ZO
ZO
... LOOKS TASTY ...
......
GUNYAAA (STRETCH)
DO (BOOM)
—!!
GUSHA (SPLAT)
FINALLY FOUND YOU.

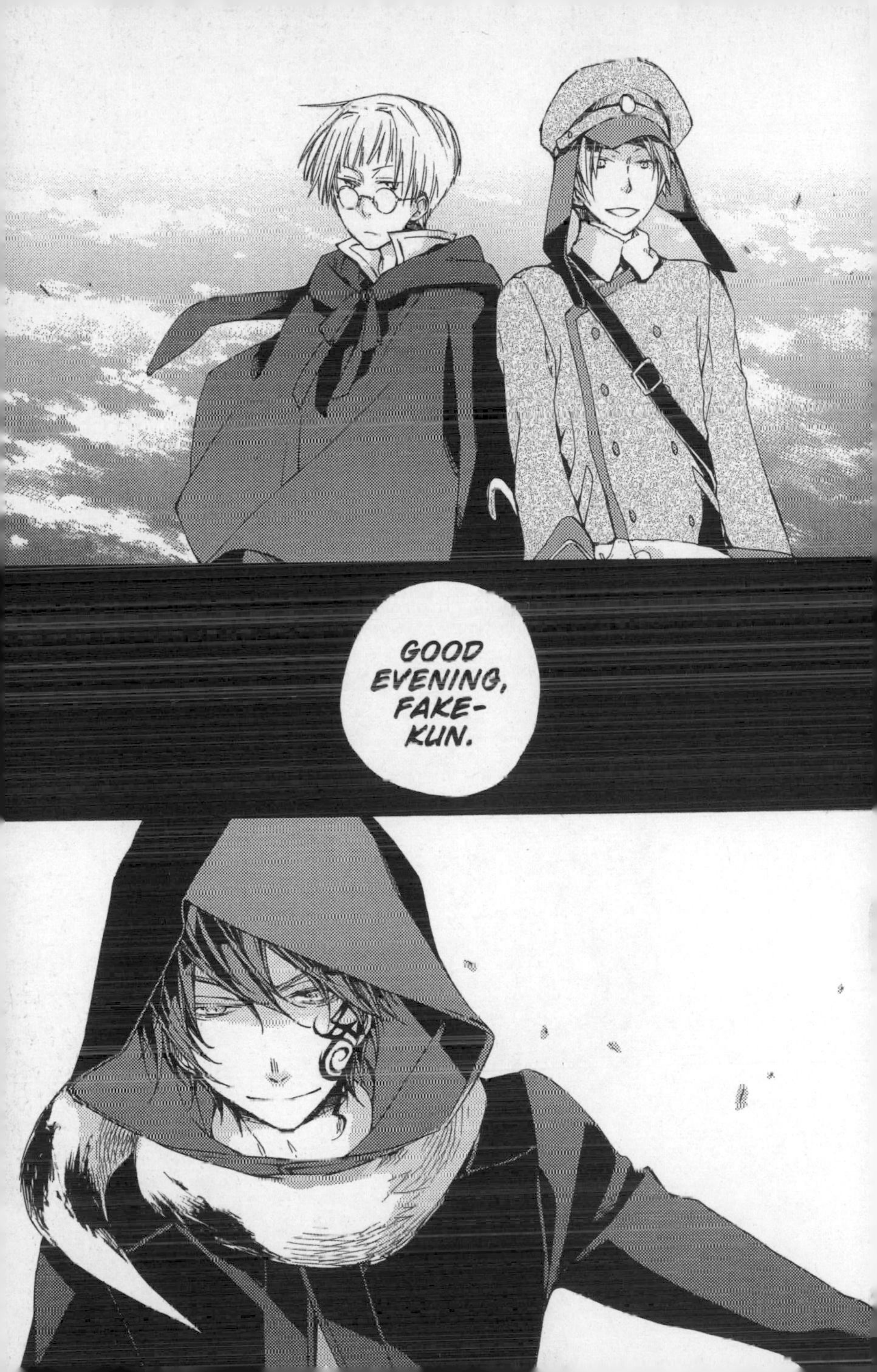
GOOD EVENING, FAKE-KUN.

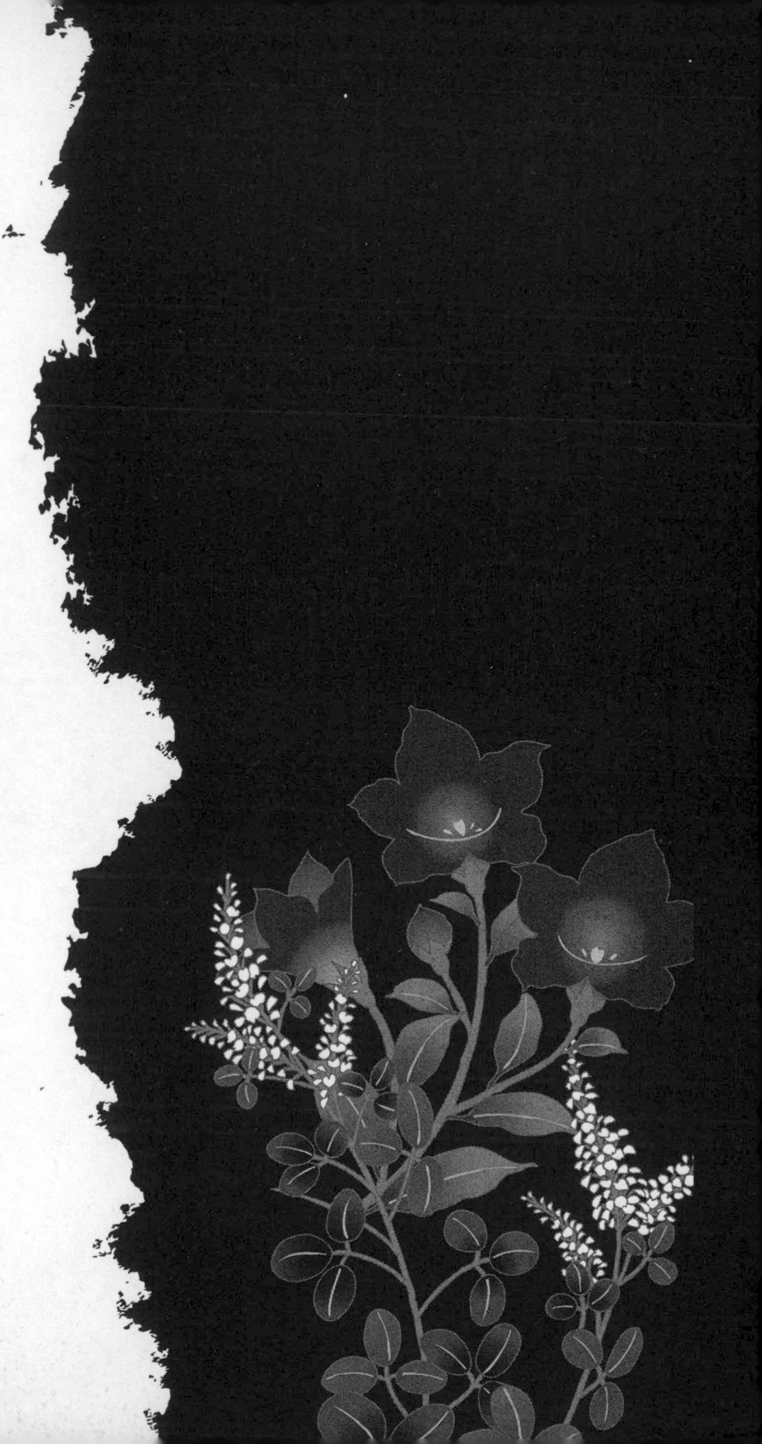

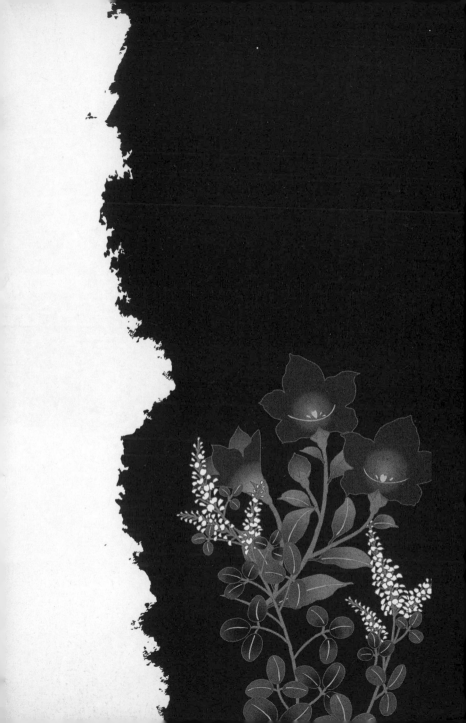

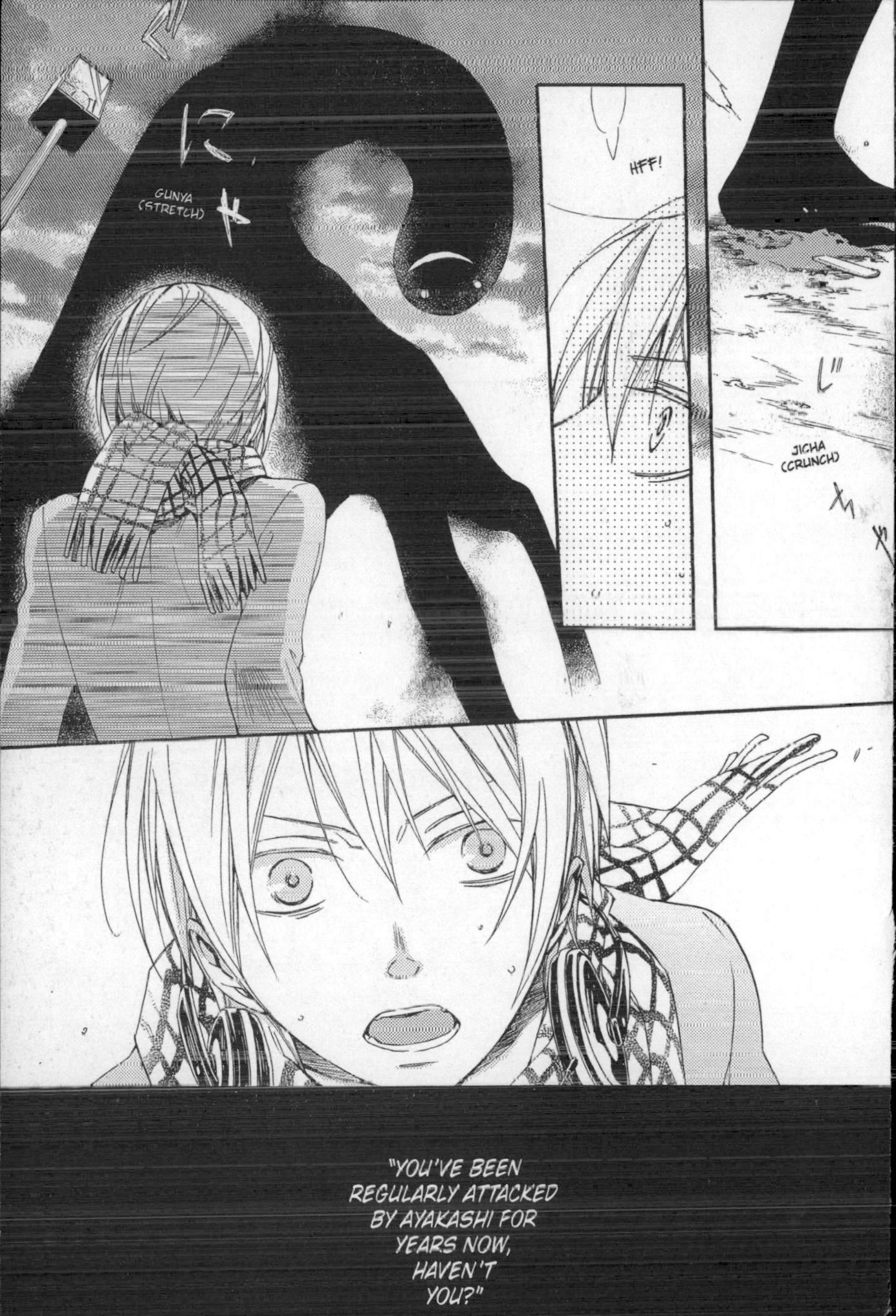
JICHA (CRUNCH)
HFF!
GUNYA (STRETCH)
"YOU'VE BEEN REGULARLY ATTACKED BY AYAKASHI FOR YEARS NOW, HAVEN'T YOU?"

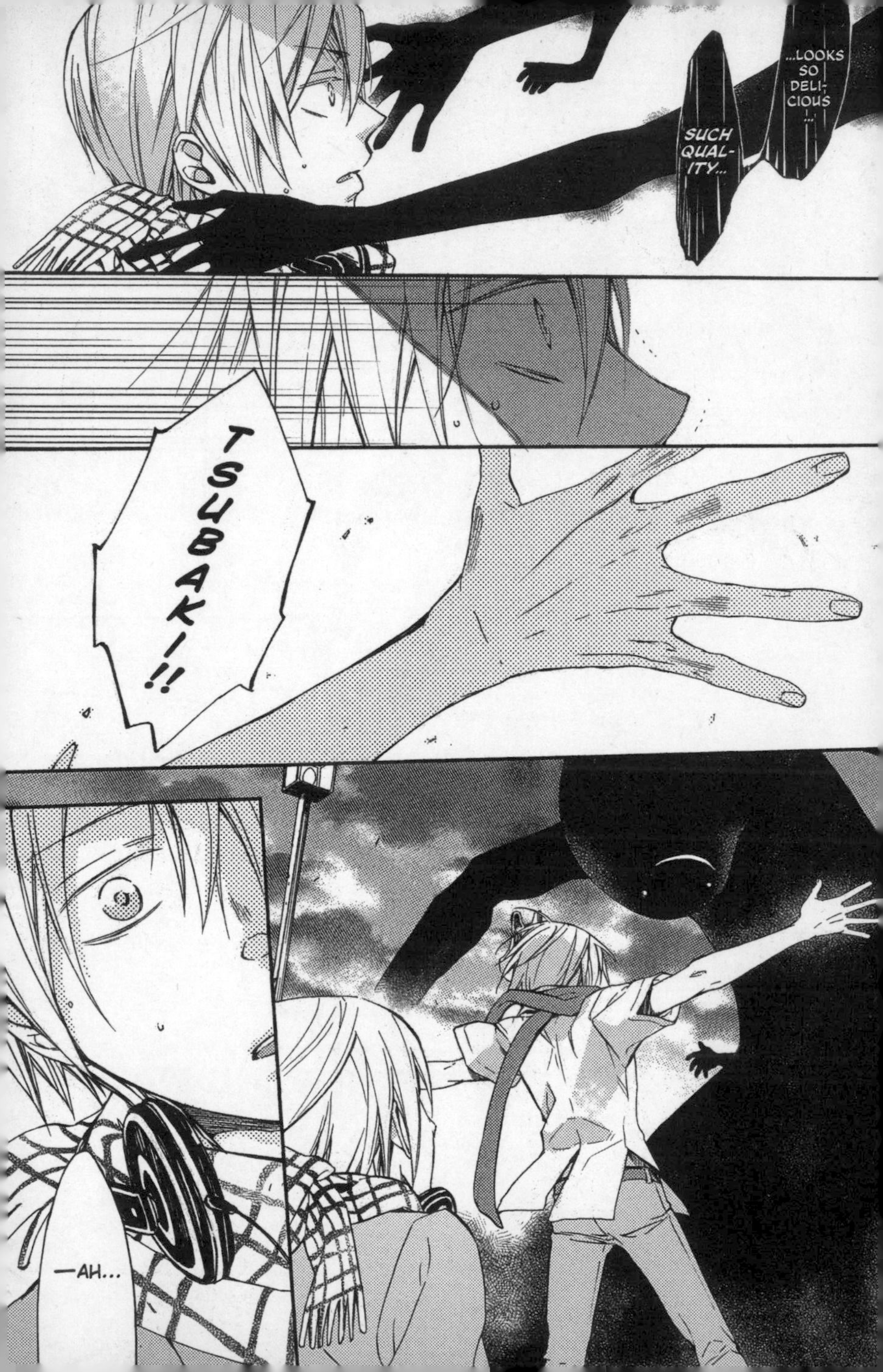
...LOOKS SO DELI-CIOUS ...
SUCH QUAL-ITY...
TSUBAKI!!
—AH...

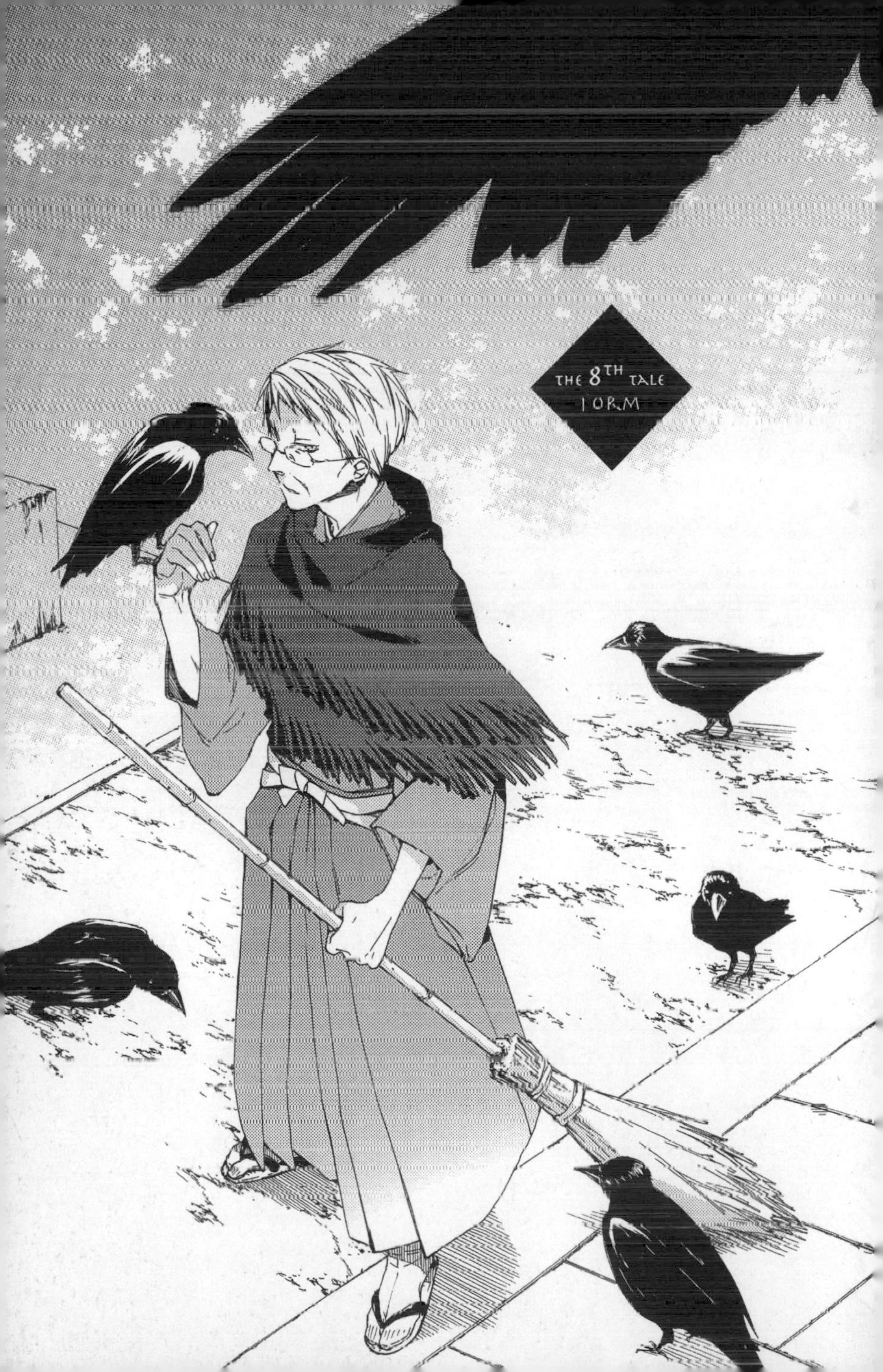
THE 8TH TALE
IORM

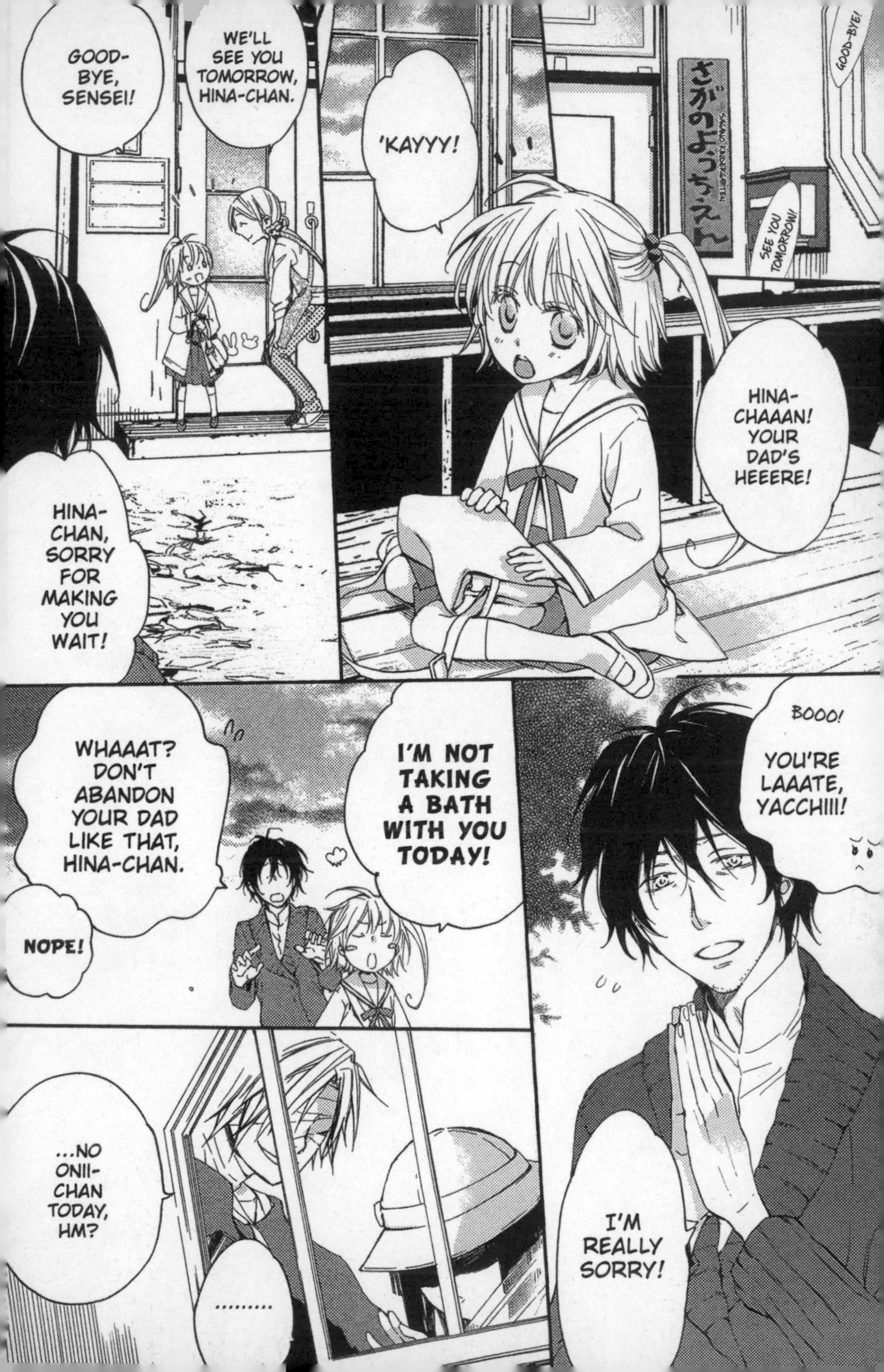

GOOD-BYE!
SEE YOU TOMORROW!
さがのようちえん
'KAYYY!
HINA-CHAAAN! YOUR DAD'S HEEERE!
WE'LL SEE YOU TOMORROW, HINA-CHAN.
GOOD-BYE, SENSEI!
HINA-CHAN, SORRY FOR MAKING YOU WAIT!
BOOO!
YOU'RE LAAATE, YACCHIIII!
I'M REALLY SORRY!
I'M NOT TAKING A BATH WITH YOU TODAY!
WHAAAT? DON'T ABANDON YOUR DAD LIKE THAT, HINA-CHAN.
NOPE!
...NO ONII-CHAN TODAY, HM?
....

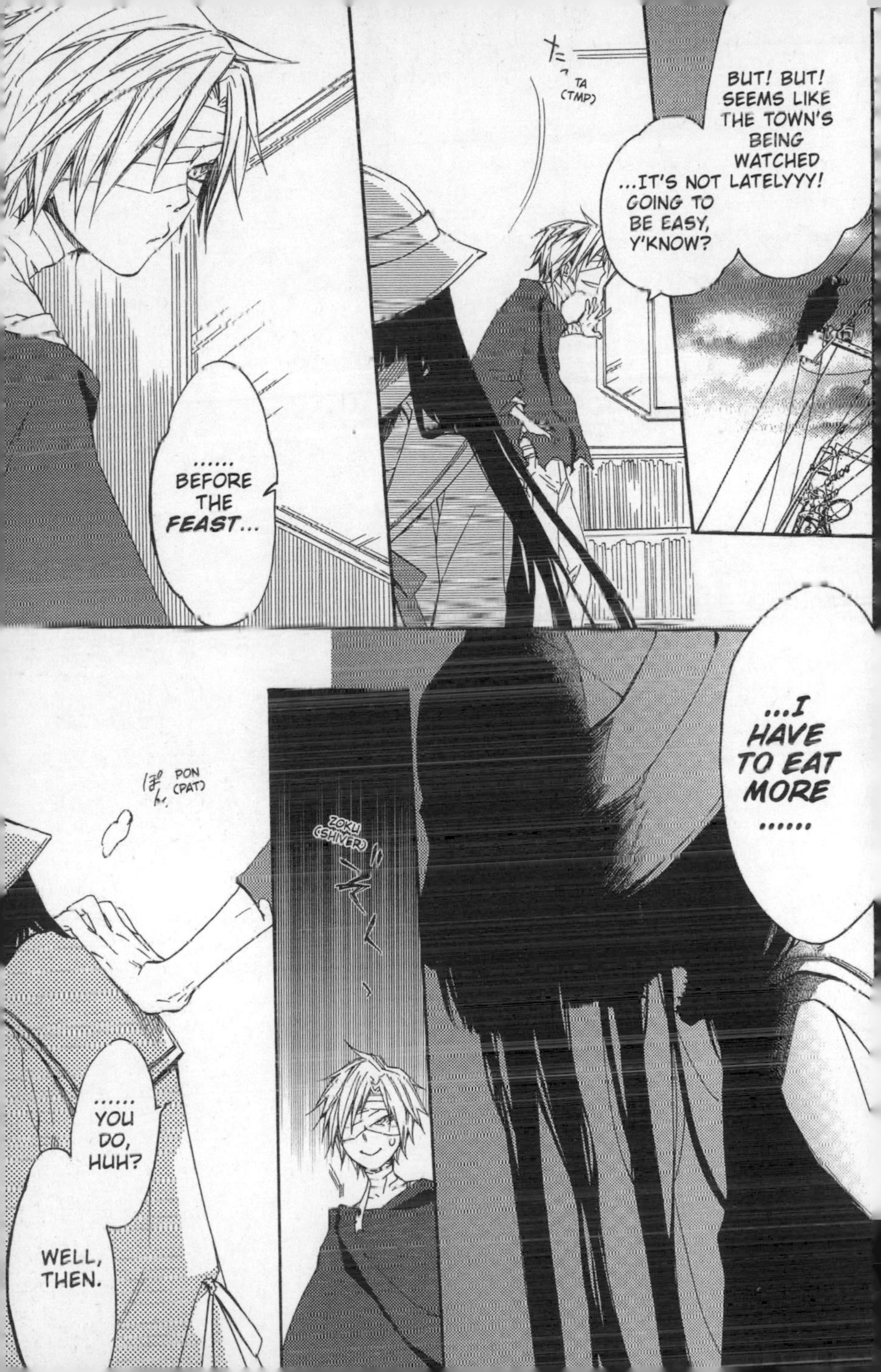
BUT! BUT! SEEMS LIKE THE TOWN'S BEING WATCHED LATELYYY!
...IT'S NOT GOING TO BE EASY, Y'KNOW?
TA (TMP)
...... BEFORE THE FEAST...
...I HAVE TO EAT MORE ......
ZOKU (SHIVER)
PON (PAT)
...... YOU DO, HUH?
WELL, THEN.

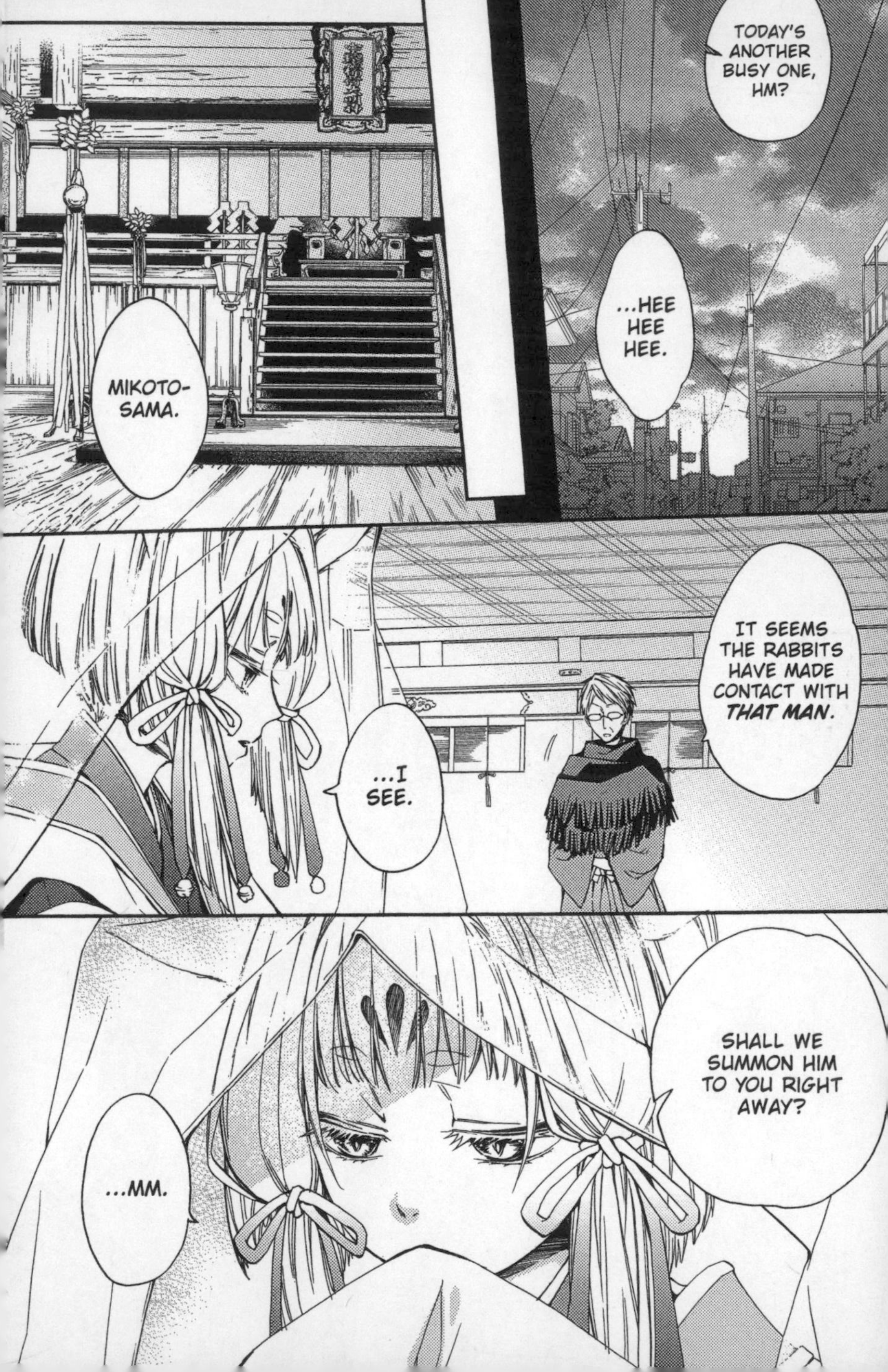
TODAY'S ANOTHER BUSY ONE, HM?
...HEE HEE HEE.
MIKOTO-SAMA.
IT SEEMS THE RABBITS HAVE MADE CONTACT WITH *THAT MAN*.
...I SEE.
SHALL WE SUMMON HIM TO YOU RIGHT AWAY?
...MM.

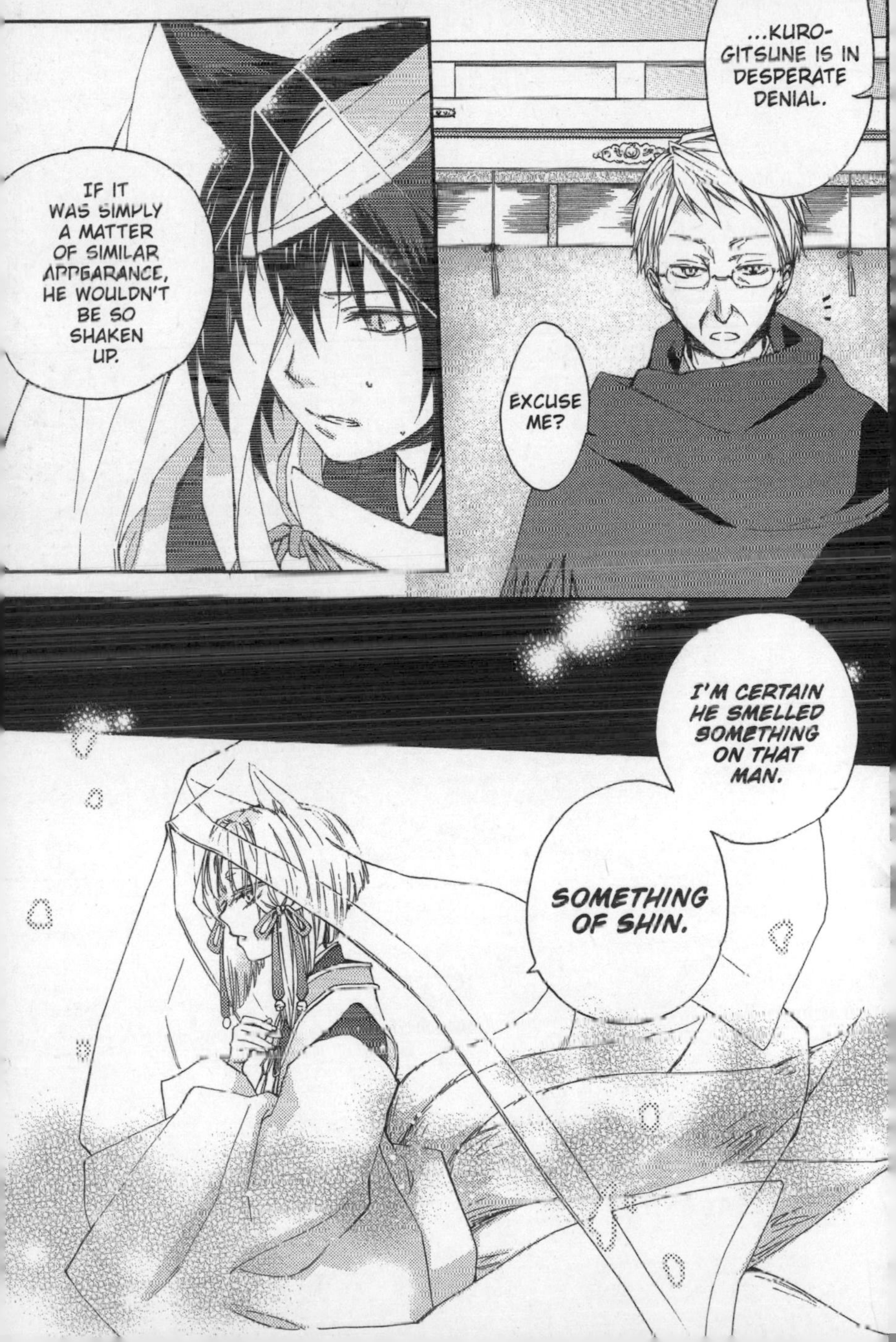
...KURO-GITSUNE IS IN DESPERATE DENIAL.
EXCUSE ME?
IF IT WAS SIMPLY A MATTER OF SIMILAR APPEARANCE, HE WOULDN'T BE SO SHAKEN UP.
I'M CERTAIN HE SMELLED SOMETHING ON THAT MAN.
SOMETHING OF SHIN.

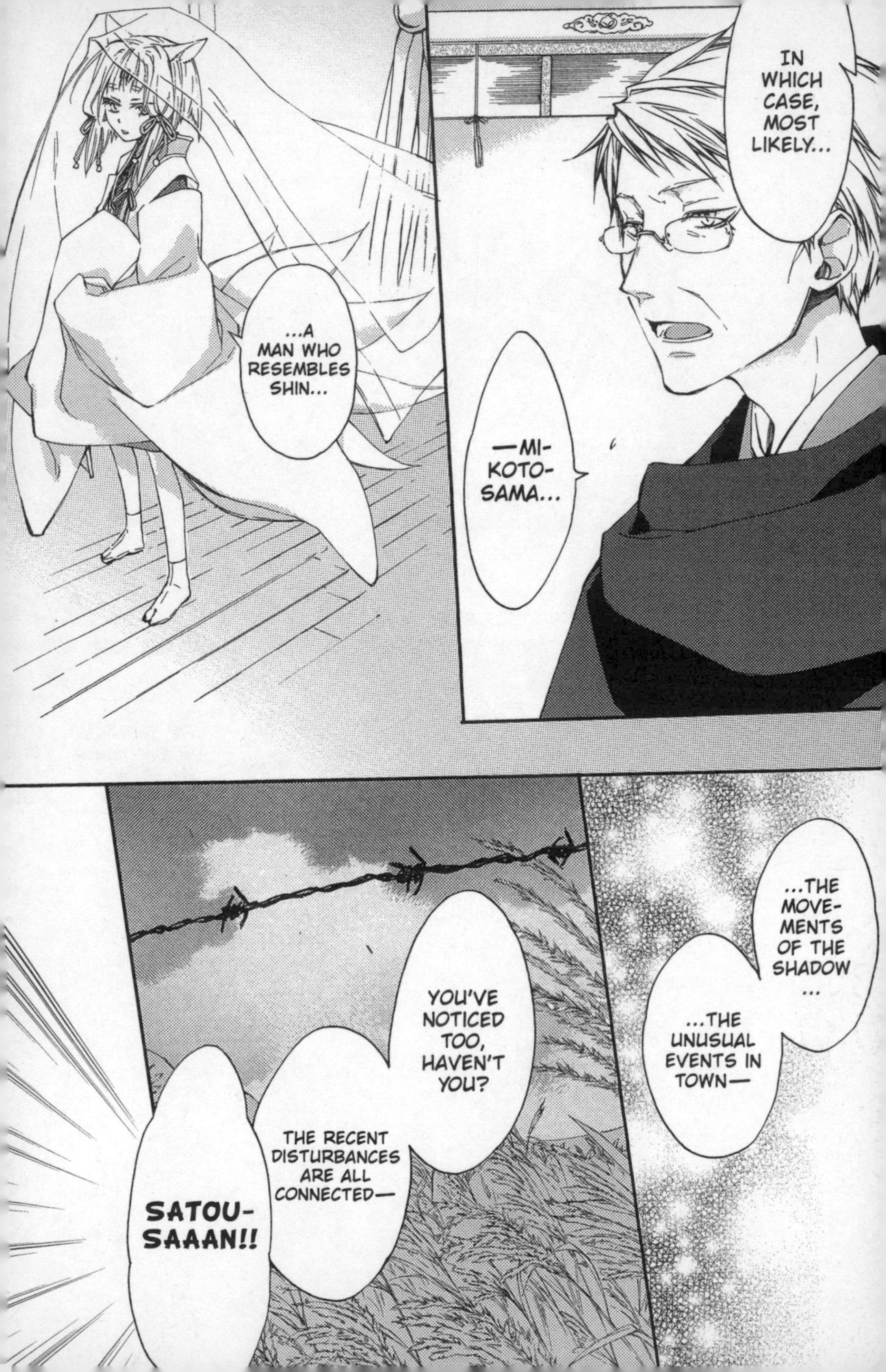
IN WHICH CASE, MOST LIKELY...
—MI-KOTO-SAMA...
...A MAN WHO RESEMBLES SHIN...
...THE MOVE-MENTS OF THE SHADOW ...
...THE UNUSUAL EVENTS IN TOWN—
YOU'VE NOTICED TOO, HAVEN'T YOU?
THE RECENT DISTURBANCES ARE ALL CONNECTED—
SATOU-SAAAN!!

SATOU-SAAAN, I'M HUNGRYYY.
ぴょこ
PYOKO (POP)
THAT'S RIGHT. I COMPLETELY FORGOT ABOUT YOUR DINNER.
WHAAAT!?
YOU'RE SOOOO MEAN!
わあぁ
WAAAH!
NO, NO, KEEMUN! SATOU AND MIKO-SAMA DON'T HAVE TIME FOR THAT NOW!
BUT I AAAM!
YOU SAY THAT, GYOKURO, BUT YOU'RE STARVING TOOOO!
ふよ
FUYO (BOB)
MY, MY.
FUYO
SATOU'S TERRIBLE. MIKO-SAMA, YOU TELL HIM TOO!
WAAAH
MM?
...YES, TRUE...
MIKO-SAMA, YOU LOOK SAD.
ARE YOU HUNGRY TOOOO?
COME NOW!

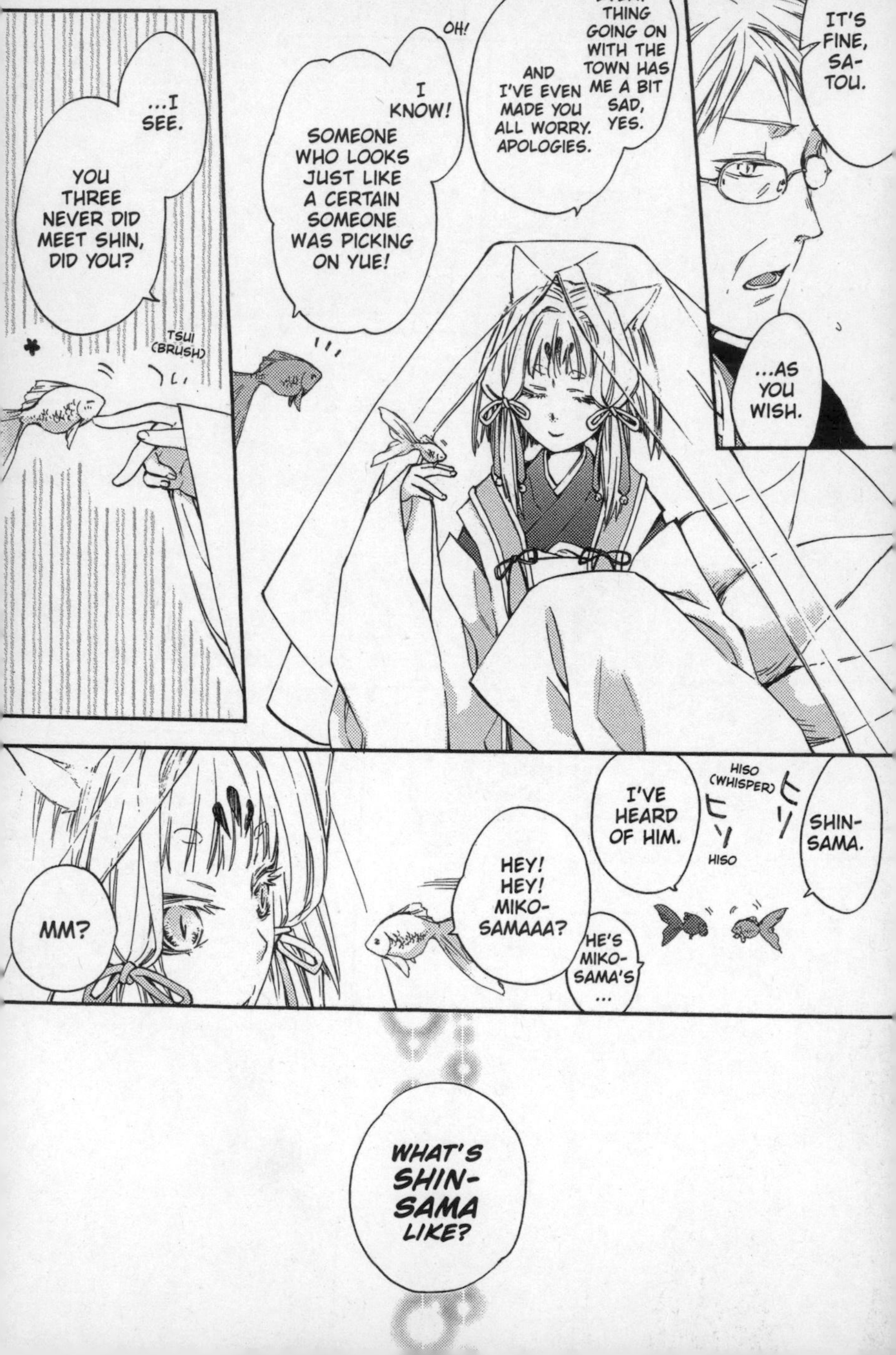
IT'S FINE, SATOU.
...AS YOU WISH.
EVERYTHING GOING ON WITH THE TOWN HAS ME A BIT SAD, YES.
AND I'VE EVEN MADE YOU ALL WORRY. APOLOGIES.
OH!
I KNOW! SOMEONE WHO LOOKS JUST LIKE A CERTAIN SOMEONE WAS PICKING ON YUE!
...I SEE.
YOU THREE NEVER DID MEET SHIN, DID YOU?
TSUI (BRUSH)
SHIN-SAMA.
HISO (WHISPER)
HISO
I'VE HEARD OF HIM.
HEY! HEY! MIKO-SAMAAA?
HE'S MIKO-SAMA'S ...
MM?
WHAT'S SHIN-SAMA LIKE?

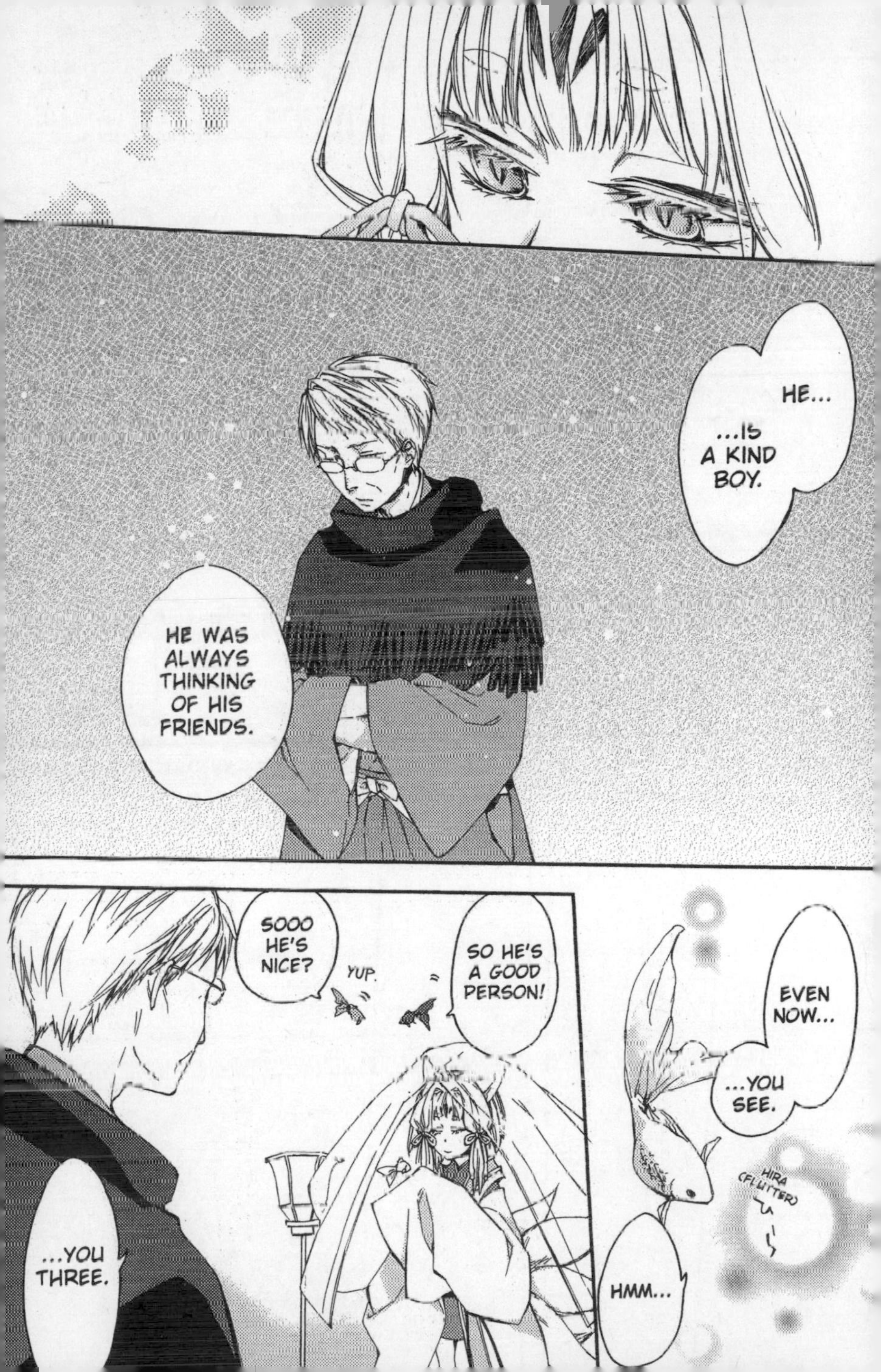
HE...
...IS A KIND BOY.
HE WAS ALWAYS THINKING OF HIS FRIENDS.
EVEN NOW...
...YOU SEE.
HIRA (FLUTTER)
HMM...
SO HE'S A GOOD PERSON!
SOOO HE'S NICE?
YUP.
...YOU THREE.

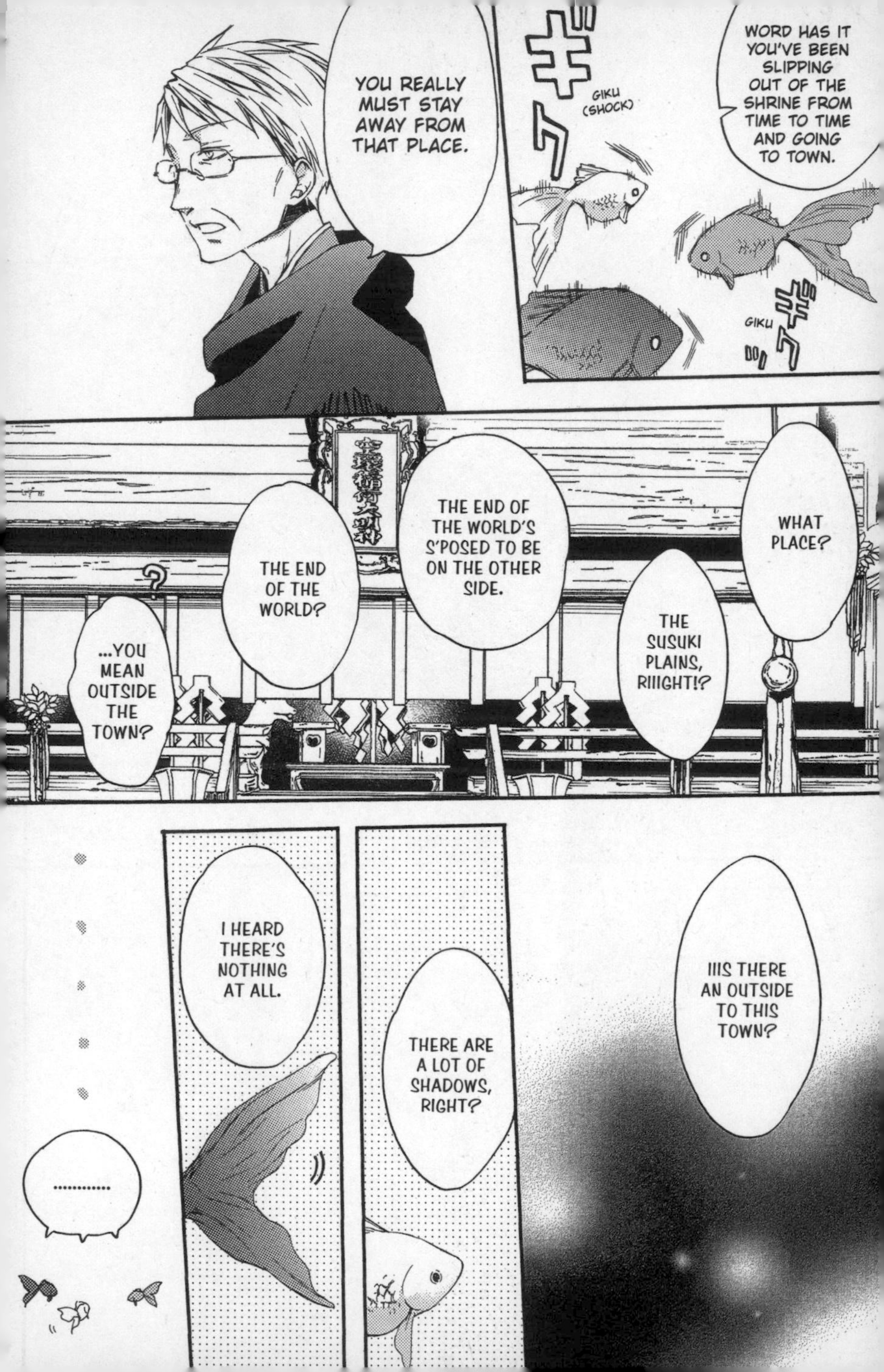
WORD HAS IT YOU'VE BEEN SLIPPING OUT OF THE SHRINE FROM TIME TO TIME AND GOING TO TOWN.
GIKU (SHOCK)
GIKU
YOU REALLY MUST STAY AWAY FROM THAT PLACE.
WHAT PLACE?
THE SUSUKI PLAINS, RIIIGHT!?
THE END OF THE WORLD'S S'POSED TO BE ON THE OTHER SIDE.
THE END OF THE WORLD?
?
...YOU MEAN OUTSIDE THE TOWN?
IIIS THERE AN OUTSIDE TO THIS TOWN?
THERE ARE A LOT OF SHADOWS, RIGHT?
I HEARD THERE'S NOTHING AT ALL.
....

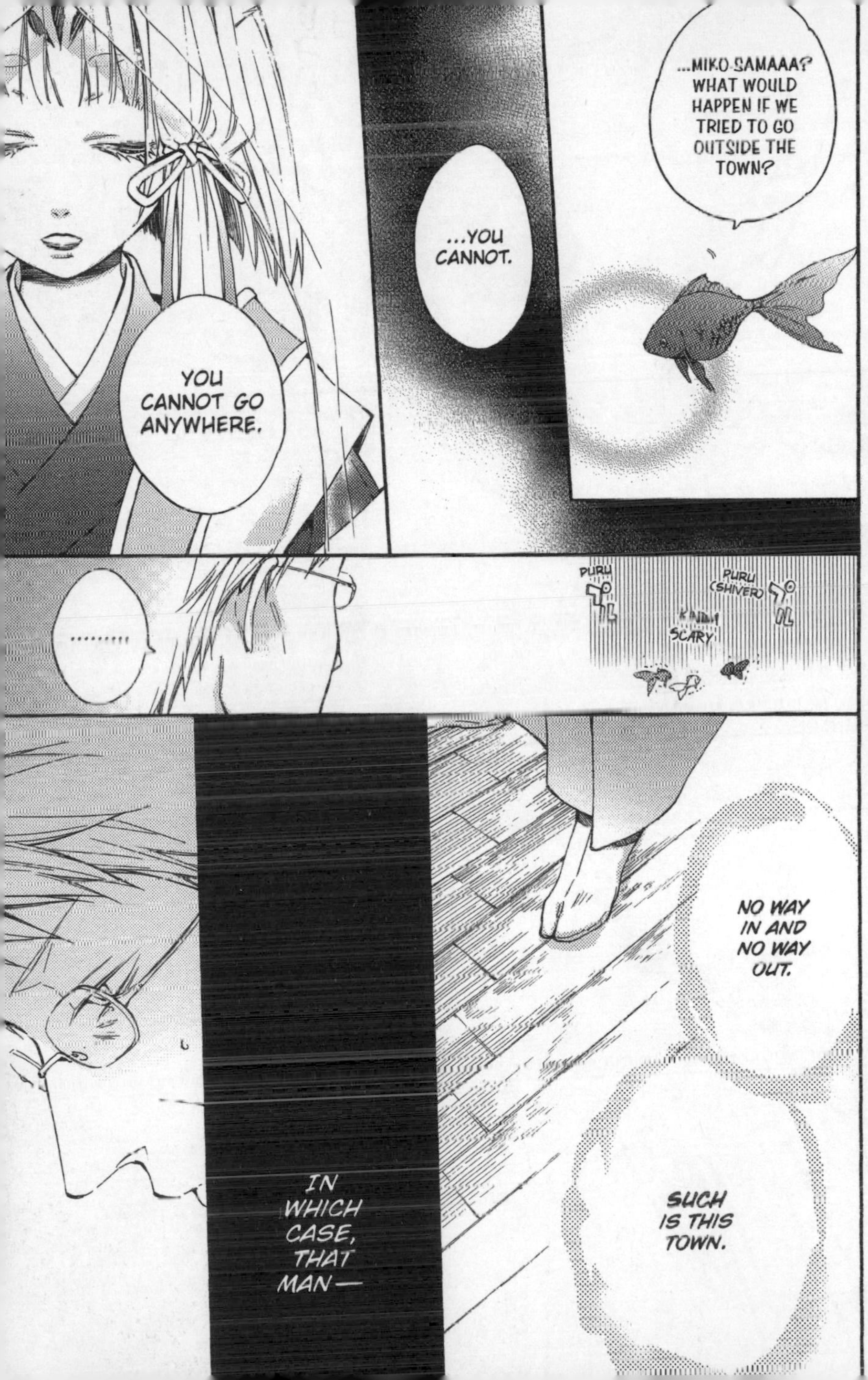
...MIKO SAMAAA? WHAT WOULD HAPPEN IF WE TRIED TO GO OUTSIDE THE TOWN?
...YOU CANNOT.
YOU CANNOT GO ANYWHERE.
PURU
PURU (SHIVER)
SCARY
....
NO WAY IN AND NO WAY OUT.
SUCH IS THIS TOWN.
IN WHICH CASE, THAT MAN—

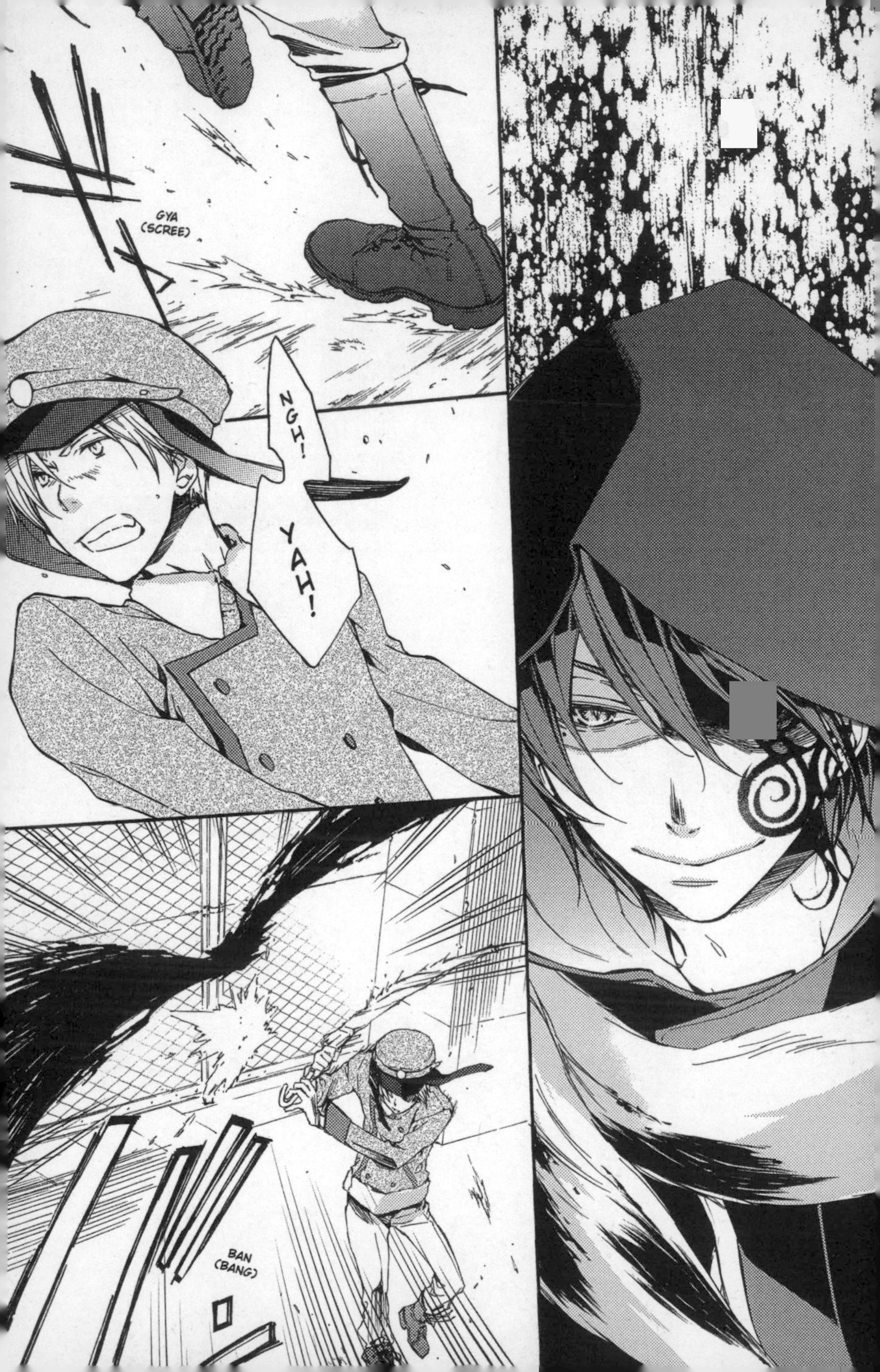
GYA
(SCREE)
NGH!
YAH!
BAN
(BANG)

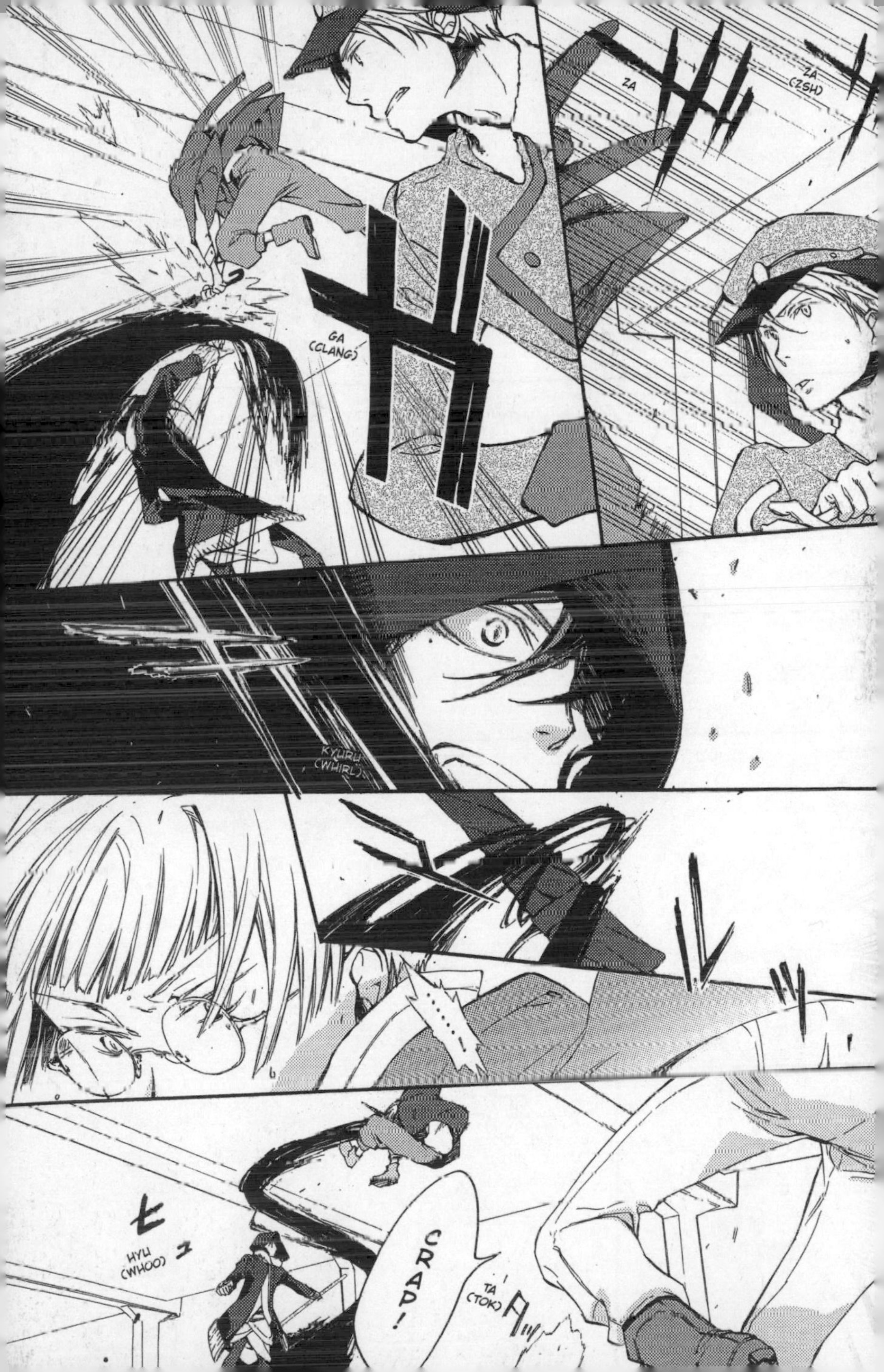
ZA (ZSH)
ZA
GA (CLANG)
KYURU (WHIRL)
......!
TA (TOK)
CRAP!
HYU (WHOO)

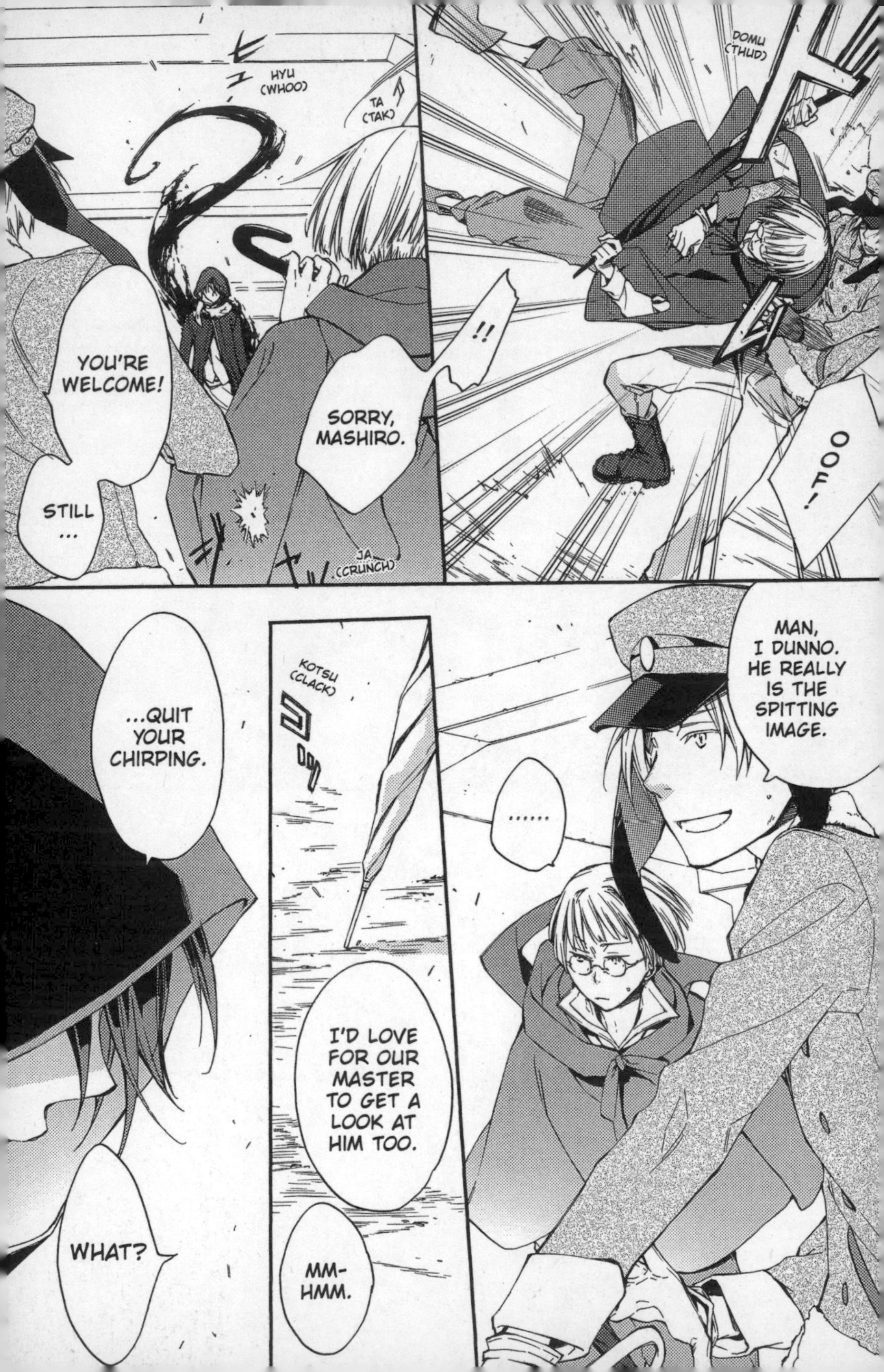
DOMU (THUD)
OOF!
TA (TAK)
HYU (WHOO)
!!
SORRY, MASHIRO.
YOU'RE WELCOME!
JA (CRUNCH)
STILL ...
MAN, I DUNNO. HE REALLY IS THE SPITTING IMAGE.
......
KOTSU (CLACK)
I'D LOVE FOR OUR MASTER TO GET A LOOK AT HIM TOO.
MM-HMM.
...QUIT YOUR CHIRPING.
WHAT?

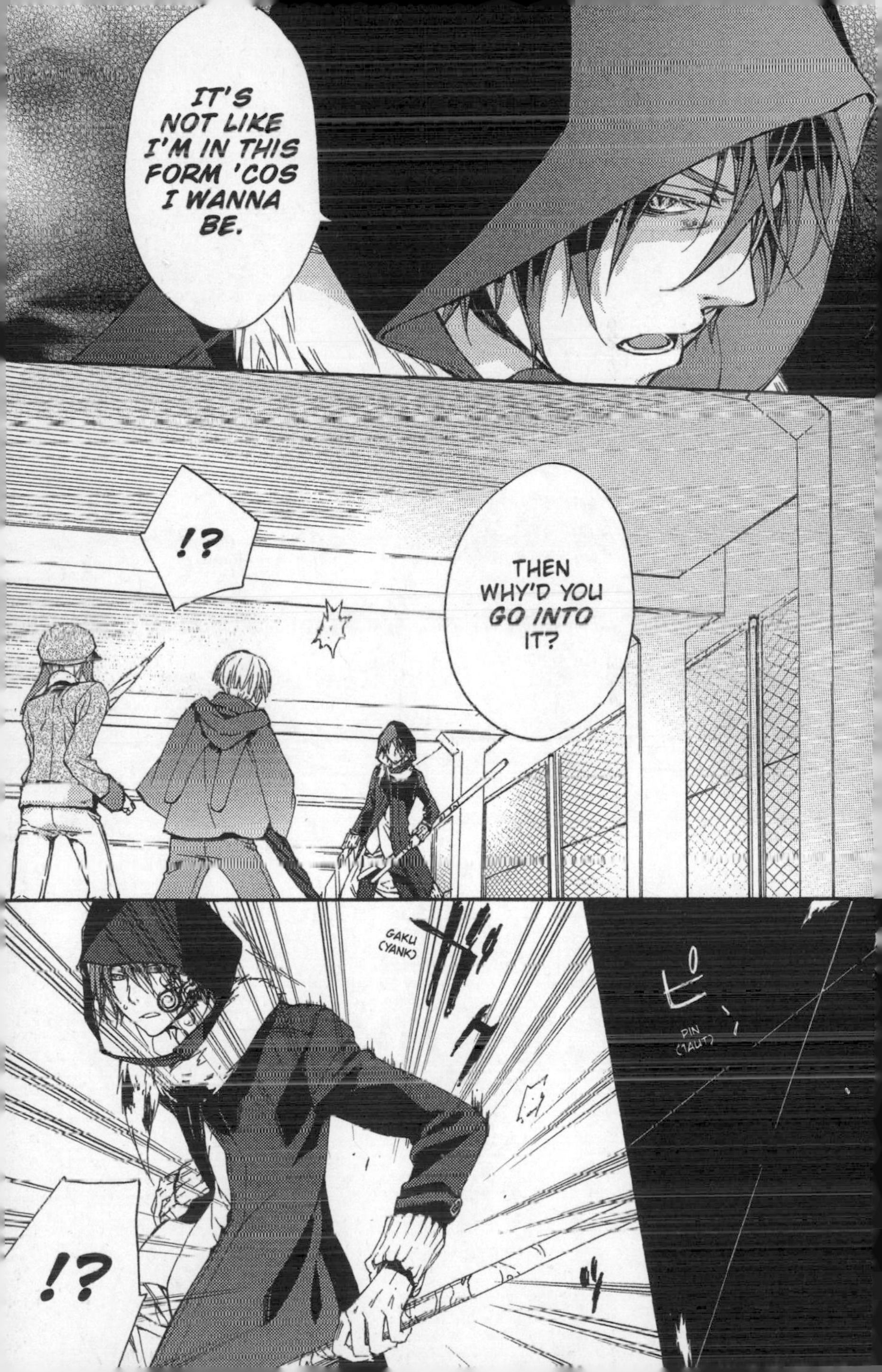
IT'S NOT LIKE I'M IN THIS FORM 'COS I WANNA BE.
THEN WHY'D YOU GO INTO IT?
!?
ピ
PIN (TAUT)
GAKU (YANK)
!?

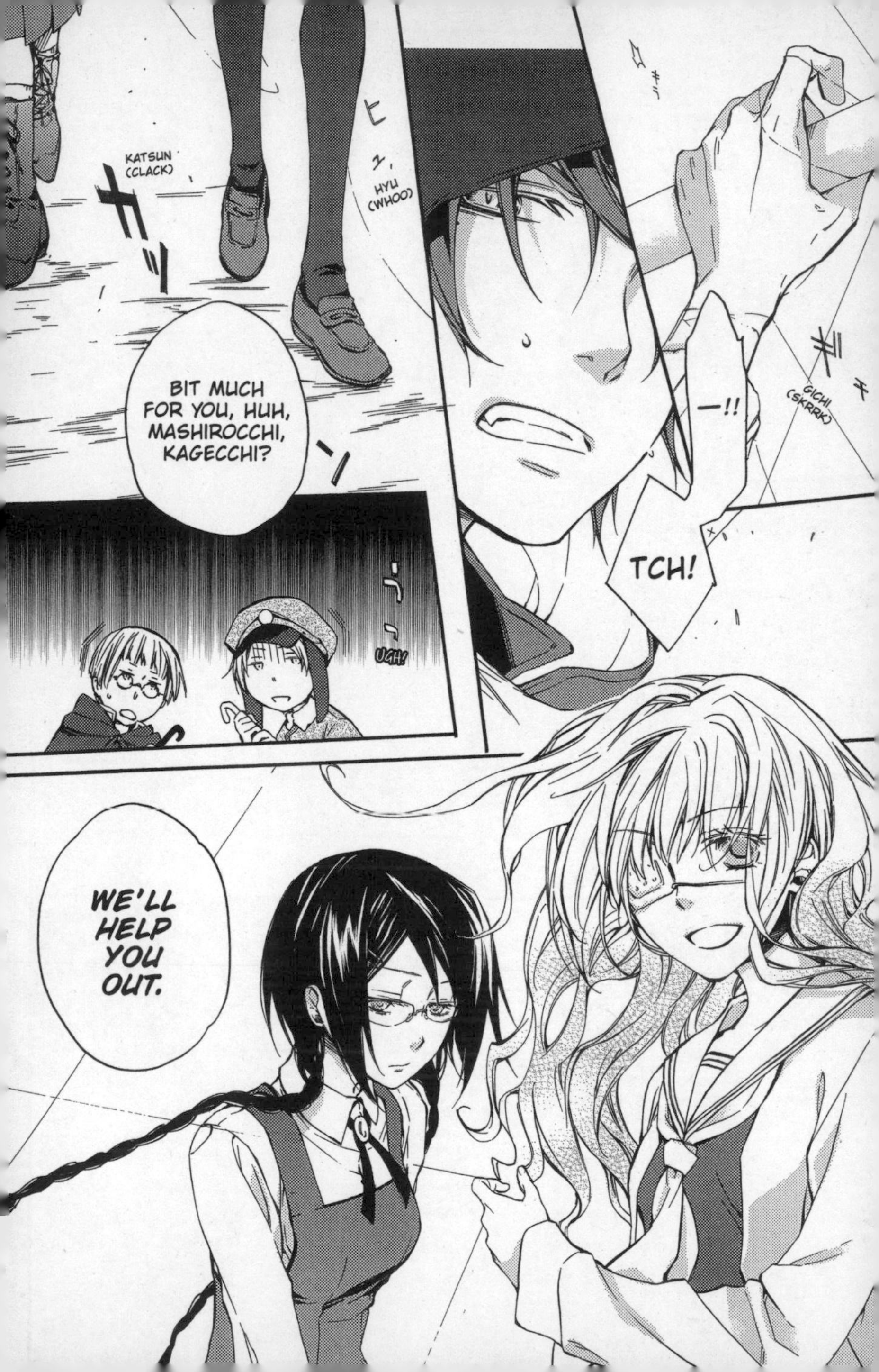
HYU (WHOO)
GICHI (SKRRK)
—!!
TCH!
KATSUN (CLACK)
BIT MUCH FOR YOU, HUH, MASHIROCCHI, KAGECCHI?
UGH!
WE'LL HELP YOU OUT.

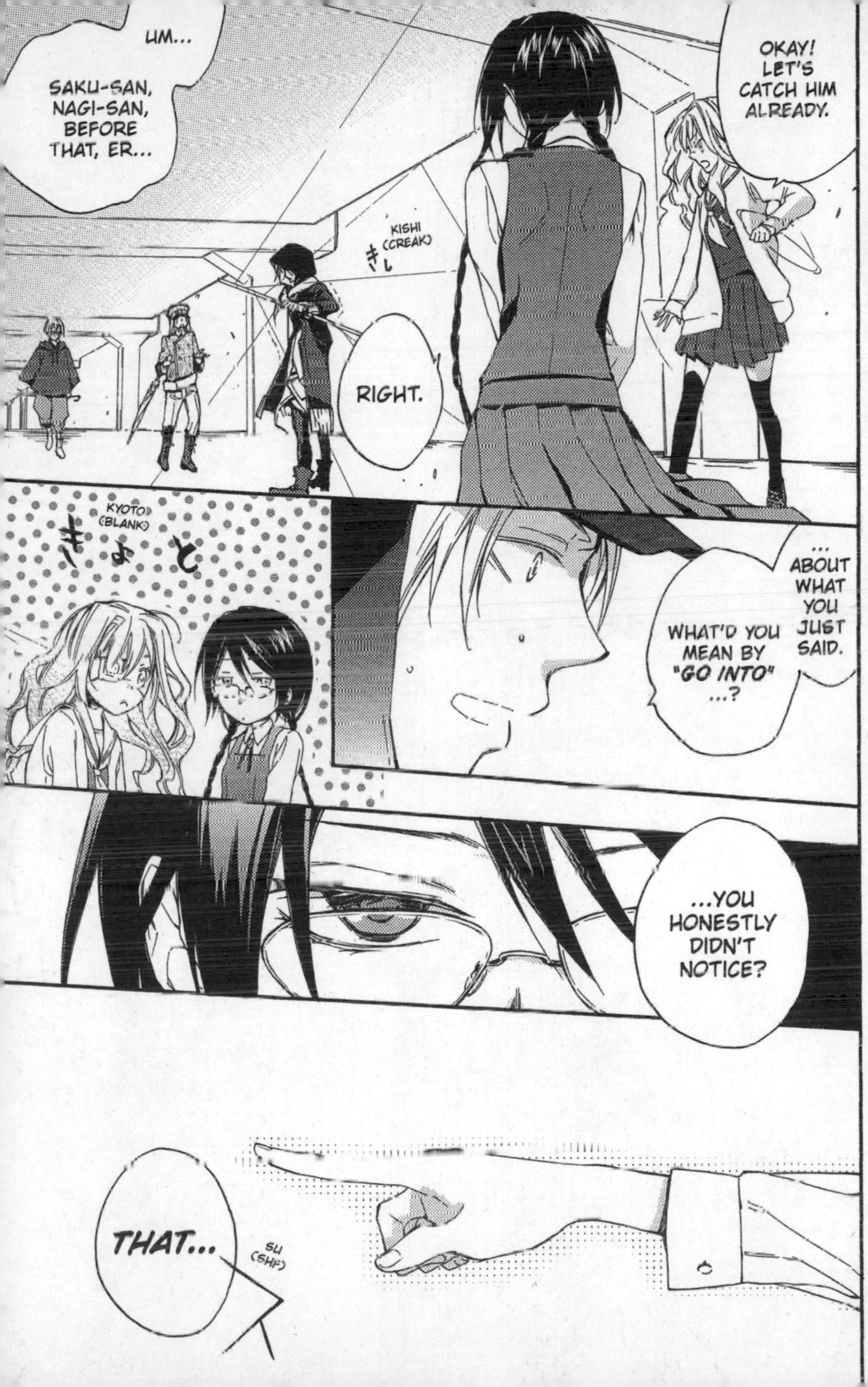
OKAY! LET'S CATCH HIM ALREADY.
KISHI (CREAK) きし
RIGHT.
UM...
SAKU-SAN, NAGI-SAN, BEFORE THAT, ER...
... ABOUT WHAT YOU JUST SAID.
WHAT'D YOU MEAN BY "GO INTO" ...?
KYOTO (BLANK) きょと
...YOU HONESTLY DIDN'T NOTICE?
THAT...
SU (SHF)

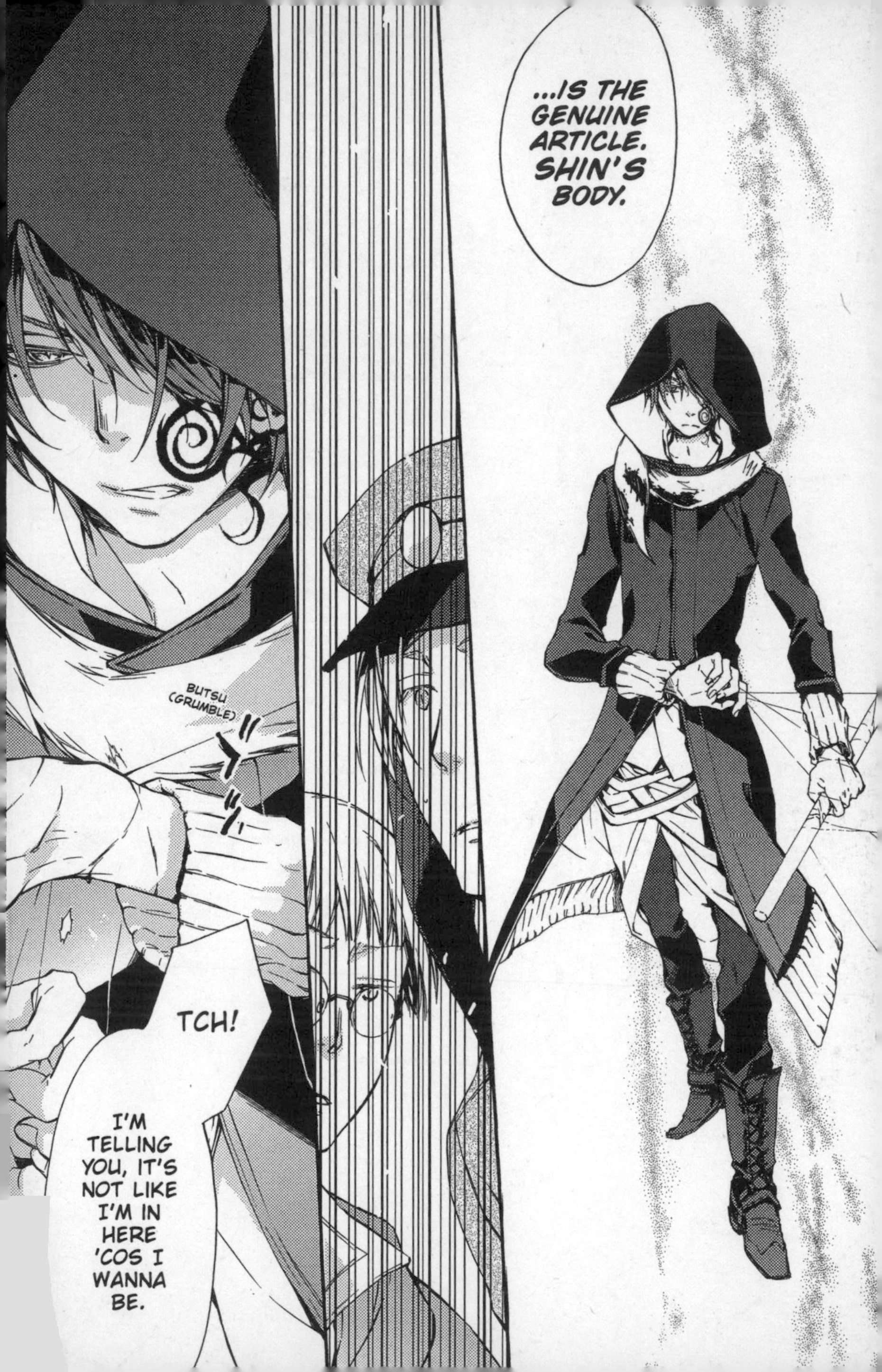
...IS THE GENUINE ARTICLE. SHIN'S BODY.
BUTSU (GRUMBLE)
TCH!
I'M TELLING YOU, IT'S NOT LIKE I'M IN HERE 'COS I WANNA BE.

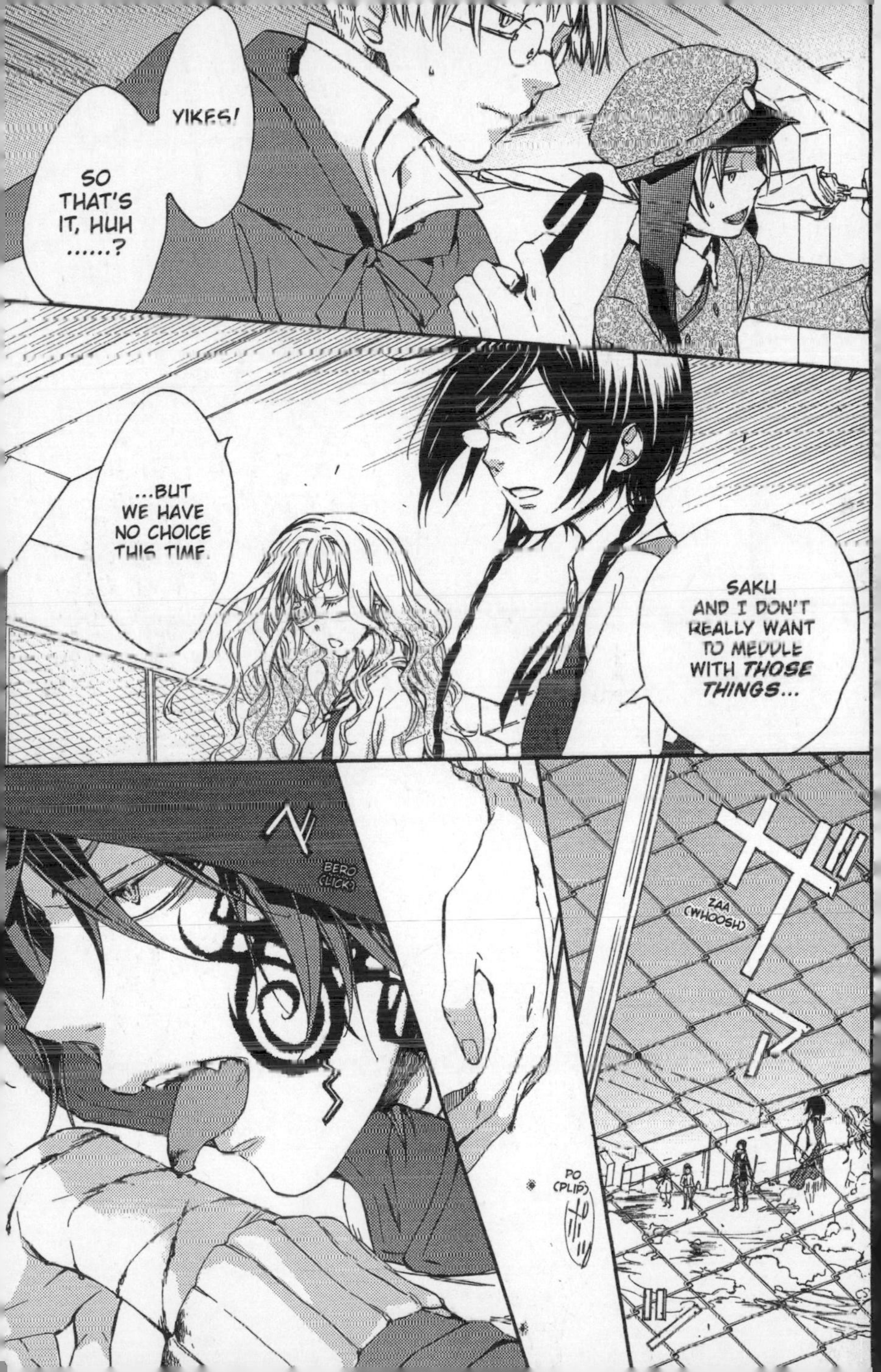
YIKES!
SO THAT'S IT, HUH ......?
SAKU AND I DON'T REALLY WANT TO MEDDLE WITH *THOSE THINGS*...
...BUT WE HAVE NO CHOICE THIS TIME.
ZAA (WHOOSH)
PO (PLIP)
BERO (LICK)

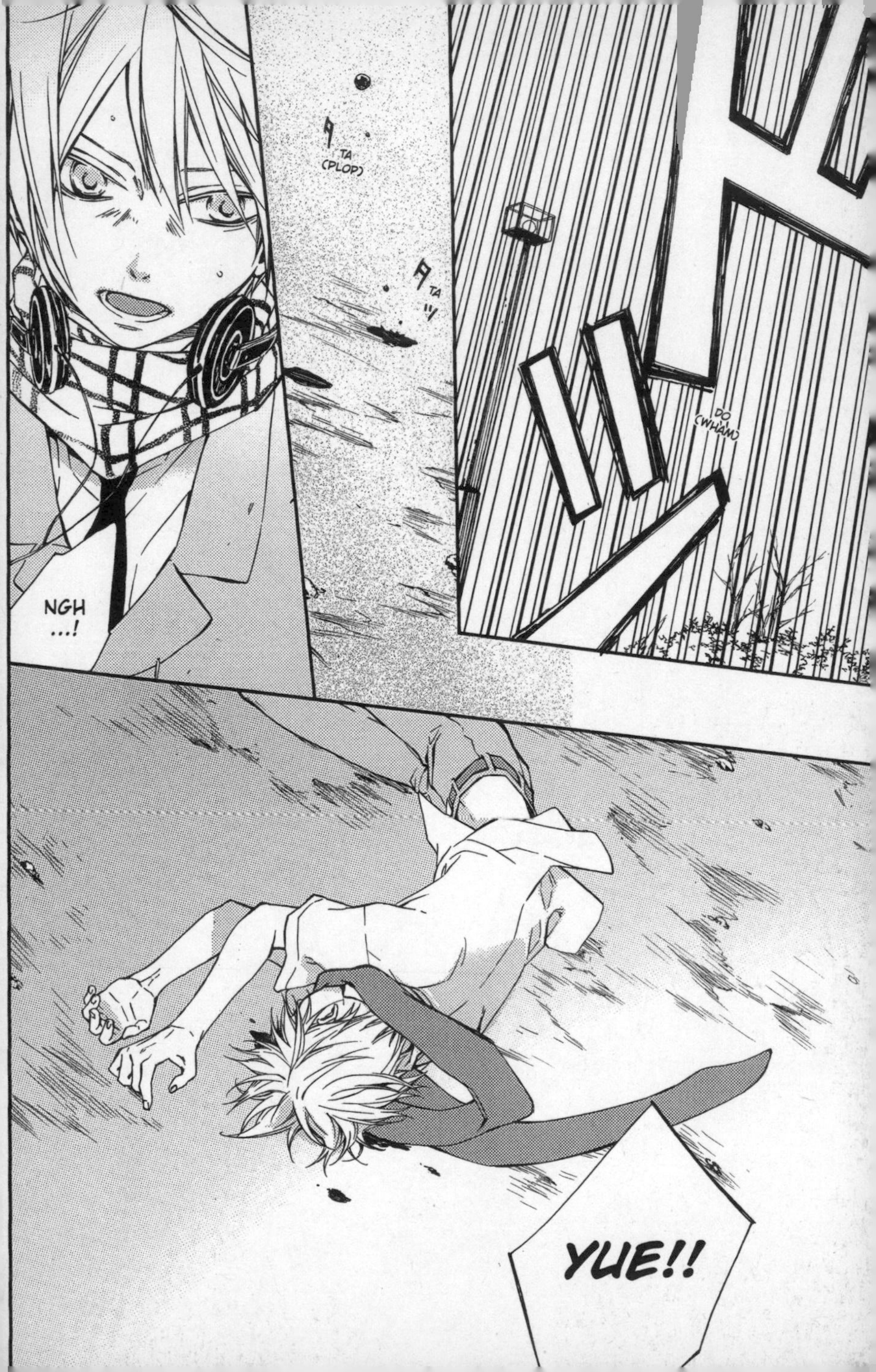
DO (WHAM)
TA (PLOP)
TA
NGH ...!
YUE!!

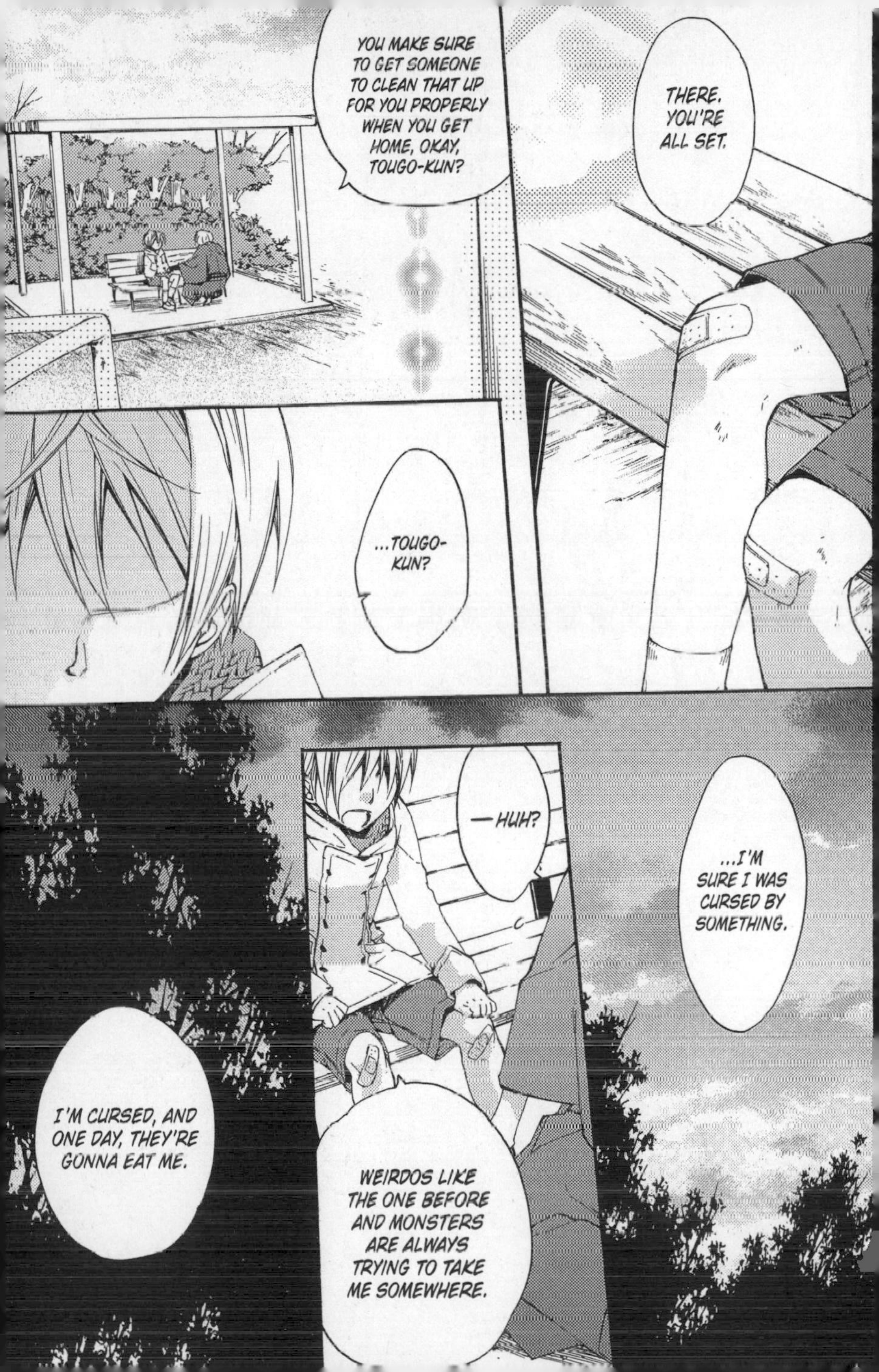
THERE. YOU'RE ALL SET.
YOU MAKE SURE TO GET SOMEONE TO CLEAN THAT UP FOR YOU PROPERLY WHEN YOU GET HOME, OKAY, TOUGO-KUN?
...TOUGO-KUN?
—HUH?
...I'M SURE I WAS CURSED BY SOMETHING.
WEIRDOS LIKE THE ONE BEFORE AND MONSTERS ARE ALWAYS TRYING TO TAKE ME SOMEWHERE.
I'M CURSED, AND ONE DAY, THEY'RE GONNA EAT ME.

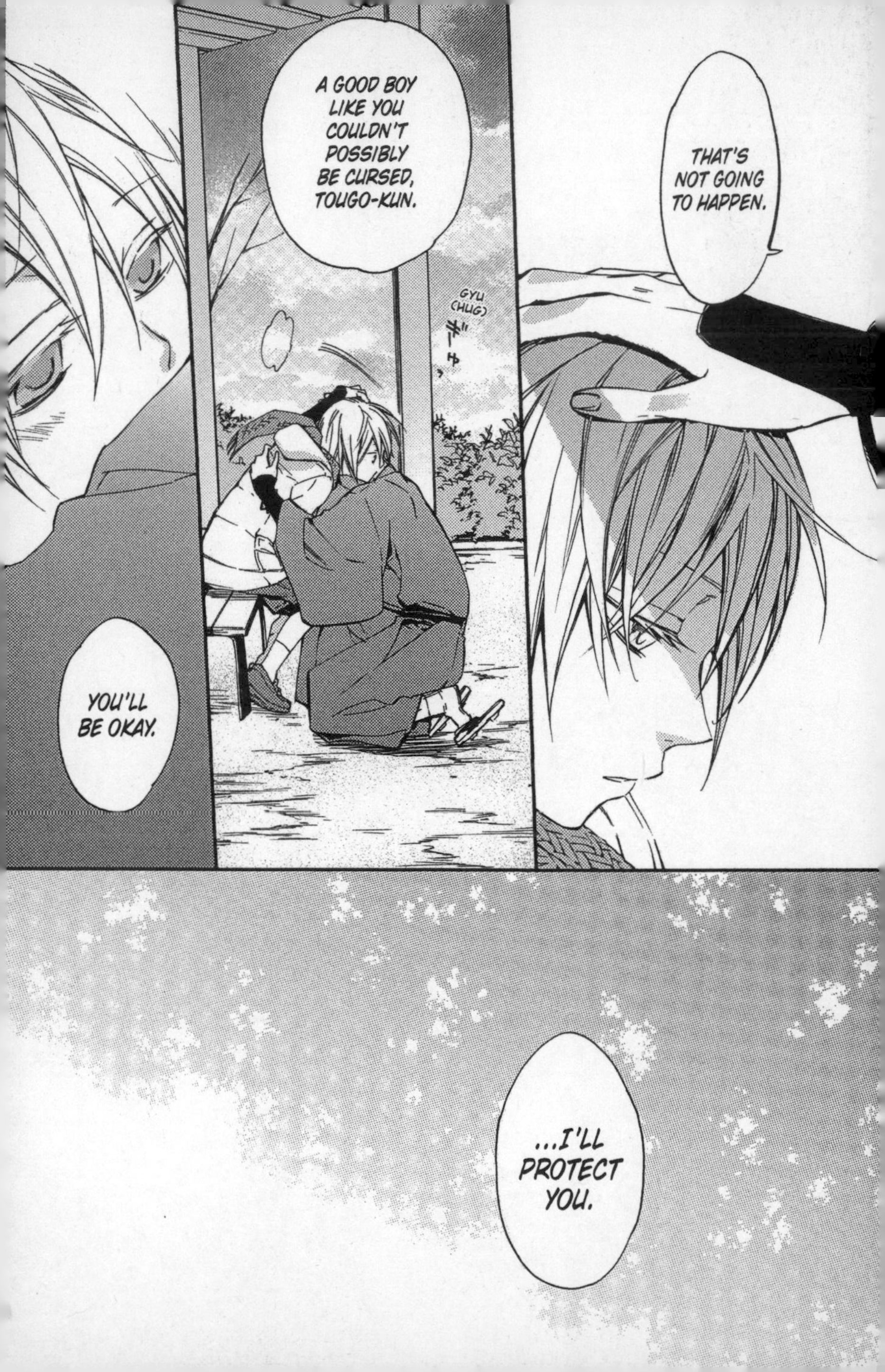
THAT'S NOT GOING TO HAPPEN.
A GOOD BOY LIKE YOU COULDN'T POSSIBLY BE CURSED, TOUGO-KUN.
GYU (HUG)
YOU'LL BE OKAY.
...I'LL PROTECT YOU.

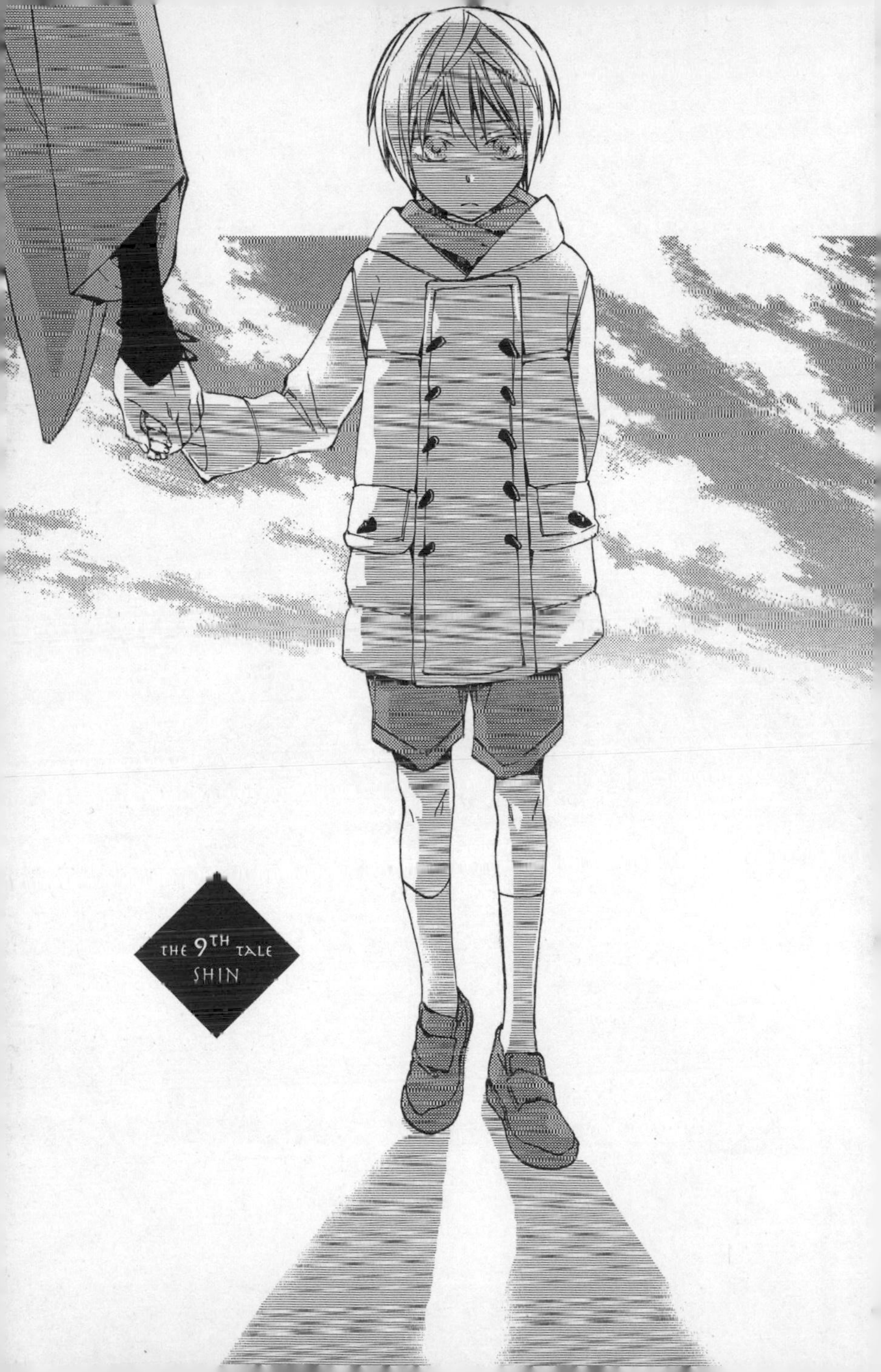
THE 9TH TALE
SHIN

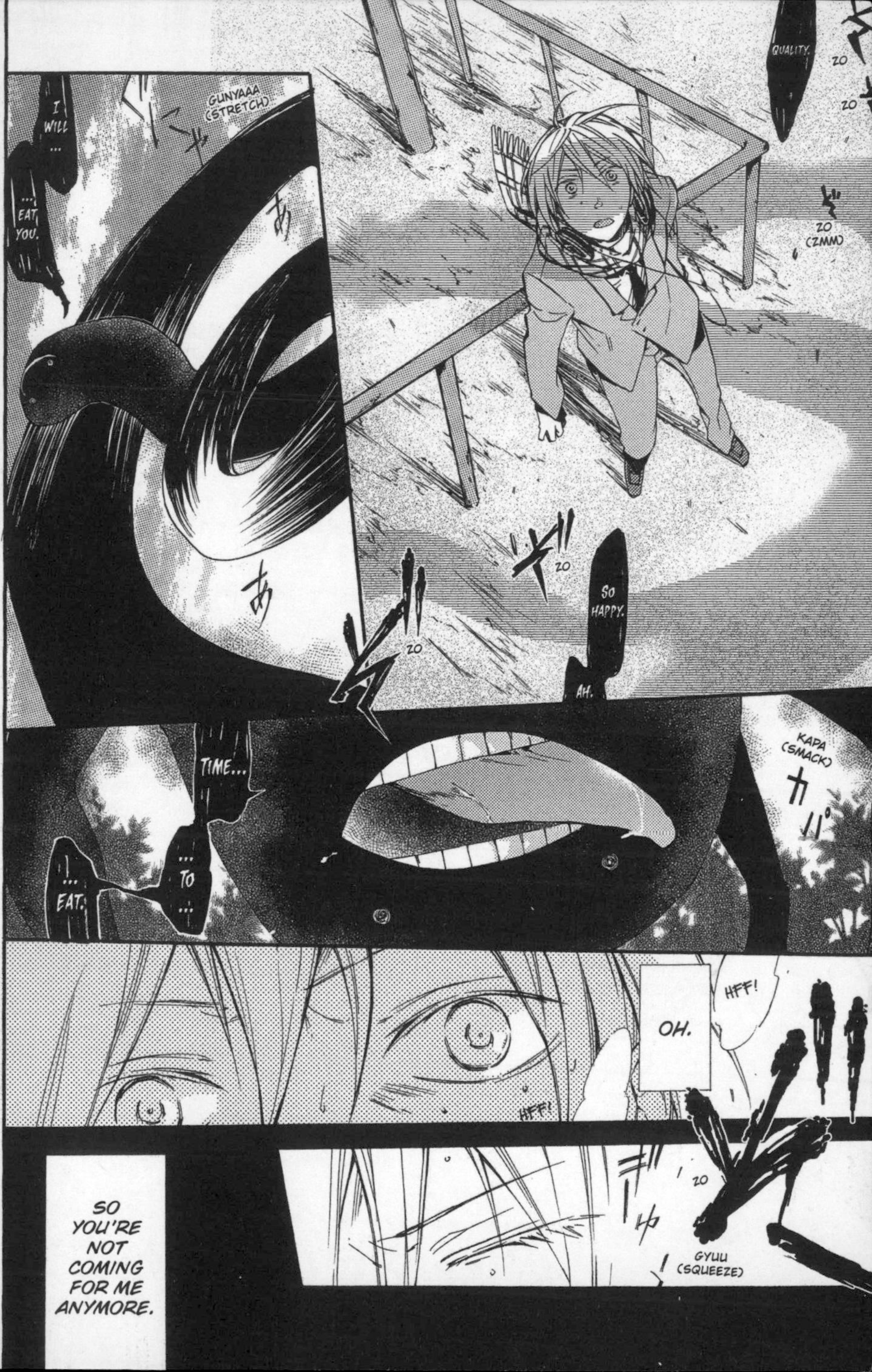
QUALITY.
ZO
ZO
ZO (ZMM)
ZO
SO HAPPY.
AH.
ZO
GUNYAAA (STRETCH)
I WILL...
...EAT YOU.
KAPA (SMACK)
TIME...
...TO...
...EAT.
HFF!
OH.
HFF!
ZO
GYUU (SQUEEZE)
SO YOU'RE NOT COMING FOR ME ANYMORE.

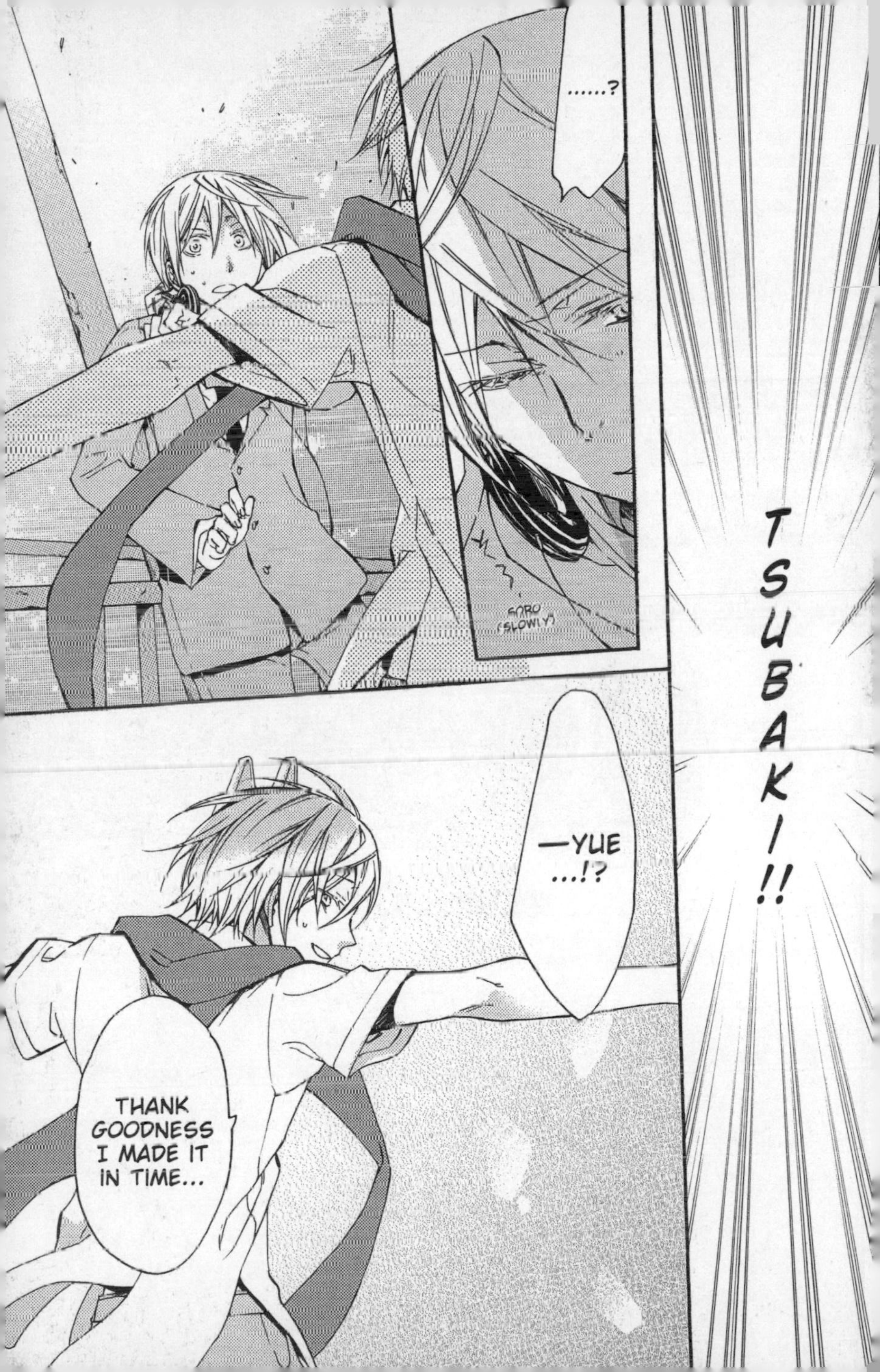
TSUBAKI!!
......?
SORO (SLOWLY)
—YUE ...!?
THANK GOODNESS I MADE IT IN TIME...

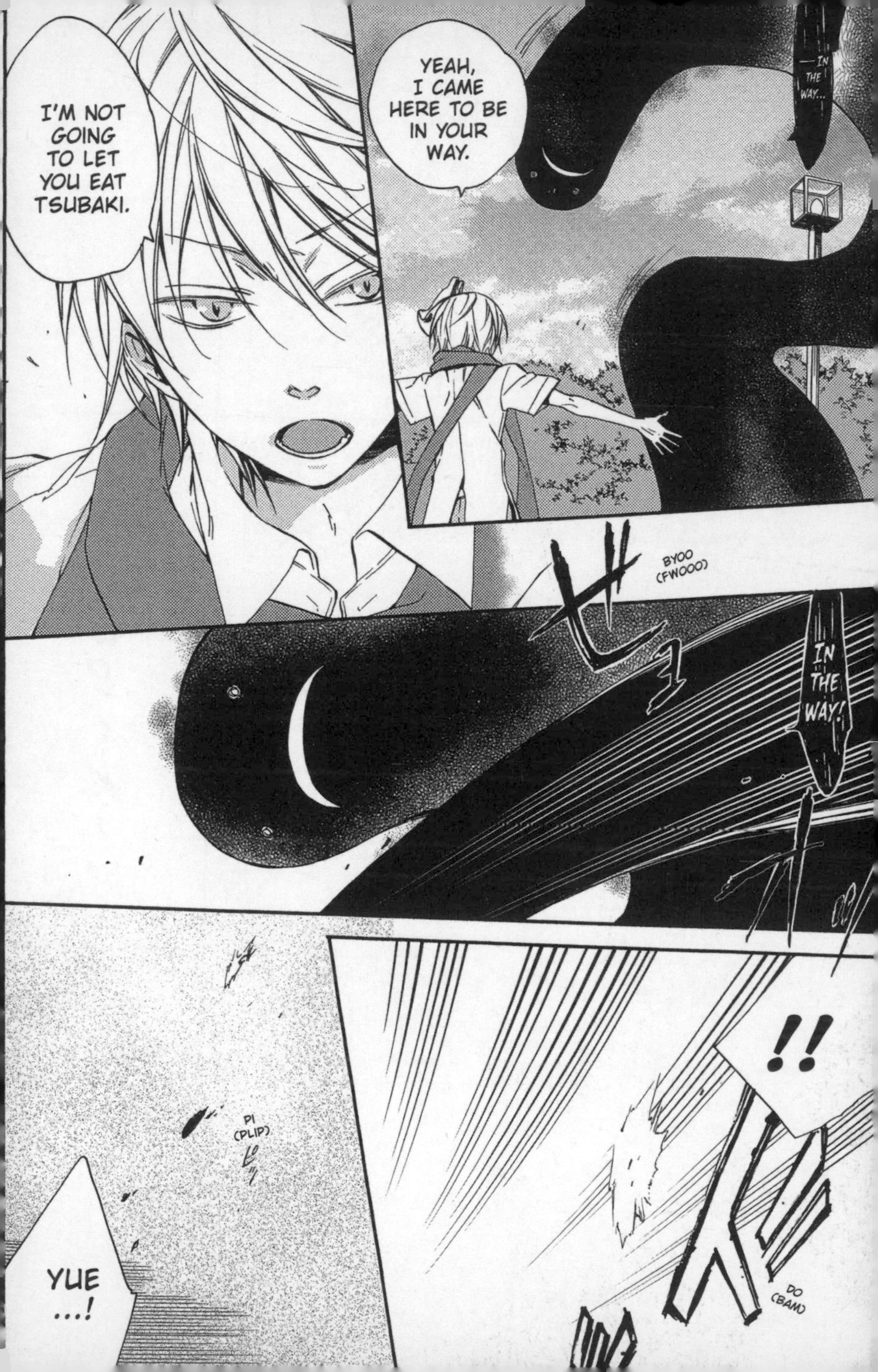
IN THE WAY...
YEAH, I CAME HERE TO BE IN YOUR WAY.
I'M NOT GOING TO LET YOU EAT TSUBAKI.
BYOO (FWOOO)
IN THE WAY!
!!
DO (BAM)
PI (PLIP)
YUE ...!

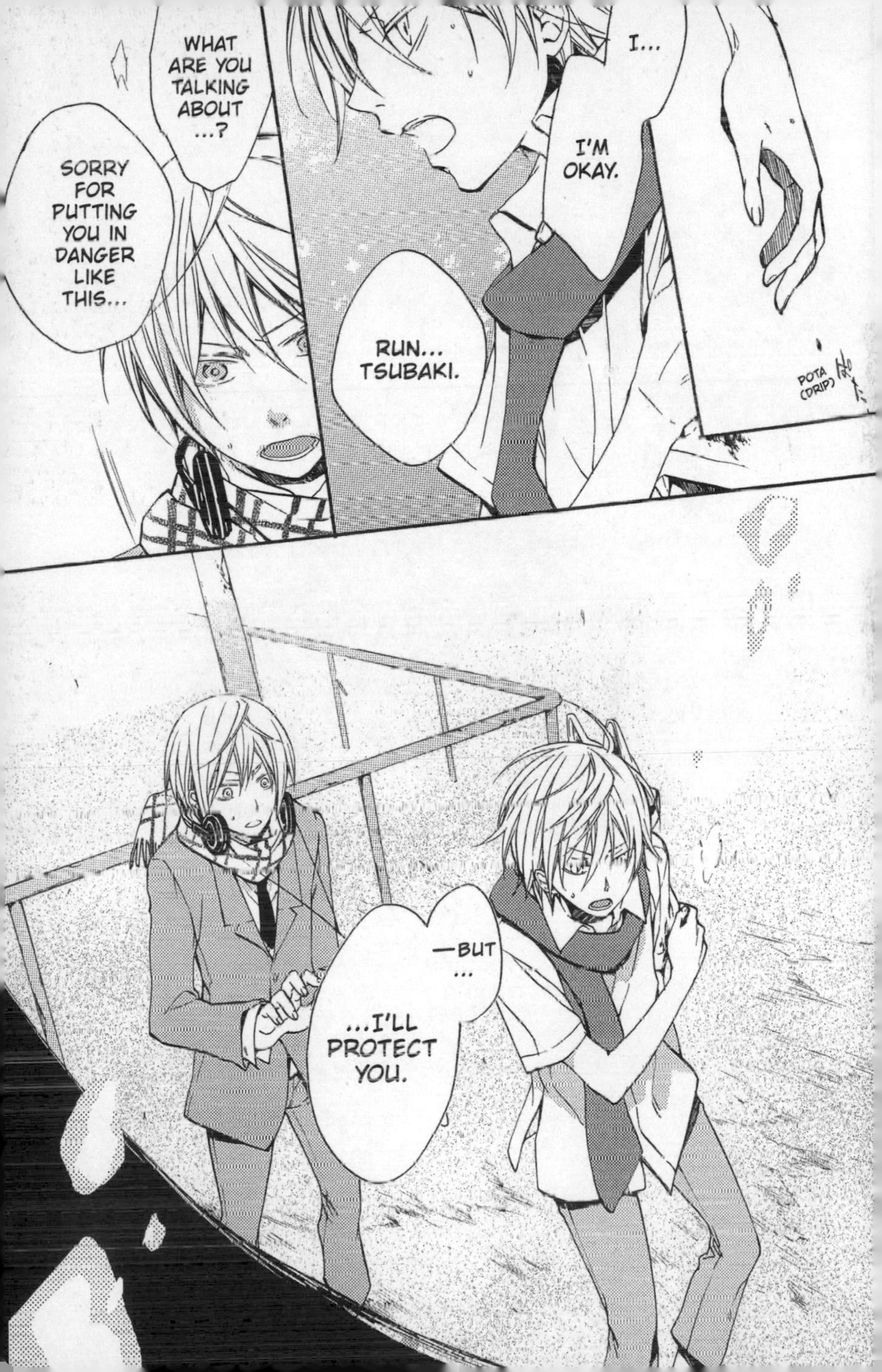
I...
I'M OKAY.
POTA (DRIP)
RUN... TSUBAKI.
WHAT ARE YOU TALKING ABOUT ...?
SORRY FOR PUTTING YOU IN DANGER LIKE THIS...
—BUT ...
...I'LL PROTECT YOU.

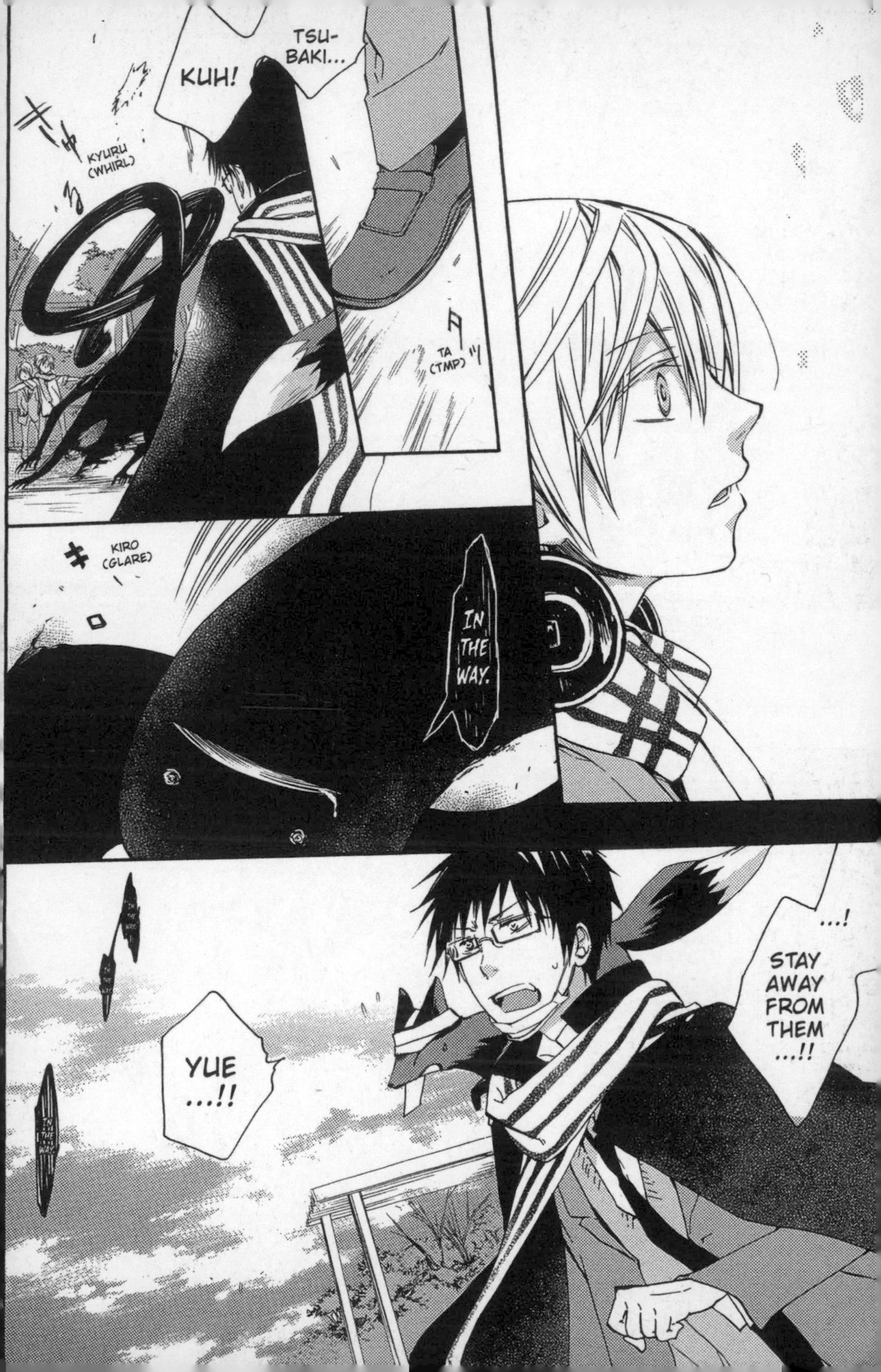
TSU-BAKI...
TA (TMP)
KUH!
KYURU (WHIRL)
IN THE WAY.
KIRO (GLARE)
...!
STAY AWAY FROM THEM ...!!
YUE ...!!

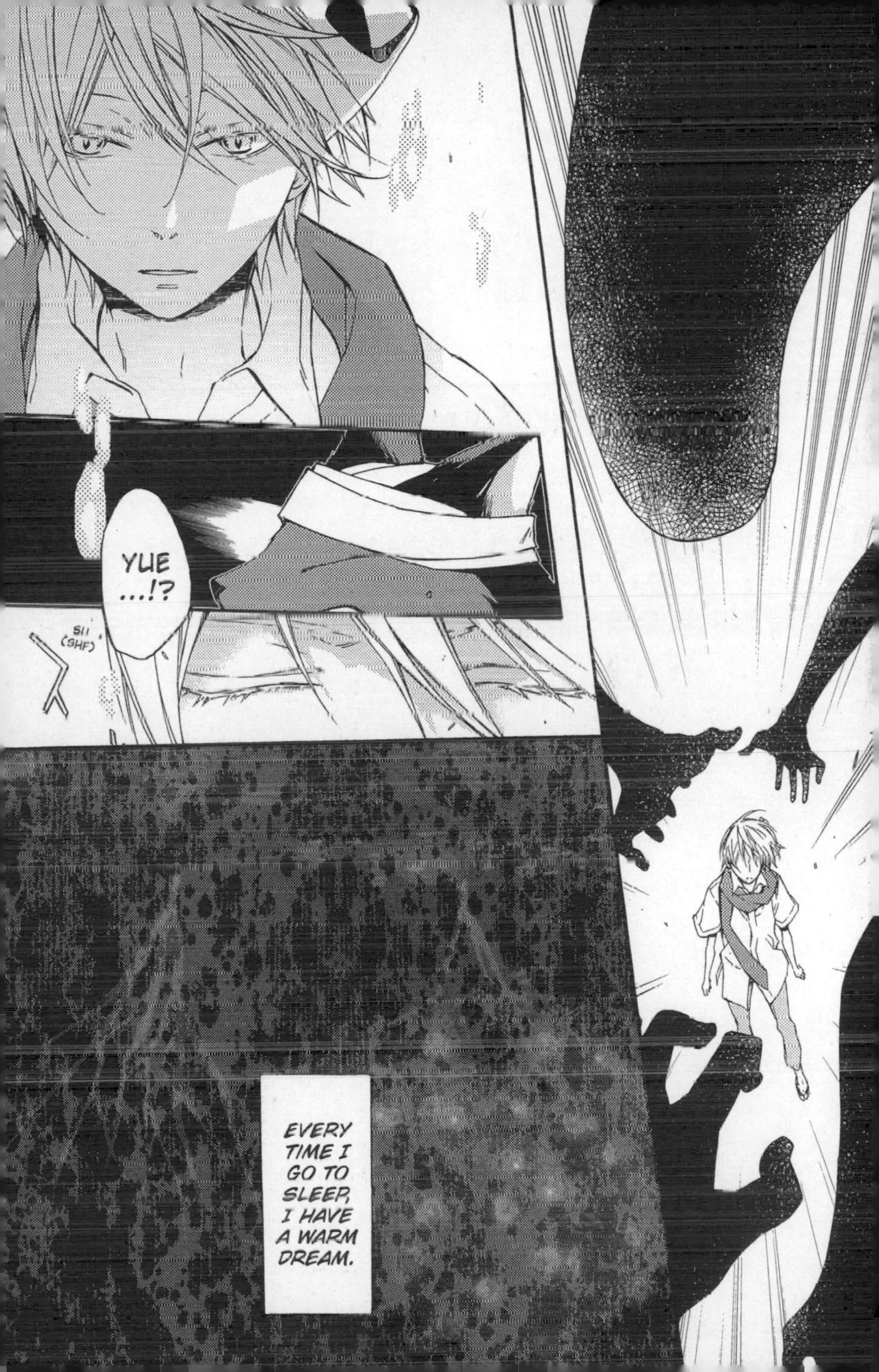
YUE ...!?
SII (SHF)
EVERY TIME I GO TO SLEEP, I HAVE A WARM DREAM.

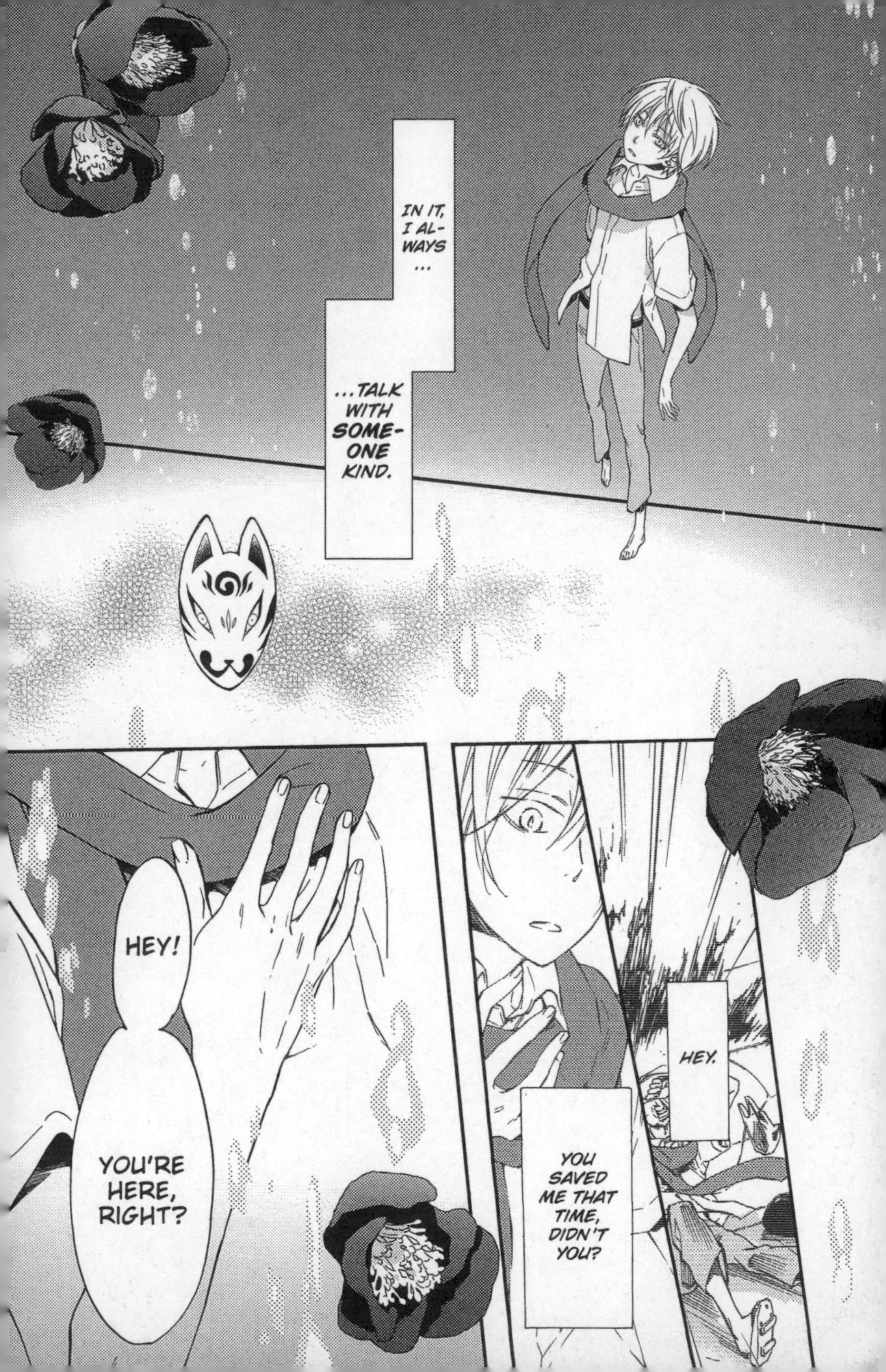
IN IT, I AL-WAYS ...
...TALK WITH SOME-ONE KIND.
HEY.
YOU SAVED ME THAT TIME, DIDN'T YOU?
HEY!
YOU'RE HERE, RIGHT?

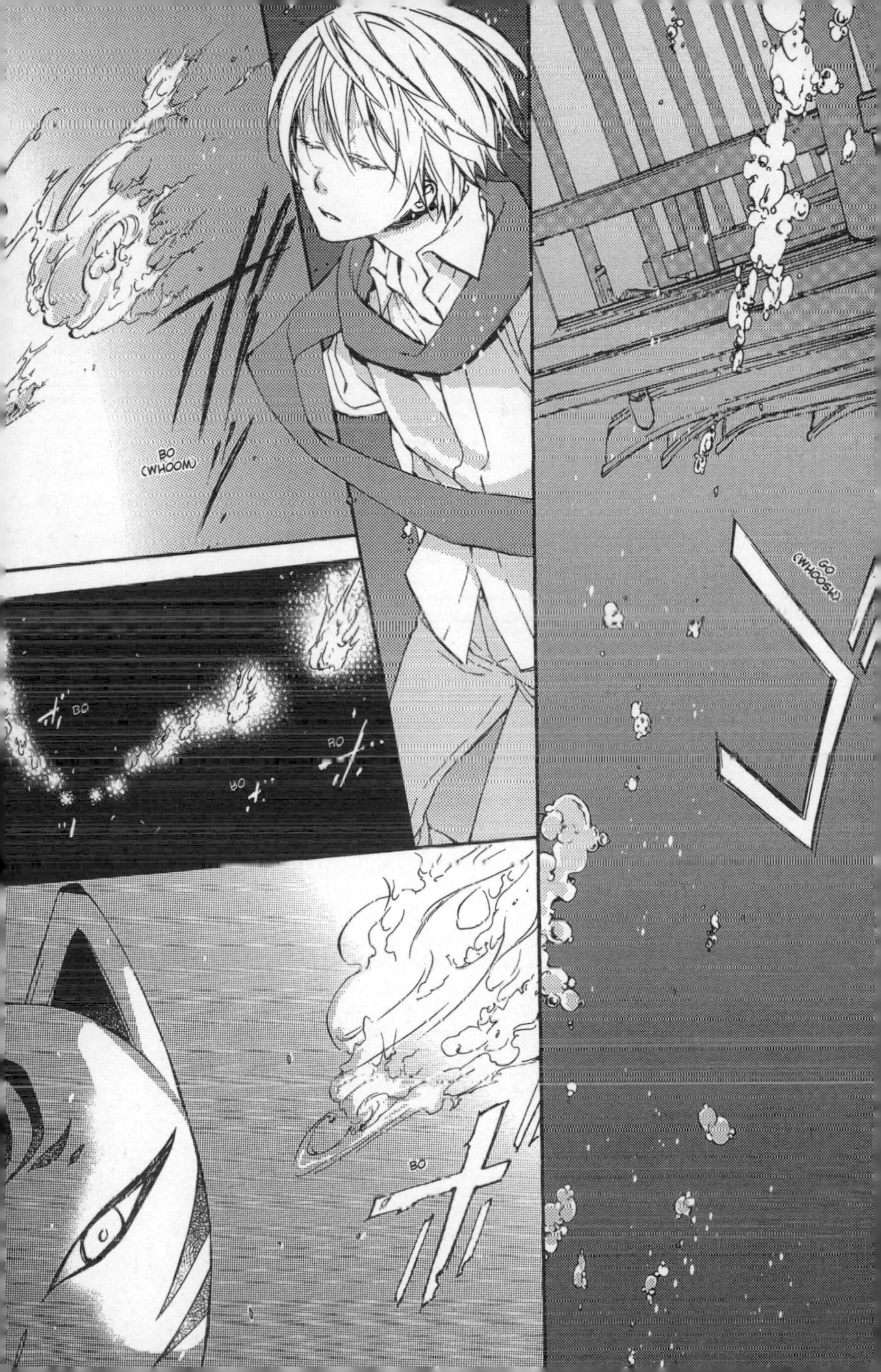
GO
(WHOOSH)
BO
(WHOOM)
BO
BO
BO
BO

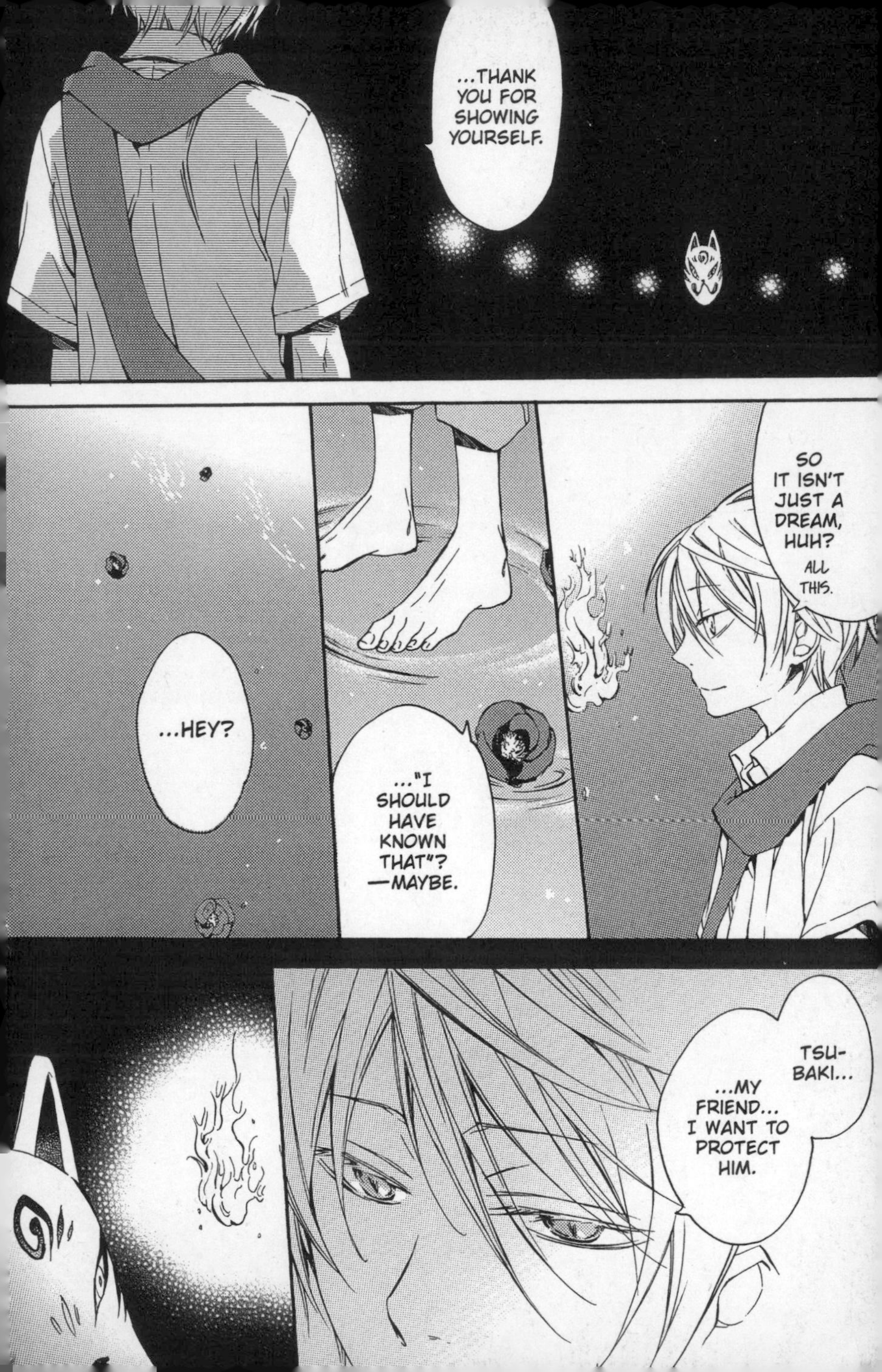
...THANK YOU FOR SHOWING YOURSELF.
SO IT ISN'T JUST A DREAM, HUH?
ALL THIS.
..."I SHOULD HAVE KNOWN THAT"? —MAYBE.
...HEY?
TSU-BAKI...
...MY FRIEND... I WANT TO PROTECT HIM.

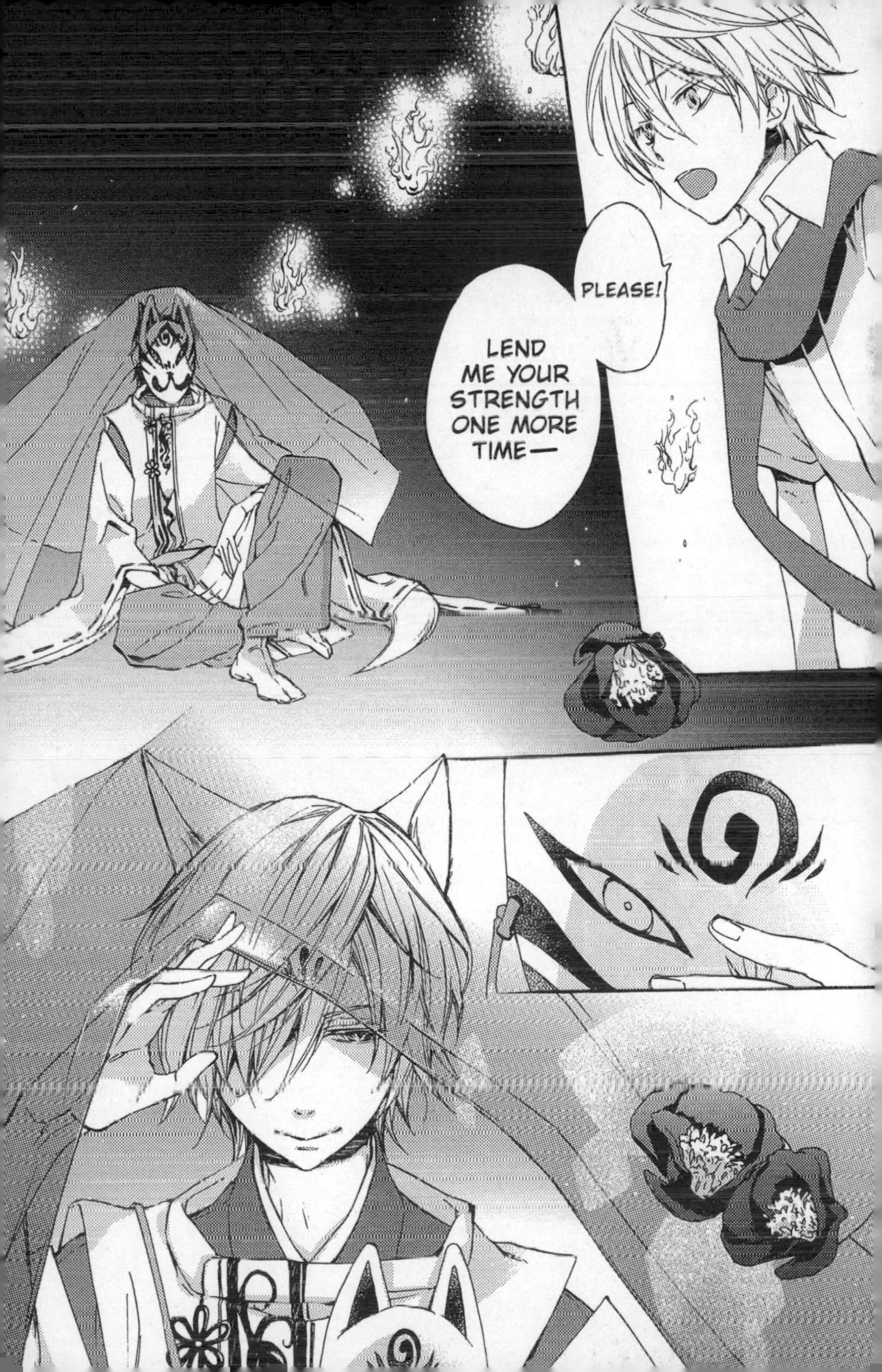
PLEASE!
LEND ME YOUR STRENGTH ONE MORE TIME—

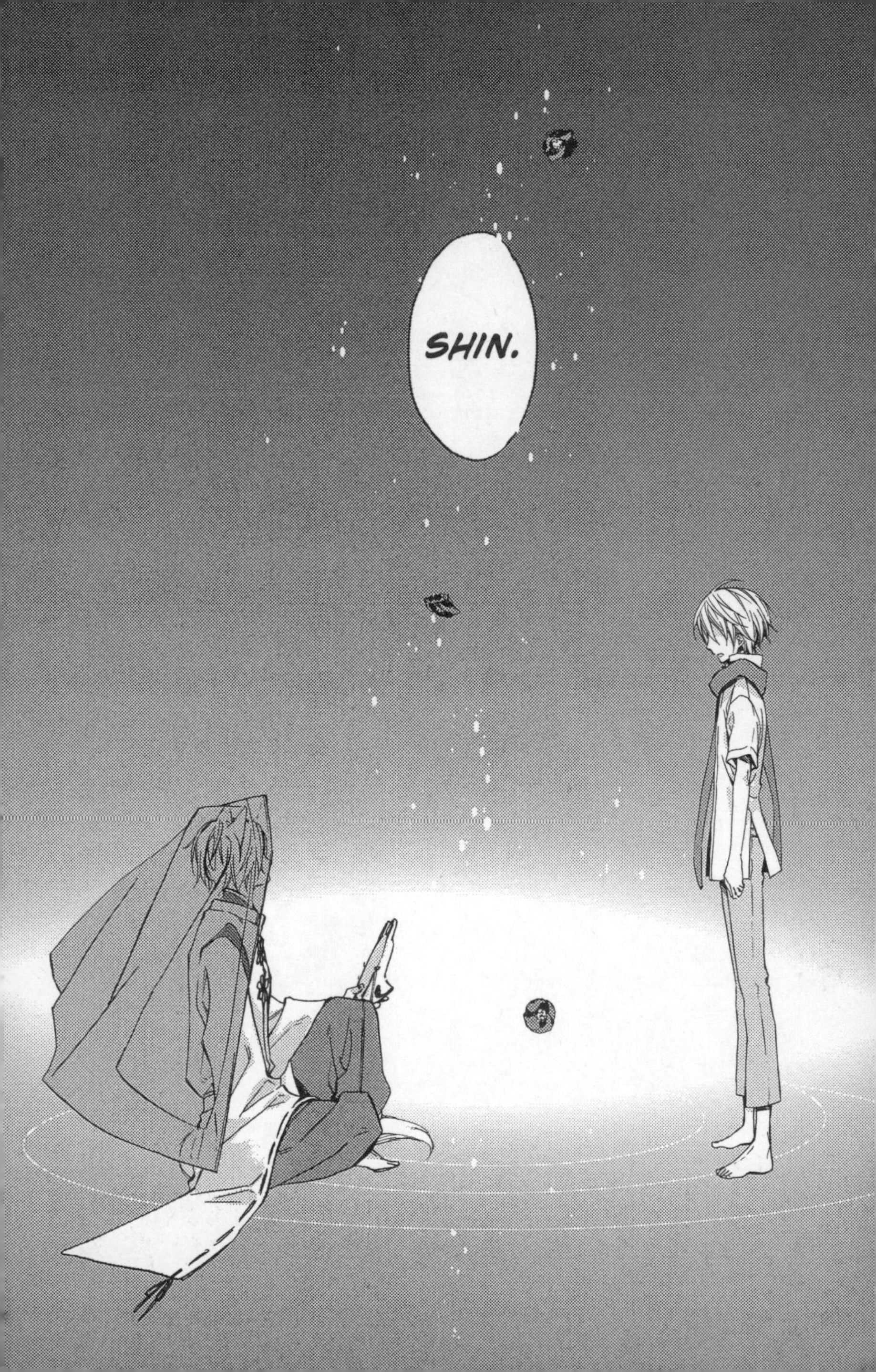
SHIN.

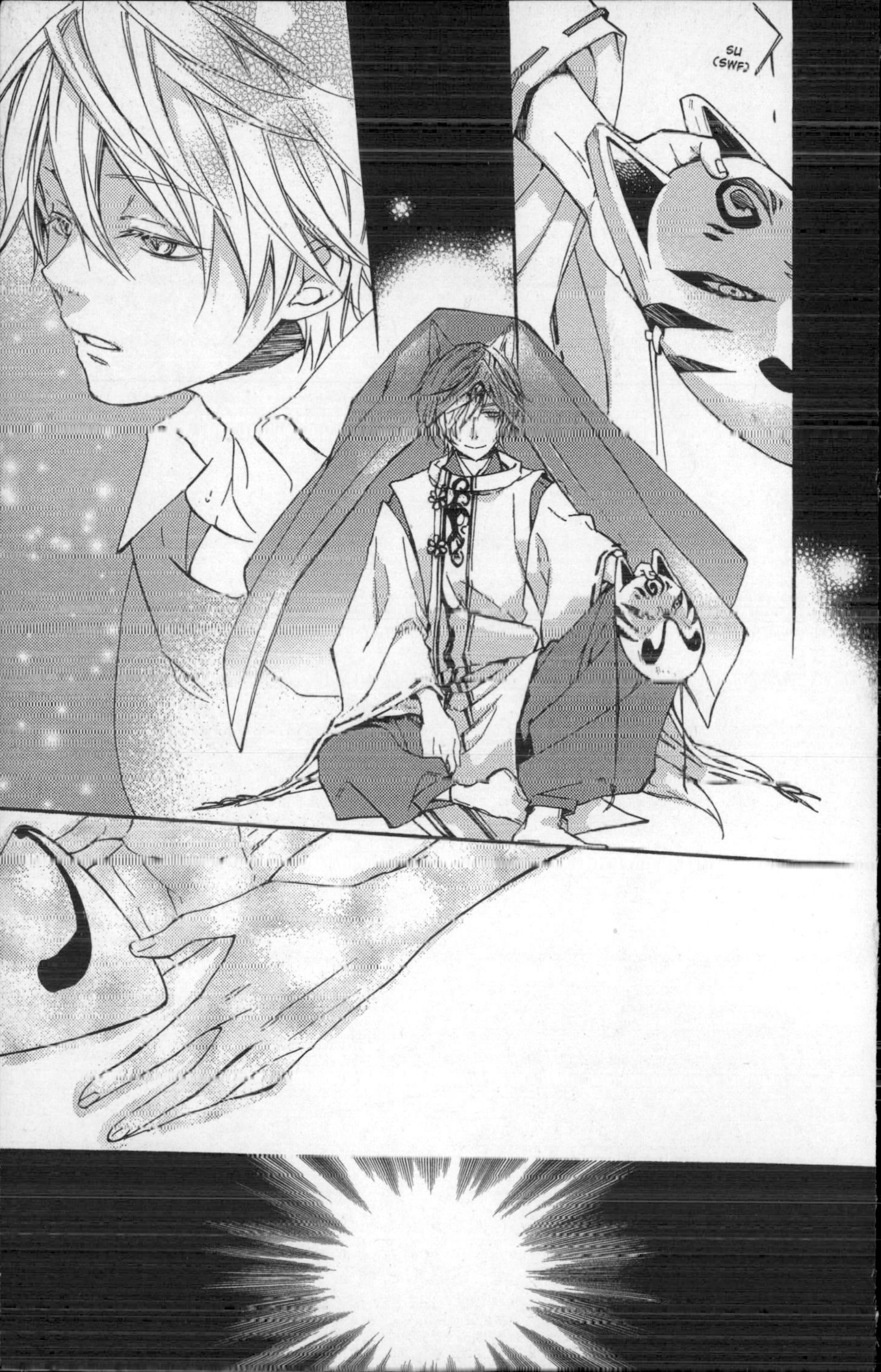
SU
(SWF)

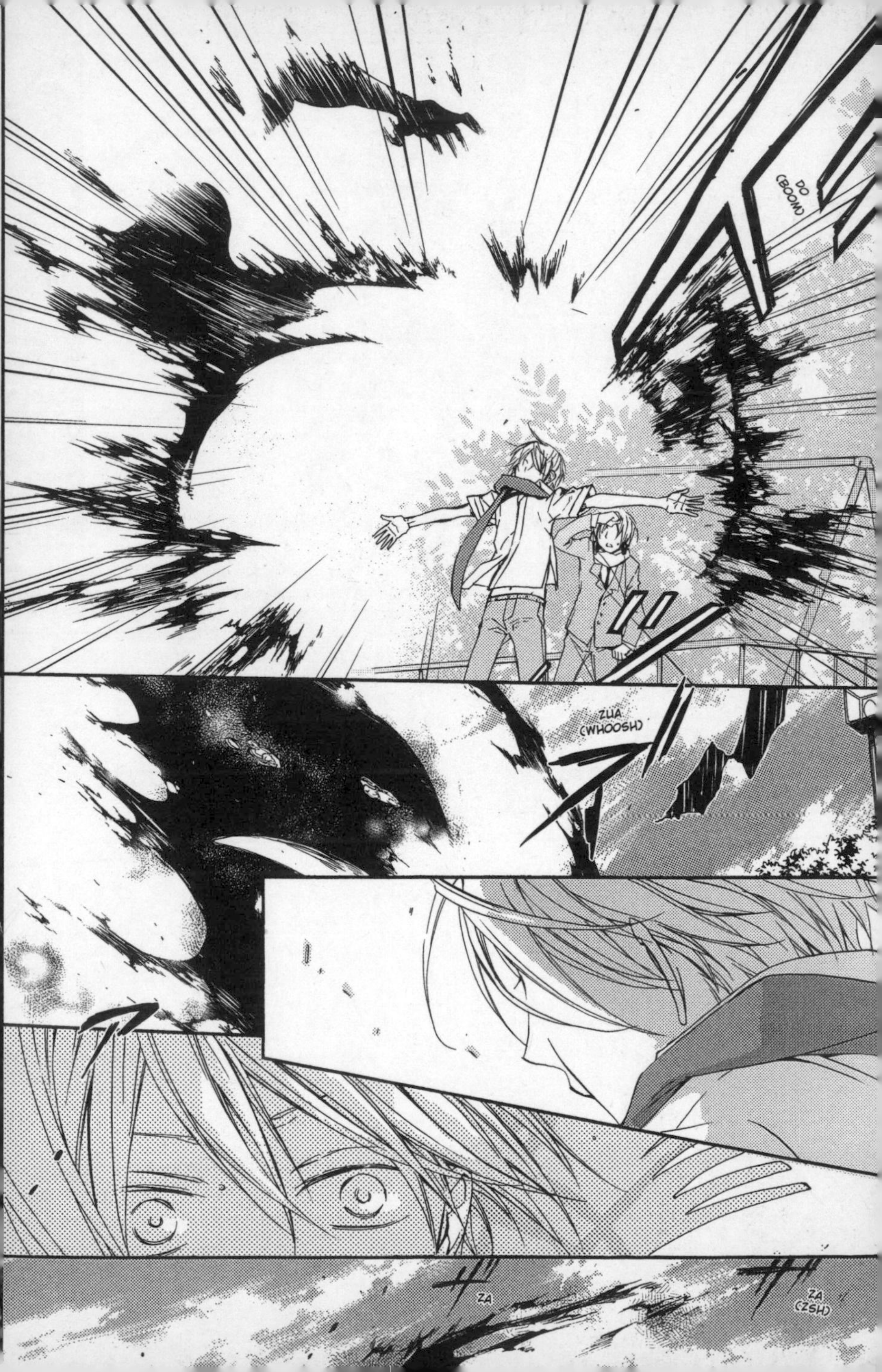
DO (BOOM)
ZUA (WHOOSH)
ZA (ZSH)
ZA

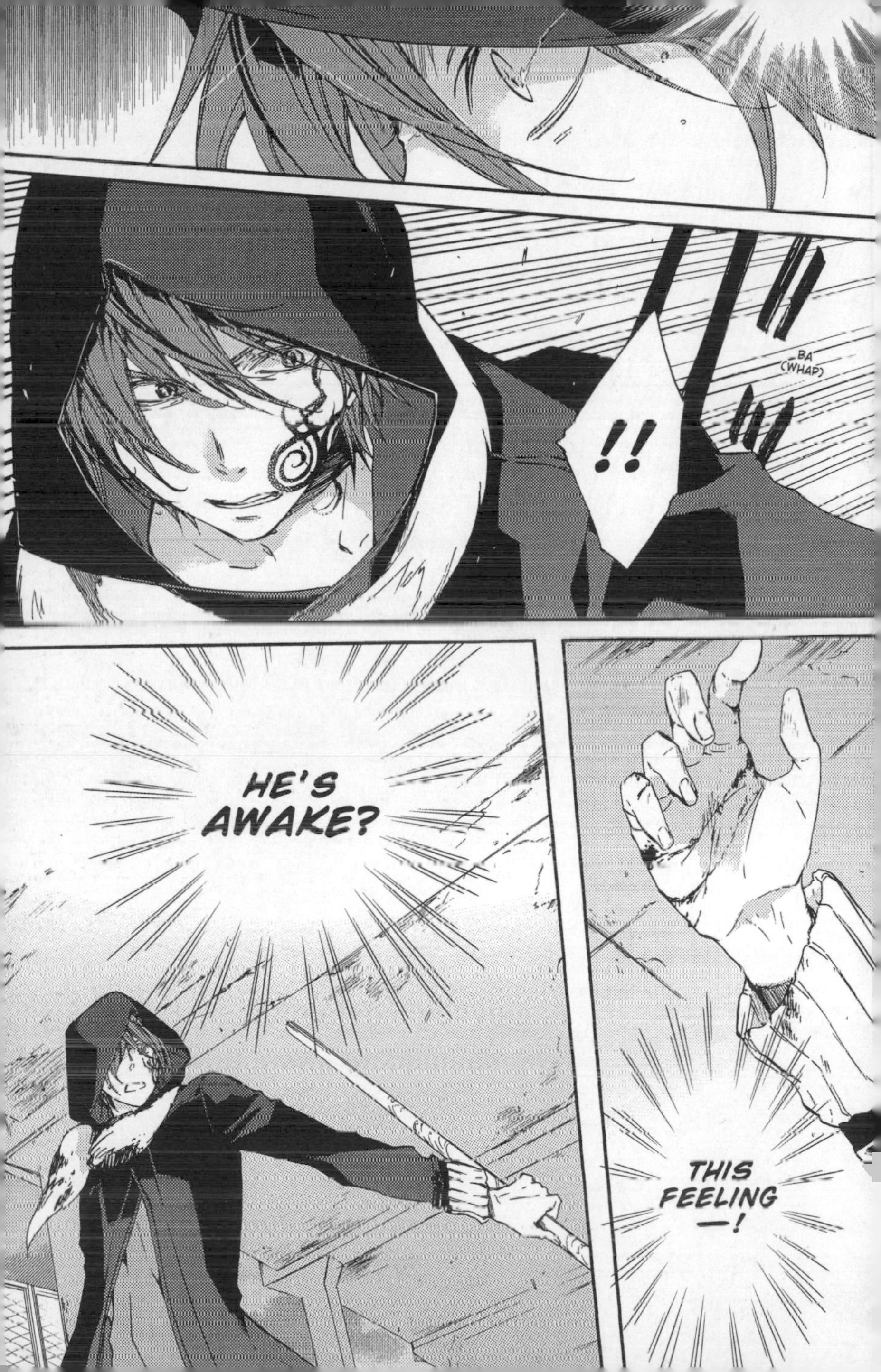
BA
(WHAP)
!!
THIS FEELING —!
HE'S AWAKE?

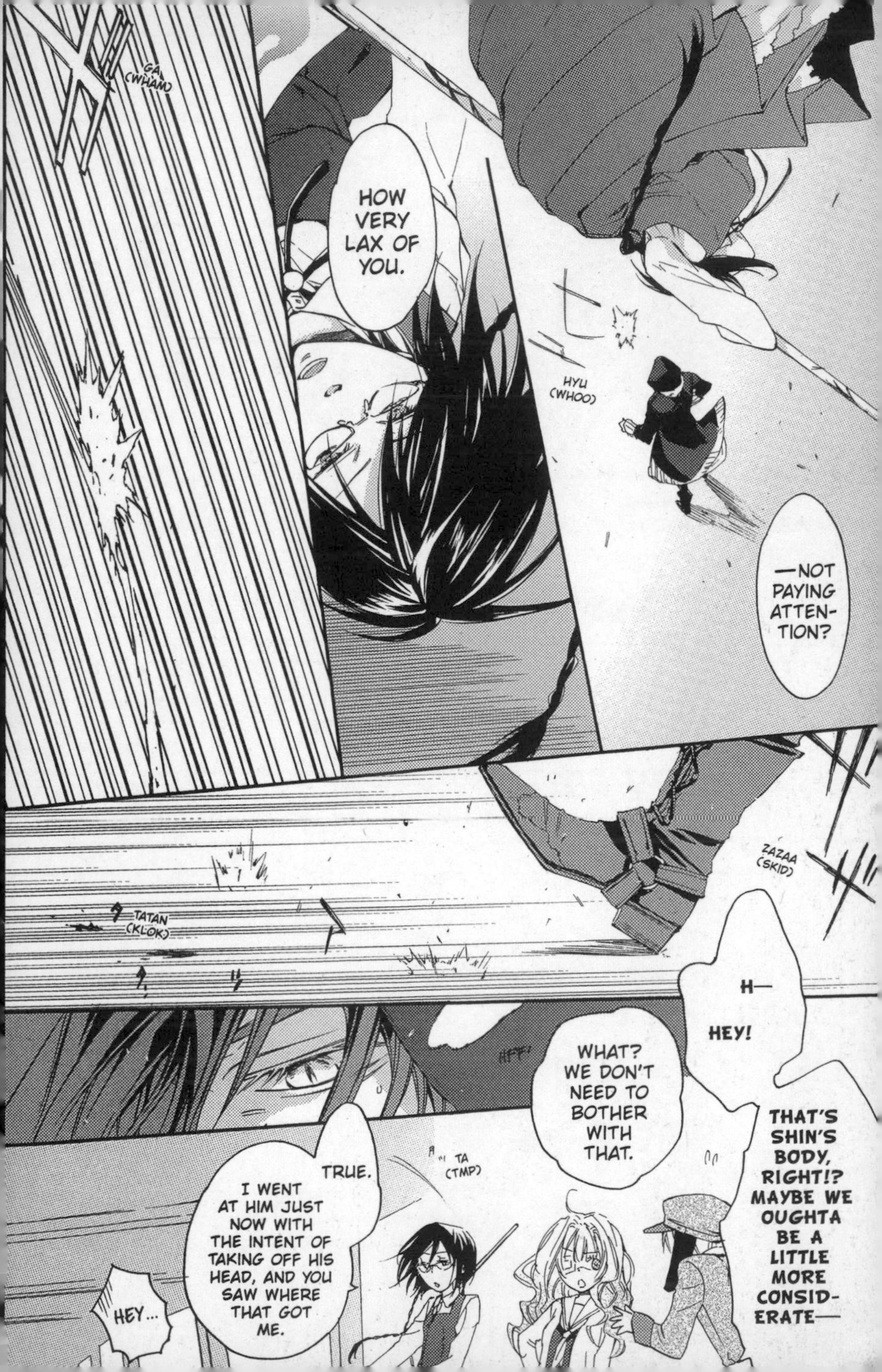
HYU (WHOO)
—NOT PAYING ATTENTION?
GA (WHAM)
HOW VERY LAX OF YOU.
ZAZAA (SKID)
TATAN (KLOK)
H—
HEY!
THAT'S SHIN'S BODY, RIGHT!? MAYBE WE OUGHTA BE A LITTLE MORE CONSID-ERATE—
WHAT? WE DON'T NEED TO BOTHER WITH THAT.
TA (TMP)
TRUE.
I WENT AT HIM JUST NOW WITH THE INTENT OF TAKING OFF HIS HEAD, AND YOU SAW WHERE THAT GOT ME.
HEY...

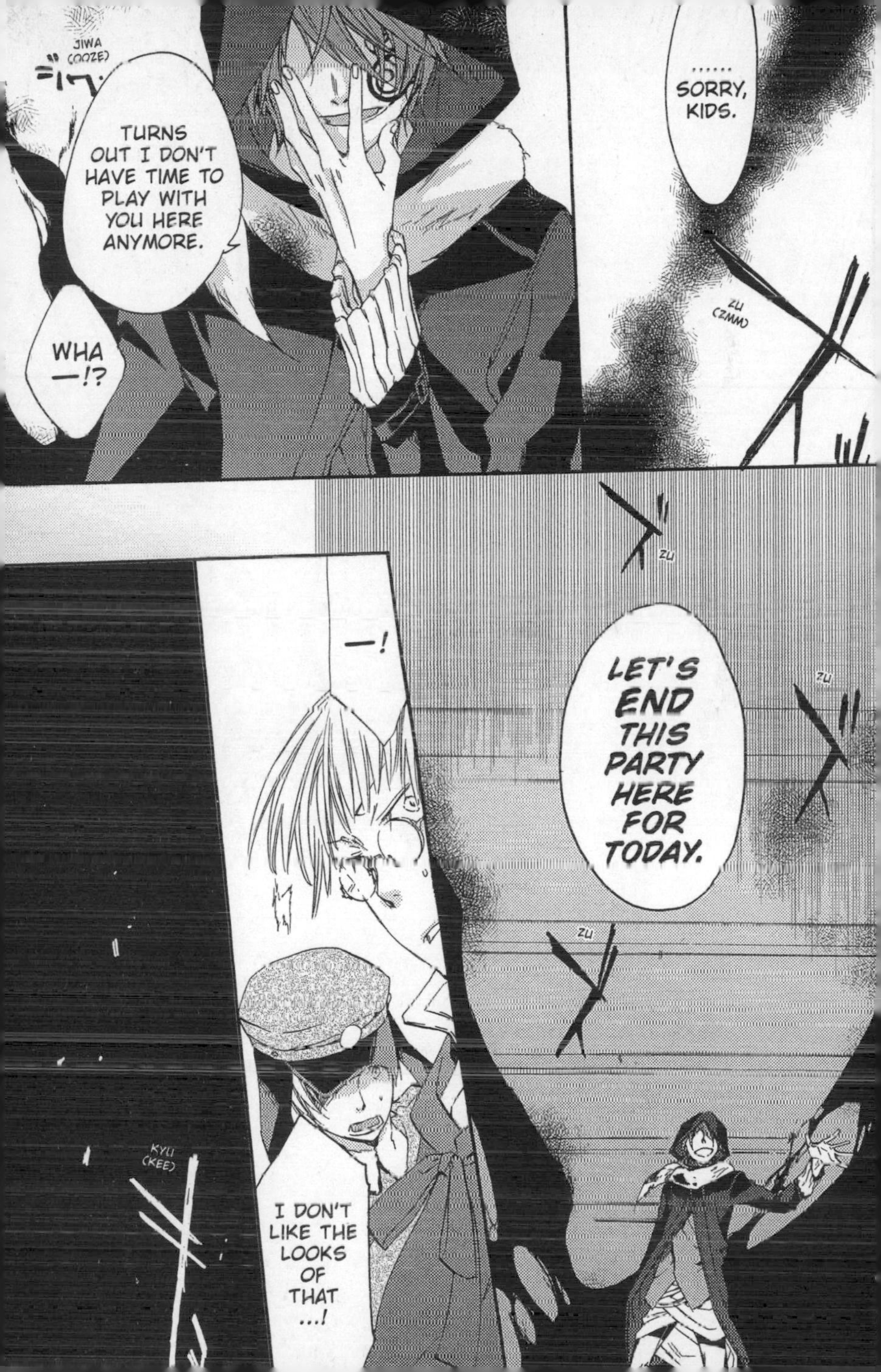

......
SORRY, KIDS.
ZU (ZMM)
JIWA (OOZE)
TURNS OUT I DON'T HAVE TIME TO PLAY WITH YOU HERE ANYMORE.
WHA —!?
ZU
LET'S END THIS PARTY HERE FOR TODAY.
ZU
ZU
—!
KYU (KEE)
I DON'T LIKE THE LOOKS OF THAT ...!

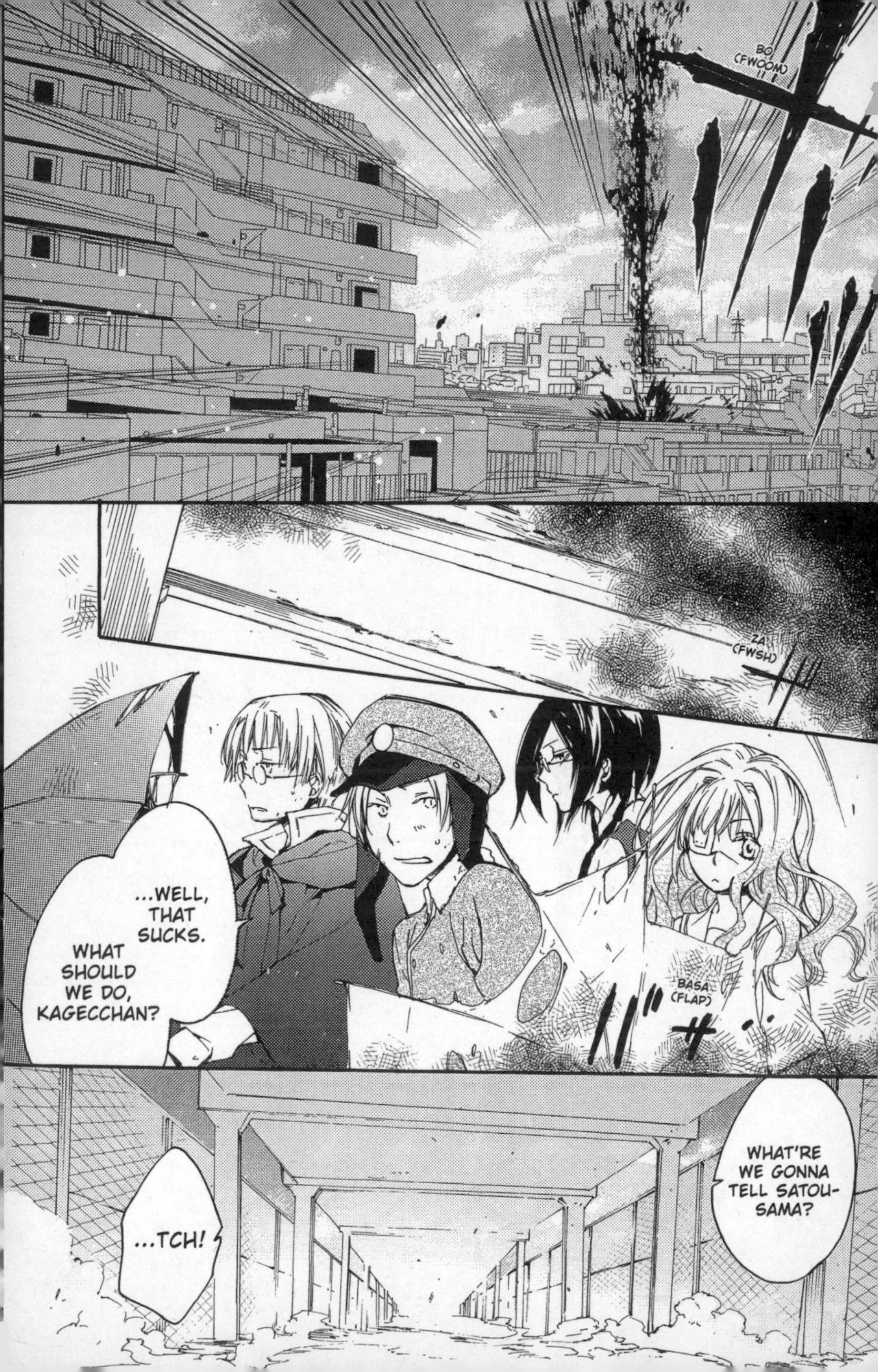
BO (FWOOM)
ZA (FWSH)
BASA (FLAP)
...WELL, THAT SUCKS. WHAT SHOULD WE DO, KAGECCHAN?
WHAT'RE WE GONNA TELL SATOU-SAMA?
...TCH!

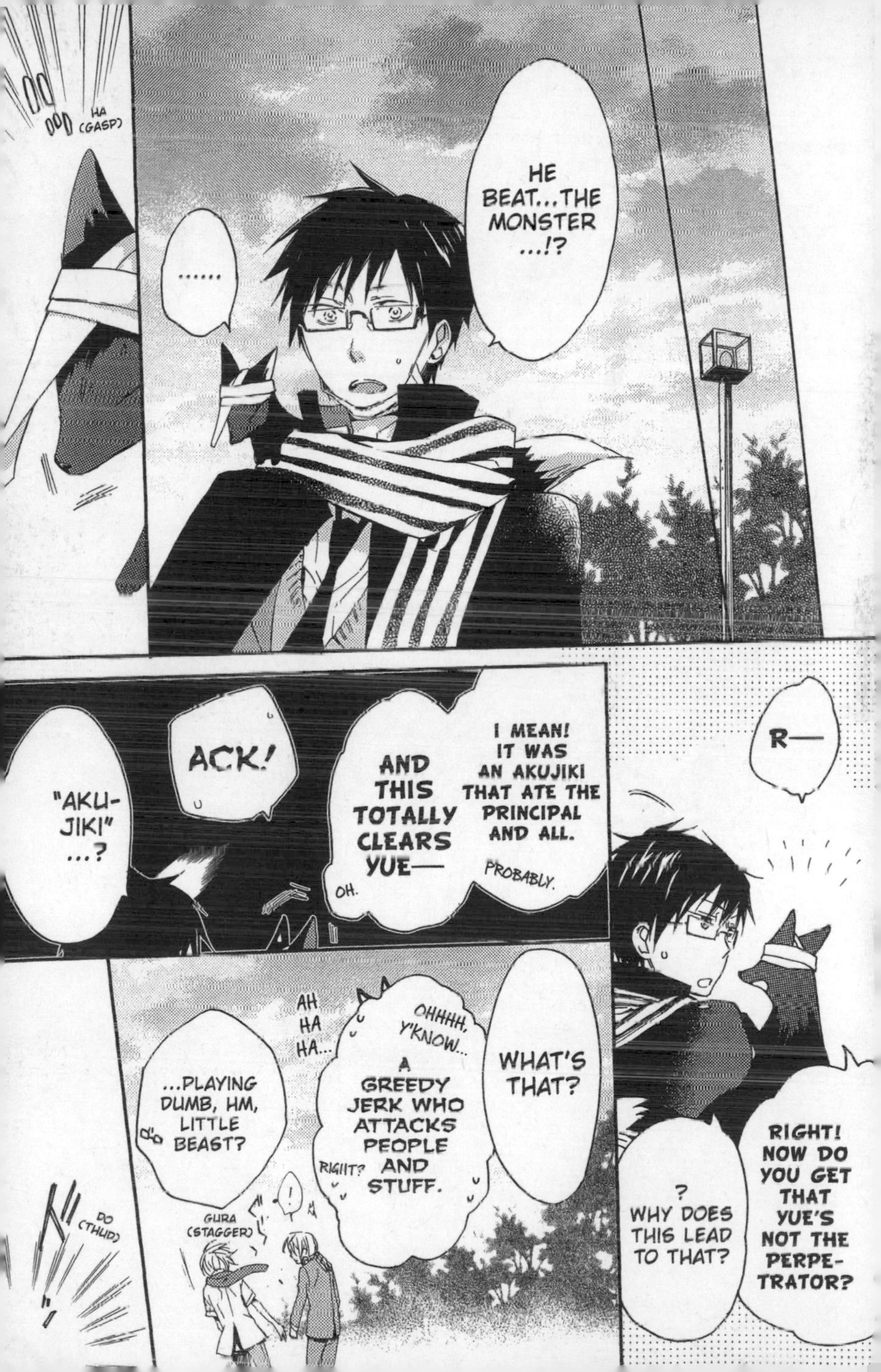
HE BEAT...THE MONSTER ...!?
......
HA (GASP)
R—
RIGHT! NOW DO YOU GET THAT YUE'S NOT THE PERPE-TRATOR?
? WHY DOES THIS LEAD TO THAT?
I MEAN! IT WAS AN AKUJIKI THAT ATE THE PRINCIPAL AND ALL.
PROBABLY.
AND THIS TOTALLY CLEARS YUE—
OH.
ACK!
"AKU-JIKI" ...?
WHAT'S THAT?
OHHHH, Y'KNOW...
A GREEDY JERK WHO ATTACKS PEOPLE AND STUFF.
RIGHT?
AH HA HA...
...PLAYING DUMB, HM, LITTLE BEAST?
!
GURA (STAGGER)
DO (THUD)

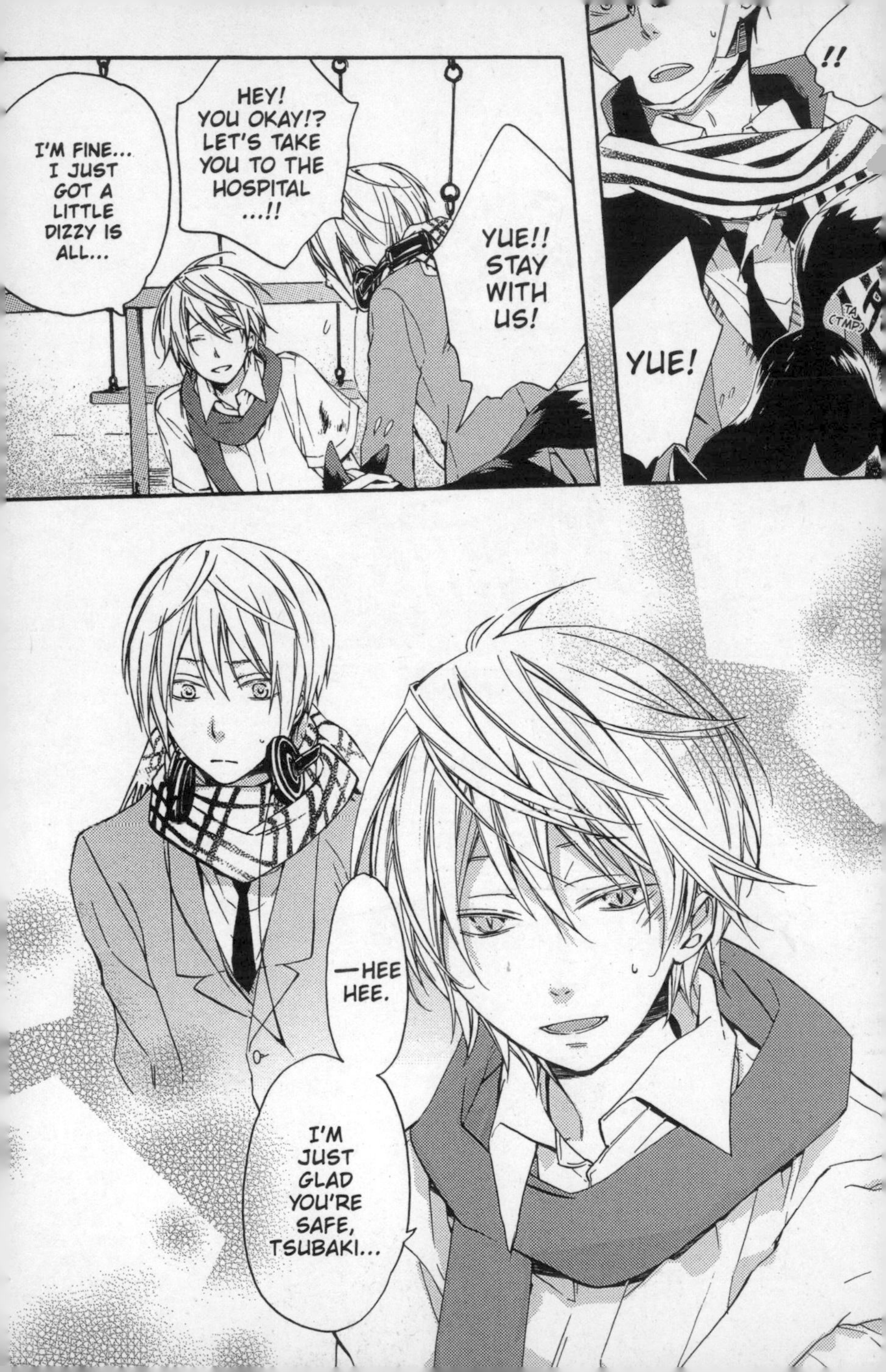
!!
TA (TMP)
YUE!
YUE!! STAY WITH US!
HEY! YOU OKAY!? LET'S TAKE YOU TO THE HOSPITAL ...!!
I'M FINE... I JUST GOT A LITTLE DIZZY IS ALL...
—HEE HEE.
I'M JUST GLAD YOU'RE SAFE, TSUBAKI...

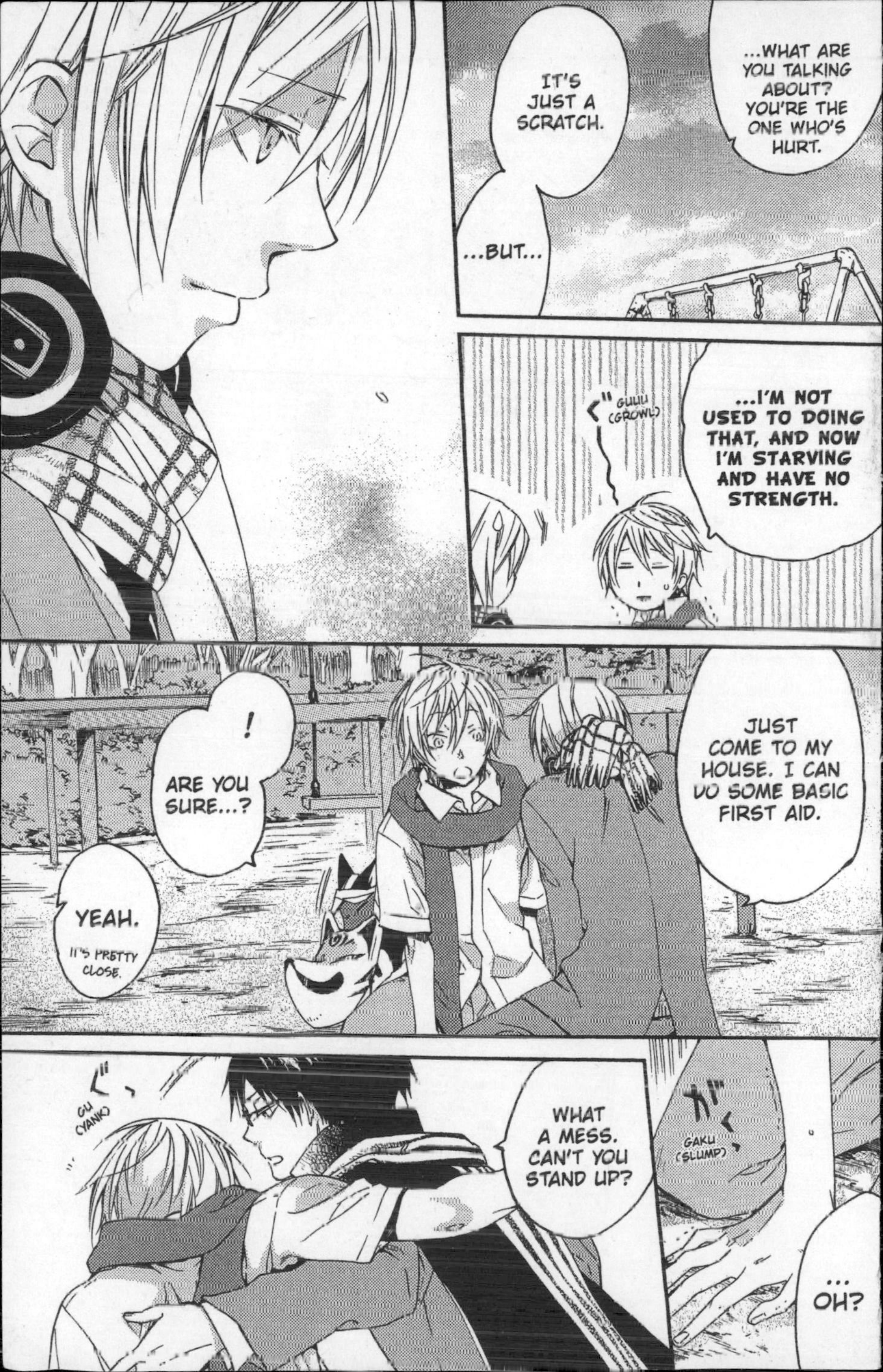
...WHAT ARE YOU TALKING ABOUT? YOU'RE THE ONE WHO'S HURT.
IT'S JUST A SCRATCH.
...BUT...
GUUU (GROWL)
...I'M NOT USED TO DOING THAT, AND NOW I'M STARVING AND HAVE NO STRENGTH.
JUST COME TO MY HOUSE. I CAN DO SOME BASIC FIRST AID.
!
ARE YOU SURE...?
YEAH.
IT'S PRETTY CLOSE.
...OH?
GAKU (SLUMP)
WHAT A MESS. CAN'T YOU STAND UP?
GU (YANK)

IT'S CREEPY SOMEHOW, YOU LENDING ME YOUR SHOULDER, AKIYOSHI.
...NOT LIKE I HAVE A CHOICE. I MEAN, YOU ARE INJURED AND ALL.
JARI (CRUNCH)
PLUS, IT SEEMS THERE'S A STORY WE NEED TO HEAR FROM THE TWO OF YOU.
HUH!? WHAT'S THAT?
THAT CAN WAIT.
COME ON.
....
THANK YOU...
...SHIN.

Of the Red,
the Light,
and the
Ayakashi

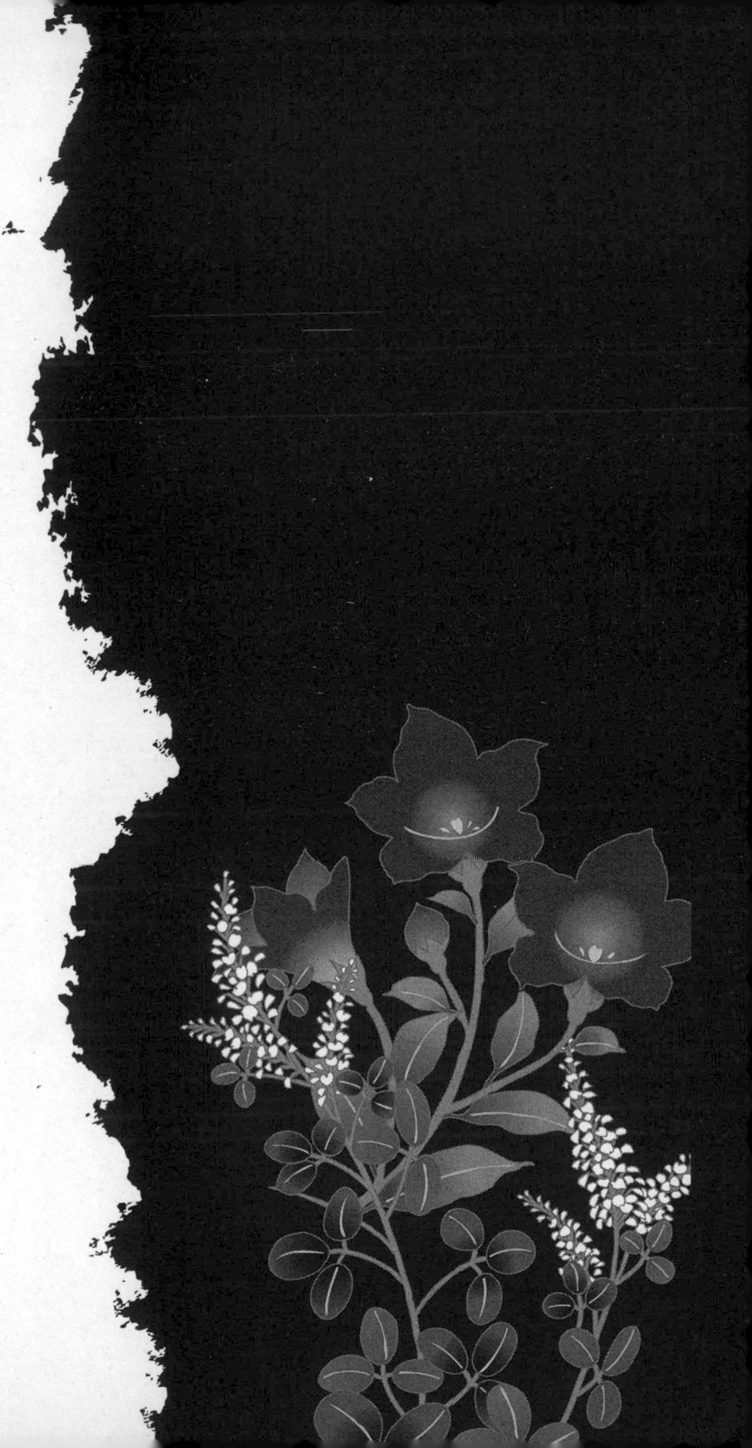

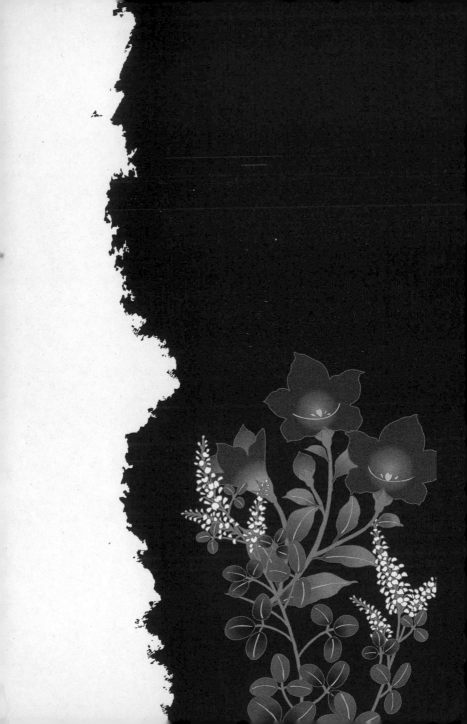

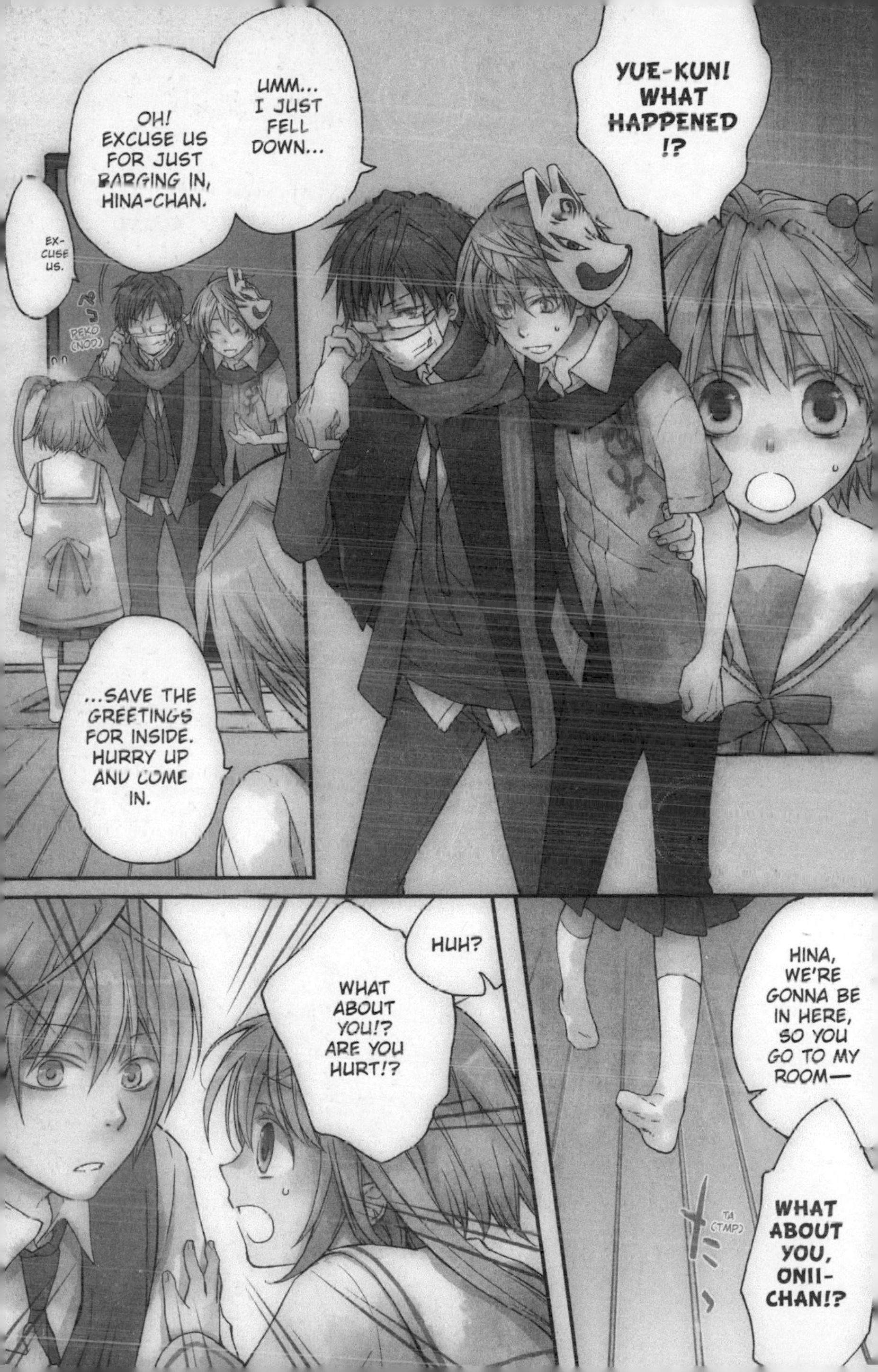
YUE-KUN! WHAT HAPPENED!?
UMM... I JUST FELL DOWN...
OH! EXCUSE US FOR JUST BARGING IN, HINA-CHAN.
EX-CUSE US.
PEKO (NOD)
...SAVE THE GREETINGS FOR INSIDE. HURRY UP AND COME IN.
HINA, WE'RE GONNA BE IN HERE, SO YOU GO TO MY ROOM—
TA (TMP)
WHAT ABOUT YOU, ONII-CHAN!?
HUH?
WHAT ABOUT YOU!? ARE YOU HURT!?

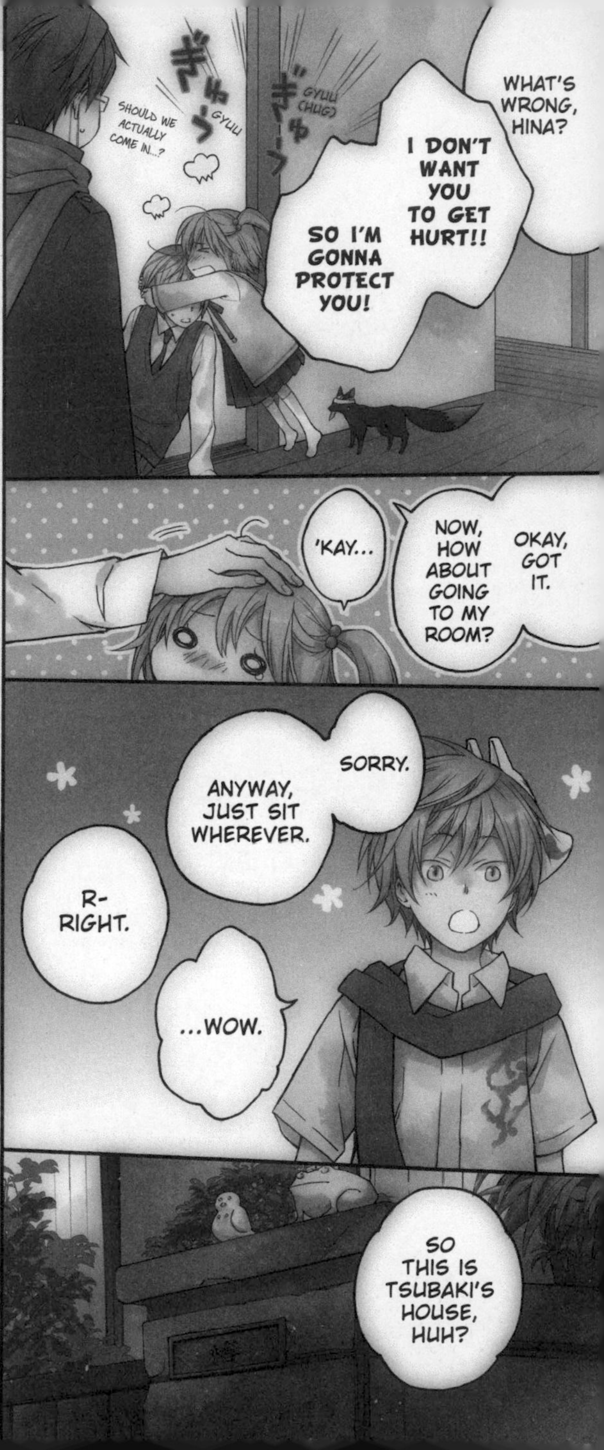
WHAT'S WRONG, HINA?
I DON'T WANT YOU TO GET HURT!!
SO I'M GONNA PROTECT YOU!
ぎゅーう
GYUU (HUG)
ぎゅう
GYUU
SHOULD WE ACTUALLY COME IN...?
OKAY, GOT IT.
NOW, HOW ABOUT GOING TO MY ROOM?
'KAY...
SORRY.
ANYWAY, JUST SIT WHEREVER.
R-RIGHT.
...WOW.
SO THIS IS TSUBAKI'S HOUSE, HUH?
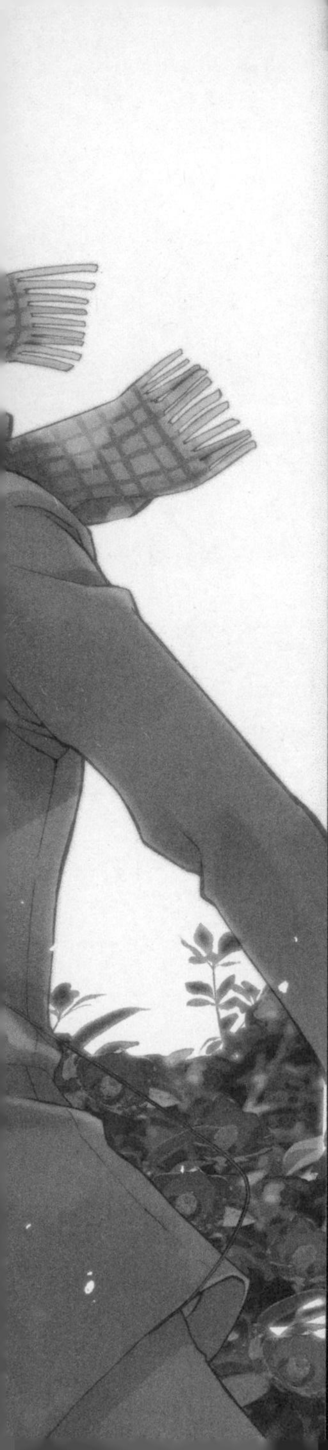

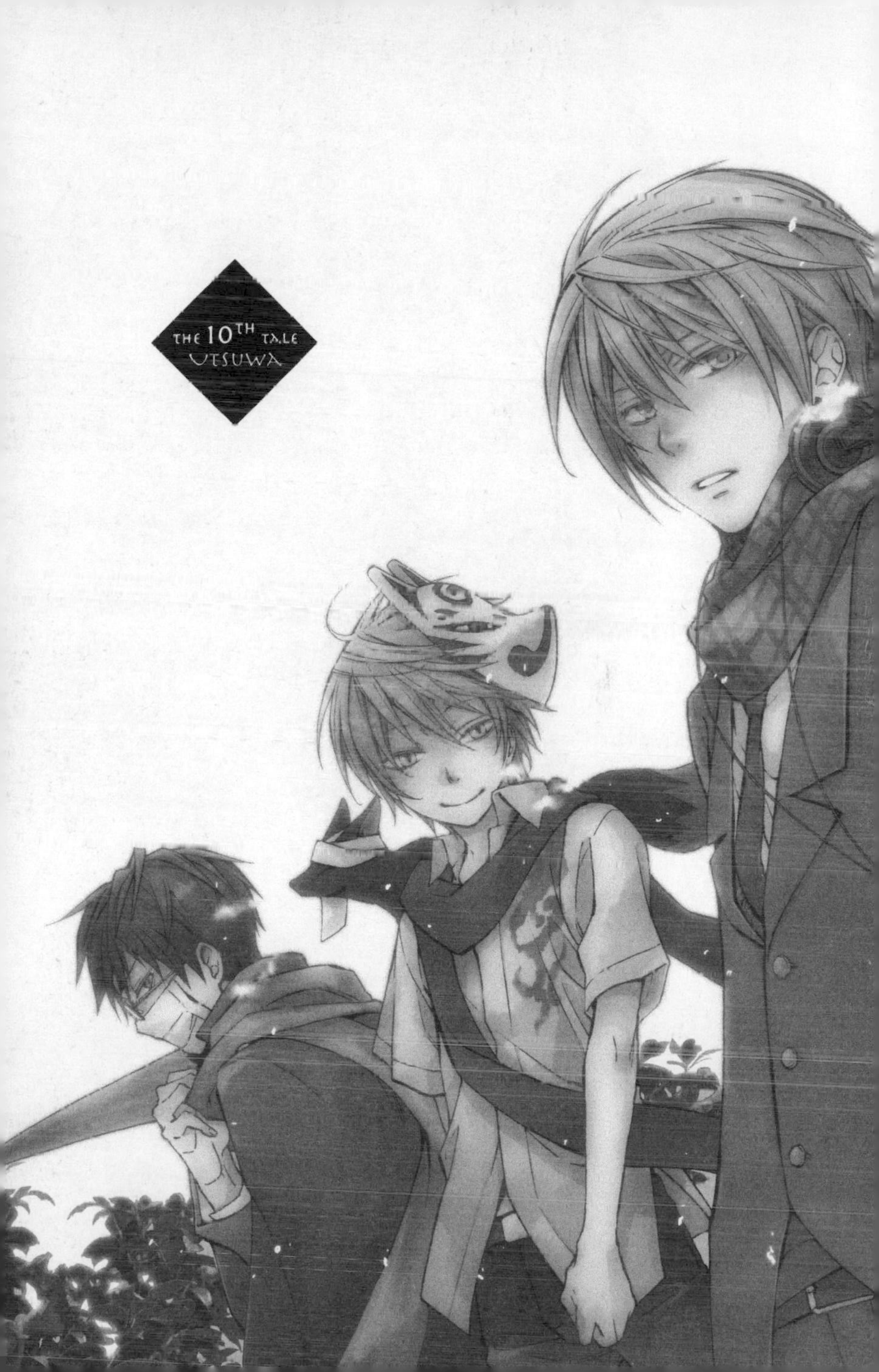
THE 10TH TALE
UTSUWA

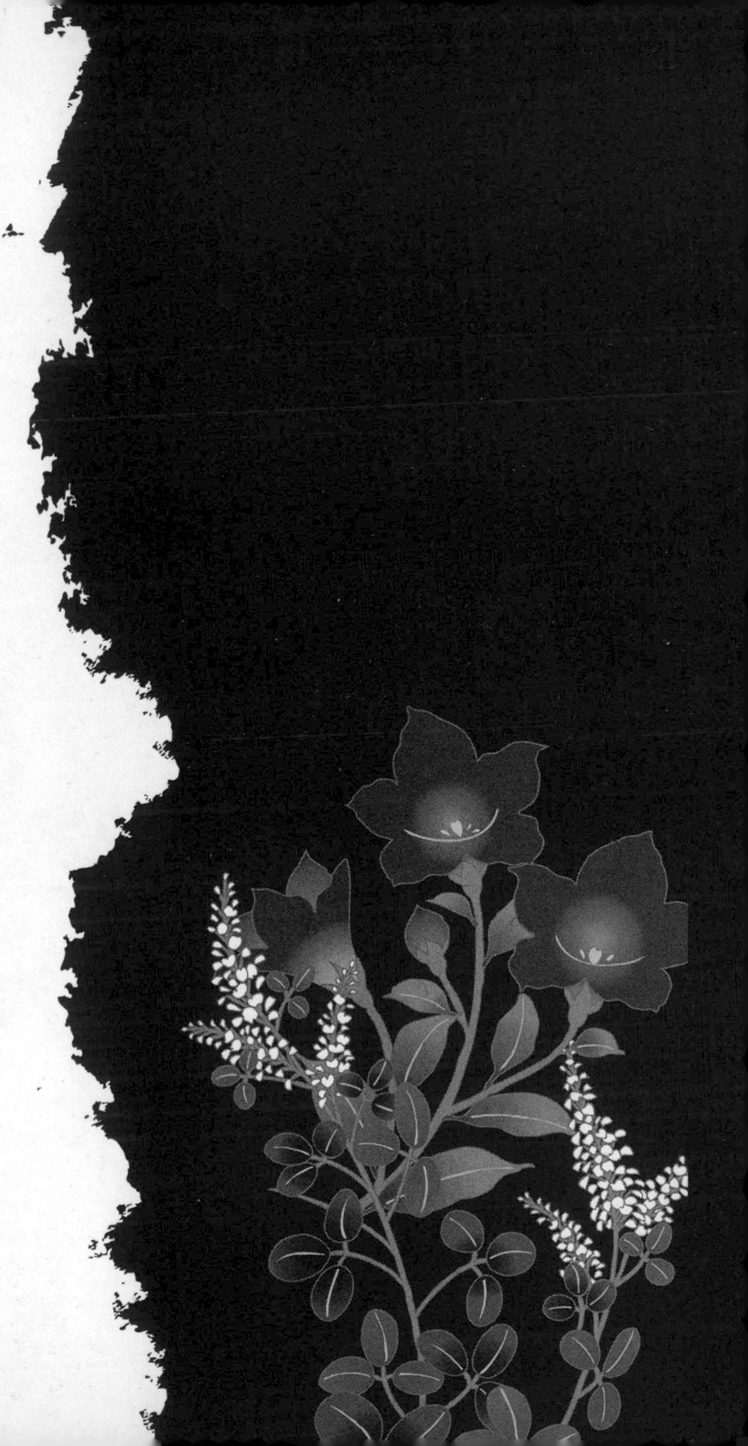

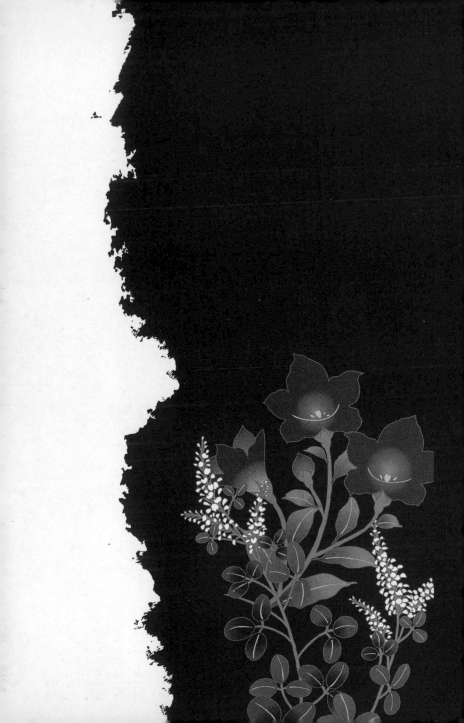

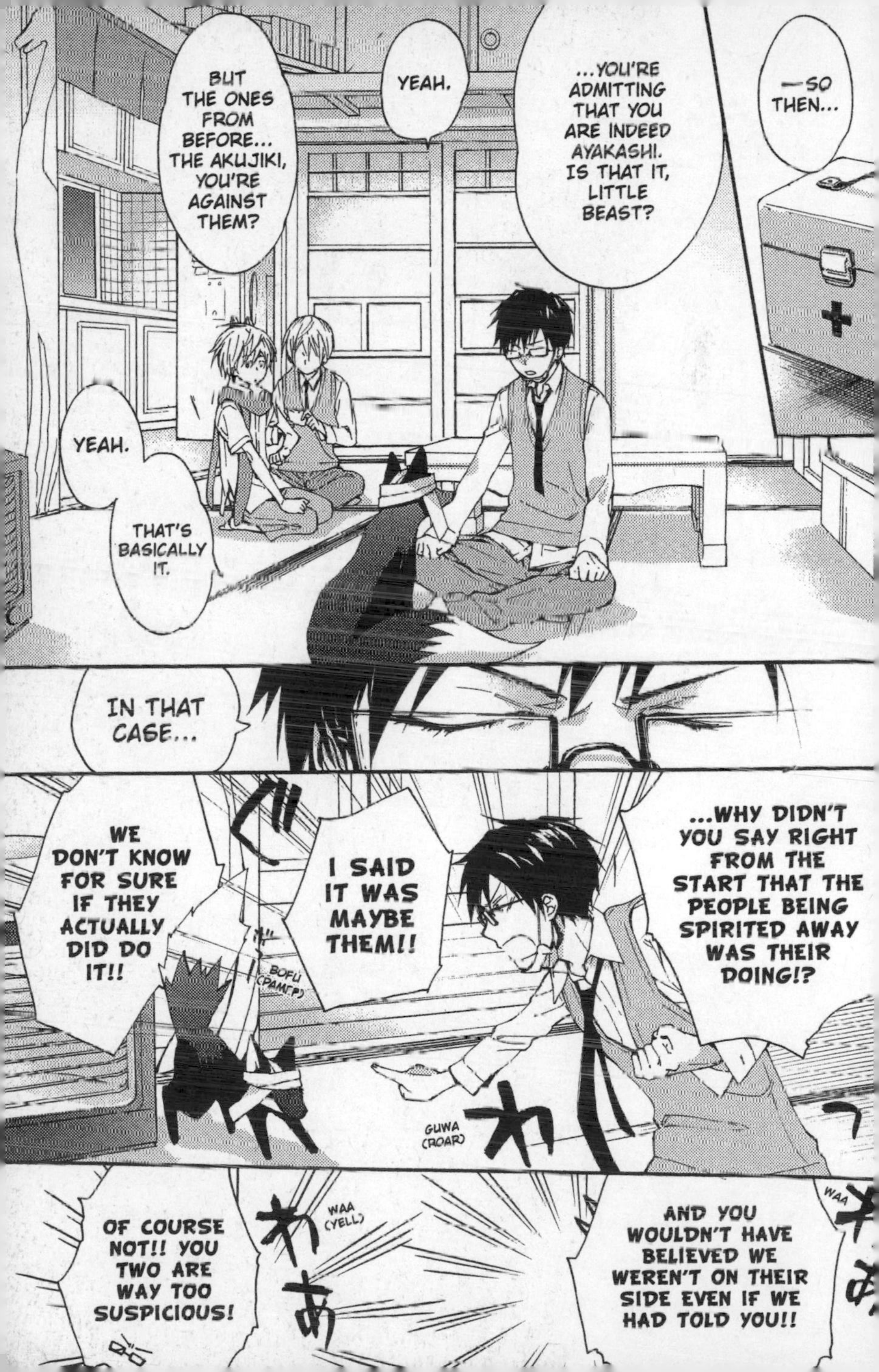
—SO THEN...
...YOU'RE ADMITTING THAT YOU ARE INDEED AYAKASHI. IS THAT IT, LITTLE BEAST?
YEAH.
BUT THE ONES FROM BEFORE... THE AKUJIKI, YOU'RE AGAINST THEM?
YEAH.
THAT'S BASICALLY IT.
IN THAT CASE...
...WHY DIDN'T YOU SAY RIGHT FROM THE START THAT THE PEOPLE BEING SPIRITED AWAY WAS THEIR DOING!?
GUWA (ROAR)
I SAID IT WAS MAYBE THEM!!
BOFU
WE DON'T KNOW FOR SURE IF THEY ACTUALLY DID DO IT!!
WAA
AND YOU WOULDN'T HAVE BELIEVED WE WEREN'T ON THEIR SIDE EVEN IF WE HAD TOLD YOU!!
WAA (YELL)
OF COURSE NOT!! YOU TWO ARE WAY TOO SUSPICIOUS!

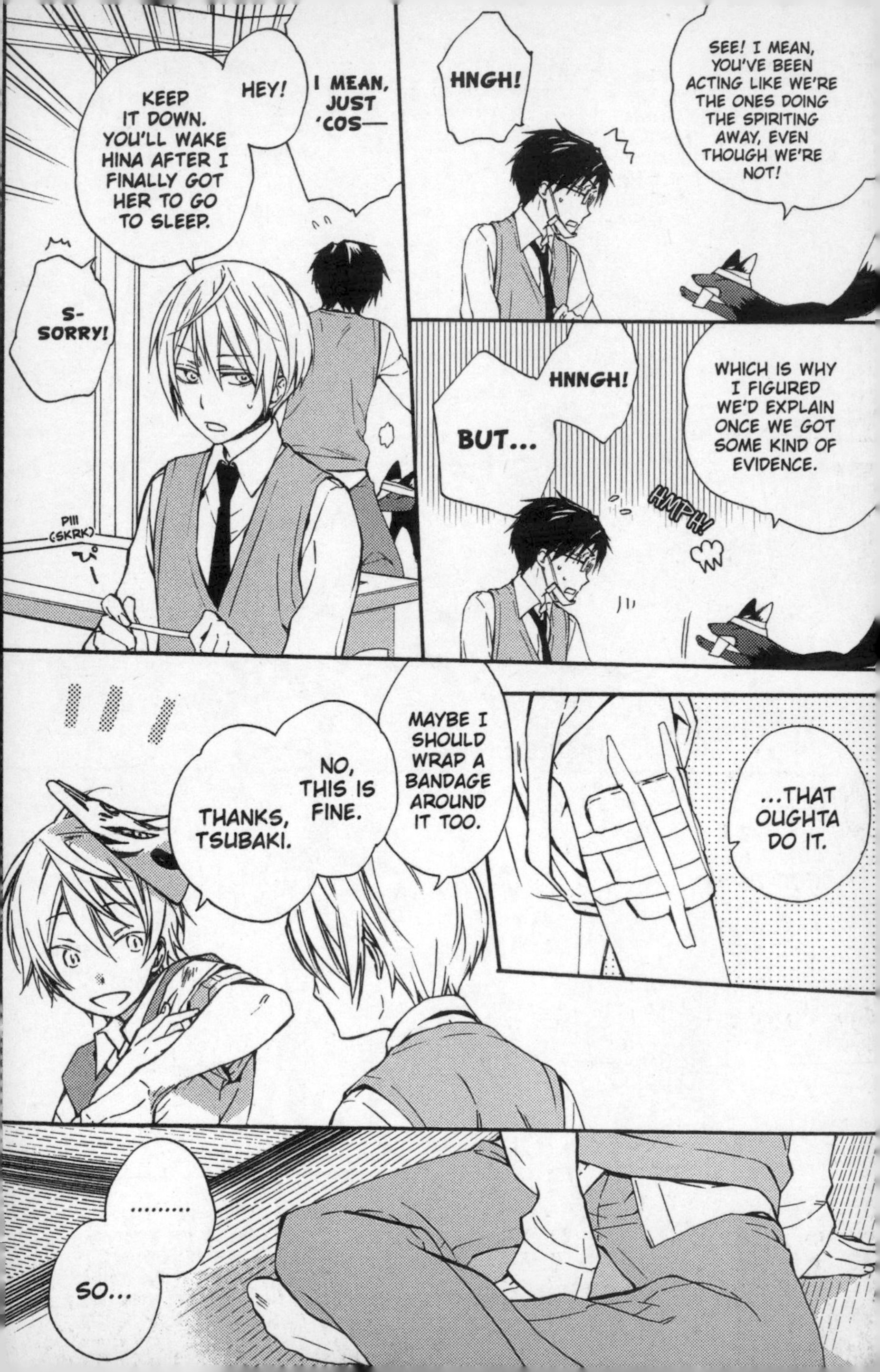
SEE! I MEAN, YOU'VE BEEN ACTING LIKE WE'RE THE ONES DOING THE SPIRITING AWAY, EVEN THOUGH WE'RE NOT!
HNGH!
WHICH IS WHY I FIGURED WE'D EXPLAIN ONCE WE GOT SOME KIND OF EVIDENCE.
HNNGH!
BUT...
HMPH!
I MEAN, JUST 'COS—
HEY!
KEEP IT DOWN. YOU'LL WAKE HINA AFTER I FINALLY GOT HER TO GO TO SLEEP.
S-SORRY!
PIII (SKRK)
...THAT OUGHTA DO IT.
MAYBE I SHOULD WRAP A BANDAGE AROUND IT TOO.
NO, THIS IS FINE.
THANKS, TSUBAKI.
....
SO...

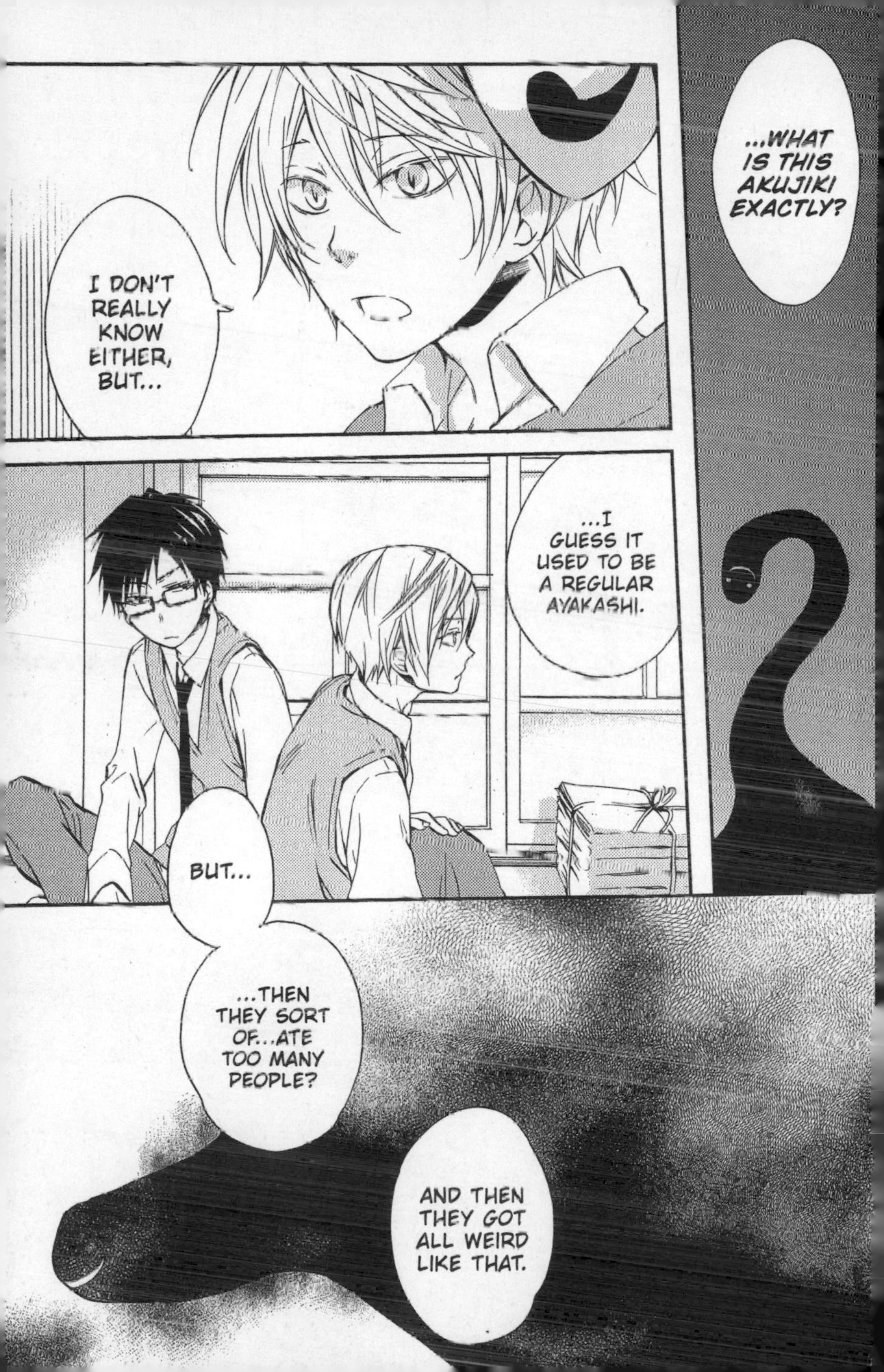
...WHAT IS THIS AKUJIKI EXACTLY?
I DON'T REALLY KNOW EITHER, BUT...
...I GUESS IT USED TO BE A REGULAR AYAKASHI.
BUT...
...THEN THEY SORT OF...ATE TOO MANY PEOPLE?
AND THEN THEY GOT ALL WEIRD LIKE THAT.

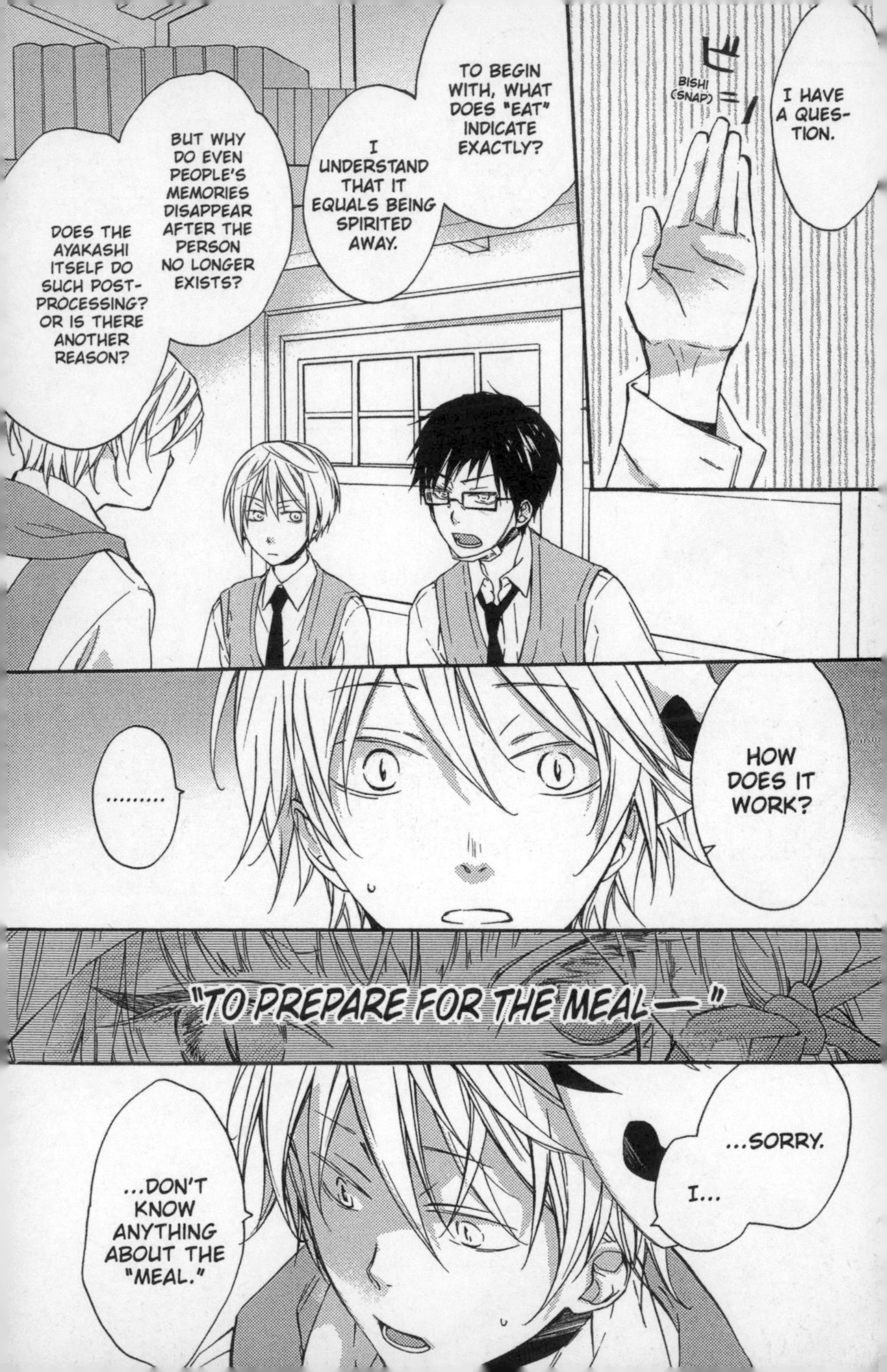
BISHI (SNAP)
I HAVE A QUESTION.
TO BEGIN WITH, WHAT DOES "EAT" INDICATE EXACTLY?
I UNDERSTAND THAT IT EQUALS BEING SPIRITED AWAY.
BUT WHY DO EVEN PEOPLE'S MEMORIES DISAPPEAR AFTER THE PERSON NO LONGER EXISTS?
DOES THE AYAKASHI ITSELF DO SUCH POST-PROCESSING? OR IS THERE ANOTHER REASON?
HOW DOES IT WORK?
....
"TO PREPARE FOR THE MEAL—"
...SORRY.
I...
...DON'T KNOW ANYTHING ABOUT THE "MEAL."

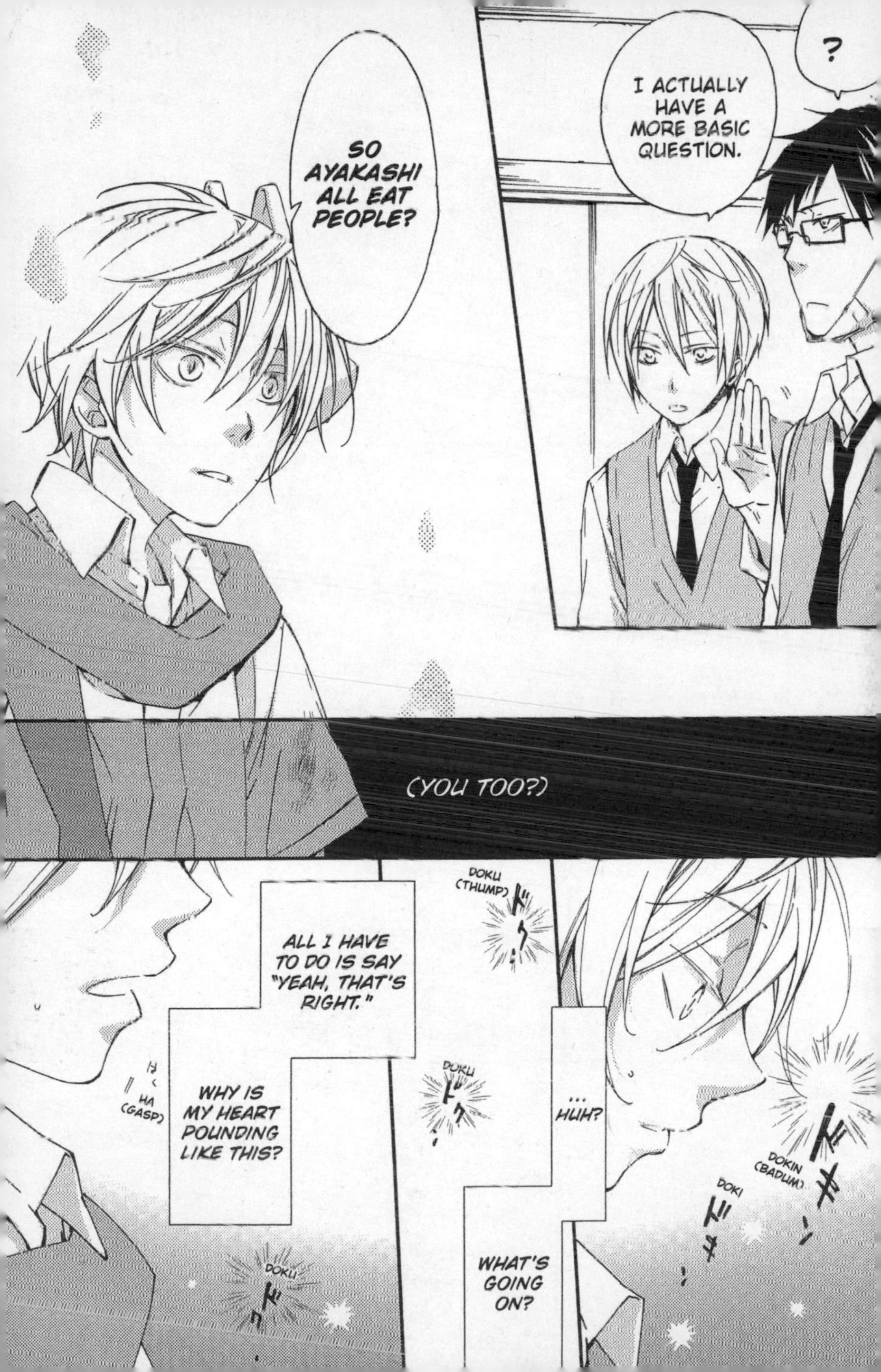
?
I ACTUALLY HAVE A MORE BASIC QUESTION.
SO AYAKASHI ALL EAT PEOPLE?
(YOU TOO?)
DOKIN (BADUM)
DOKI
...HUH?
WHAT'S GOING ON?
DOKU (THUMP)
ALL I HAVE TO DO IS SAY "YEAH, THAT'S RIGHT."
DOKU
WHY IS MY HEART POUNDING LIKE THIS?
HA (GASP)
DOKU

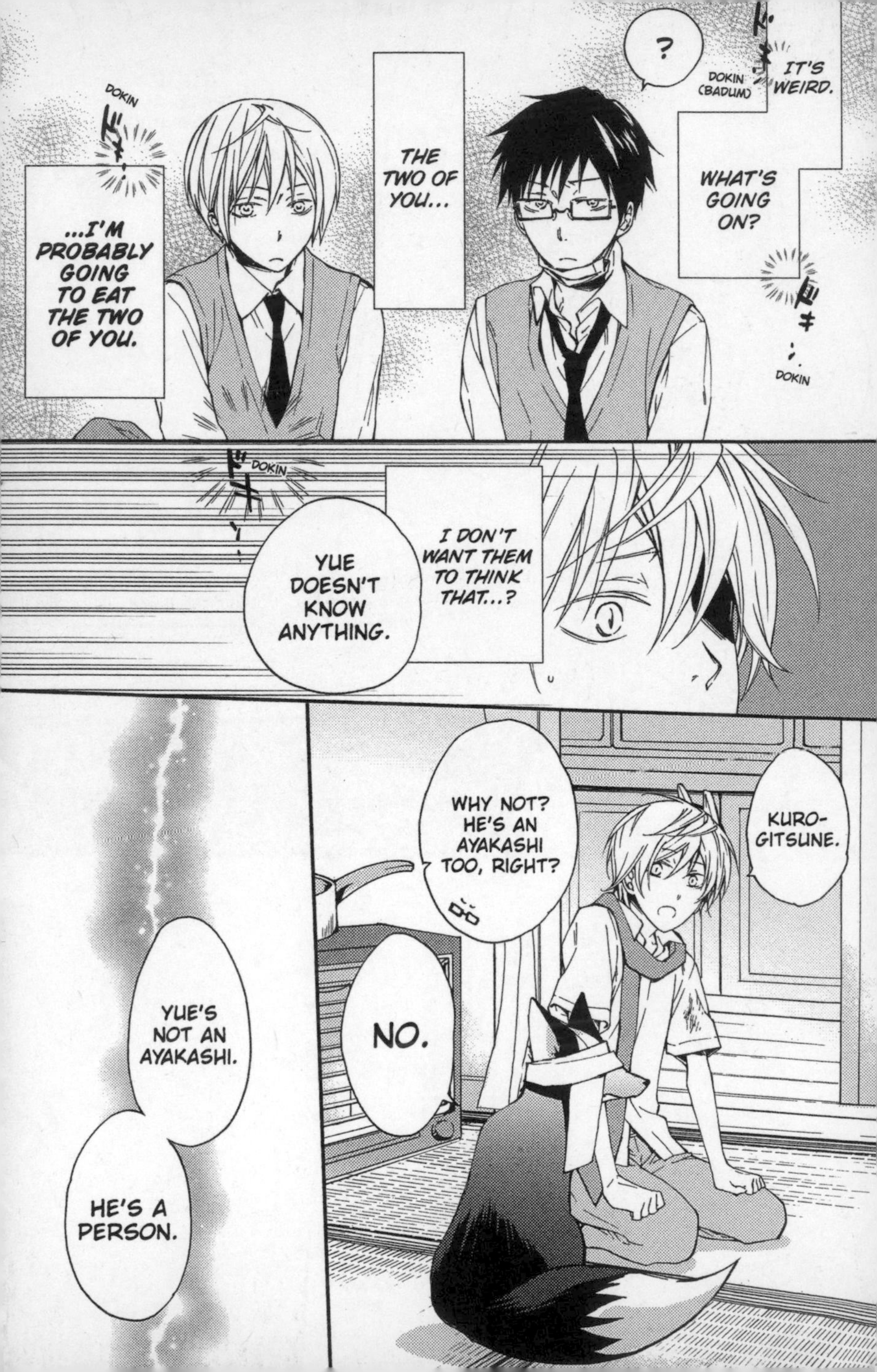
?
DOKIN (BADUM)
IT'S WEIRD.
WHAT'S GOING ON?
DOKIN
THE TWO OF YOU...
DOKIN
...I'M PROBABLY GOING TO EAT THE TWO OF YOU.
I DON'T WANT THEM TO THINK THAT...?
DOKIN
YUE DOESN'T KNOW ANYTHING.
KURO-GITSUNE.
WHY NOT? HE'S AN AYAKASHI TOO, RIGHT?
NO.
YUE'S NOT AN AYAKASHI.
HE'S A PERSON.

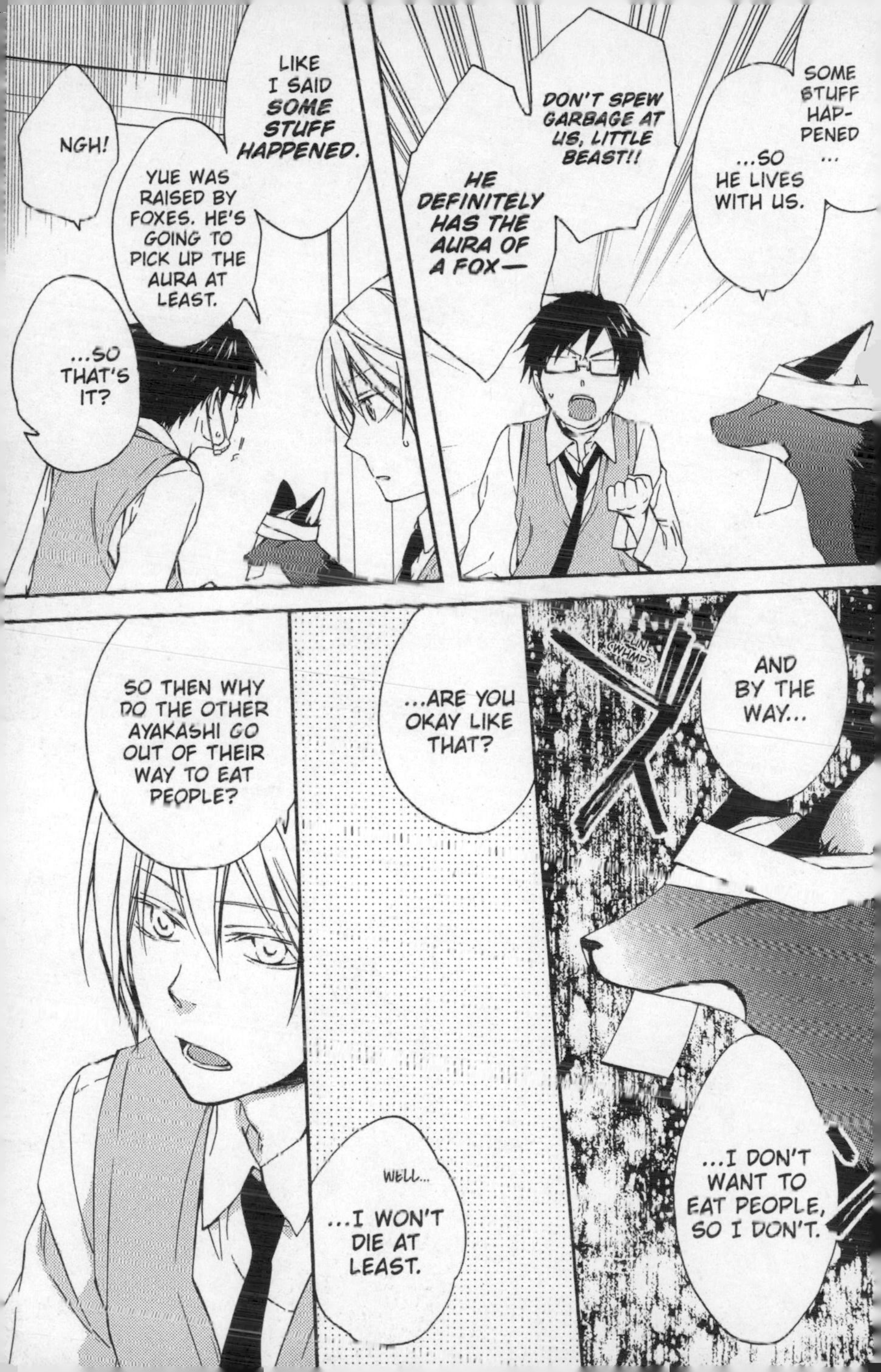
SOME STUFF HAPPENED ... ...SO HE LIVES WITH US.
DON'T SPEW GARBAGE AT US, LITTLE BEAST!!
HE DEFINITELY HAS THE AURA OF A FOX—
LIKE I SAID SOME STUFF HAPPENED.
NGH!
YUE WAS RAISED BY FOXES. HE'S GOING TO PICK UP THE AURA AT LEAST.
...SO THAT'S IT?
AND BY THE WAY...
(WHMP)
...I DON'T WANT TO EAT PEOPLE, SO I DON'T.
...ARE YOU OKAY LIKE THAT?
WELL...
...I WON'T DIE AT LEAST.
SO THEN WHY DO THE OTHER AYAKASHI GO OUT OF THEIR WAY TO EAT PEOPLE?

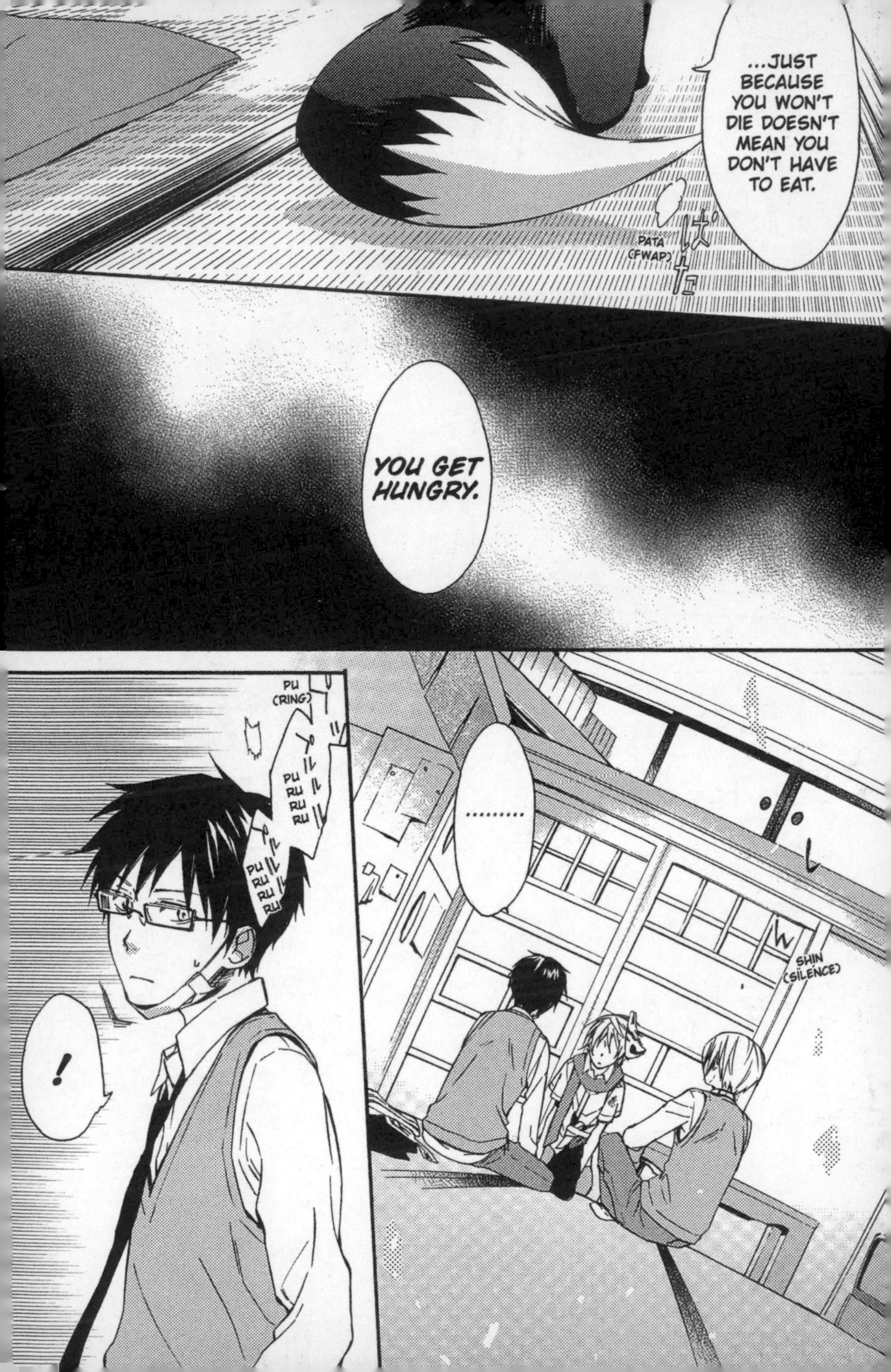
...JUST BECAUSE YOU WON'T DIE DOESN'T MEAN YOU DON'T HAVE TO EAT.
PATA (FWAP)
YOU GET HUNGRY.
....
SHIN (SILENCE)
PU (RING)
PU RU RU RU
PU RU RU RU
!

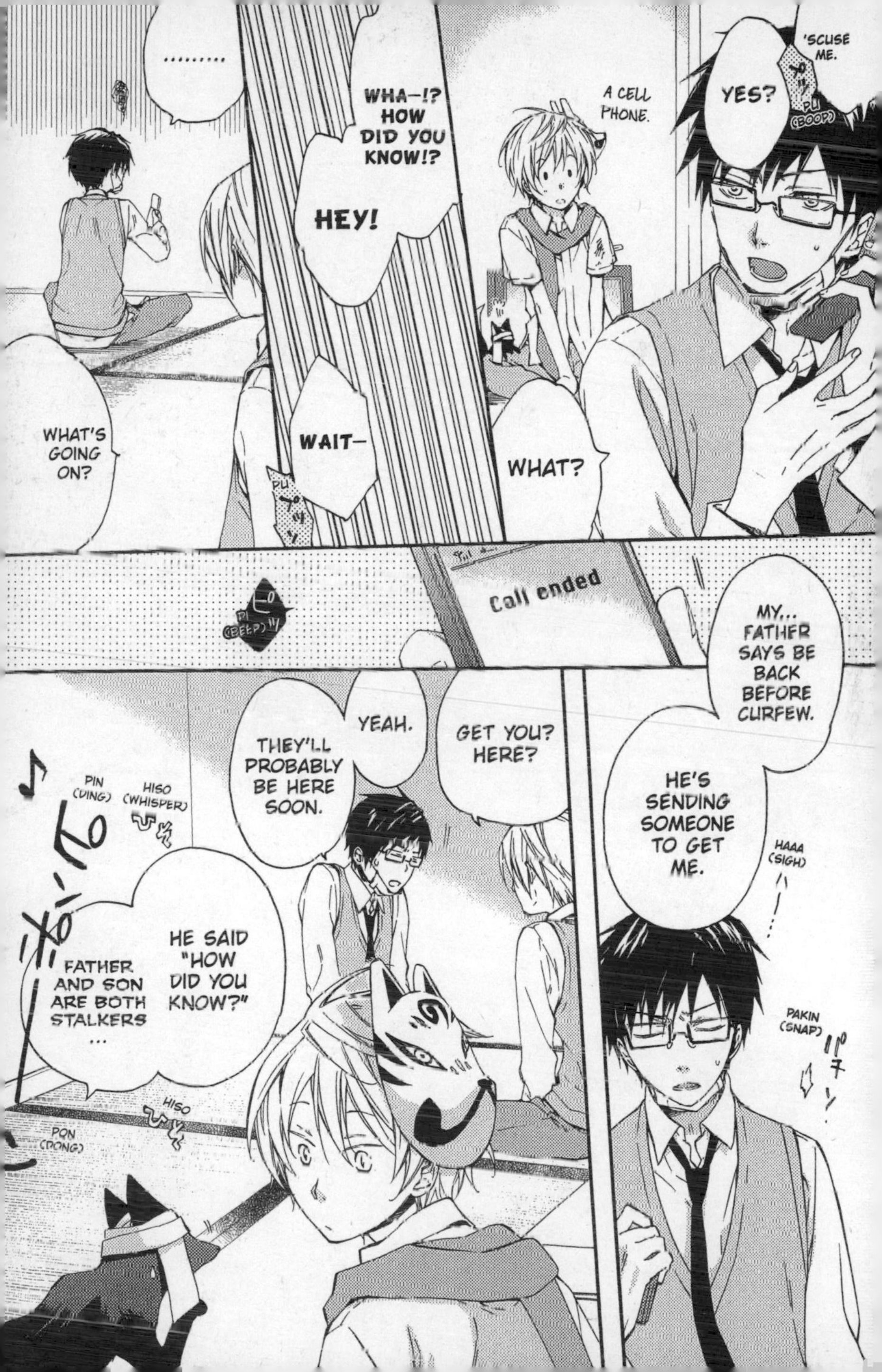
'SCUSE ME.
PU (BOOP)
YES?
A CELL PHONE.
WHAT?
WHA-!? HOW DID YOU KNOW!?
HEY!
WAIT-
PU
....
WHAT'S GOING ON?
MY... FATHER SAYS BE BACK BEFORE CURFEW.
Call ended
PI (BEEP)
HE'S SENDING SOMEONE TO GET ME.
HAAA (SIGH)
PAKIN (SNAP)
GET YOU? HERE?
YEAH.
THEY'LL PROBABLY BE HERE SOON.
PIN (DING)
HISO (WHISPER)
HE SAID "HOW DID YOU KNOW?"
FATHER AND SON ARE BOTH STALKERS ...
HISO
PON (PONG)

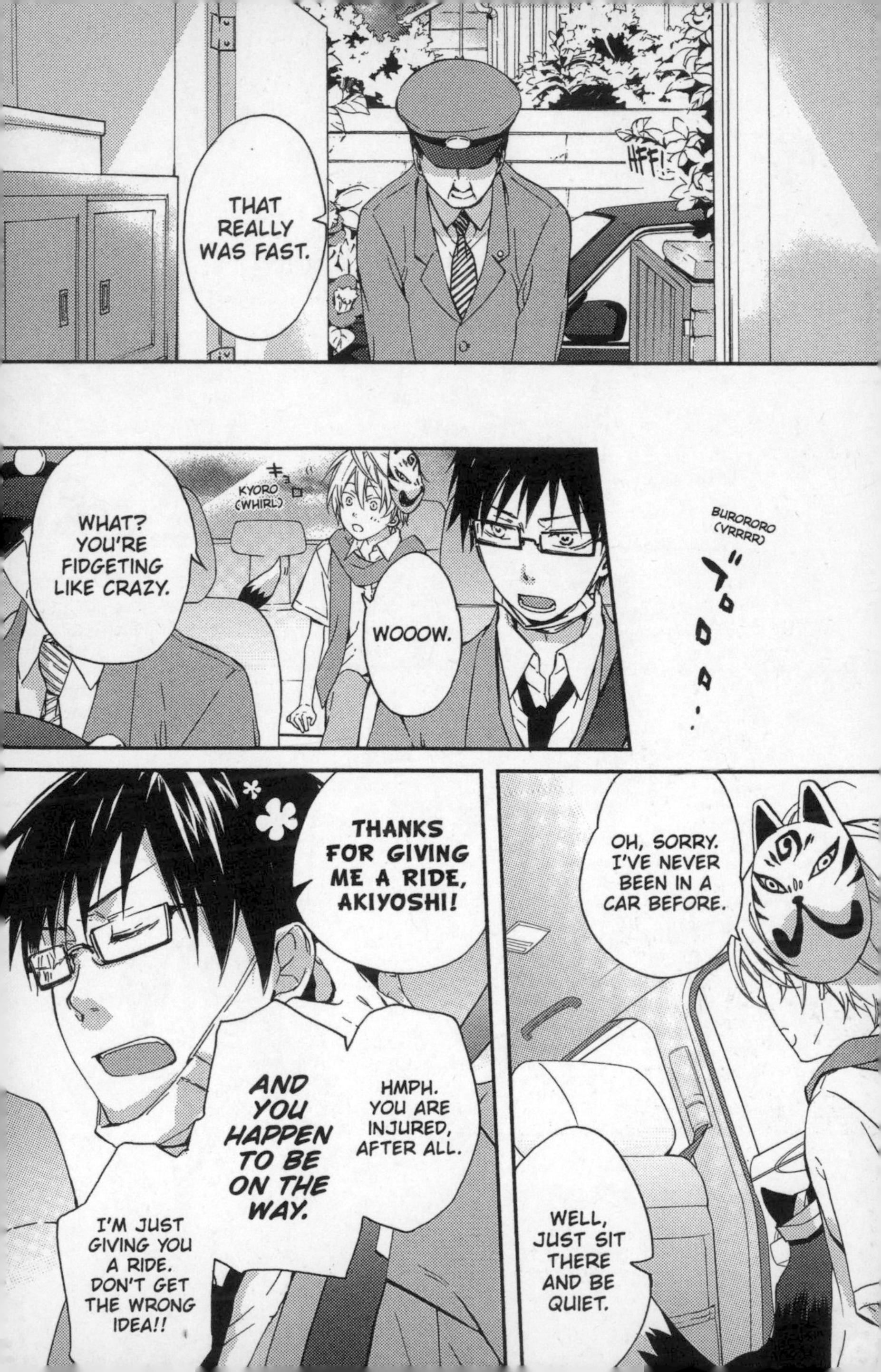
HFF!
THAT REALLY WAS FAST.
BURORORO (VRRRR)
KYORO (WHIRL)
WOOOW.
WHAT? YOU'RE FIDGETING LIKE CRAZY.
OH, SORRY. I'VE NEVER BEEN IN A CAR BEFORE.
WELL, JUST SIT THERE AND BE QUIET.
THANKS FOR GIVING ME A RIDE, AKIYOSHI!
HMPH. YOU ARE INJURED, AFTER ALL.
AND YOU HAPPEN TO BE ON THE WAY.
I'M JUST GIVING YOU A RIDE. DON'T GET THE WRONG IDEA!!

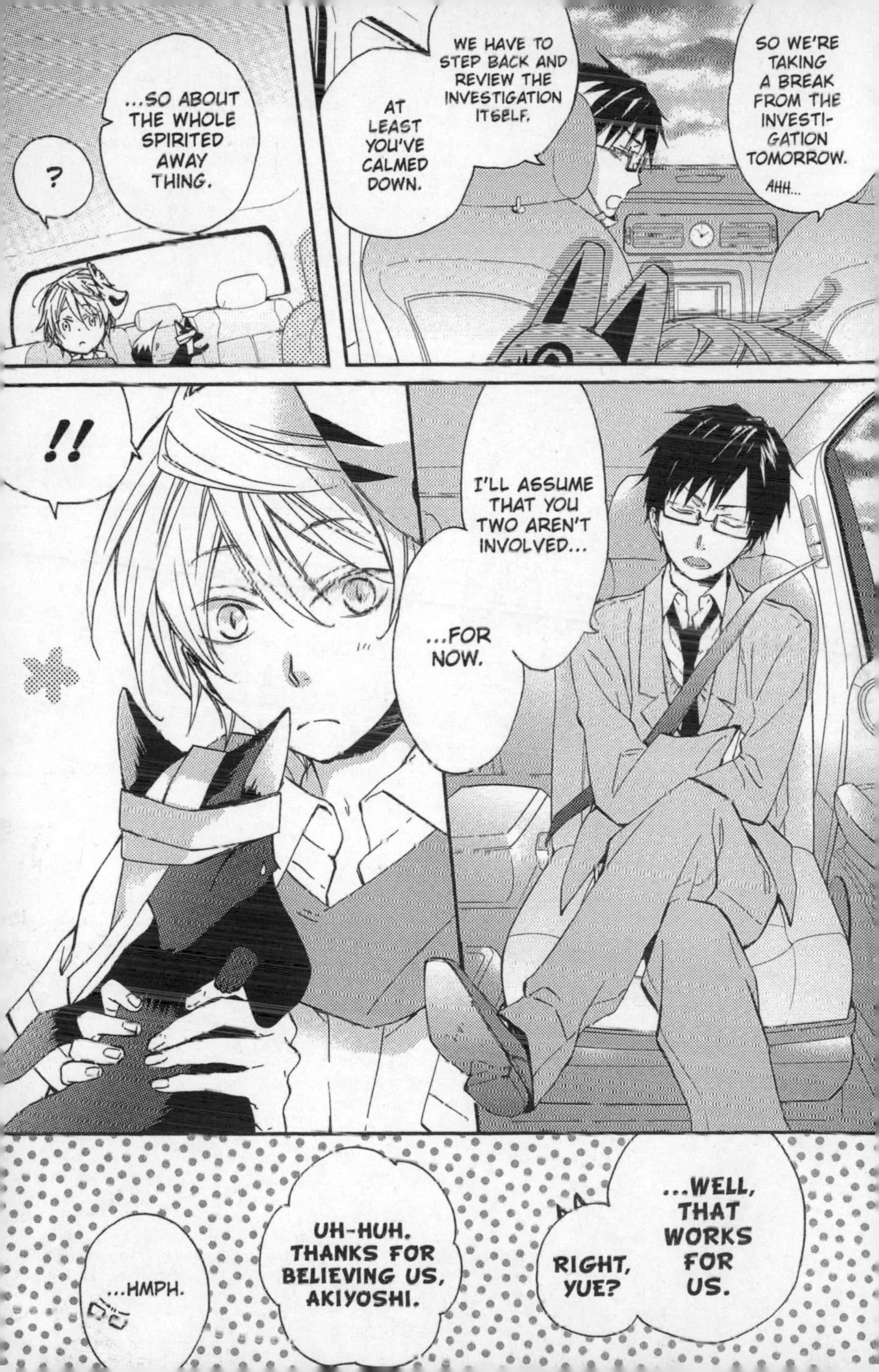
SO WE'RE TAKING A BREAK FROM THE INVESTI-GATION TOMORROW.
AHH...
WE HAVE TO STEP BACK AND REVIEW THE INVESTIGATION ITSELF.
AT LEAST YOU'VE CALMED DOWN.
...SO ABOUT THE WHOLE SPIRITED AWAY THING.
?
I'LL ASSUME THAT YOU TWO AREN'T INVOLVED...
...FOR NOW.
!!
...WELL, THAT WORKS FOR US.
RIGHT, YUE?
UH-HUH. THANKS FOR BELIEVING US, AKIYOSHI.
...HMPH.

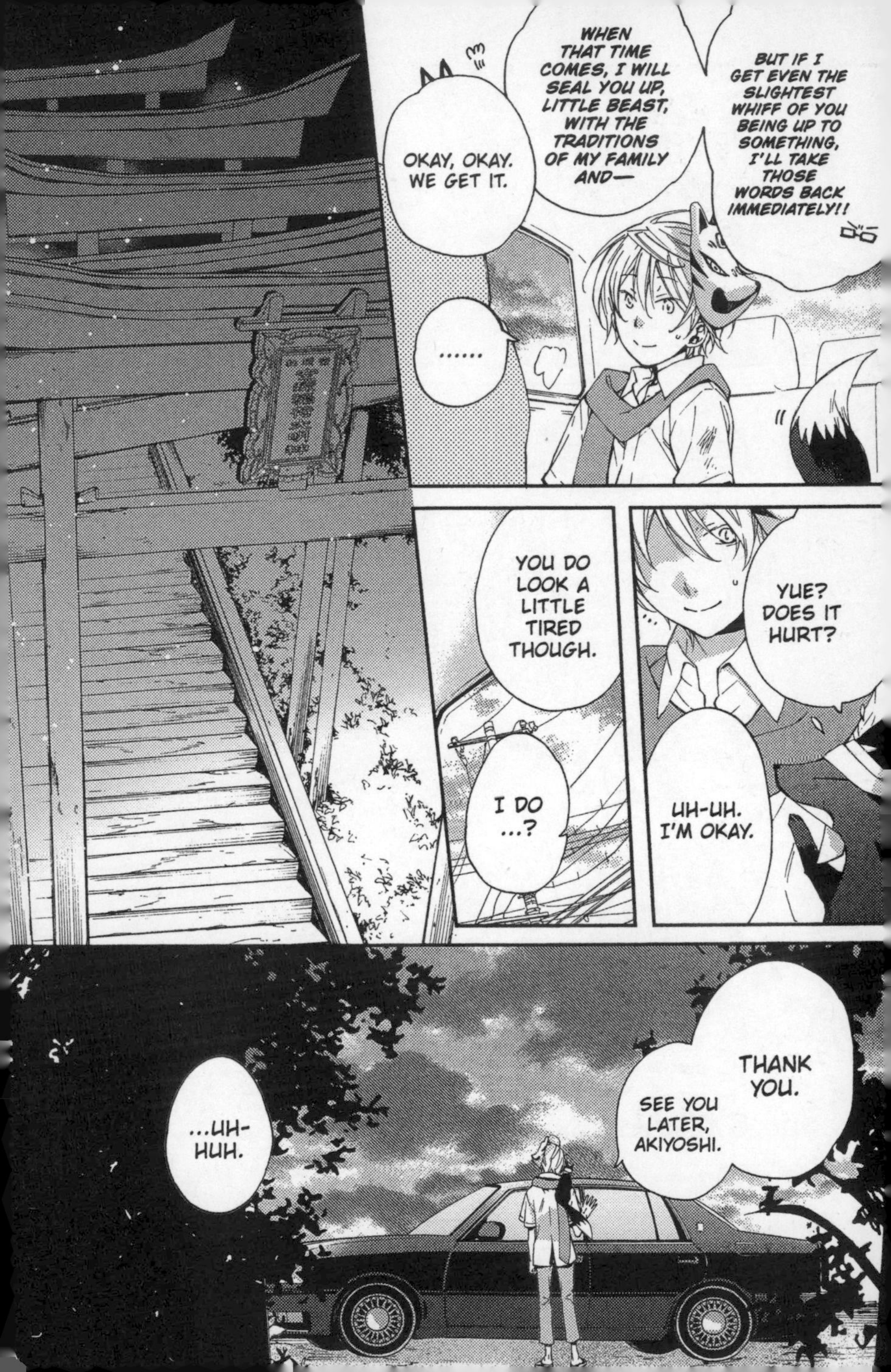
BUT IF I GET EVEN THE SLIGHTEST WHIFF OF YOU BEING UP TO SOMETHING, I'LL TAKE THOSE WORDS BACK IMMEDIATELY!!
WHEN THAT TIME COMES, I WILL SEAL YOU UP, LITTLE BEAST, WITH THE TRADITIONS OF MY FAMILY AND—
OKAY, OKAY. WE GET IT.
......
YUE? DOES IT HURT?
UH-UH. I'M OKAY.
YOU DO LOOK A LITTLE TIRED THOUGH.
I DO ...?
THANK YOU.
SEE YOU LATER, AKIYOSHI.
...UH-HUH.

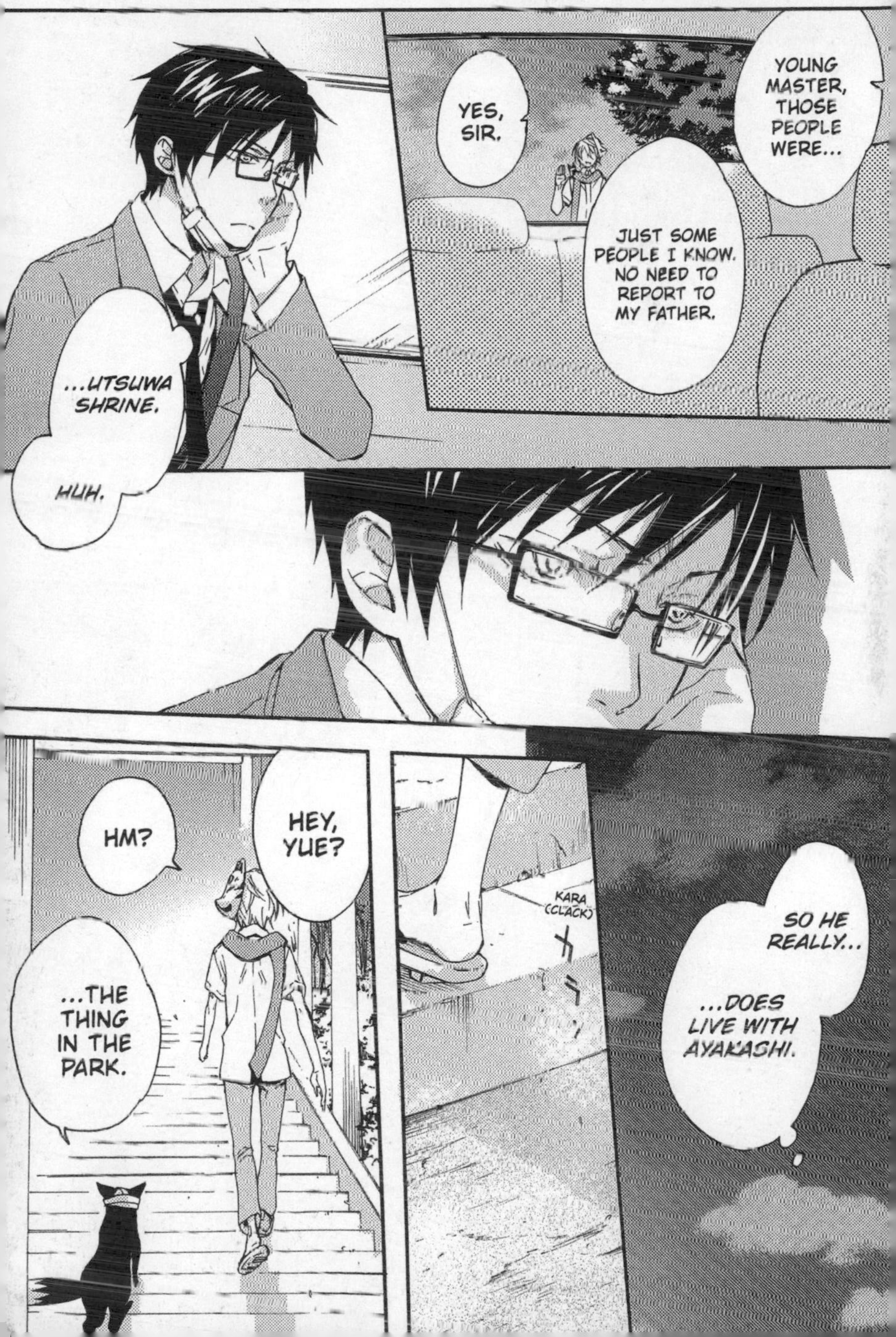
YOUNG MASTER, THOSE PEOPLE WERE...
JUST SOME PEOPLE I KNOW. NO NEED TO REPORT TO MY FATHER.
YES, SIR.
...UTSUWA SHRINE.
HUH.
SO HE REALLY...
...DOES LIVE WITH AYAKASHI.
KARA (CLACK)
HEY, YUE?
HM?
...THE THING IN THE PARK.

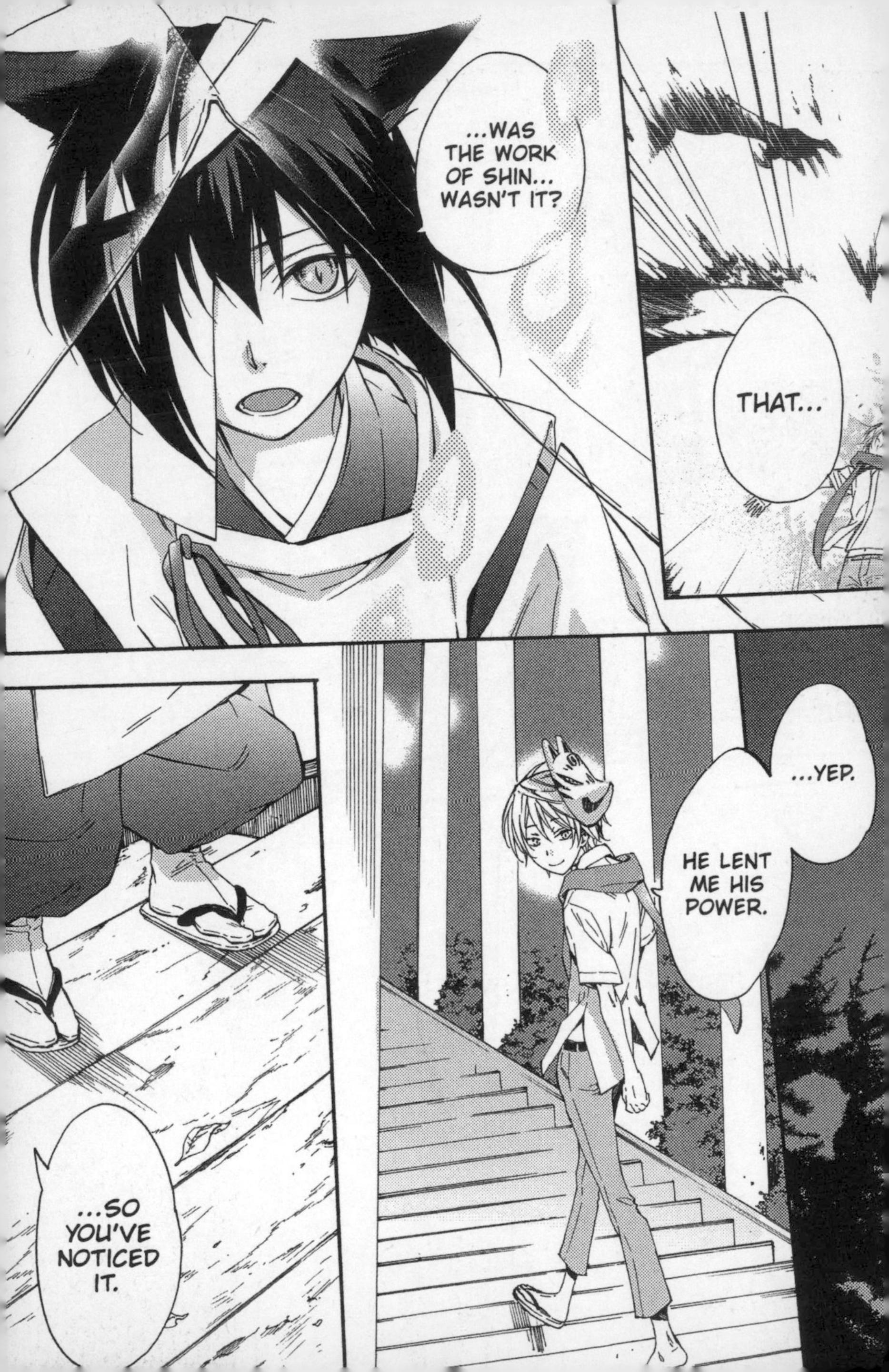
THAT...
...WAS THE WORK OF SHIN... WASN'T IT?
...YEP.
HE LENT ME HIS POWER.
...SO YOU'VE NOTICED IT.

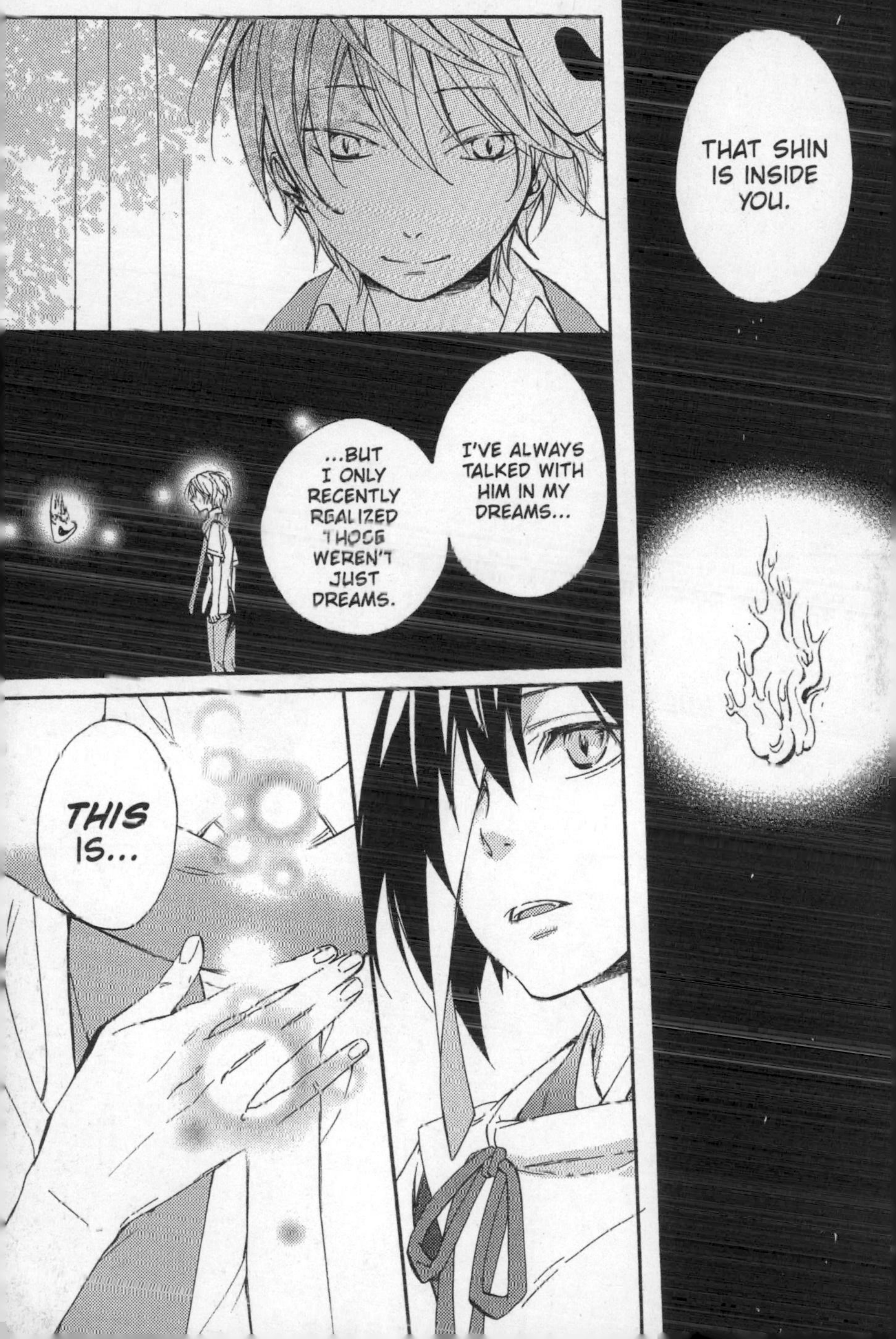
THAT SHIN IS INSIDE YOU.
I'VE ALWAYS TALKED WITH HIM IN MY DREAMS...
...BUT I ONLY RECENTLY REALIZED THOSE WEREN'T JUST DREAMS.
THIS IS...

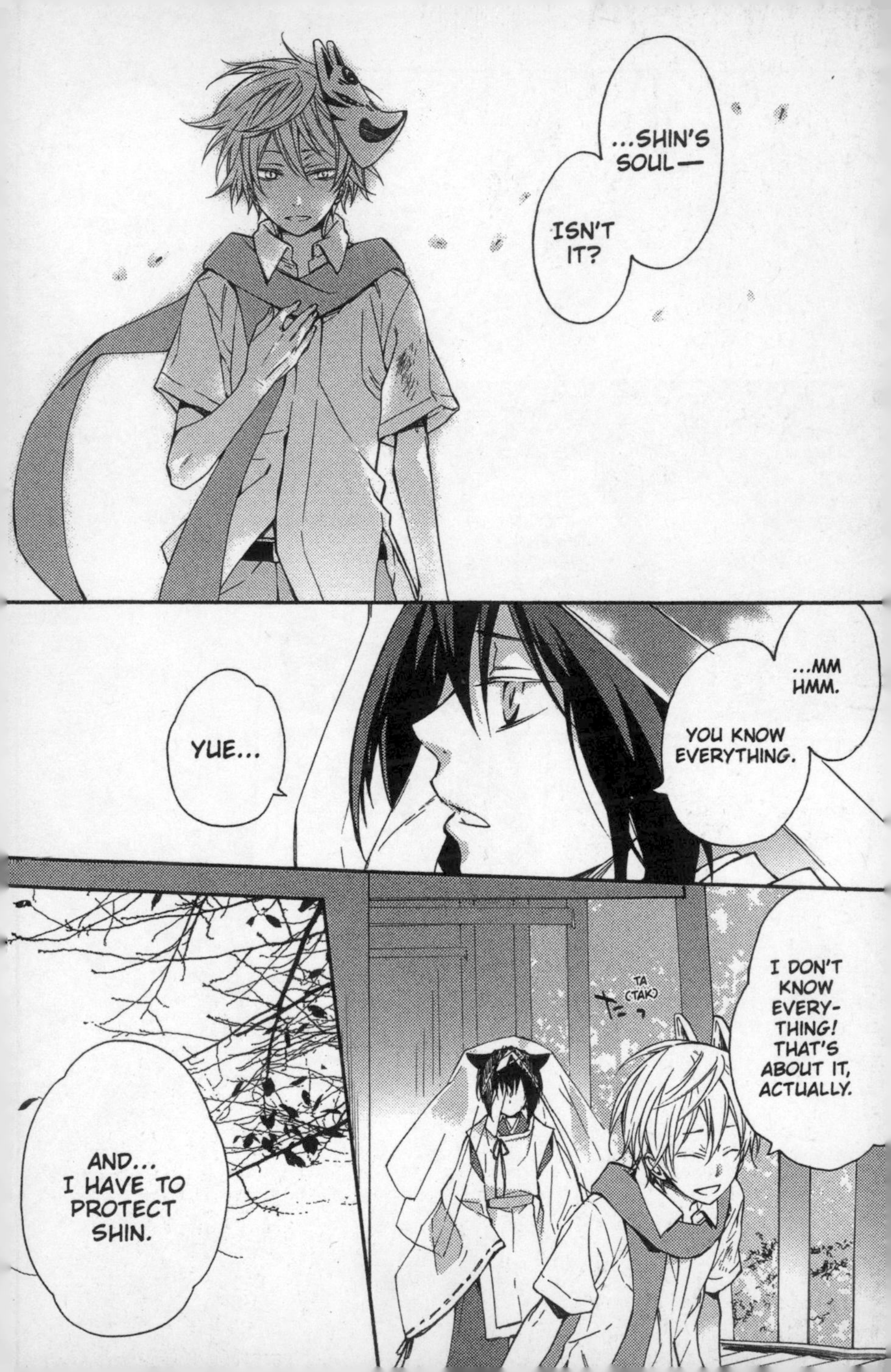
...SHIN'S SOUL—
ISN'T IT?
...MM HMM.
YOU KNOW EVERYTHING.
YUE...
I DON'T KNOW EVERY-THING! THAT'S ABOUT IT, ACTUALLY.
TA (TAK)
AND... I HAVE TO PROTECT SHIN.

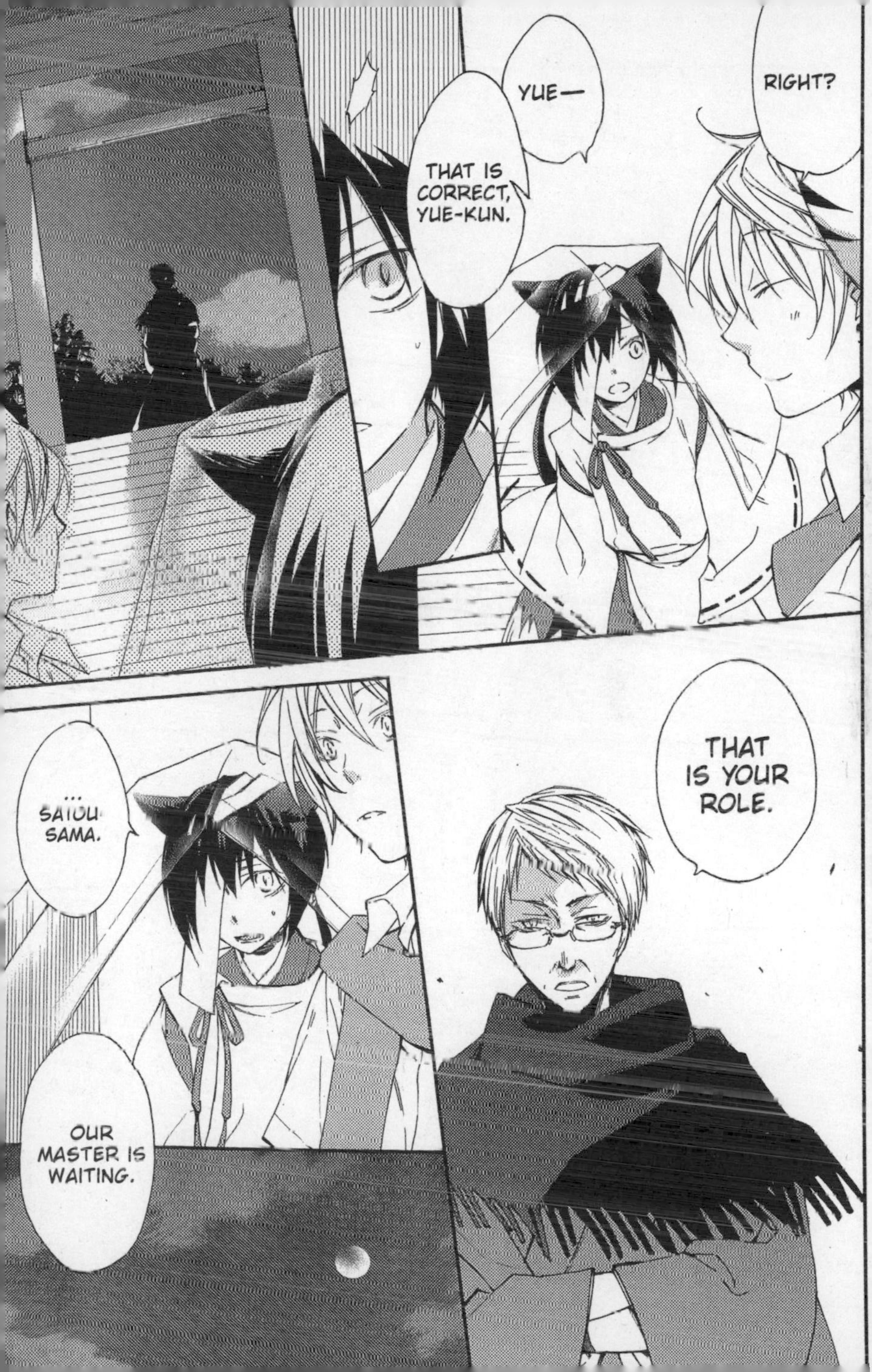
RIGHT?
YUE—
THAT IS CORRECT, YUE-KUN.
THAT IS YOUR ROLE.
... SAIOU-SAMA.
OUR MASTER IS WAITING.

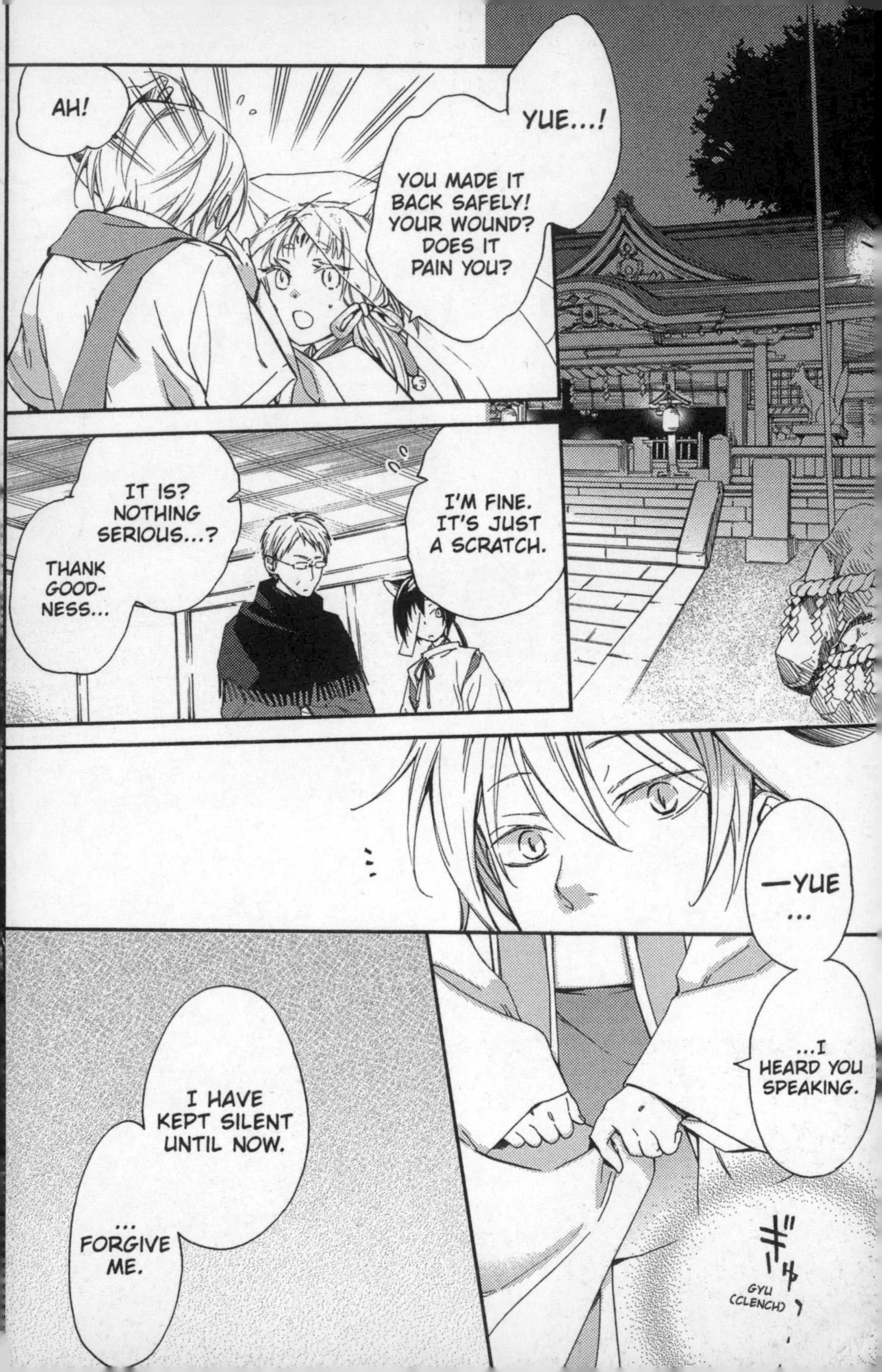
AH!
YUE...!
YOU MADE IT BACK SAFELY! YOUR WOUND? DOES IT PAIN YOU?
I'M FINE. IT'S JUST A SCRATCH.
IT IS? NOTHING SERIOUS...?
THANK GOODNESS...
—YUE ...
...I HEARD YOU SPEAKING.
GYU (CLENCH)
I HAVE KEPT SILENT UNTIL NOW.
... FORGIVE ME.

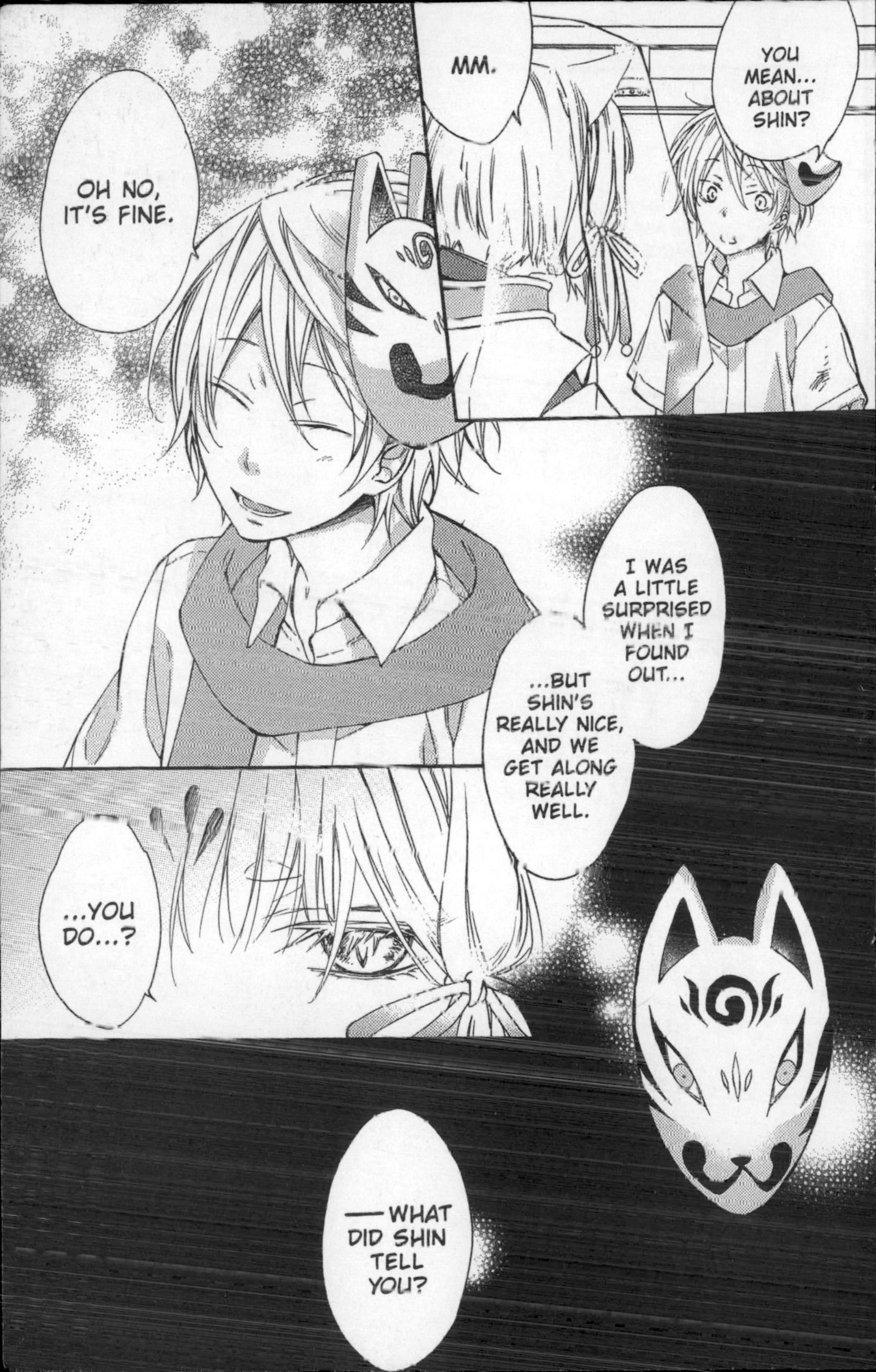
YOU MEAN... ABOUT SHIN?
MM.
OH NO, IT'S FINE.
I WAS A LITTLE SURPRISED WHEN I FOUND OUT...
...BUT SHIN'S REALLY NICE, AND WE GET ALONG REALLY WELL.
...YOU DO...?
—WHAT DID SHIN TELL YOU?

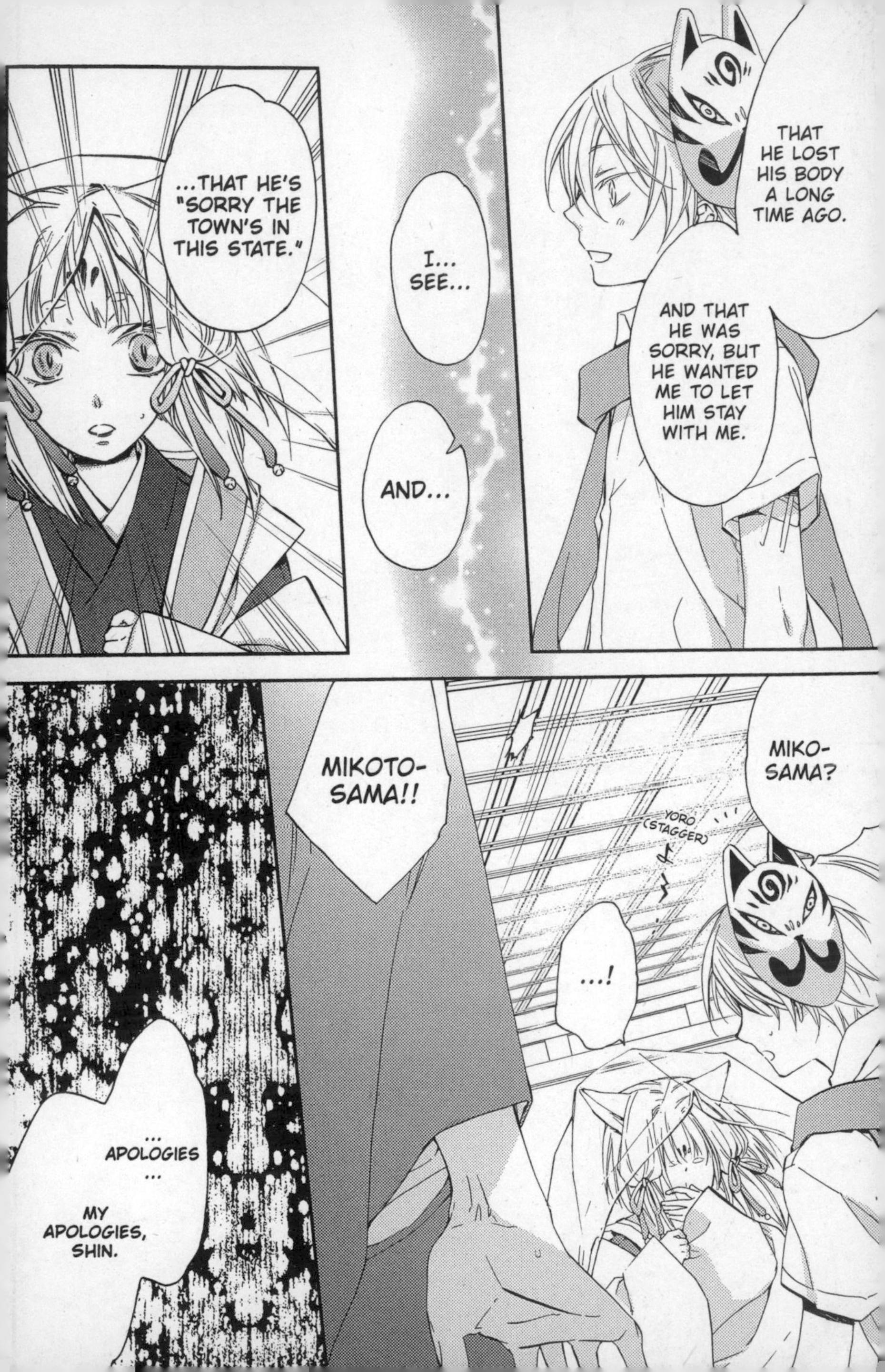
THAT HE LOST HIS BODY A LONG TIME AGO.
AND THAT HE WAS SORRY, BUT HE WANTED ME TO LET HIM STAY WITH ME.
I... SEE...
AND...
...THAT HE'S "SORRY THE TOWN'S IN THIS STATE."
MIKO-SAMA?
YORO (STAGGER)
...!
MIKOTO-SAMA!!
... APOLOGIES ...
MY APOLOGIES, SHIN.

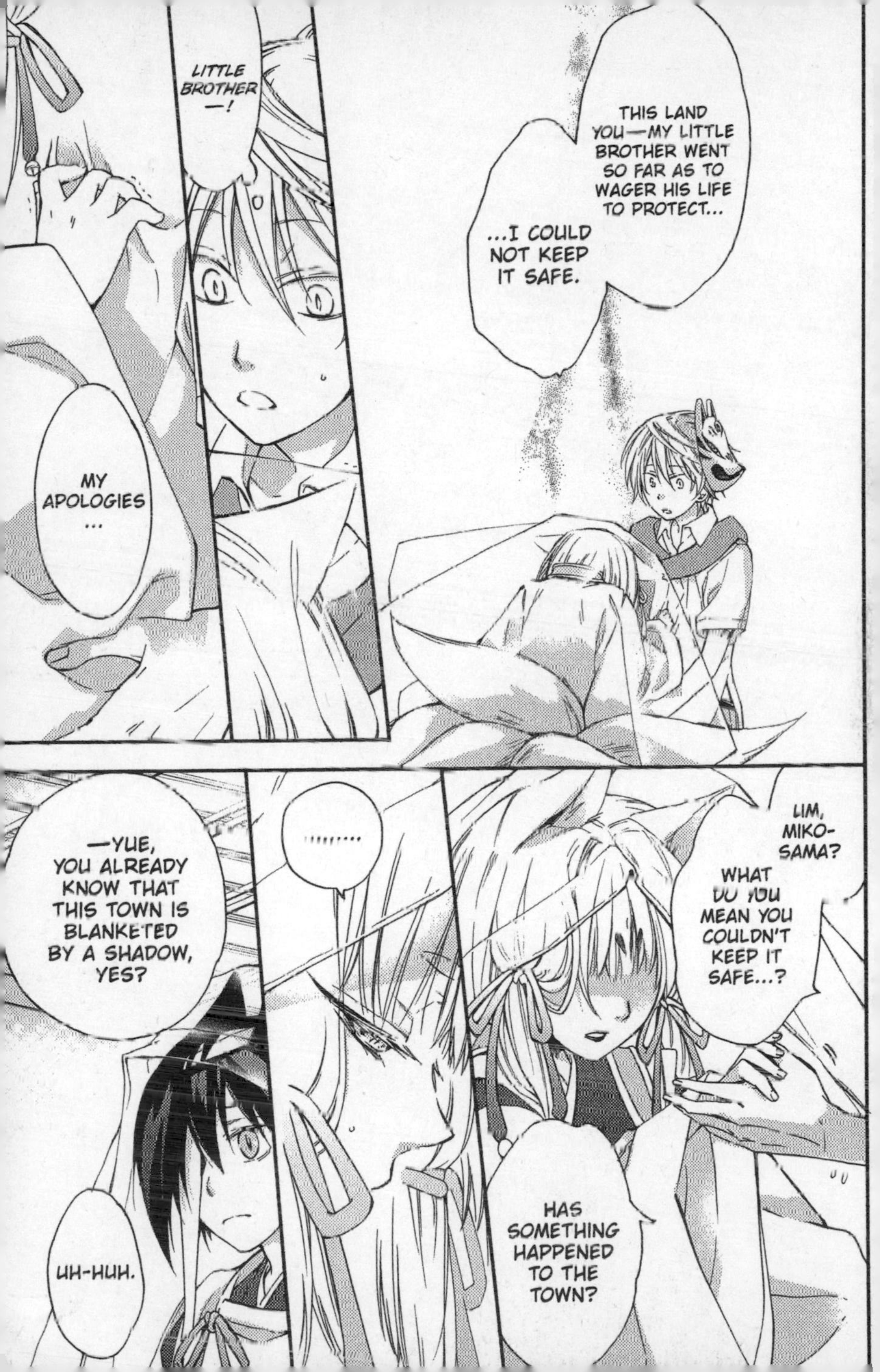
THIS LAND YOU—MY LITTLE BROTHER WENT SO FAR AS TO WAGER HIS LIFE TO PROTECT...
...I COULD NOT KEEP IT SAFE.
LITTLE BROTHER—!
MY APOLOGIES...
UM, MIKO-SAMA?
WHAT DO YOU MEAN YOU COULDN'T KEEP IT SAFE...?
HAS SOMETHING HAPPENED TO THE TOWN?
......
—YUE, YOU ALREADY KNOW THAT THIS TOWN IS BLANKETED BY A SHADOW, YES?
UH-HUH.

THAT SHADOW WAS CREATED BY SHIN FOR OUR BENEFIT.
HEY, LISTEN.
YOU HEAR ABOUT THE DISAPPEAR-ANCES?
WHICH ONES? I MEAN, THERE ARE WAY TOO MANY RUMORS ABOUT THAT STUFF.
AH HA HA
AREN'T THOSE JUST RUNAWAYS OR WHATEVER? THE RUMORS'LL BE GONE SOON TOO.
ZAWA (CHATTER)
ザワ
TOO TRUE.
WE'VE NEVER HAD A PRINCIPAL, EVEN WHEN YOU ATTENDED THIS SCHOOL, TOUGO-KUN.
"I DON'T REALLY KNOW WHO.
"BUT I'M SAD AND LONELY,"
...IS WHAT WE WERE TOLD...
AND BECAUSE OF THIS SHADOW, THIS TOWN...
...WE ARE ABLE TO MEET A PART OF THE HUMAN WORLD.

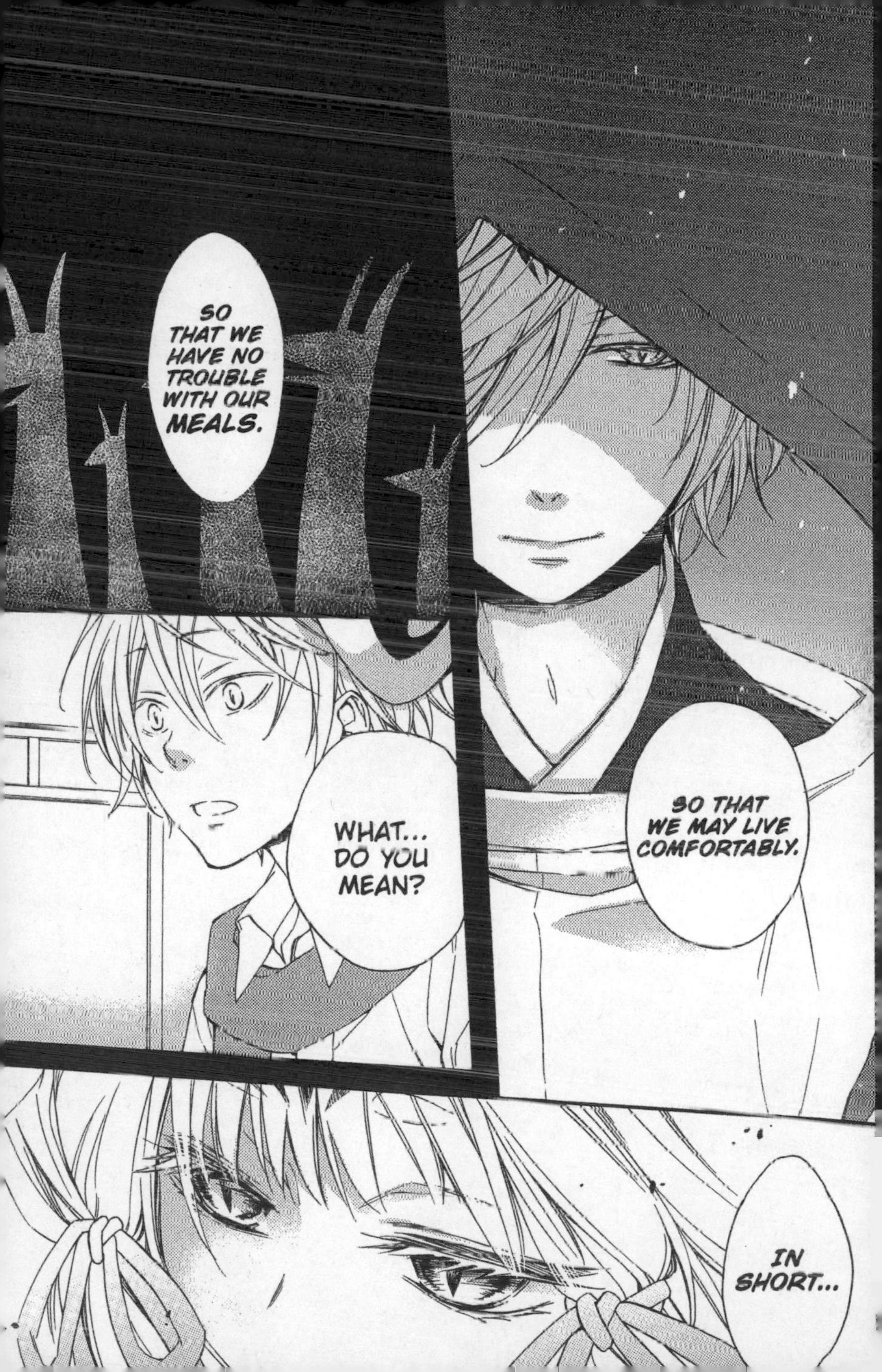
SO THAT WE MAY LIVE COMFORTABLY.
SO THAT WE HAVE NO TROUBLE WITH OUR MEALS.
WHAT... DO YOU MEAN?
IN SHORT...

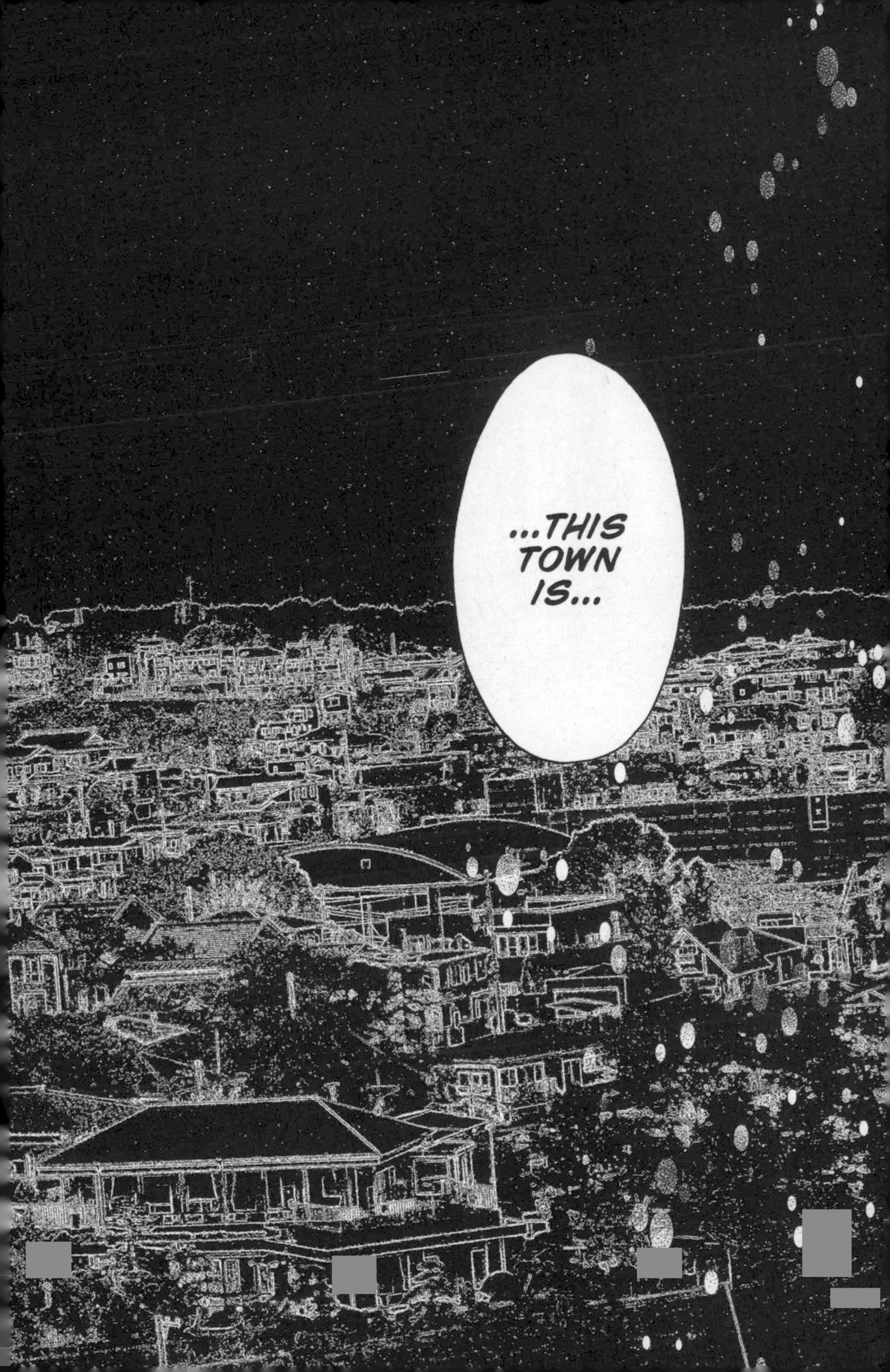
...THIS TOWN IS...

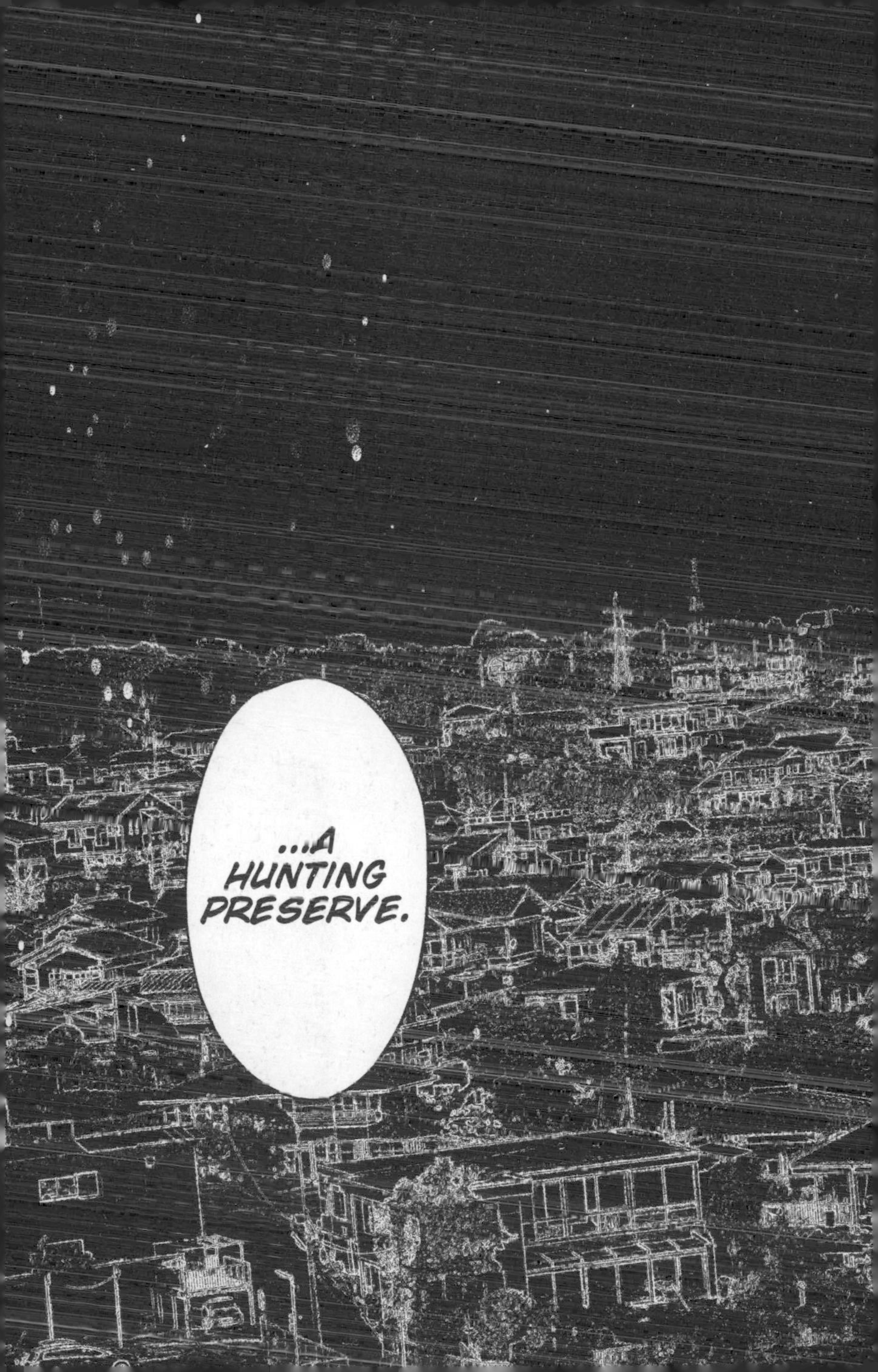
...A HUNTING PRESERVE.

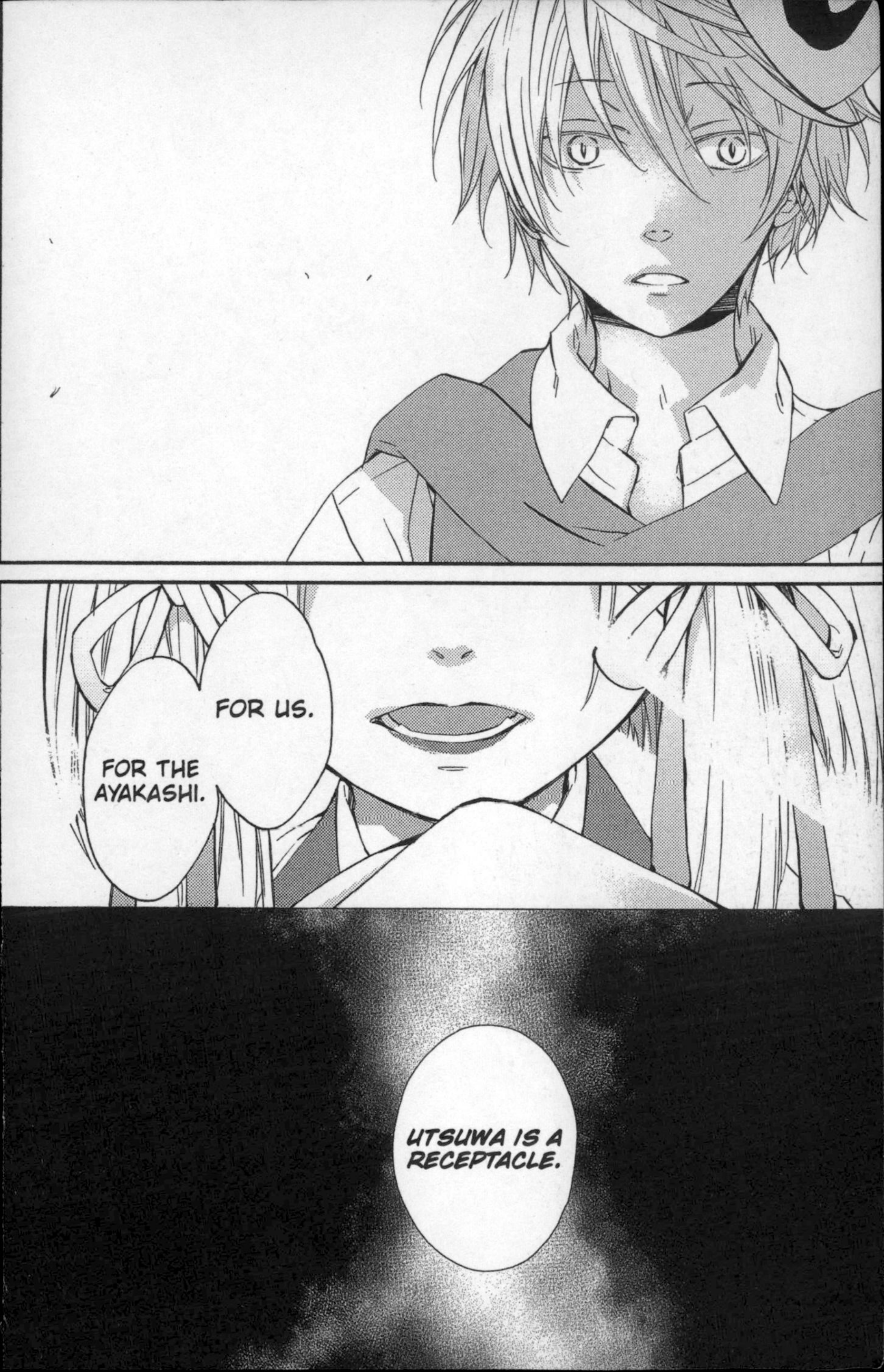
FOR US.
FOR THE AYAKASHI.
UTSUWA IS A RECEPTACLE.

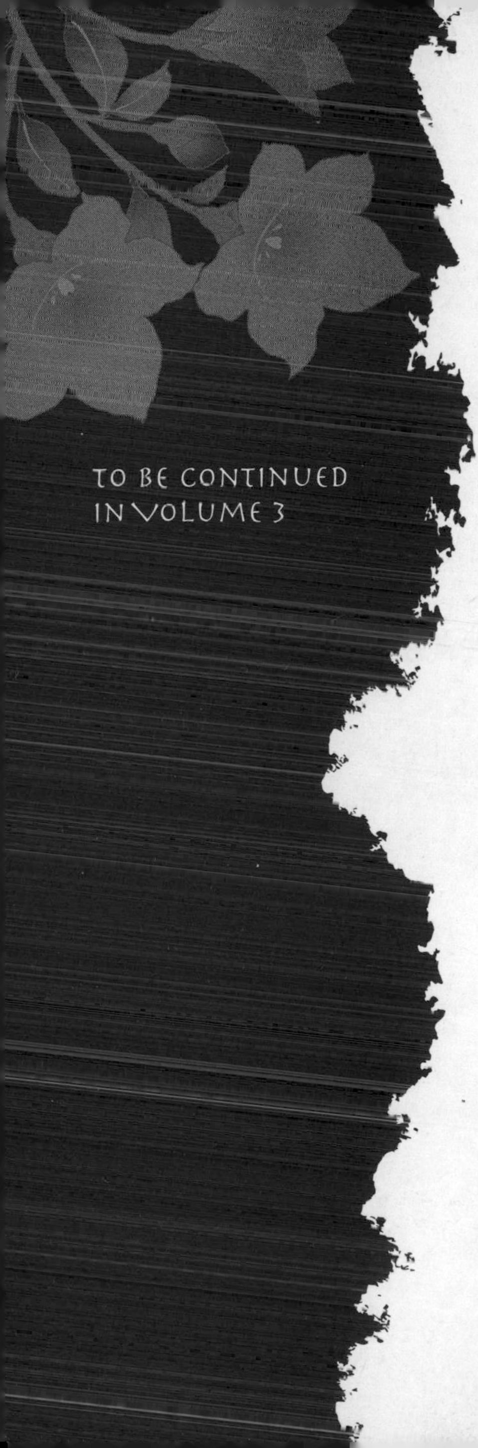
TO BE CONTINUED
IN VOLUME 3

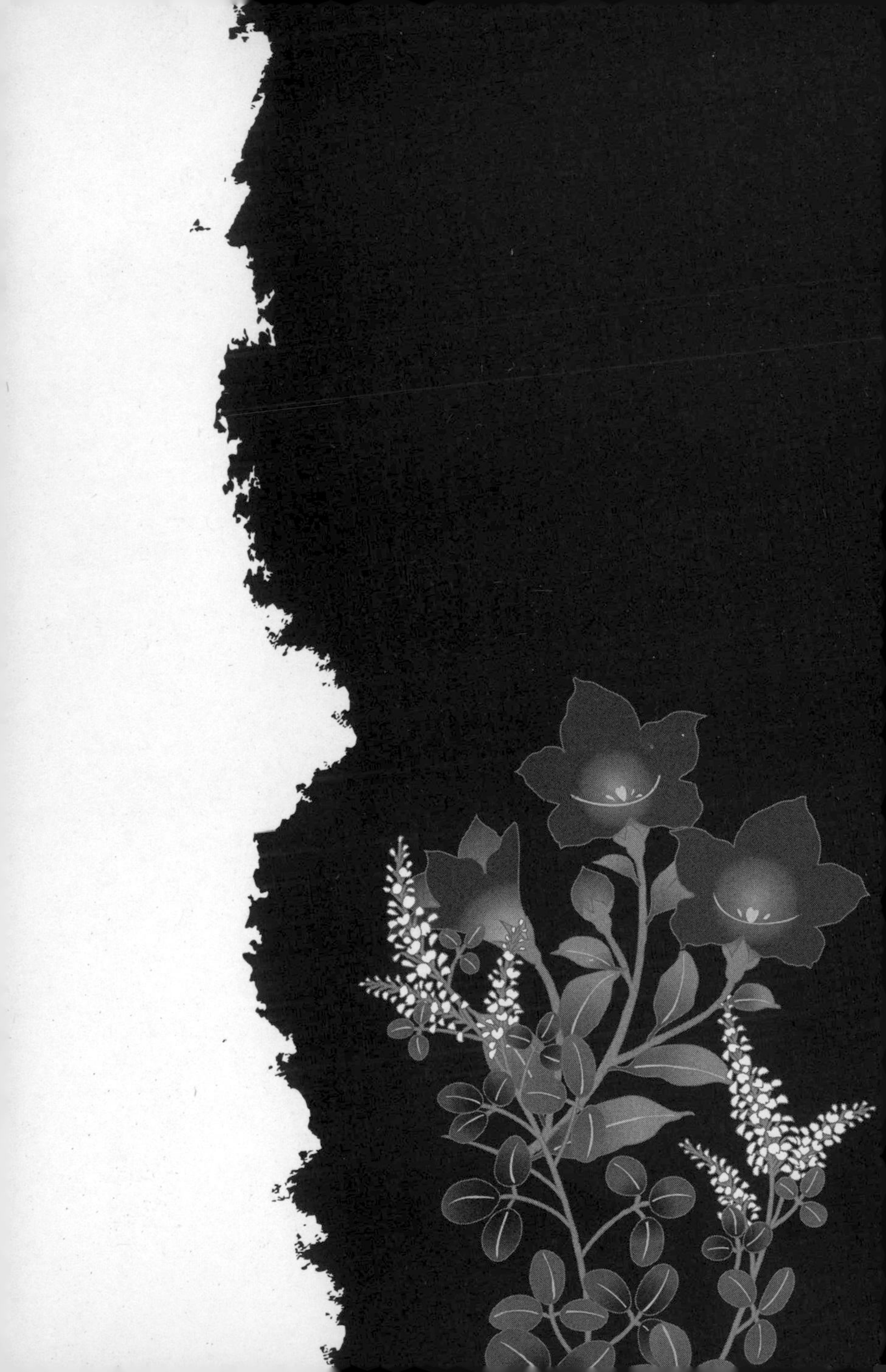

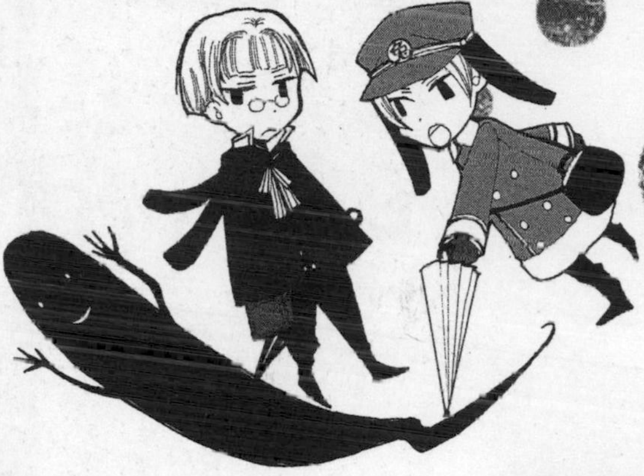

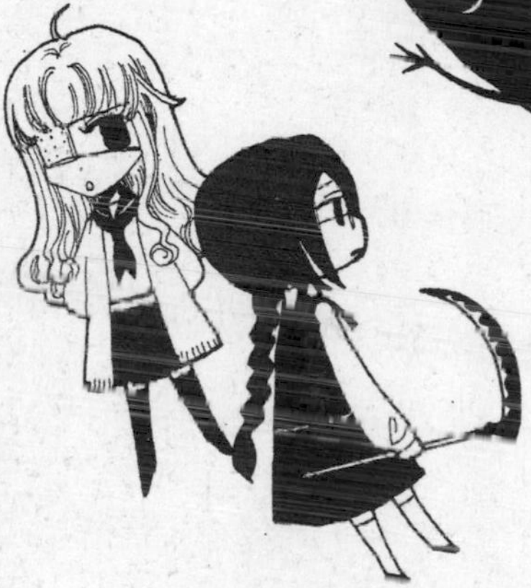
I REALLY FEEL HOW COOL THE RABBITS ARE IN THE MANGA VERSION.

RELEASE OF VOLUME TWO

CONGRATULATIONS!

I'M STILL SO DELIGHTED AT HOW SKILLFULLY NANAO-SENSEI DEPICTS ALL THE DETAILS IN THE WORLD OF OF THE RED! IT'S STILL A WAYS OFF, BUT I CAN'T WAIT FOR VOLUME THREE.

I WONDER WHAT THE FLOWERS ON THE NEXT COVER WILL BE... (LOL)

DECEMBER 2012
HaccaWorks*

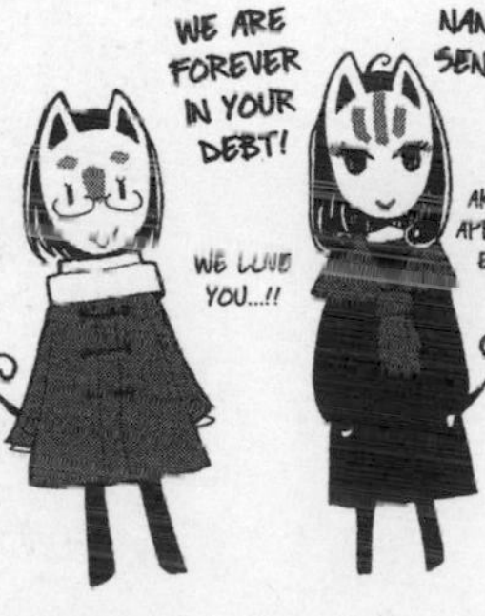
WE ARE FOREVER IN YOUR DEBT!
NANAO-SENSEI!
EDITOR Y-TA-SAN
WE LOVE YOU...!!
AKIYOSHI'S APPARENTLY EASY TO DRAW.
WE GET EXCITED PHONE CALLS ABOUT HOW GREAT THE COVER OR THE COLOR PAGES ARE.

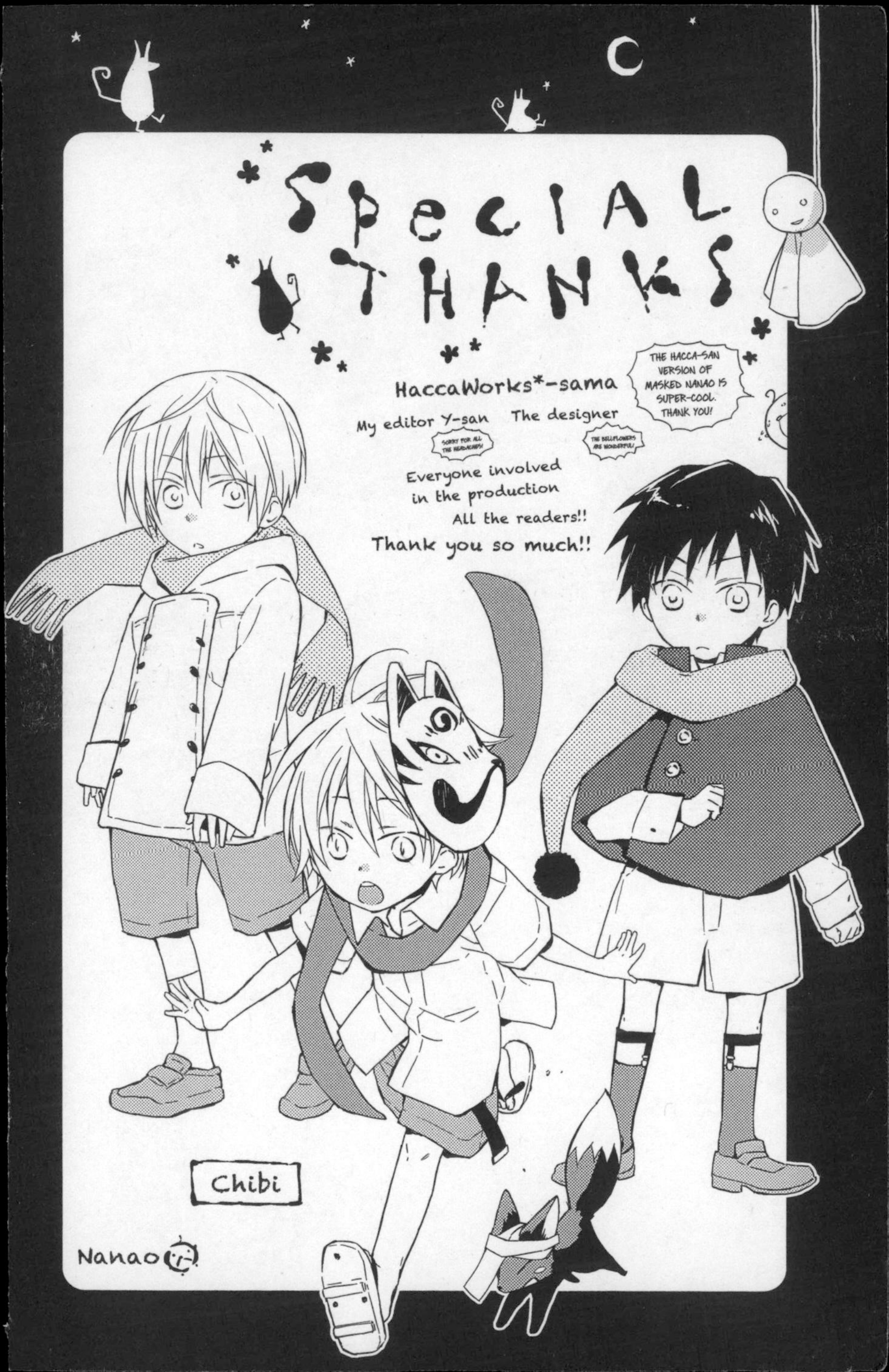
SPECIAL THANKS
HaccaWorks*-sama
THE HACCA-SAN VERSION OF MASKED NANAO IS SUPER-COOL. THANK YOU!
My editor Y-san
SORRY FOR ALL THE HEADACHES!
The designer
THE BELLFLOWERS ARE WONDERFUL!
Everyone involved in the production
All the readers!!
Thank you so much!!
Chibi
Nanao

TRANSLATION NOTES

COMMON HONORIFICS

no honorific: Indicates familiarity or closeness; if used without permission or reason, addressing someone in this manner would be an insult.

-san: The Japanese equivalent of Mr./Mrs./Miss. If a situation calls for politeness, this is the fail-safe honorific.

-sama: Conveys great respect; may also indicate that the social status of the speaker is lower than that of the addressee.

-kun: Used most often when referring to boys, this indicates affection or familiarity. Occasionally used by older men among their peers, but it may also be used by anyone referring to a person of lower standing.

-chan, -tan: An affectionate honorific indicating familiarity used mostly in reference to girls; also used in reference to cute persons or animals.

Ayakashi is a general term for ghosts, monsters, haunted objects, mythical animals, and all sorts of uncanny things from Japanese folklore.

PAGE 5

The **goldfish** are all named after varieties of tea. Gyokuro is an expensive high-grade Japanese green tea. Shui Hsien is a variety of dark oolong tea produced in China and Taiwan. Keemun is a popular variety of black tea from China.

PAGE 67

Sennen literally means "a thousand years" in Japanese.

PAGE 67

The text on **the slip of paper** on the cat's forehead is a type of charm. This prayer that many customers will come to the shop often accompanies a *maneki-neko*, a cat statue that beckons good fortune and customers to businesses. However, the way in which the slip is stuck to the forehead of the cat also resembles an *ofuda*, a slip of paper used to exorcise bad spirits.

PAGE 154

Utsuwa, the town name, is also the word for "vessel" in Japanese.

Of the Red, the Light, and the Ayakashi

ART BY Nanao
STORY BY HaccaWorks*

Translation: Jocelyne Allen ✦ Lettering: Alexis Eckerman

AKAYA AKASHIYA AYAKASHINO
© Nanao 2013
© Hacca Works* 2013
Edited by MEDIA FACTORY
First published in Japan in 2013 by KADOKAWA CORPORATION. English translation rights reserved by HACHETTE BOOK GROUP, INC. under the license from KADOKAWA COPORATION, Tokyo through TUTTLE-MORI AGENCY, Inc., Tokyo.

Translation © 2016 by Hachette Book Group, Inc.

Yen Press
Hachette Book Group
1290 Avenue of the Americas
New York, NY 10104

www.HachetteBookGroup.com ✦ www.YenPress.com

Yen Press is an imprint of Hachette Book Group, Inc.
The Yen Press name and logo are trademarks of Hachette Book Group, Inc.

The publisher is not responsible for websites (or their content) not owned by the publisher.

Library of Congress Control Number: 2015956851

First Yen Press Edition: March 2016

ISBN: 978-0-316-31007-9

10 9 8 7 6 5 4 3 2 1

BVG

Printed in the United States of America